ROUTLEDGE LIBRARY EDITIONS:
ROMANTICISM

Volume 15

THE ROMANTIC REVIEWERS

THE ROMANTIC REVIEWERS
1802–1824

JOHN O. HAYDEN

LONDON AND NEW YORK

First published in 1969 by Routledge & Kegan Paul Limited

This edition first published in 2016
by Routledge
2 Park Square, Milton Park, Abingdon, Oxon OX14 4RN

and by Routledge
711 Third Avenue, New York, NY 10017

Routledge is an imprint of the Taylor & Francis Group, an informa business

British Library Cataloguing in Publication Data
A catalogue record for this book is available from the British Library

ISBN: 978-1-138-64537-0 (Set)
ISBN: 978-1-315-62815-8 (Set) (ebk)
ISBN: 978-1-138-19380-2 (Volume 15) (hbk)
ISBN: 978-1-138-19382-6 (Volume 15) (pbk)
ISBN: 978-1-315-63912-3 (Volume 15) (ebk)

Publisher's Note
The publisher has gone to great lengths to ensure the quality of this reprint but points out that some imperfections in the original copies may be apparent.

Disclaimer
The publisher has made every effort to trace copyright holders and would welcome correspondence from those they have been unable to trace.

The Romantic Reviewers 1802-1824

JOHN O. HAYDEN

London
Routledge & Kegan Paul

First published 1969
by Routledge *& Kegan Paul Limited*
Broadway House, 68–74 Carter Lane
London, E.C.4
Printed in Great Britain
by Butler & Tanner Limited
Frome and London

SBN 7100 6037 8

This book is for

J. N. L.

Acknowledgments

Every book with pretensions to scholarship has obligations to many scholars both past and present. This book is no exception. Debts to past scholars are generally represented, however inadequately, in footnotes and in the bibliography; obligations to those who have assisted more directly by reading and advising need a more direct presentation.

The idea for this study originated in a research paper written for a graduate seminar in Romantic literature at Columbia University under Jacques Barzun and Lionel Trilling. The advice and encouragement they gave me at that time are greatly appreciated. More considerable assistance was provided by my graduate supervisor at Columbia University, Carl Woodring, and by my research supervisor at Cambridge University, Ian Jack of Pembroke College, both of whom gave freely of their time and advice. Donald Davie, now of the University of Essex, and Anthony Spearing of Queens' College, Cambridge, were good enough to read several chapters in earlier versions. My greatest debt, however, is to an old friend, George Dekker, also of the University of Essex; his encouragement and advice were invaluable.

Mention of my obligations should not in any way suggest that these scholars agree with all I have said in my study or are in the least responsible for any errors I have made.

To the Trustees of the Edward John Noble Foundation of New York I also express my gratitude. Without their extension of an already generous scholarship, I would not have been able to pursue my research in the British Isles. A grant from the Council on Research and Creative Work of the University of Colorado paid for the typing of this study. That grant is greatly appreciated.

My thanks also to the staffs of the Cambridge University Library and of the Reading Room of the British Museum, as well as those of the Bodleian Library, the Edinburgh University Library, the Library of the Victoria and Albert Museum, the London Library, and the New York Public Library. With the help of these librarians, research became an easier and more enjoyable task.

Davis, California
June, 1967

Contents

Introduction

Though the extent of the importance and influence of literary reviewing in Britain in the early nineteenth century will never be known precisely, there is little doubt that it must have been considerable. Many prose works of the period—from Southey's *Letters from England* and Coleridge's *Biographia Literaria* to Hazlitt's *Table Talk* and Peacock's *Nightmare Abbey* —contain passages or entire chapters that concern contemporary literary reviewing. Frequently prefaces to volumes of poetry, such as those written by Keats for his *Endymion* and by Shelley for his *Adonais*, are also concerned with the Romantic reviewers either directly or by implication, further evincing their importance to writers of the time. Copious references to literary reviews in contemporary correspondence and the amount of space given to the reviews by later biographers of Romantic writers provide additional evidence of the importance and influence of the Romantic reviewers.

The early nineteenth century was in fact the heyday of periodical reviewing; never before or since has it been so energetic and widespread. The *Edinburgh Review* and the *Quarterly Review* were the two most important periodicals concerned, but there were at least sixty other periodicals between 1802 and 1824 that carried reviews of literature.[1] Yet, except for

[1] In keeping with the custom of commentators on reviewing, the word 'review' when referring to a periodical will be capitalized (Review) and when referring to a critical article in a periodical will be lower-cased (review).

a few studies touching on individual writers or periodicals, this critical activity during so important a time as the Romantic period has been largely overlooked and nowhere explored with the thoroughness it deserves.[1]

The objective here is a study broad enough to provide a reliable representation of reviewing practices in the period, yet sufficiently delimited to avoid becoming mired in consideration of minor writers who were of little interest to their contemporaries and of even less interest today. To this end reviews of the works of the following writers were selected: Wordsworth, Coleridge, Byron, Shelley, Keats, Hazlitt, Lamb, Scott, Crabbe, Hunt, Southey, and Moore. That these were truly the most popular writers of the age is partly evidenced by the frequent references in reviews to other members of this group than the writer under review, in sharp contrast to infrequent mention of other writers.

This selection of authors proves highly advantageous since it permits the most representative coverage of the literary critiques. Reviews of the more popular writers' works tended to be considerably longer and more elaborate than reviews of the works of those less prominent, often relegated to monthly catalogues of brief notices. The variety of forms used by the writers selected, moreover, is the widest possible: they wrote romances, ballads, narrative poems of all lengths, satires in verse and prose, dream visions, short lyric poems, burlesques, dramas, essays, and historical works. The only genre excluded from consideration in this study is the novel. The reviewers, in short, had a wide field in which to display their critical talents, and almost the entire field is surveyed here.

The reviewing periodicals covered in this study have also been delimited slightly. The *Westminster Review*, although begun in 1824, was not considered since it represents in a sense a new era in the history of reviewing. Another omission, perhaps more important, is that of the criticism in the daily newspapers. As far as I have been able to determine, no dailies carried reviews before 1815, and very few after that date.[2]

The span of years, from 1802 to 1824, was selected to give the largest practicable coverage, both from the standpoint of the Reviews and from that of the writers. The beginning date (1802) was the year of the founding of the *Edinburgh Review*, which in turn marked the beginning of a new era

[1] William S. Ward's Duke dissertation (1943), 'The Criticism of Poetry in British Periodicals, 1798–1820' (microcards, University of Kentucky, 1955), is the only previous study with any claim to a wide view of the subject. His list of reviews was helpful as a check-list.

[2] Another limit is the exclusion of Reviews not published in the two metropolitan centers, London and Edinburgh; for reasons discussed at the beginning of Chapter 2, such Reviews could not have been in any way influential. The only exception to the limitation is the *Oxford Review*, which was run by Sir Richard Phillips in London.

in periodical criticism—the only exception being reviews of the *Lyrical Ballads*. The terminal date (1824) was both the year in which William Gifford retired as editor of the *Quarterly Review* and the year of Byron's death. Within the period, all the published works of Byron, Shelley, and Keats are included, all the poetry of Scott, and almost all the most important works of the remaining writers. By 1824 the astonishing creativity of the Romantic age was at an end.

The construction of this study falls into three sections. The first, 'The Historical Background of the Reviewing Periodicals' (Chapters 1 and 2), is an attempt at a thorough compilation of available information concerning the general background—for example, contributors, affiliations, and editors—of the reviewing periodicals. (Attributions of authorship of reviews form, I believe, a considerable part of the value of this section; for the first time in this study a large number are made and brought together.) This background information for the major and for most of the minor periodicals is presented as part of the text; but information on the very minor periodicals (those containing few relevant reviews) has been relegated to Appendix I, which also contains a complete list of the abbreviations of periodical titles used in the notes and in Appendix II.

The second section, 'The Reviews and Schools' (Chapters 3–6), discusses reviews of the works of each of the twelve writers selected. Complete lists of those reviews are found in Appendix II. Because the reviews and the works cannot adequately be discussed in a critical vacuum, an attempt has been made to evaluate briefly the works themselves and, on the strength of the evaluations, to judge the validity of the critical conclusions reached by the reviewers. Both judgments are an integral part of my general approach to the reviewers. However, the strictly factual information concerning the critical reception accorded the writers can easily be extracted by the reader, should he consider some of my evaluations questionable. In this respect, the study provides detailed information on an important aspect of the career of each of the writers.

The third section (Chapter 7) contains a brief account of the 'Attitudes, Policies, and Practices' of the reviewers. To some extent this section, I am aware, may read like an apology for the reviewers. The only possible excuse for this is that almost all other commentators either have taken an adverse, though usually mistaken, stand on many aspects of the reviewing or have indulged in undue condescension. I can only hope that I am not guilty of having gone to the other extreme; at least there has been no conscious attempt to whitewash the reviewers.

There are, however, some who will object to any kind of evaluation or attempt at objectivity as being fundamentally irrelevant. To such critical relativists, no critical judgments of any kind have validity but are merely of historical interest. Aside from the philosophical difficulties of such a viewpoint, it will, I believe, prevent one from arriving at an adequate appreciation of the Romantic reviewers.[1] For they themselves were operating in the humanist critical tradition as it had been passed down from Aristotle, Horace, Dryden, and Dr. Johnson, and thus considered themselves to be criticizing *sub specie aeternitatis*. And since some point of view, call it opinion *or* judgment, will of necessity be taken by everyone (like it or not), the prejudice against the reviewers will continue if nurtured by relativism, and a great mass of criticism of the works of the English Romantic writers will be lost as a result.

[1] For some of the problems involved in historical relativism, see Appendix One, 'Criticism, History, and Critical Relativism', in Cleanth Brooks, *The Well Wrought Urn* (New York: Reynal and Hitchcock, 1947).

Part I

The Historical Background of the Reviewing Periodicals

A secret history of criticism, for some twenty years at a time, with its favouritisms, its animosities, and its hesitations, would make a very curious book; but the subject would be so disagreeable, that it would require almost as disagreeable a person to write it.

Leigh Hunt, *Autobiography*

1

The 'Edinburgh Review' and the 'Quarterly Review'

At the beginning of the nineteenth century the state of periodical reviewing left something to be desired. Some of the more outstanding eighteenth-century monthlies, it is true, were still in existence; both the venerable *Monthly Review* and the *Critical Review* had survived and were responsible critical organs. More recently established periodicals, the *British Critic* and the *Antijacobin Review and Magazine*, had a political *raison d'être*, but on the whole they provided competent appraisals of non-political works. There were, as well, magazines, such as the *Gentleman's Magazine* and the *Monthly Magazine*, which had short but serious reviewing sections. And yet, although it is perhaps unfair to compare the state of the reviewing periodicals as it existed in 1800 with that existing a mere fifteen years later, in the heyday of reviewing, nevertheless, if the comparison is made, something unmistakably is missing in reviewing at the turn of the century.

For one thing, little attempt was made to go beyond providing readers with an idea of the content and relative worth of recent publications—the merest practical function of reviewing. This function was undoubtedly of value to rural subscribers, who had no other means of keeping up with the latest books, but the Reviews seem to have made little impression on metropolitan readers and even less on the literature being produced. Writers and professional men who were later to make their mark on the age, such as S. T. Coleridge, Robert Southey, Francis Jeffrey, and William Taylor of

Norwich, were, to be sure, contributing to the Reviews about this time; and yet there was little of the excitement and stimulation that reviewing was soon to provide. Most of the testimony of those living at the time was anything but favorable; it seems in fact even to exaggerate the inferiority of the Reviews in question.[1]

In 1802 a drastic change took place; the *Edinburgh Review* began a career that was to last until 1929, and not only transformed the reviewing periodicals already in existence but became the model of all Reviews of the nineteenth century.[2]

The time was ripe and the location favorable. Edinburgh had for some years been a provincial center of culture and intellectual activity; and though the Scottish eighteenth-century renaissance was over—David Hume and Adam Smith gone from the scene—a substantial reputation was retained by such names as Dugald Stewart, John Playfair, and Adam Ferguson; and Edinburgh was still a metropolitan center of intellectual life, the 'Athens of the North'.[3] For that very reason, Sydney Smith, the originator of the idea of the *Edinburgh Review*, had come there with the young man he was tutoring in 1798, when the customary continental Grand Tour was made impossible by the war.

The intellectual climate in Edinburgh in the early nineteenth century was somewhat more attractive than the political. The Tory party was in complete control and ruled Scotland through the benevolent despotism of Dundas. Political reaction was the order of the day, and any sort of liberal viewpoint was seen as Jacobin.[4] Almost all liberals (who were not radicals) were perforce Whigs—a situation quite different from that in England at the same period.[5]

[1] Lord Cockburn, in his *Life of Lord Jeffrey*, I, 129, observed of the reviewing at this time: 'There were reviews in England; but, though respectable according to the notions at that time of critical respectability, they merely languished in decent feebleness.' Walter Scott, in a letter to George Ellis of Nov. 18, 1808 (H. J. C. Grierson [ed.], *The Letters of Sir Walter Scott*, II, 128) remarked that by 1802 'the common Reviews . . . had become extremely mawkish; and, unless when prompted by the malice of the bookseller or reviewer, gave a dawdling, maudlin sort of applause to everything that reached even mediocrity.'

[2] Walter Graham, *English Literary Periodicals*, pp. 238, 248.

[3] Cockburn, I, 156–60. See also John Clive, *Scotch Reviewers*, pp. 17–19. Clive's study of the *Edinburgh Review* (1802–15) should be consulted for a more detailed account of the history of the founding and early years of the periodical, particularly its political, economic, and historical attitudes.

[4] Cockburn, I, 73–84. See also Clive, pp. 22–24.

[5] Chester W. New, *The Life of Henry Brougham to 1830*, p. 32.

The liberal, or Whig, circle in Edinburgh was small but active. The younger Whigs belonged to several societies, such as the Academy of Physics and the Speculative Society. It was at the meetings of these societies that Sydney Smith met with the other young men who were to found the *Edinburgh Review*. Among the members of both groups were Francis Jeffrey, Francis Horner, and Henry Brougham, all of whom were lawyers practising at the Scottish bar, or trying to practice, since they had to pay the price of their avowedly liberal opinions. Smith was at this time occupied only in tutoring one student, so all four young men—Smith (thirty-one), Jeffrey (twenty-nine), Brougham (twenty-four), and Horner (twenty-four)—were, in 1802, 'masters of their own time'.[1]

An account of the actual founding of the *Edinburgh Review* can only be based on contradictory testimony given, most of it years later, by those involved. John Clive, in an appendix to his *Scotch Reviewers*, sifted the evidence and came to the following conclusion:

> . . . Sydney Smith first proposed the idea of the *Edinburgh Review* to Jeffrey and Horner while the three of them were discussing various literary projects late in 1801 or early in 1802. Some time in March the suggestion was taken up by a larger group, and Jeffrey's hesitations overridden. The principal editing work on the first three numbers was carried out by Smith and Jeffrey, though Horner, as one of the three founders, retained throughout certain prerogatives. Since he was in London from late March to early May (1802), he had less concern than did the other two with the editing of the first number in which various other associates—soon to become simply contributors—participated. However, Brougham alone was admitted to the inner circle of founding editors, though not until June, 1803, and not until he had previously been readmitted, after a temporary break, as a mere contributor. Jeffrey was appointed sole editor some time after the appearance of the third number. Brougham, Smith, and Horner, though all of them left Edinburgh for London, remained his closest and most powerful advisers.[2]

After months of preparation and postponement, the first number appeared on October 10, 1802. It contained twenty-nine reviews of a variety of books, including works of economics, politics, science,

[1] Cockburn, I, 126.

[2] Clive, p. 197. The 'larger group' mentioned in the quotation as involved in the founding of the *Edinburgh Review*, included Thomas Brown, John A. Murray, Webb Seymour, John Thomson, and Thomas Thomson (Clive, p. 195).

and literature; at least seven were written by Smith, five by Jeffrey, four by Horner, and six by Brougham. Nothing quite like it had been seen before; 'the learning of the new Journal, its talent, its spirit, its writing, its independence, were all new.'[1] 'The effect was electrical', both positively, in terms of its immediate popularity, and negatively, in terms of the attacks which the *Edinburgh Review* drew upon itself for the severity of much of its criticism; for the *Edinburgh* began shortly to be attacked by pamphlets and newspapers in a manner even more severe than its own.[2]

Lord Brougham later wrote that its success was as much a surprise to its founders as to anyone else; Jeffrey, for example, 'was utterly dumfounded'.[3] To its originators, the *Edinburgh* was 'only a matter of temporary amusement', although they were also concerned for their own 'improvement—joined with the gratification of some personal, and some national, vanity'.[4] At the beginning, in fact, the reviewers were to receive no remuneration for their articles: 'It was to be all gentlemen, and no pay.'[5] Then, in the spring of 1803, Sydney Smith suggested in a letter to Constable, the publisher, that he pay the contributors and editor well, and Constable complied.[6]

One of the three novelties of the *Edinburgh* often cited as responsible for its success was this high rate of pay, which all contributors, regardless of wealth or position, had to accept. Another was the *Edinburgh*'s independence of booksellers, in an age in which Reviews were charged with 'puffing' the wares of the booksellers who owned

[1] Cockburn, I, 131.

[2] Thomas Constable, *Archibald Constable and His Literary Correspondents*, I, 52. See also Leonard Horner (ed.), *Memoirs and Correspondence of Francis Horner*, I, 212.

[3] Henry Brougham, *The Life and Times of Henry Lord Brougham*, I, 252.

[4] Horner, I, 218 (Francis Horner to James Loch, Dec. 12, 1802). Cockburn, II, 83 (Jeffrey to Horner, Sept. 8, 1803).

[5] Cockburn, I, 133.

[6] Nowell C. Smith (ed.), *The Letters of Sydney Smith*, I, 79–80 (Smith to A. Constable). N. C. Smith dates this letter as '1803, before Aug. 8th', and Clive (p. 33, n. 3) follows the tentative dating given in Constable (I, 51): 'soon after the publication had been started, and before the rate of remuneration to contributors had been determined'. The letter, however, can be dated more closely than that. Jeffrey mentioned Smith's negotiations with Constable, to Horner, on May 11, 1803 (Cockburn, II, 70); he said that they had taken place 'during [his] absence'. I cannot discover which 'absence' Jeffrey refers to; but since the previous letter by Jeffrey in Cockburn's collection was also to Horner, dated Apr. 1, 1803, it seems likely that Smith's letter to Constable was written sometime between those two dates, i.e., between Apr. 1 and May 11, 1803.

these periodicals.[1] A final point of originality often cited was the one that the *Edinburgh* itself saw fit to announce in the Advertisement to its first number: that unlike all other Reviews, the *Edinburgh* wished 'to be distinguished, rather for the selection, than for the number of its articles', and 'to confine [its] notice, in a great degree, to works that either have attained, or deserve, a certain portion of celebrity'. The Advertisement further pointed out that, since the articles would be fewer, longer, and not dependent on 'the earliness of [their] intelligence', it was decided to publish quarterly rather than monthly.[2] The *Edinburgh* thus became the only quarterly Review on the British scene.

In his memoirs, Brougham chose still another aspect of the *Edinburgh* as most original: articles were often dissertations based on the subject of a book rather than strictly critical reviews of the books themselves. Brougham added that this was in fact the major attraction for 'men who would not think of publishing a book', but who needed 'a place ready to receive their writings, and a place of respectability, in which their works appeared in decent company'.[3] This aspect was present in the first number, and gained in importance as articles became fewer and longer. A gradual trend in this direction set in; by 1810, the quantity of articles per issue had shrunk from the twenty-nine of the first issue to an average of eleven, in about the same total number of pages. And yet there were always some reviews that were solely descriptions and evaluations of books.

In the passage quoted above, Brougham also mentions that the anonymity afforded by the *Edinburgh* was an added attraction to writers.[4] Anonymity was certainly no novelty in reviewing periodicals; in fact, the one periodical in which anonymity had been discarded, the *London Review* of 1809, had a very short existence.[5]

[1] To my knowledge, the charge of puffery was never made against a specific Review.

[2] The Advertisement follows the lists of contents in the first number. It should be pointed out, in connection with the *Edinburgh Review*'s policy of not reviewing all books published, that after the fourth number the publication began to append a 'Quarterly List of New Publications'.

[3] Brougham, I, 260. For possible predecessors to this 'original' aspect of reviewing, see Clive, p. 32, n. 1.

[4] Brougham was himself jealous of his anonymity. When in 1813 one of the London publishers of the *Edinburgh Review* seems to have been careless of the secrecy involved, Brougham flew into a rage (Constable, II, 224–26).

[5] Graham, *Periodicals*, p. 240. Scott considered the *London Review*'s proposal to eliminate anonymity 'extraordinary' (Grierson, *Letters*, II, 143).

Reasons for anonymity were many. The most obvious is the protection it afforded contributors when they set forth unpopular viewpoints. John Clive offers three additional reasons: reviewing was considered ungentlemanly—thus no gentleman would wish his name used; some professions frowned upon contributions to periodicals by members; anonymity lent the reviewers 'oracular authority'.[1] Still another reason for anonymity was the small size of the literary world of the period; the critics would very likely be acquainted with the writer criticized or with his friends—anonymity would afford a degree of objectivity otherwise impossible.[2]

The only names given in the *Edinburgh Review* were those of the publishers, both in Edinburgh and in London. Archibald Constable, the Edinburgh publisher, had been chosen (after another publisher had turned down the project's innovators) because his energetic business methods appealed to the group, as did his liberal political views.[3] Constable was young—very nearly of an age with the founders of the *Edinburgh*—and was already the publisher of two magazines.[4] He was soon to become one of the greatest publishers in Great Britain by publishing the *Encyclopaedia Britannica* and the works of Godwin, Hazlitt, Hogg, Maturin, John Wilson, and, above all, Sir Walter Scott. This was a great age of publishers, an age that saw the rise of publishers from their previous degraded, purely commercial standing. Constable, by his patronage and generosity, was one of those who made it so.

Constable took over the business end and financial responsibilities of the *Edinburgh*, and, as previously mentioned, had the foresight to agree to pay the editor and contributors well. He became a good friend of Jeffrey and was acquainted with most of the contributors.[5] To what extent, then, could the *Edinburgh* have been free from the influence of booksellers? There is an early instance of the damning by the *Edinburgh* of a book published by Constable, and we have

[1] Clive, pp. 32, 34.

[2] There is something of this desire for anonymity on personal grounds in Walter Scott's letter to John Murray, in reference to an article on Sir John Carr, which Scott contributed to the first number of the *Quarterly Review*: 'He is an incomparable goose, but as he is innocent and good-natured, I would not like it to be publicly known that the flagellation comes from my hand. Secrecy therefore will oblige me.' Samuel Smiles, *A Publisher and His Friends: Memoir and Correspondence of John Murray*, I, 146n.

[3] Constable, I, 49; Brougham, I, 248.

[4] Constable, I, 49n.

[5] *Ibid.*, II, 214, 226.

Constable's own later testimony: 'With regard to the Edinburgh Review, you have not at this time to learn that it has ever been placed above the partiality and influence of booksellers.'[1] Constable was several times asked by friends to have books reviewed in the *Edinburgh*, and in one recorded instance in which he went as far as to request such a review from Jeffrey—in the case of Scott's edition of Swift—the editor complied. Constable commented on this to Lockhart: 'It was, I think, the first time I ever asked such a thing of him, and I assure you the result was no encouragement to repeat such petitions.'[2]

The London publisher of the *Edinburgh* was at first Joseph Mawman, but after the initial number, the publishing rights were transferred to Longman, a distant relative of Sydney Smith. He published the *Edinburgh* in London until 1808.[3] It was subsequently published by various other firms in London until 1814, when Longman regained the London sale. The entire rights to the *Edinburgh* became Longman's property in 1826 when Constable went bankrupt.[4]

Of the four friends involved in the founding of the *Edinburgh*, Francis Horner wrote the fewest articles—an estimated fifteen. A lawyer by profession, he had been called to the Scottish bar in 1800 but had left for the greener pastures of English practice in March, 1803. In 1806, Horner became a Whig M.P. and served with great esteem in Parliament for most of the years before his death in 1817 at the age of thirty-eight. Since most of his work in Parliament was concerned with economic measures, it is not surprising that Horner's *Edinburgh* articles deal mainly with political economy. He wrote no reviews of literature.[5]

Sydney Smith, the originator of the idea of the *Edinburgh* and the only Englishman of the inner circle, was both an Anglican minister

[1] *Ibid*, pp. 248, 265. (A. Constable to Sir Richard Phillips, Nov. 6, 1822). The confident tone of the remark makes this testimony, I believe, more reliable than it would otherwise be.

[2] J. G. Lockhart, *Life of Sir Walter Scott, Bart.*, IV, 165 (Chap. XXVII). Jeffrey, however, seems to have been financially involved with Constable's firm at its collapse in 1826, but it is not clear whether or not this was merely a matter of his payment as editor of the *Edinburgh Review* (Cockburn, I, 278).

[3] Brougham, I, 248; Constable, I, 55.

[4] Constable, I, 55–56. Graham's remark in *English Literary Periodicals* (p. 238) that 'during its entire career the *Edinburgh* was associated with the house of Longman' is incorrect.

[5] For more detailed information of Horner's life, see Leonard Horner (ed.), *Memoirs and Correspondence of Francis Horner, M.P.*

and one of the wits of the age. His wit and his political liberalism seem to have combined to keep him from advancing in his church. After leaving Edinburgh in 1804, he spent several years in London giving a series of lectures on moral philosophy before receiving a country living in Yorkshire in 1806 through the influence of Lord Holland. Smith wrote the *Letters of Peter Plymley* (in favor of Catholic emancipation) before leaving London for Yorkshire, where he was 'village parson, village doctor, village comforter, village magistrate, and Edinburgh Reviewer'.[1] He reached the height of his career in 1831 as canon of St. Paul's.

Smith wrote approximately eighty reviews for the *Edinburgh* before 1825. They covered a variety of subjects, including religion (especially attacks on Methodism), travel, education, America, and social abuses. Smith was a popularizer, an occupation which his genius for wit made doubly effective.[2] It was this wit that made Jeffrey look to Smith to supply the *Edinburgh* with light articles to offset the frequently long-winded articles by others.[3] Smith himself saw this as no disgrace; in 1824, he reminded Jeffrey that 'lightness and flimsiness are *my line of reviewing*', and a little over a year later claimed that his articles were 'sparrow-shot' compared to Jeffrey's 'cannon and mortars'.[4] No more than sparrow-shot was called for in his only reviews of contemporary English literature—one on Moore's *Memoirs of Captain Rock* and several others on novels of secondary importance.[5]

Henry Brougham, the most indefatigable of the reviewers for the *Edinburgh*, was called by his most recent biographer 'the most vital personality of [the] period'.[6] Allowing somewhat for the exaggeration of biographers, something like that distinction is perhaps owed to Brougham. After leaving Edinburgh in 1804 for the English bar, he immediately became connected with slave-trade

[1] Lady Holland, *Memoir of the Reverend Sydney Smith*, I, 161. The biographical information on Smith contained in this paragraph is taken from this memoir by Smith's daughter.

[2] *Ibid.*, pp. 35–36.

[3] Cockburn, II, 81, 84 (Jeffrey to Horner, Sept. 2 and Sept. 8, 1803).

[4] N. C. Smith, I, 408, 422 (Smith to Jeffrey, Sept. 22, 1824, and 'probably about' Feb. 12, 1826).

[5] All attributions of authorship of literary reviews in the *Edinburgh* are taken from Walter E. Houghton (ed.), *The Wellesley Index to Victorian Periodicals 1824–1900*, pp. 416–66.

[6] New, p. v. The biographical information in this paragraph is based on New's study.

abolition, the first of many movements he joined and led. He became a Whig M.P. in 1810—the beginning of a fifty-four-year parliamentary career—and used his considerable energy in the cause of parliamentary reform, education, law reform, the abolition of slavery itself, and the reform of any number of government abuses. He was also a practising lawyer, defending the Hunts twice and acting as one of the defense lawyers at the Queen's trial in 1820. He was made Lord Chancellor in 1830, when the Whigs came to power.

By 1825, Brougham was also the most prolific contributor to the *Edinburgh*, with a probable total of over two hundred articles.[1] In the earlier issues, Brougham wrote on science, travels, and economics; but as he became more involved with his various crusades, there was a preponderance of political articles, especially on projects for reform. He in fact made the *Edinburgh* his mouthpiece, which brought about much of the animosity directed against the publication.[2] Even his one review of contemporary English literature had repercussions: his review of Byron's *Hours of Idleness* brought forth Byron's satiric *English Bards and Scotch Reviewers*.

The last of the original projectors to be considered is also the most important, for Francis Jeffrey was the sole editor of the *Edinburgh* after the third number in 1803 until the ninety-eighth number in 1829, except for numbers thirty-three and thirty-four in the winter of 1813–14, when he was in America.[3] That Jeffrey should have been

[1] Brougham's contributions to the *Edinburgh Review* (to 1830) are listed in an appendix to New's study, from which the sum in the text is derived. New's research for these attributions seems to be thorough, but there is a mistake on p. 433 (a double entry of art. 5 for No. XXXVII); therefore New's totals listed on p. 446 are incorrect. Twenty-two of the articles New ascribes to Brougham before 1825 and included in my approximate 'over two hundred', are listed by New as 'more likely than not'. Jeffrey, on the other hand, had contributed about 185 articles by the same date, most of them fairly certain attributions, and may even have contributed more. It is possible that Jeffrey actually contributed a greater number of articles than Brougham by 1825.

[2] New, pp. 15, 28, 40, 60, 131, 149, 204, 300, 348, 365.

[3] The temporary editor for these two numbers is difficult to determine. Cosmo Innes, in his *Memoir of Thomas Thomson, Advocate*, says (p. 138) that Jeffrey left Thomson as 'his viceregent'; and Clive (p. 45) accepts this claim. But Cockburn (I, 215) names both Thomson and John A. Murray. Murray seems definitely to have participated; Smith says to him in a letter on July 12, 1813: 'I understand you are one of the Commissioners for managing the Edinburgh Review' (N. C. Smith, I, 237; see also I, 241). Sir James Mackintosh seems also to have been involved (Constable, II, 214–15), but from evidence in R. J. Mackintosh (ed.), *Memoirs of the Life of the Right Honourable Sir James Mackintosh*, II, 262–70, Sir

chosen as editor was not a matter of chance. He was the center of the group toward which all the others gravitated. As Lord Cockburn pointed out, 'several of them surpassed him in individual qualities, but none in general power'.[1] A lawyer at the Scottish bar, he was nonetheless interested and competent in many fields. Lord Brougham later testified that 'if we had searched all Europe, a better man, *in every respect*, could not have been found'.[2]

Some of the apparent exaggeration of Brougham's testimony disappears when Jeffrey's editorial responsibilities, as set forth by Lord Cockburn, are taken into account:

> He had not only to revise and arrange each number after its parts were brought together, but before he got this length, he, like any other person in that situation, had much difficult and delicate work to perform. He had to discover, and to train, authors; to discern what truth and the public mind required; to suggest subjects; to reject, and, more offensive still, to improve, contributions; to keep down absurdities; to infuse spirit; to excite the timid; to repress violence; to sooth jealousies; to quell mutinies; to watch times; and all this in the morning of the reviewing day, before experience had taught editors conciliatory firmness, and contributors reasonable submission. He directed and controlled the elements he presided over with a master's judgment. There was not one of his associates who could have held these elements together for a single year.[3]

Jeffrey held the *Edinburgh* together for twenty-six years and delivered it over to his successor a successful and smoothly running periodical.

And yet with all the powers that his duties imply, Jeffrey never had absolute power over the *Edinburgh*. Although in 1803 Jeffrey, feeling his new power as editor, jokingly told Horner, 'I am the master', he also admitted to Horner in 1810 that 'I am but a feudal monarch at best, and my throne is overshadowed by the presumptuous crests of my nobles'.[4] One noble in particular, Brougham, had considerable influence with Jeffrey in directing the policies of the

---

James seems to have been in London during the time in question and no reference is made to an editorial function. Thomson and Murray may have been co-editors again in 1824 when Jeffrey was abroad. See Martha H. Gordon, *Christopher North*, II, 72.

[1] Cockburn, I, 143.

[2] Brougham, I, 264.

[3] Cockburn, I, 301–2.

[4] *Ibid.*, II, 67, 129 (Jeffrey to Horner, Apr. 1, 1803, and July 20, 1810).

Edinburgh, chiefly because he was a dependable contributor.[1] But Jeffrey in general disliked interference with his editorial authority.[2]

Jeffrey was the only one of the original projectors of the *Edinburgh Review* to remain in Edinburgh. Along with his editorial duties, he managed to practise law in spite of prejudices arising from his connections with the *Edinburgh*; and by 1811 his practice was increasing steadily.[3] From the beginning, he had scruples as to the possible degradation connected with his editorship; and in 1827, when the chance of a judicial promotion was in view, he was still aware of this possibility.[4] But in July, 1829, Jeffrey was made Dean of the Faculty of Advocates, an honorary position. He then resigned as editor of the *Edinburgh*, having decided that the two positions were incompatible. In 1830, with the Whigs back in office, he was made Lord Advocate, which was the highest position of dignity in Scotland.[5] Finally, in 1833, Jeffrey was made Judge of the Court of Session, and along with the position came the title 'Lord'.

Either of these careers—editing or law—would have been enough for any one man to cope with. Jeffrey, however, managed also to be one of the major contributors to the *Edinburgh* during the years under study.[6] By the end of 1824, he had written about 185 articles, a large percentage of which were on biographies, letters, and memoirs, fewer on law and politics, and others on travel, philosophy, and religion. But far and away the largest group of his reviews was on literature, mainly English, but also classical and continental. That Jeffrey should have written so many reviews considering his other two full-time careers is not surprising when his critical bent is considered; for even as a boy, he wrote a great deal in a systematic way, and most of the writing is either critical itself or followed by self-criticism.[7] Jeffrey had both a habit of writing and a critical nature.

Of some sixty-seven reviews in the *Edinburgh* before 1825 that deal with significant works of contemporary English literature,

[1] Clive, pp. 63–64. See also New, p. 46.

[2] Smith, I, 369 (Sydney Smith to Edward Davenport, Dec. 15, 1820).

[3] Cockburn, I, 144, 199.

[4] *Ibid.*, II, 71–72, 74, 84; I, 280. [5] *Ibid.*, I, 305, 307.

[6] See p. 15, note 1, above.

[7] Cockburn, I, 19–33. Jeffrey was already a contributor to the *Monthly Review* before the first number of the *Edinburgh Review* was published. A list of thirteen articles by Jeffrey published in the *Monthly Review* from June, 1802, to Jan. 1803, is contained in the introduction to D. Nichol Smith, *Jeffrey's Literary Criticism*, p. ix.

about fifty were written by Jeffrey.[1] They cover most major works of the Romantic writers now considered of greatest importance. The only other such review by any of the original group was Brougham's review of Byron's *Hours of Idleness*, previously mentioned.

Both Jeffrey and Brougham were lawyers trained for the Scottish bar, a fact that tends to substantiate Brougham's claim that there was an especially close relationship between law and literature in Scotland.[2] Two other literary reviewers also were connected with Scottish law. Walter Scott, a colleague of Jeffrey at the Scottish bar, wrote at least thirteen articles before he ceased contributing in 1808. However, only two of these review contemporary literary works of any importance: one translated, the other edited by Southey.[3] Thomas Brown, although a physician, philosopher, and poet, had also studied law in Scotland; he reviewed Lamb's *John Woodvil*.[4]

Still other *Edinburgh* reviewers of literature were lawyers at the English bar. Thomas Noon Talfourd, who reviewed Hazlitt's *Lectures on Elizabethan Drama* in 1820, and is now best known as an early editor of Lamb and Hazlitt, was also a lawyer—he became a judge in 1849—as well as poet and playwright. Another lawyer, Sir James Mackintosh, also led a varied, energetic career in philosophy, education, and politics; he wrote a review of Rogers' *Poems* of 1812. Sir John Stoddart, who reviewed Scott's *Minstrelsy*, was journalist as well as lawyer. Henry Hallam, famed writer of medieval history, was a lawyer before acquiring the independent means necessary for his other career; he reviewed Scott's edition of Dryden.

The remainder of the literary reviewers for the *Edinburgh* before 1825 were more particularly connected with the literary life of the times. George Ellis, the reviewer of Scott's edition of *Sir Tristrem*, and John Wilson, the reviewer of Canto IV of Byron's *Childe Harold*,

[1] By 'significant works of contemporary English Literature' I mean works written, edited, or translated by Wordsworth, Coleridge, Byron, Keats, Shelley, Scott, Southey, Hunt, Hazlitt, Lamb, Campbell, Rogers, Moore, Crabbe, Jane Austen, or Maria Edgeworth. The following attributions to Jeffrey are questionable: reviews of Hunt's *Rimini*, Southey's *Carmen Triumphale*, and the joint review of Moore's *Loves of the Angels* and Byron's *Heaven and Earth*. See Houghton under appropriate vol. and P. P. Howe (ed.), *The Complete Works of William Hazlitt*, XVI, 420–21.

[2] Brougham, I, 243.

[3] Reviews of Southey's translation of *Amadis of Gaul* and of his edition of Chatterton's works.

[4] Biographical information on Brown, Talfourd, Mackintosh, Stoddart, and Hallam was taken from the *D.N.B.*

will be discussed later in their more significant relationships with the *Quarterly Review* and *Blackwood's Magazine*, respectively. William Hazlitt reviewed Coleridge's *Biographia Literaria* and the *Statesman's Manual*, and Shelley's *Posthumous Poems*. Finally, there are contributions that have not yet been identified: reviews of Southey's *Specimens of English Poetry* and Coleridge's *Christabel*.

There were, of course, other reviews of works of literature—such as the poetry of James Montgomery and of Amelia Opie—that have not survived the test of time and will not therefore concern us here. Reviews of literary works in fact appeared in almost every number of the *Edinburgh*, as did also reviews of political books and pamphlets.

Since the political aspect of most of the reviewing in the *Edinburgh* has been emphasized by later commentators on the publication, a brief sketch of its political background is necessary here. The frequency of the political articles, for example, combined with the buff and blue colors of the Foxites on the *Edinburgh*'s cover, are often used as evidence of this periodical's political partisanship—evidence that the *Edinburgh* was a Whig organ. But it is not as simple as that.

In December, 1808, when rumors of the impending establishment of the rival *Quarterly Review* were circulating, Walter Scott wrote to a friend that Jeffrey, apparently in a funk, had promised him that no more party politics would appear in the *Edinburgh Review*.[1] Years after Lockhart had published the letter in his *Life of Scott*, Jeffrey insisted that Scott had misunderstood him and that what he had really said was that the *Edinburgh* would avoid, not party politics, but excessively violent and unfair politics.[2] And yet, oddly enough, Jeffrey made the very distinction that Scott claimed he had, in letters to Horner and Smith at about the same time.[3] In these letters, Jeffrey

[1] Lockhart, III, 150 (chap. XVIII).

[2] Francis Jeffrey, *Contributions to the Edinburgh Review*, I, xiii–xvii. Clive's rendering of this episode (p. 69) is misleading because he confuses *politics* and *party politics*, when he states that Jeffrey claimed that 'the notion that he should have offered to renounce politics altogether at that time was "palpably ridiculous"'. In the introduction to his *Contributions*, Jeffrey was quite explicit (p. xvi): he had often told Scott of the impossibility 'of excluding politics (which of course could mean nothing but party politics) from the Review'. The reason for Jeffrey's later insistence on the partisan nature of the *Edinburgh Review* at that early period was most likely a compression of the whole period of his editorship in his memory after a lapse of more than thirty years; for the publication did become more partisan later on.

[3] Horner, I, 465 (Jeffrey to Horner, Dec. 6, 1808); Smith, I, 147 (Smith to

resolved to avoid *party* politics but not political discussion altogether. This distinction is, I believe, an important one.

Sydney Smith called the *Edinburgh* 'a sort of magazine of liberal sentiments', and Horner termed it 'a most useful channel for the circulation of liberal opinions'.[1] The *Edinburgh* was, from the beginning, supposed to be liberal, not Whig. Lockhart, in his *Life of Scott*, quotes a letter from an unidentified correspondent that describes the publication's early policy:

> Neutrality, or something of the kind, as to party politics, seems to have been originally asserted—the plan being, as Scott understood, not to avoid such questions altogether, but to let them be handled by Whig or Tory indifferently, if only the writer could make his article captivating in point of information and good writing.[2]

In any case, a strong Tory, such as Scott, could write for the *Edinburgh* without scruples, at least until 1808. By that time, Brougham, who had been undecided about party affiliation, had gone over to the Whig party; and since there was an understanding that he was to be the main contributor on political subjects and had become that in fact, he caused the *Edinburgh* gradually to assume more strictly Whiggish views.[3] This was the situation in 1808, when Jeffrey, confronted with the possibility of a rival Review and censured by Scott, as well as by Smith and Horner, for the increasing partisanship of the *Edinburgh* told them he was resolved to avoid party politics in the future.

Even with Brougham exerting his strong influence, the publication never became a strictly Whig organ, for the very good reason that Brougham never became a strictly orthodox Whig. He was much too liberal for the Whig leaders, and he rarely had their full support.[4] For example, anti-slavery was one of Brougham's favorite

Jeffrey, Nov. or Dec., 1808). Smith's letter to Jeffrey contains the following statement: 'I heard from you and from many other Quarters that you was resolved there should be no more politics in the review,—*party* politics omitted in your first Letter you have added in your explanation and this little word makes all the difference.' Since Smith had a policy of destroying all letters he received, the two letters from Jeffrey to which he refers have probably suffered that fate.

[1] Smith, I, 323 (Smith to Jeffrey, Apr. 2, 1819); Horner, I, 430 (Horner to Jeffrey, June 5, 1807). See also Brougham, I, 259, and Cockburn, II, 151–52.

[2] Lockhart, III, 65 (chap. XVI).

[3] New, p. 46. See also Clive, pp. 62–63.

[4] New, pp. 40, 146.

crusades, both in Parliament and in the *Edinburgh*; but he had to align himself with Wilberforce and the Evangelicals, who were nearly all Tories. The Whigs, some of whom were absentee slave-owners themselves, were not, as a party, abolitionists.[1] Another instance of the *Edinburgh*'s independent politics was the Don Cevallos article (written by Jeffrey and Brougham), which caused such a furor in October, 1808; it is significant that it offended the Whigs as much as the Tories.[2]

To see the *Edinburgh Review* as a party organ is to confuse its discussion of politics in general with the presentation of a partisan position; and this confusion of the periodical's politics is helped along by a further mistaken identification of Whiggism with liberalism as they existed in the early part of the nineteenth century. Just as the Tories were not merely reactionaries, the Whigs then were by no means a group of liberals fighting for social and political reforms.[3] Both parties shared aristocratic conceptions of government and can best be seen as the 'ins' and the 'outs', the 'Government' and the 'Opposition'.[4] In both parties there were factions; both Whigs and Tories had some members who were liberal and some who were conservative.[5]

The main contributors to the *Edinburgh* were all Whigs and they were all liberals. When they began the publication, however, they launched it as a liberal, not a Whig, periodical; and referred to it in terms of 'liberal' rather than 'Whig'. As previously mentioned, Brougham introduced some distinctly Whiggish issues into the *Edinburgh* by 1808, but as Jeffrey later pointed out to Horner (1815), referring to a further trend away from *general* political questions: 'In such times as we have lived in, it was impossible not to mix them, as in fact they mix themselves, with questions which might be considered as of a narrower and more factious description.'[6] The *Edinburgh*, when dealing with general political questions, was sometimes Whiggish by virtue of this inevitable mixing process, but its premises were always liberal. Sydney Smith, a Whig and a good friend of the Hollands, summed up, I think, the political position of

[1] *Ibid.*, pp. 22, 33, 128. See also Clive, pp. 88–89.
[2] New, p. 48. See also Clive, p. 112.
[3] Elie Halévy, *England in 1815* (London: Benn, 1949), p. 199.
[4] New, pp. 32, 147; Halévy, pp. 171, 173–74.
[5] Clive, pp. 72–74, 78.
[6] Cockburn, II, 151 (Jeffrey to Horner, Mar. 12, 1815).

the inner circle of the *Edinburgh*. In 1812, he wrote Jeffrey, referring to a political article he had contributed:

Pray tell me if it is much complained of by the Whigs. I shall not regret having written it if it is; but if I reconcile the interests of *truth* with the feelings of party, so much the better; I am sure it is the good sense and justice of the question.[1]

While the *Edinburgh* was beginning to increase its 'witty Whiggery', there were signs among the Tories that countermeasures were thought necessary in the form of a rival Review. On September 25, 1807, John Murray II, a successful young publisher in London, wrote to George Canning, who was then Secretary of Foreign Affairs. Murray pointed out the 'radically bad' principles of the *Edinburgh* and proposed the establishment of a rival, but only if Canning and his 'friends' would help.[2]

There was apparently no direct answer from Canning, but contact was made with Murray through a cousin, Stratford Canning, who seems to have taken part in a similar idea for a rival periodical while 'walking one day in Pall Mall with two of [his] Eton friends', although it is not quite clear which of them first had the inspiration. The three Etonians discussed the idea, and Stratford talked it over with George Canning, who referred him to William Gifford, 'who in his turn approved the proposal'.[3] In January, 1808, Stratford Canning introduced Gifford to Murray, and the latter two men began to have frequent consultations.[4]

By 1808, there were other plans for rivals to the *Edinburgh*; in fact, the idea seems to have been pervasive. In late 1807 Robert Southey had suggested such a scheme to Coleridge, but Coleridge had already

[1] Smith, I, 226 (Smith to Jeffrey, Sept., 1812). See also W. H. Auden, 'Portrait of a Whig', p. 153.

[2] Smiles, I, 93. Murray later said he had been thinking about a new Review for a year before writing to Canning (Smiles, I, 109).

[3] Stanley Lane-Poole, *Life of Stratford Canning*, I, 192. There is no date given to the inspiration on Pall Mall, but it seems likely that it occurred after Murray's letter to George Canning, since nothing was done before January, 1808, despite Stratford Canning's own previous acquaintance with Murray (see Smiles, I, 67). Stratford Canning also claimed that the name of the *Quarterly Review* originated with him and his two friends.

[4] Smiles, I, 94. Murray wrote to Stratford Canning in 1809 that the *Quarterly Review* owed 'its birth to [his] obliging countenance and introduction [of himself] to Mr. Gifford' (Smiles, I, 152).

considered something of that nature; the *Friend* of 1809–10 was the outcome.[1] Both Richard Cumberland and the Wilberforce group had their individual plans for a rival; and Walter Scott had advocated the establishment of a periodical to counteract the *Edinburgh*, with the publication of the *Edinburgh Annual Register* as one result.[2]

The planning of what was eventually to become the *Quarterly Review* was in the meantime getting nowhere. The initial impetus of the combined efforts of the Cannings, Murray, and Gifford seems to have petered out, possibly because George Canning had more than enough to keep him occupied on the political scene and because Stratford Canning left England as secretary of a mission to Turkey in June, 1808. Perhaps what was needed was the support of a man like Walter Scott.

Scott was a logical candidate for major participation in setting up the new Review, if not also for its first editorship. Murray told Lockhart 'that when he read the article on Marmion, and another on general politics, in the same number of the Edinburgh Review [April, 1808], he said to himself—"Walter Scott has feelings both as a gentleman and a Tory, which these people must now have wounded: —the alliance between him and the whole clique of the Edinburgh Review, its proprietor included, is shaken." '[3] Scott did indeed break off as a contributor to the publication shortly after that issue, but his irritation at the review of *Marmion* seems not to have been a major factor in his switch to the *Quarterly Review*, as has been often claimed ever since, because he and Jeffrey had gone over the review in question and had 'had a hearty laugh at the revisal of the flagellation'.[4] Scott himself said that he quit the *Edinburgh* 'when their politics became so warm'.[5]

In any case, Scott was to become one of the main supporters of the new Review; in fact, the history of that periodical from October,

[1] Jack Simmons, *Southey*, pp. 125–26.

[2] Grierson, *Letters*, II, 120, 123, 129, 143. Lockhart, III, 126 (chap. XVIII). Smiles, I, 117. The *Edinburgh Annual Register* seems to have originally been planned as a joint effort involving Constable, Jeffrey, Brougham, and Horner *and* Scott, Ellis, and Canning (Constable, I, 111, 117, 119).

[3] Lockhart, III, 124 (chap. XVIII).

[4] Grierson, *Letters*, II, 54 (Scott to Robert Surtees, Apr. 1808); see also II, 51, 66. Lockhart, III, 62 (chap. XVI). Southey denied that the review of *Marmion* had anything to do with Scott's separation from the *Edinburgh Review* (John Wood Warter (ed.), *Selections from the Letters of Robert Southey*, II, 132).

[5] Grierson, *Letters*, II, 71 (Scott to Lady Abercorn, June 9, 1808).

1808, to the publication of the first number must be traced mainly in Scott's correspondence.[1] For, after nearly eight months of apparent inactivity, the plan got under way again in the middle of October, 1808, when Murray visited Scott at Ashestiel. Murray asked Scott to be editor; Scott declined but offered his wholehearted assistance.[2]

While Murray was with Scott, the October issue of the *Edinburgh* arrived, containing the famous article, 'Don Cevallos on the French Usurpation of Spain'. The book being reviewed, a propagandistic account by the First Secretary of State to the exiled King Ferdinand VII, was used by Jeffrey and Brougham, the co-reviewers, to attack the war effort—England made war with France 'for the purpose of sharing in the plunder' of Spain; to point out that Napoleon had merely miscalculated and that with larger forces he could easily recapture Spain; and, most galling of all, to show that England, by her support of the Spanish uprising, which was in some respects a popular undertaking, was in fact supporting the rights of a people to overthrow an unjust government. This review was thus directed against the first favorable event in years in the long, depressing war with France. Scott withdrew his subscription to the *Edinburgh*; the Earl of Buchan, 'personally, *kicked* the [*Edinburgh Review*] out to the centre of the street, where he left it to be trodden into the mud'; and Sydney Smith reported that the *Edinburgh* was 'not only discontinued by many people but returned to the Bookseller from the very first volume: the library shelves fumigated, &c.'[3]

[1] In a letter to the Rev. Polwhele, dated July 21, 1808 (Grierson, *Letters*, II, 81–82), Scott discusses the *Quarterly Review* by name and mentions Gifford as editor. The letter is undoubtedly misdated, since by all indications, both the name and editor of the *Quarterly Review* were not definitely decided upon until the fall of 1808. The mention of recent residence in London—Scott was not in London in 1808—would indicate that the letter probably should be dated 1809.

[2] Grierson, *Letters*, II, 101n (letter from William Erskine to A. C. Colquhoun, Oct. 23, 1808). In a note on p. 130, in reference to Scott's statement to his brother that he had been asked to be editor of the *Quarterly Review*, Grierson says, 'Murray knew nothing of this.' And yet in a prefatory remark to the letter from Erskine on p. 101n, in which Erskine states that Murray offered Scott the editorship, Grierson says, 'The following letter of Erskine shows that Murray had thought of Scott as editor.' Smiles (I, 96) makes no mention of Murray's offer of the editorship, but implies instead that Murray told Scott that Gifford was to be editor. Cyrus Redding, in *Fifty Years Recollections, Literary and Personal*, I, 69, claimed that the editorship was offered to a 'Dr. Grant' before it was offered to Gifford.

[3] Lockhart, III, 126 (chap. XVIII); Cockburn, I, 190n; Smith, I, 152. John Wain, in *Contemporary Reviews of Romantic Poetry* (pp. 18–19), says of the violent

The political reaction to the *Edinburgh* number of October, 1808, gave added impetus to the planners of the *Quarterly Review*. By October 25, 1808, A. C. Colquhoun, the Lord Advocate of Scotland, had heard from George Canning and had in turn contacted Scott and requested him to write to Gifford. Scott has been called 'the master strategist of the Tory Camp'[1]—this title undoubtedly given because of the letter which he sent to Gifford on the date referred to above. The letter should be read in full, for it outlines the policies of the new Review as Scott saw them: that the new publication should follow the *Edinburgh* in freedom from booksellers' influence, and in payment for all contributions; that the editor must have absolute control and should add spice to dull articles; that access to inside political information was necessary; that the new Review should not at first be exclusively political nor ever merely pro-ministry; finally, that the criticisms should reflect the value of the works reviewed. Scott also listed the Roses, Malthus, George Ellis, the Hebers, and Oxford scholars as possible contributors.[2]

About a week later, Scott wrote his friend, George Ellis, and introduced him to the plans for the new Review, stressing its non-partisan nature and 'its principles English and constitutional'.[3] On the same day, he wrote to Murray, announcing approval of his letter to Gifford by the Lord Advocate.[4] About this same time, Gifford was busy soliciting contributions. He sought out Southey through Grosvenor Bedford, a mutual friend. Southey accepted the offer but laid down his political position, which was anti-partisan but in favor of both the war with Napoleon and Reform.[5] This position was, however, to change after 1810, when Southey became a Tory reactionary and an anti-Reformist.[6]

reaction to the Don Cevallos article: 'It is hard to see why; in fact a glance at this article is the quickest way for a modern reader to assure himself of the eagerness with which heresies were sniffed out and denounced.' This is true only if one ignores the political situation, especially the state of war with France. See Geoffrey Carnall, *Robert Southey and His Age*, pp. 85–98; and John Clive, 'The Earl of Buchan's Kick: A Footnote to the History of the *Edinburgh Review*'.

[1] Walter Graham, *Tory Criticism in the Quarterly Review, 1809–1853*, p. 6.

[2] The letter of policy from Scott to Gifford (Oct. 25, 1808) is in two versions: Lockhart, III, 133–42 (chap. XVIII) and Grierson, *Letters*, II, 100–9. For differences between the two versions, see Grierson, *Letters*, II, 100, n. 1.

[3] Grierson, *Letters*, II, 121 (Scott to Ellis, Nov. 2, 1808).

[4] *Ibid.*, p. 123 (Scott to Murray, Nov. 2, 1808).

[5] Simmons, p. 128; Smiles, I, 107–8.

[6] Carnall, pp. 100, 120. See also Simmons, p. 152.

Scott received from Gifford approval of his letter of policy on November 13 and two days later wrote to Murray complaining of the amount of help Gifford seemed to anticipate from him; Scott also said that he would not be able to come to London before spring.[1] Murray had written Scott that same day, and he also had something to say about Gifford; he expressed doubts concerning his editorial abilities. He also added a reassurance that he agreed with Scott about the freedom of the new Review from the influence of booksellers.[2] Scott informed Ellis on November 18 that Canning had read the letter of policy to Gifford and had 'promised such aid as is therein required'. Scott also had some doubts of his own about Gifford.[3]

By the end of November, 1808, Gifford was in constant contact with George Canning; and Gifford, Canning, and Ellis spent four days together at Ellis's house working on a political article.[4] Both Scott and Murray were busy for the next few months soliciting articles from their acquaintances (in the case of Scott, also writing articles), as a glance at both sets of correspondence shows. That most of the requests for contributions were made to friends was owing to the secrecy that was thought necessary and was insisted upon throughout their correspondence. No plan, however, of such a scope and involving so many people could remain a secret for long; in December, 1808, Jeffrey had heard of the new Review and swore to avoid partisan politics.[5]

The first number of the *Quarterly Review* appeared in late February, 1809. A copy reached Scott on March 2; after a glance through, he was well satisfied with it, except that it appeared to have been the result of haste.[6] This first number was generally well received; a second edition was soon called for; but the total sale of the first number was not large enough to make the *Quarterly Review* an outstanding success.[7] Scott reported that the sales were better in Edinburgh than in London, but asked Murray to inform the Lord

[1] Grierson, *Letters*, II, 124–27 (Scott to Murray, Nov. 15, 1808).

[2] Smiles, I, 109–12 (Murray to Scott, Nov. 15, 1808).

[3] Grierson, *Letters*, II, 127–30 (Scott to Ellis, Nov. 18, 1808).

[4] Smiles, I, 116, 118.

[5] See above p. 20. For Jeffrey's knowledge of the projected *Quarterly Review*, see Horner, I, 465 (Jeffrey to Horner, Dec. 6, 1808).

[6] Grierson, *Letters*, II, 173–74; Smiles, I, 146.

[7] Smiles, I, 147, 148. See also Holland, II, 51 (Smith to John Allen, Feb. 21, 1809): 'The Quarterly Review is out also; not good, I hear.' This statement is for some reason not included in N. C. Smith's version of Smith's letter (I, 155).

Advocate that it would be to the advantage of the *Quarterly* if Scott could go to London.[1] Scott was in London in April, May, and part of June, 'was much with George Ellis, Canning, and Croker', and conferred with Murray and Gifford.[2]

The second number was late, appearing at the end of May, but apparently all of the conferences had a good effect, for Number Two was generally considered an improvement.[3] The numbers continued to be late for some years, but in spite of the delays and early friction among the staff, the *Quarterly* continued to grow until, by early 1818, it achieved the same circulation as the *Edinburgh*.[4]

After this brief history of the genesis of the *Quarterly Review*, the political connections of this periodical should be obvious. George Canning's relationship with the *Quarterly* was a closely guarded secret; and when viewing his extensive political career, that relationship can scarcely be called even an episode. Yet it is evident that Canning was pulling the strings at least during the planning stages, from the introduction of Murray to Gifford to setting the tone of the political articles. He may have directed Murray to offer Scott the editorship, for Canning and Scott had become friends in 1807; and it was Canning who finally chose Gifford.[5] In the summer of 1809, Canning told John Barrow that he was 'deeply, both publicly and personally, interested' in the *Quarterly* and had 'taken a leading part' in its founding.[6] But the operation of political connections becomes most blatant in Scott's request to Murray, mentioned above, that Scott be sent to London through the influence of Government officials.

Tory politicians in office were clearly involved, and yet it is a

[1] Grierson, *Letters*, II, 182–84 (Scott to Murray, Mar. 19, 1809).

[2] Lockhart, III, 187, 188 (chap. XIX).

[3] Smiles, I, 157–60.

[4] *Ibid.*, II, 4. Conflicting testimony concerning the circulation figures is given in the *British Stage*, III (Aug., 1819), 234, where it is claimed that in Aug., 1819, the *QR* (about thirteen to fourteen thousand) is only *nearly* equal to the *ER* (about fifteen thousand). See also Kenneth Curry (ed.), *New Letters of Robert Southey*, II, 178, 180. For a short account of the problems encountered in getting the *QR* under way, see Roy B. Clark, *William Gifford*, pp. 171–77.

[5] H. J. C. Grierson, *Sir Walter Scott, Bart.*, pp. 91–92; Smiles, I, 138. In a letter to George Canning on Sept. 8, 1824, Gifford says, 'It is now exactly sixteen years ago since your letter invited or encouraged me to take the throne' (Smiles, II, 163).

[6] Sir John Barrow, *Autobiographical Memoir of Sir John Barrow*, p. 499. Also quoted in Smiles, I, 166.

mistake to see the *Quarterly* as having been set up as a mere partisan mouthpiece. The principal founders concurred in disapproval of such a policy; Scott, whose letter of policy to Gifford had been approved by the Tory politicians in question, had made a point of denouncing any such tie, which point had been seconded by Gifford, the editor, and was apparently approved by all of the others involved—at least there is no record of any disapproval. And Southey and Croker, both of them important contributors, were against making the *Quarterly* a partisan organ.[1]

But if the *Quarterly* was not to be partisan, it was to stand for certain principles—'English and constitutional', as Scott phrased them. Behind the framing of those principles, however, there stands the primary purpose of the new Review, which was explicit throughout the planning stage: the counteracting of the 'pernicious' doctrine of the *Edinburgh Review*. As has already been mentioned, some of the latter's political views were objectionable to both Whigs and Tories; but, under the influence of Brougham, some of those views were distinctly Whiggish. And so it is only to be expected that many of the political articles in the rival *Quarterly* should have had a distinctly Tory bias. Add to this natural rivalry the fact that many of the political articles in the first twelve numbers were written in collaboration by George Ellis and George Canning, an active Tory politician, and the likelihood of a partisan line is bound to be great.[2]

Since from 1809 to 1830 the Tories were the party in power—the 'ins', the 'Government'—reviewers in early issues of the *Quarterly* would thus be in a position of defending the ministry and could not afford the amount of freedom of political views enjoyed by the *Edinburgh* reviewers as part of a divided 'Opposition'. The evidence does seem to indicate that the former publication was more partisan than the latter; but, like the *Edinburgh*, the *Quarterly* managed to retain a certain amount of political independence of viewpoint.[3] Walter Graham, in his study of the *Quarterly*, states:

The *Quarterly* did not keep close to the Tories of the various ministries. After 1822 it cannot be said to have represented the Government. But it spoke always for a certain very conservative attitude of mind, opposed

[1] Simmons, pp. 128–29; Anon., 'The Centenary of the "Quarterly Review" ', 756; Graham, *Tory Criticism*, p. 8.

[2] Hill Shine and Helen C. Shine, *The 'Quarterly Review' under Gifford*, p. xii.

[3] Graham, *Periodicals*, p. 245.

to innovation and change—it was a pattern of old fidelity to British institutions.[1]

That is, the *Quarterly* had by the 1820's become reactionary and then remained so after the liberal segment of the Tories had gained control of the party.[2]

As we have seen, it was Brougham who influenced the *Edinburgh Review*'s politics by virtue of his dependable contributions; in the same way, it was dependable Southey who 'helped to give the [*Quarterly*] *Review* thruout a number of years the character of narrowness and intolerance which was peculiarly his own'.[3] Again it is a question, not so much of parties, as of political attitudes. Both Reviews were sometimes partisan; but when taking an independent line, the *Edinburgh*, which was controlled by liberal Whigs was naturally liberal; the *Quarterly*, which was controlled by Tories who happened to be conservatives, was naturally conservative when it was not distinctly partisan.

Like the *Edinburgh*, the *Quarterly* did not take shape overnight; the first number was published well over a year after the introduction of Gifford to Murray. But, unlike its rival, the *Quarterly* was not the brainchild of a gathering of friends. And yet those involved in its founding—the Cannings, Murray, Scott, Ellis, Gifford, and Croker—were not merely far-flung men with only a political affiliation or attitude in common. Most of them were friends, and almost all of them had some previous connection with the others.

Most of the connections have their roots back in the *Anti-Jacobin; or, Weekly Examiner*, a violently reactionary periodical set up in 1797 to counteract seditious publications—that is, for somewhat the same reasons as the *Quarterly Review* was later founded. The *Anti-Jacobin* had a short existence, lasting only eight months, but it brought together George Canning, William Gifford, and George Ellis. This association led to further ones; for example, it was through a mutual friendship with Ellis that Scott and Canning met in 1806, an acquaintanceship that later grew to friendship in 1807.[4]

Of those involved in founding the *Quarterly*, John Murray was the

[1] Graham, *Tory Criticism*, p. 17.

[2] In *Ibid.*, Graham says (p. vi, n.) that the *Quarterly Review* had 'remained loyal to the old-line Tories of the Eldon type'.

[3] *Ibid.*, p. 6.

[4] Lockhart, II, 63 (chap. X), 312 (chap. XV); Grierson, *Scott*, pp. 91–92.

most nearly an outsider. He and George Canning seem to have been acquainted when Murray wrote to him in 1807, but Murray had helped a group of Etonians, among them Stratford Canning, to publish a volume of essays, the *Miniature*, in 1805.[1] As mentioned above, Murray met Gifford for the first time through Stratford Canning in 1808; and Murray and Ellis were likewise strangers prior to the launching of the *Quarterly*. But Murray knew Scott through his part in the publication of *Marmion*; they had met in London in 1807.[2]

John Murray is most famous as Lord Byron's publisher, but was also publisher of works by Scott, Southey, Jane Austen, Leigh Hunt, and Washington Irving. He was apparently the originator of the *Quarterly* and was certainly one of its chief supporters. It was he who financed this publication and did much of the soliciting of articles, both at the outset and later.[3]

His relationship to the *Quarterly*, beyond being its publisher, is difficult to define, but it seems to have been closer than that of Constable to the *Edinburgh*. In a letter to Scott in 1818, he referred to the *Quarterly* as 'my *Review*'; and in 1836, John Wilson Croker, after a dispute with Murray, acknowledged that 'he is master of his own publication' and conceded 'Murray's *sovereignty* over the *Review*', adding 'but 'tis a constitutional sovereignty, and must be exercised through his *ministers*'.[4] In any case, any influence which Murray exerted over the *Quarterly* would probably not have been of a political nature; even though Murray's letter to Canning proposing this new Review brought up the matter of parties, Murray convincingly set forth in several letters his nonpartisan position.[5] R. B. Clark, in *William Gifford*, states that Murray had 'no direct control over the nature of the reviews', and since the statement is made in reference to Murray's publishing of Hunt's *Story of Rimini* despite the probability of the poem being damned by the *Quarterly*, it seems likely that the statement is true.[6]

[1] Smiles, I, 67–69. Smiles here claims that Stratford Canning introduced Murray to George Canning, apparently in 1805; but Murray's letter to George Canning of Sept. 25, 1807 (see p. 22, note 2, above) does not indicate any previous acquaintanceship.

[2] *Ibid.*, p. 76.

[3] *Ibid.*, pp. 154, 157, 165, 181, 337; Clark, p. 170.

[4] Smiles, II, 12 (Murray to Scott, June 6, 1818). *Ibid.*, p. 382 (Croker to Lockhart, Jan. 31, 1836).

[5] *Ibid.*, I, 424; II, 263.

[6] Clark, p. 212. It is curious, however, that Murray's name, as publisher, is omitted at the head of reviews in the *Quarterly*, of works which he published.

William Gifford, like Murray, was well known in the literary world of the period. He was the author of two satires against the Della Cruscans—the *Baviad* and the *Maeviad*; an editor of the *Anti-Jacobin; or, Weekly Examiner* in 1797–98; a translator of Juvenal and Persius; and an editor of Massinger, Jonson, Ford, and Shirley. As editor of the *Quarterly* from its founding until 1824, he wielded the real control over that publication: in a letter to Canning, in 1824, he called himself 'King Gifford'.[1]

He was not crowned at the beginning of his editorship, however; just as his position with the *Anti-Jacobin* had actually been a subordinate one, so too was his editorship of the *Quarterly* at first. He lacked the wholehearted support of both Murray and Scott, as well as of other early *Quarterly* supporters; and pressure was exerted on him in the early choice of articles.[2] This situation was cleared up as the periodical gradually became a success, and eventually Gifford even became one of Murray's most valued literary advisors in his publishing business.[3]

Gifford wrote only eight articles himself, but there are at least thirty-nine in which he collaborated to some extent.[4] Of the former, none deal with major works of contemporary literature; of those articles on which he collaborated, only two are important for this study. It was not his writing that was significant for the *Quarterly*, but rather, as R. B. Clark points out, 'His importance and influence are to be explained by the fact that his own spirit and personality were largely merged into and expressed by the *Quarterly*.'[5]

And so, measure of Gifford's 'spirit and personality' becomes of some importance if one is to understand the publication itself. The testimony given by Gifford's contemporaries is 'conflicting' and 'likely to be tinged with prejudice, for it is furnished by close personal friends and admirers, or by bitter personal or political enemies'.[6] But it seems on the whole to have been favorable.[7] Later scholars have also held conflicting views: Samuel Smiles, the biographer of Murray, generally presents Gifford as a kindly old man; Clark, who

[1] Smiles, II, 162 (Gifford to Canning, Sept. 8, 1824).

[2] Clark, pp. 170–74, 177.

[3] Smiles, I, 127.

[4] Shine, pp. xvi–xvii. For different kinds of editing performed by Gifford, see p. xvii. All attributions of articles in the *Quarterly Review* are derived from the Shines' study.

[5] Clark, p. 200.

[6] *Ibid.*, p. 28.

[7] *Ibid.*, pp. 28–33

has done the only full-length study of Gifford, is less favorable; and Malcolm Elwin, writing over a hundred years after Gifford's death, seems almost to have been personally injured by Gifford and suggests that he had an inferiority complex.[1]

All in all, Gifford seems to have had an irascible nature, which was aggravated, if not caused, by physical deformity and chronic ill-health. He was evidently very friendly and tractable personally, displaying his irascibility mainly in his writings—in an age in which such 'personality' in literature was common, but soon to be on the way out. He was, like Scott, vitally interested in principles; and where these seemed in danger in politics, religion, or literature, he could become violent.[2] But there is also evidence that he sometimes toned down the severity of the *Quarterly* articles.[3]

During the term of Gifford's editorship, the tenor of the *Quarterly* was noticeably serious, with many articles on theology and classical studies.[4] Like the *Edinburgh*, the *Quarterly* reviewed books of all kinds and had contributors from all walks of life. Some, such as John Barrow, who contributed the most reviews during this period, never reviewed books of literature. The 112 of Barrow's reviews accepted by Gifford deal with travel, exploration, and naval matters—all subjects he was eminently qualified to handle as Second Secretary of the Admiralty.[5]

Robert Southey, who supported himself in part by his reviewing, wrote fifty-eight articles for Gifford; but in spite of his status as a professional man of letters, he did not review in the *Quarterly* a single work by any writer covered in this study.[6] His other articles deal mostly with history, travels, biography, religion, and social problems; and he was considered by Gifford one of the most valuable contributors, partly because of the well-wrought prose of his articles. These Gifford nevertheless saw fit to edit considerably, to Southey's great annoyance.[7] Southey was in fact the most incompatible of the *Quarterly* group; he did not get on well with Murray, Gifford, Ellis,

[1] Malcolm Elwin, 'The Founder of the "Quarterly Review"—John Murray II', p. 10.

[2] Clark, pp. 164–65, 176, 245–47.

[3] Smiles, I, 162; II, 130.

[4] Clark, pp. 243–44. M. F. Brightfield, *John Wilson Croker*, p. 336. For an early reference to the deep seriousness, i.e., dullness, of the *Quarterly Review*, see *QR*, III (May, 1810), 339.

[5] Shine, pp. xv–xvi.

[6] *Ibid.*, p. xiii.

[7] Clark, pp. 179–81. Simmons, pp. 129–30.

or Canning, which leaves Scott and Croker as his only friendly contacts with the *Review*.[1]

After John Barrow, the most prolific contributor to the *Quarterly* under Gifford was Barrow's superior at the Admiralty, John Wilson Croker, the First Secretary. He held that important post in the Admiralty from 1809 to 1830. In spite of the heavy duties involved there, as well as the duties of an M.P., which he performed for many years, Croker managed to find time to be a Fellow of the Royal Society, to help found the Athenaeum Club, to write and publish poetry, to edit numerous memoirs and Boswell's *Life of Johnson*, and to become an authority on the history of the French Revolution. In addition to these accomplishments, Croker wrote seventy-nine articles for the *Quarterly* during Gifford's editorship alone.[2]

After such an astonishingly active life, it is ironic that Croker should be remembered mainly for his review of Keats' *Endymion*. John Wain even adds to the indignity by claiming that Croker was 'nowhere liked',[3] but this claim at least can be refuted, based on his relations with the *Quarterly* group. Croker and Canning had met in 1807 and had quickly become both friends and political allies; it was probably Canning who introduced Croker to the *Quarterly* in 1809.[4] Gifford had contributed to an unimportant weekly magazine, the *Cabinet*, which Croker had edited briefly in 1803—a coincidence that is another indication of the size of the literary world of the time; but they did not meet until 1809 during the early stages of the *Quarterly*, after which time they seem to have gotten along well.[5] Southey and Croker probably met for the first time in 1811; Croker was instrumental in obtaining the laureateship for Southey, and Southey dedicated his *Life of Nelson* to Croker.[6] Scott and Croker were friends from their first meeting in 1809 until Scott's death, with only one period of misunderstanding; and Croker and George Ellis were good friends.[7]

[1] Owen Holloway, 'George Ellis, *The Anti-Jacobin* and the *Quarterly Review*', p. 61.

[2] Shine, p. xiv. Altogether Croker wrote about 270 articles for the *Quarterly Review* (Brightfield, p. 317).

[3] Wain, p. 23.

[4] Brightfield, p. 28. Croker had many other friends in politics, among them George IV, Wellington, and Peel (Brightfield, p. 119).

[5] *Ibid.*, pp. 10, 205. Clark, pp. 177, 178.

[6] Brightfield, pp. 207, 210–12.

[7] *Ibid.*, pp. 216–28. For Croker's friendship with Ellis, see 'The Croker Papers', *QR*, CLVIII (Oct. 1884), 527.

Of the seventy-nine articles written by Croker for the *Quarterly* under Gifford, most dealt with history, especially recent French history, and with memoirs.[1] Some ten articles review significant contemporary English literature, mainly the novels of Scott and Maria Edgeworth and the poetry of Leigh Hunt and Keats. It was one of Croker's jobs to provide light articles in the form of short, ironic reviews of easily assailable new writers, or 'fools', as they were called by the inner circle of the *Quarterly Review*.[2] The review of *Endymion* was undoubtedly one of these.

When Canning left office in the autumn of 1809, the *Quarterly* lost its most important contact with the government, and Croker had to perform this function.[3] He did not write any strictly political articles before 1825, but Croker was definitely a party man—like Canning, a liberal Tory.[4]

Walter Scott, who had taken such an active part in the founding of the *Quarterly*, rivaled Croker in the distinction of being the most important contributor on significant contemporary literature during Gifford's editorship. During that time, Scott wrote nineteen articles altogether, many of them on Scottish history and on balladry.[5] About ten of the articles dealt with contemporary literature, the most important being reviews of the poetry of Campbell, Southey, and Byron, the novels of Jane Austen, and his own *Tales of My Landlord.*

It is perhaps significant that Scott was financially involved in the *Quarterly* through his partnership with the Ballantynes, who were the Edinburgh publishers of the *Quarterly* from its beginning until the spring of 1810.[6] During this time, roughly covering the first six numbers, Scott wrote nine of the nineteen articles identified as his; and his financial interests could be partly accounted for by this initial activity and its subsequent decline.

After Croker and Scott, the most important reviewer of contemporary literature was George Ellis, who had been prominent in the founding of the *Quarterly*. Before his death in 1815, he wrote or had a part in at least twenty-six articles, some dealing with Russia and with the West Indies, and some, in collaboration with Canning, on English politics.[7] He wrote six important literary reviews—four on

[1] Shine, p. xiv.

[2] Brightfield, pp. 336–37.

[3] *Ibid.*, pp. 164–65; Anon., 'The Centenary of the "Quarterly Review" ', p. 744. See also Smiles, II, 53.

[4] Brightfield, pp. 52, 264.

[5] Shine, pp. xi–xii

[6] Smiles, I, 85, 142, 175.

[7] Shine, p. xii.

Scott's poetry and two on Byron's. Ellis, the oldest of the founders of the *Quarterly*, was by 1809 already established as a well-known politician and writer of the period, and was, like Croker, a Fellow of the Royal Society. In 1790 he published his *Specimens of the Early English Poets*, which in time went through six editions and brought about his acquaintanceship with Scott.[1]

As the *Quarterly* got under way, it gained many contributors, most of whom were prominent in one walk of life or another. Of those who reviewed contemporary literature, Reginald Heber was perhaps the most prominent. He was to become the Bishop of Calcutta in 1822, and before that time was a Fellow at Oxford, the author of several volumes of poetry, and an hymnologist. Of Reginald Heber's eighteen articles, most were reviews of travels and history, but he also reviewed Byron's dramas and Southey's *History of Brazil* (Vol. II) and *Life of Wesley*.[2]

Two other high-ranking churchmen once wrote literary reviews for the publication. William Lyall, who became Dean of Canterbury in 1845, wrote in 1815 the review of Wordsworth's *White Doe* and *Poems* of 1815. Richard Whately, who wrote the review of two of Jane Austen's novels in 1821, succeeded Nassau Senior (see below) in the chair of political science at Oxford in 1829, which position he left in 1831 to become Archbishop of Dublin.

Including Scott and Croker, a vast majority of the literary reviewers for the *Quarterly* before 1825 were connected with the law. Nassau Senior, who wrote three reviews of Scott's novels, was a lawyer whose interest in economy led him to be the first professor of political economy at Oxford in 1825. Sir John Taylor Coleridge, who became the editor of the *Quarterly* for about a year, after Gifford's retirement, became a judge in 1835. He was the nephew of Samuel Taylor Coleridge and wrote reviews of his uncle's *Remorse* and of Shelley's *Revolt of Islam*. James Russell, who was probably the reviewer of Hazlitt's *Round Table* and *Characters of Shakespear's Plays*, was a law reporter in the Courts of the Lord Chancellory. Scott's friend and literary advisor, William Erskine (later Lord Kinneder), became a judge in 1822. He was probably the author of a review of Scott's *Vision of Don Roderick*.

The close ties between the *Quarterly* and the government are

[1] Smiles, I, 125–26. The biographical information which follows concerning the reviewers of literature in the *Quarterly Review* was derived from the *D.N.B.*

[2] Shine, p. xii.

reflected in the number of civil servants and politicians who wrote literary reviews. Grosvenor Bedford, a close friend of both Southey and Gifford, and a functionary in the Exchequer, reviewed Southey's *Curse of Kehama* and *Roderick*, the former in collaboration with Scott. Another friend of Southey, Sir Henry Taylor, was often in government service, besides being a fairly prominent writer later. He reviewed Moore's *Irish Melodies* (Numbers V to VIII) in 1822. The first four numbers of the *Irish Melodies* had been reviewed in 1812 by Horace Twiss, an M.P. from 1820 to 1831 and a well-known wit of the day. John Ward (later Lord Dudley) was also an M.P. for many years and Foreign Secretary in 1827–28. He wrote reviews of Maria Edgeworth and Rogers.

The last group of literary reviewers under Gifford's editorship consists of writers and scholars. Charles Lamb, at present the most famous of these, wrote a review of Wordsworth's *Excursion* (heavily edited by Gifford). Eaton Barrett, a poet of some note at the time, collaborated with Gifford on a review of Hazlitt's *Table Talk*. William Walker, a Cambridge Fellow and Shakespearean critic, was the reviewer of Shelley's *Prometheus Unbound*.

The *Quarterly* and the *Edinburgh* are most often seen in contrast as the two major and rival reviewing periodicals of the early nineteenth century, but many of their dissimilarities are largely superficial. For example, they both used the same form and technique of reviewing, which is not surprising since the *Edinburgh* was the model for the *Quarterly*, as it was for most of the Reviews after 1802.[1] The history of the *Quarterly*'s founding evinces a few differences, such as its slow and difficult beginning; yet, even in its inception, the *Quarterly* was, like its northern rival, largely the work of friends. By 1809 the *Edinburgh* and the *Quarterly* were alike in having both some partisan affiliation and some political independence.

Another incidental dissimilarity between the two lies in the age of those most involved in their respective foundings. The *Edinburgh* was launched in 1802 by young men in their twenties and early thirties; yet though the founders of the *Quarterly* were for the most part very nearly their contemporaries, by the time of the beginning of the *Quarterly* in 1809—that is, seven years later—most of them were in their late thirties. Such were Scott (thirty-eight), George Canning (thirty-nine), and Southey (thirty-five). Murray (thirty-one)

[1] See p. 8, note 2, above. The *Quarterly Review* was conspicuously modeled after the *Edinburgh Review* (see Grierson, *Letters*, II, 102–4).

and Croker (twenty-nine) were more nearly the same age as the *Edinburgh* group at its founding, and Stratford Canning (twenty-three) was as young as any in either group. Two of the most important members of the *Quarterly* in 1809, however, were considerably older: Gifford was fifty-three and Ellis fifty-six.[1] This comparative seniority of the *Quarterly* group may help to account for the more serious tone of the publication itself.

Not only did the two rivals have much in common, but the rivalry was not always as bitter as it might first appear from their political differences. From the very beginning, the *Quarterly* group were admirers of the *Edinburgh Review*, if only grudgingly. To realize just how influential and talented the latter appeared to its contemporaries, one has only to read the correspondence of the projectors of the *Quarterly*. Such expressions as 'unquestionable talent', 'so much ability', and 'only valuable literary criticism which can be met with' are continually used to refer to the *Edinburgh*, although always accompanied by a statement deploring that periodical's politics.[2]

And then there are previous connections with the *Edinburgh*, some of which continued after the founding of the *Quarterly*. Scott, for example, was a close friend of both Jeffrey and Sydney Smith and wrote at least fourteen articles for the *Edinburgh* before his break with it in 1808, and even one later on in 1818.[3] Ellis also wrote for the *Edinburgh* in 1804; and Murray not only had business dealings with Constable, its publisher, but he 'pushed the sale' of the *Edinburgh* in 1803, sent books for reviewing by the *Edinburgh* in 1807, and even became its London publisher in 1808.[4]

Furthermore, neither the *Edinburgh* nor the *Quarterly* was a closed shop. Many reviewers contributed to both in the period before 1825: included are T. R. Malthus, Richard Chenevix, Francis Cohen (Sir Francis Palgrave), Henry Hallam, Ugo Foscolo, even Macvey Napier, who became editor of the *Edinburgh* on Jeffrey's retirement.

The rivalry was not always as bitter as it is supposed to have been, but it was always keen. This distinction must be made in order to

[1] In the article in the *Quarterly Review* cited above (p. 34, note 3), the anonymous writer for some reason remarks (p. 746) that George Ellis died at an early age in 1815. He was sixty-two.

[2] Smiles, I, 93; Grierson, *Letters*, II, 121.

[3] Lockhart, I, 241 (chap. VI); II, 134 (chap. XII); VI, 6 (chap. XLIII); Cockburn, I, 143–44.

[4] Smiles, I, 58–59, 77–80, 83; Constable, I, 55, 337, 367.

counteract the still prevalent notion that the two great Reviews, the *Edinburgh* and the *Quarterly*, were party organs manned by party zealots giving out the straight party line, and therefore locked in irrational mortal combat.

It would be too much, however, to claim that the editors and contributors of these two Reviews were unaffected by party prejudices. In an age of rapid political and social transition and of great political and social stress, with a war raging abroad for many years and revolution imminent at home, few men could help but have strong political ideas—and some prejudices. The fact is that politics pervaded the age, its literature, and its criticism. But to view as party hacks such men as Jeffrey, Brougham, Horner, Smith, Scott, Gifford, Croker, and Ellis is palpably absurd. They were all men of talent and intelligence; and most of them were eminently successful in their various careers, as well as diligent in their services to the Reviews. They in fact made the *Edinburgh* and *Quarterly* what they were: the two greatest periodicals in the history of English journalism and the two greatest critical influences on English Romantic literature.

2

The Lesser British Reviewing Periodicals 1802-1824

Besides the *Edinburgh Review* and the *Quarterly Review*, whose vast superiority is reflected in the deference often paid them by lesser journals, at least sixty other periodicals carried reviews between 1802 and 1824.[1] Some of these were founded in the eighteenth century; some survived the first quarter of the nineteenth; still others saw both their birth and death within the period under study; a few lasted only a year or less. There were all kinds, from regular Reviews to Sunday papers with only an occasional review; the majority, however, fall into the category of monthly publications, either Reviews or magazines with regular reviewing sections. With all of these reviewing periodicals contending for readership, it was obviously an age vitally interested in literature and literary criticism, for periodicals are a business venture and supply never exceeds demand for long.

The importance and influence of any of these secondary periodicals are almost impossible to determine exactly. Circulation figures are scanty, when they exist at all.[2] One of the best supplementary

[1] Josiah Conder, later editor of the *Eclectic Review*, in a short work published in Oxford in 1811 (pseud. John Charles O'Reid, *Reviewers Reviewed*) wrote (p. 54) that the *Edinburgh Review* and the *Quarterly Review* 'form a distinct class by themselves, equal or more than equal, in power and influence, to the combined host of monthly critics'. For a list of all the reviewing periodicals and for information concerning the very minor ones, see Appendix I.

[2] C. H. Timperly, in his *Encyclopedia of Literary and Topographical Anecdotes*,

criteria is the number of years a periodical survived. If it lacked subscribers it could hardly have been very influential, considering the large public demand for critical assistance at the time. But, even here, the test would only be valid for Reviews, since magazines or weekly newspapers with all of their other features would not survive on the strength of their reviews alone. Another criterion, which holds for all types of periodicals, is the survival of copies in libraries in Britain and the United States: the law of averages would influence survival in ratio with the number of copies published, and the contemporary estimate of a periodical would determine to some extent whether sets would be collected. Final evidence is the written testimony of contemporaries.

Early in 1802, the most important Review in existence, judged by the above criteria, was the *Monthly Review* (1749–1845).[1] Published and edited by Ralph Griffiths from 1749 until his death in 1803, it could boast of having once had Goldsmith as a contributor. The *Monthly* was a family concern for over three-quarters of a century; George Edward Griffiths, the son of the founder, began to assume many of the editorial duties in the last decade of the eighteenth century, became editor in fact in 1803, and remained so until he sold the *Monthly* in 1825.[2]

A further indication of the *Monthly*'s importance can be had by a glance at the list of contributors of all its articles up to 1815, which has fortunately survived.[3] Besides the reviewers of specialized works, most of whom had established reputations in their fields, the reviewers of the more important literary works themselves form an impressive group.[4] Thomas Denman, who reviewed many of the

lists the following circulation figures for 1797: *Monthly Review*, 5000; *Monthly Magazine*, 5000; *Gentleman's Magazine*, 4550; *British Critic*, 3500; *European Magazine*, 3250; *Critical Review*, 3500; *Universal Magazine*, 1750. No authority is given for these figures. See also R. D. Altick, *The English Common Reader*, Appendix C.

[1] For high estimates of the *Monthly Review* about the turn of the century by Southey and William Taylor, see J. W. Robberds, *A Memoir of the Life and Writings of the Late William Taylor of Norwich*, I, 265–66, 387. Conder (pp. 37–39) praises the *Monthly Review* but notes a decline in sale. In 1817, the *Monthly Review* was said to retain 'a circulation more extensive than that of all its rivals united' (*British Stage*, I [July, 1817], 207). In 1821, the circulation of the *Monthly Review* was estimated at 2500 (Margaret Oliphant, *Annals of a Publishing House*, I, 498).

[2] Benjamin C. Nangle, *The Monthly Review, Second Series, 1790–1815*, p. v.

[3] Nangle has catalogued the attribution of articles 1790–1815, as found in the editorial copies preserved in the Bodleian Library.

[4] Nangle, p. viii.

works of Byron, Campbell, Crabbe, and Lamb, was a young man when reviewing for the *Monthly*, but went on to become a highly successful lawyer, and finally Chief Justice in 1832.[1] Two other principal reviewers of important literary works were close friends of Denman from undergraduate days at Cambridge. John Merivale, like Denman a lawyer, reviewed *Marmion*, *The Excursion*, and *Roderick*. Francis Hodgson, a Cambridge don and poet in his own right, reviewed four of Scott's poems, as well as the *Curse of Kehama*, *Remorse*, and the *Irish Melodies*. All three friends, especially Francis Hodgson, were on good terms with Byron, who himself wrote two relatively unimportant reviews for the *Monthly*, in 1812 and 1813.

The other most important literary reviewers for the *Monthly* were of various professions. William Taylor of Norwich, who was, like his friend Southey, a professional man of letters, wrote at least three hundred and fifty reviews for the *Monthly* between 1810 and 1824, but those on the works of important English literary figures were limited mainly to Hazlitt's.[2] The reviewer of most of Byron's Eastern Tales was John Hodgson, a lawyer; Lockhart Muirhead, librarian and professor at the University of Glasgow, reviewed four of Scott's works. Another Scotsman, John Ferriar, was a doctor; he contributed reviews of Moore's poems and Southey's *Metrical Tales* and *Madoc*. Still another Scotsman, Francis Jeffrey, reviewed Southey's *Thalaba* while the *Edinburgh Review* was just getting under way.

Many of the *Monthly*'s reviewers also contributed to the *Edinburgh* and *Quarterly*. Considering this sharing of contributors with the successful new Reviews, it is surprising to find a decline in the *Monthly*'s fortunes by 1815.[3] B. C. Nangle, in the Preface to his *Monthly* index of contributors, attributes a great deal of this decline to the editorial policies of George Griffiths, especially his insistence on uniformity of style and opinion.[4] Griffiths' view, inherited from his father and shared with most editors of other Reviews, was that reviewers were supposed to reflect the corporate opinion of the publication for which they wrote, the editor alone being responsible for that opinion. This was one of the main reasons for the anonymity of the contributors. Views set forth by one reviewer should not be

[1] All of the biographical information (including a few of the attributions of reviews) in this chapter is from the *D.N.B.* unless otherwise indicated. The attributions of reviews for the *Monthly Review* to 1815 are from Nangle.

[2] Robberds, I, 126; II, 498n–99n, 521n.

[3] Nangle, p. ix.

[4] *Ibid.*, pp. x–xii.

contradictable by the next on the same subject. Since reviews frequently made reference to previous articles, it is probable that such references were most often inserted by the editor. The matter of consistency of style was a minor issue; Nangle cites the case of William Taylor, whose style was egregiously individual.[1]

Some of Griffiths' other policies, such as his insistence on strict reviewing ethics (no reviewer, for example, was allowed to review his own works or those of a friend) could not have hurt the *Monthly* in its rivalry with the newer Reviews.[2] But the uniformity of opinion must have been a serious drawback, as Nangle contends. And yet, although the reviews never turned into essays in the manner of the *Edinburgh*, the *Monthly* allowed its contributors a greater latitude of theorizing than most of the other Reviews. William Taylor was in fact a pioneer of the new 'philosophical criticism'.[3]

But the *Monthly* was in general the prototype of the other monthly Reviews, especially in the range of books reviewed and in its physical make-up. When it began its new series with a size increase in 1790 the *Monthly* announced that despite its new size it would have to ignore many publications, since the number of books published had increased greatly. An attempt was to be made, however, to overlook as few publications as possible, even though this often might mean only short notices for works of lesser importance.

To cope with as many works as possible, the size of the *Monthly* ranged from about ninety-six to one hundred and twenty octavo pages a month, with about ten to fifteen longer (five to twenty pages each) reviews, plus a 'Monthly Catalogue' of short reviews and notices. Only the *Critical Review* followed this pattern very closely—down to the hundred-page Appendix on foreign literature to each volume (every four months, that is)—but most of the monthlies did not vary from it greatly.

The *Critical Review* (1756–1817) was for many years the chief rival of the *Monthly*. Before it entered the nineteenth century, it could,

[1] Robberds, II, 184.

[2] *Ibid.*, pp. 317, 483–84.

[3] *Ibid.*, I, 127. In a footnote, Robberds quotes Hazlitt's remark in the *Spirit of the Age*: 'The style of philosophical criticism, which has been the boast of the Edinburgh Review, was first introduced into the Monthly Review about the year 1796, in a series of articles by Mr. William Taylor of Norwich' (William Hazlitt, *Complete Works*, ed. P. P. Howe, XI, 127). See also Robberds, I, 434; II, 26.

like the *Monthly*, boast some famous names. Smollett was the first editor, and both Coleridge and Southey were contributors in the 1790's.[1]

Its career, however, was very unlike that of the *Monthly*, with father passing on to son the duties of publisher and editor. The *Critical* had a more eventful history: between 1802 and 1817, the year it expired, it had at least five different editors and as many different publishers, and suffered a fire in its offices and a bankruptcy. In 1803, the year of the fire, Samuel Hamilton was editor and apparently co-publisher with George Robinson, although Robinson's name does not appear on the title page to the volumes.[2] The bankruptcy in 1805 caused the *Critical* to change hands: J. Mawman was the new publisher; the new proprietor and editor was John Higgs Hunt, previously a Fellow at Cambridge. Under his direction the periodical began a decline, and he was replaced in 1807 by Robert Fellowes, who began to put the *Critical* back on its feet.[3] Then, in 1814, began a series of changes of publishers and editors along with attempts to introduce other than review features, all indications of the impending end.[4]

During these years, however, the publication had a fairly impressive list of contributors. Although no such list of attributions as that of the *Monthly* has survived, a sketchy list can be made from various sources. Denman, Merivale, and Francis Hodgson wrote for both the *Critical* and the *Monthly*; and William Taylor of Norwich wrote sixty-four reviews altogether, including one of Southey's *Thalaba*, for the *Critical* in 1803, 1804, and 1809.[5] Southey was a contributor until 1804; and Charles LeGrice, an Anglican minister and former

[1] See Derek Roper, 'Coleridge and the *Critical Review*'; D. V. Erdman, 'Immoral Acts of a Library Cormorant'; and Jacob Zeitlin, 'Southey's Contributions to "The Critical Review" '.

[2] Robberds, I, 460–61, 477; II, 68. Derek Roper (in 'The Politics of the *Critical Review*, 1756–1817', p. 122) states that Samuel Hamilton was editor by 1801. John M. Good, however, writing to Dr. Drake (Jan. 29, 1803) states, 'I have edited the Critical Review, besides writing several of its most elaborate articles' (Olinthus Gregory, *Memoirs of the Life, Writings, and Character of John Mason Good*, p. 81).

[3] Robberds, II, 223. In a letter dated Oct. 26, 1807, Southey calls Fellowes 'joint editor' (J. W. Warter, *Selections from the Letters of Robert Southey*, II, 23).

[4] George Frederick Busby was said to be one of the editors in the last two years (*British Stage*, I [July, 1817], 208).

[5] J. T. Hodgson, *Memoir of the Reverend Francis Hodgson, B.D.*, I, 94; J. Arnould, *Memoir of Thomas, First Lord Denman*, I, 68; Robberds, I, 126; II, 26n.

schoolfellow of Coleridge and Lamb at Christ's Hospital, reviewed *Madoc*.[1]

Both periodicals were, by 1802, organs of liberal opinion.[2] They were run and supported for the most part by dissenters, who had least reason, because of their own position outside of the Establishment, to fall into the political reaction brought about by the French Revolution. William Taylor, writing to Southey in November, 1801, in answer to his suggestion to found a new Review, says, 'Both the Monthly and the Critical are in the main well conducted, and as low in their politics as the times will yet patronize.'[3]

To emphasize his reluctance, Taylor continues, 'To vie with the British Critic or the Antijacobin will not be the amusement of *my* leisure'; and thus we are presented with the two other monthlies which survived the eighteenth century.

The *British Critic* (1793–1826) was established at the height of the reaction to the French Revolution. It was, according to Thomas Rees, 'professedly intended to uphold the tenets of the Established Church and the Tory politics of the ruling government', and to counteract the *Monthly*, *Critical*, and *Analytical Review*.[4] It was founded as a by-product of a 'Society for the Reformation of Principles by Appropriate Literature', which was established by William Stevens and other followers of William Jones of Nayland about 1792.[5] The first editor was an Anglican divine, William Beloe; his editorship may, however, have been shared by Robert Nares, later Archdeacon of Stafford.[6] Nares, in any case, eventually replaced Beloe and moderated the original High Church position of the *British Critic*.[7] Late in 1811, Joshua Watson and H. H. Norris purchased the Review and replaced Nares with Dr. William Van Mildert,

[1] Robberds, I, 500–1; Warter, I, 381. J. Conder (p. 41) mentions Robert Woodhouse and William Frend, both Cambridge dons, and Mawman, the publisher, as occasional contributors.

[2] Robberds, I, 120. Roper, 'Politics of the *Critical Review*', pp. 120–22. There was apparently a slight reactionary set-back in the *Monthly Review* in 1801 (Robberds, I, 381) and in the *Critical Review* in 1805–7 (Robberds, II, 73, 223).

[3] Robberds, I, 387.

[4] Thomas Rees, *Reminiscences of Literary London*, pp. 32–33. There is, however, nothing political in the Preface to Volume I.

[5] William Stevens, *A Short Account of the Life and Writings of William Jones*, pp. xxxv–xxxvi.

[6] F. E. Mineka, *The Dissidence of Dissent*, p. 51n; Septimus Rivington, *The Publishing Family of Rivington*, p. 100.

[7] Mineka, p. 51.

later Bishop of Durham, who served as editor for only a short period but was editor again in 1820.[1] The editorship during the intervening years is difficult to determine, but among the editors were Thomas F. Middleton, ordained Bishop of Calcutta in 1814, William Lyall, later Deacon of Canterbury, and Thomas Rennell.[2] The publishers, aptly enough, were Francis and Charles Rivington, who dealt 'chiefly in books relating to the established church'.[3] Among the contributors were various Oxford and Cambridge dons, and the Reverend John Whitaker, the historian of Manchester.[4] The literary reviewers are unknown.

The extent of its dependence on political support is difficult to determine; but it may have been considerable, since Francis Hodgson, writing to William Gifford in 1809, warns the new editor of the *Quarterly* that the cause of the *British Critic*'s decline is its lack of independence.[5] In any case, it seems to have been one of the least popular of the Reviews which had any title to respect.[6]

Even below this level of respect, if lack of mention by contemporaries is a just indication, was the *Antijacobin Review and Magazine* (1798–1821).[7] As the name would imply, the *Antijacobin* was highly political in nature; its religious bias became more obtrusive with the change of title in Volume XXXVI: *The Antijacobin Review and True Churchman's Magazine*. It was explicitly the successor to that nursery of the *Quarterly*, *The Anti-Jacobin; or Weekly Examiner*; and its sponsors did not hesitate to confess, or rather to brag of, their bias: 'We are deeply prejudiced in favour of our country; and are highly

[1] Edward Churton, *Memoir of Joshua Watson*, I, 96; John H. Overton, *The English Church in the Nineteenth Century*, p. 37n. A different account of the matter was that T. F. Middleton replaced Nares (C. W. Le Bas, *Life of T. F. Middleton*, I, 19).

[2] Le Bas, I, 19; Mineka, p. 53n. In 1821, Nares was said to be still secretly editing the *BC* (Oliphant, I, 499).

[3] Rees, p. 32. Septimus Rivington (*The Publishing House of Rivington*, p. 17), claims that 'Nares and Beloe were conjoint partners with Francis and Charles Rivington.'

[4] J. Conder (p. 42) lists Abraham Robertson, Thomas Rennell, Francis Wollaston, Samuel Vince, and Dr. Glegg. Rees (p. 34) claims Dr. Parr supported the *BC*. See also Churton, II, 148.

[5] Hodgson, I, 115. See also William Beloe, *The Sexagenarian*, I, 296–98, where Beloe claims the *BC* had the support and gratitude of the Government and Church.

[6] See Warter, I, 287; J. Conder, p. 42; Oliphant, I, 499.

[7] J. Conder (p. 42) was not even sure if the *Antijacobin Review* was still being published in 1811.

partial to her constitution and laws, to her religion and government.'[1]

Its title indicates an additional difference from the other monthlies; for *The Antijacobin Review and True Churchman's Magazine* had features other than reviews. The section of 'Original Criticism' was the largest (generally, however, with reviews shorter than the other monthlies), but there were also departments of 'Original Poetry' and 'Miscellanies'. Its closest similarity to the weekly *Anti-Jacobin* was the section entitled 'Reviewers Reviewed', wherein their 'object is to subject [British Jacobinical] *monthly* and *annual* publications to a similar process' to that used by *The Anti-Jacobin; or Weekly Examiner* on daily papers.[2] The *Monthly* and the *Critical* are referred to specifically as Reviews to be scrutinized.

The names of contributors of articles for the first six volumes (1798–1800) of the *Antijacobin Review* are contained in a staff copy now in the British Museum. Most of the reviews were then done by John Gifford (pseud. John Richards Green), one of the founders and the first editor, and by Dr. Robert Bisset and John Bowles. Among later contributors were James Mill, the utilitarian philosopher, who wrote for the publication in 1802, and John Bowles, who was still contributing in 1811.[3] The amount of support it received from the government was very likely small, for the editor's 'Farewell Address to the Public' in 1821 contains a long complaint of ministerial indifference.[4] As early as 1811, Josiah Conder thought it moribund, an observation substantiated by a constant change of publishers.[5]

The year 1802 saw the founding of the *Edinburgh Review*, and earlier that same year the *Christian Observer* (1802–74) began. The title page of the latter announces that it is 'conducted by members of the Established Church', and the Prospectus leaves no doubt about its religious program: 'It is intended so to combine information upon general subjects, with religious instruction, as to furnish such an interesting view of Religion, Literature, and Politics, free from the contamination of false principles, as a clergyman may without scruple recommend to his Parishioners, and a Christian introduce into his family. . . .' To this general intention is added, in the Preface to Volume IX, the promotion of slave-trade abolition.

[1] 'Prospectus', *AjR*, I (1798), 1, 5.

[2] *Ibid.*, p. 2.

[3] Alexander Bain, *James Mill*, pp. 41, 48. J. Conder, p. 43.

[4] *AjR*, LXI (1821), 355–59.

[5] J. Conder, p. 43.

The original idea of founding the *Christian Observer* was introduced by Josiah Pratt at a meeting of the Eclectic Society, London, in 1799: Pratt, a clergyman, was its first editor.[1] It was supported and conducted by Evangelicals within the Church of England, members of the 'Clapham Sect'. Zachary Macaulay, the abolitionist, replaced Pratt within a few months and remained editor until 1816, when Samuel C. Wilkes, an Evangelical minister, took over (to 1850). Contributors included Wilberforce, Lord Teignmouth, and Hannah More.[2]

The *Christian Observer* differed from the other monthlies in several ways. It was, for one thing, shorter, ranging from sixty to seventy pages. It was, like the *Antijacobin*, partially a magazine, with original poetry and even an obituary section. But most important was the emphasis given to reviewing religious works; in fact, the reviewing section was entitled 'A Select Review of New Publications, connected with Religion and Morals . . .', and so should not have contained reviews of works of general literature at all. From 1809 to 1815, however, and sporadically thereafter, some dozen important literary works were reviewed.

Following in the footsteps of the *Christian Observer* was another monthly Review with a religious background, the *Eclectic Review* (1805–68), the organ of the Eclectic Society, which was founded in 1783.[3] Although its selection of books to be reviewed was not so closely confined to religion, the *Eclectic* nevertheless announced in the Preface to Volume II: 'To induce the religious world to cultivate literature, and the literary world to venerate religion, was the entire object and hope of the [projectors'] most sanguine ambition.' A more sanguine ambition, however, was to have the cooperation of members of both the Established Church and the nonconformist sects. Neutrality, at first thought necessary on only a few theological points, soon became a necessity on important social and ecclesiastical issues;

[1] For an account of the meeting and other details, see J. H. Pratt, *Eclectic Notes*, pp. 92–93.

[2] Besides the three contributors named in the text, Zachary Macaulay lists Isaac Milner and Charles Grant (Letter to the editor of the *CO*, Mar. 16, 1830—quoted in Pratt, p. 93). J. Conder (p. 54) also lists John Bean, Henry Venn, John Owen, Henry Thornton, and William Stevens. All of these contributors were connected with the Clapham Sect. See also, Mineka, pp. 53, 58; Overton, p. 201. William Hey was said to be influential in the founding of the *CO* (John Pearson, *The Life of William Hey*, I, 197–98).

[3] Overton, p. 285.

yet criticisms of the Church were made in the Review anyway; and the Church contributors soon dwindled away.[1] In 1814, this attempt at cooperation was explicitly dropped, and a new series begun.[2] It eventually became an organ of the Congregationalists.[3]

Founded in 1805, under the proprietorship of Adam Clarke, W. A. Hankey, and others, the *Eclectic* was unsuccessful under Samuel Greathead, editor for the first year.[4] Luckily, for the *Eclectic*, Greathead, who became ill, was replaced in 1806 by Daniel Parken, who was a mere twenty-one years old at the time.[5] Parken's youth and talents, plus the talents of John Foster and James Montgomery, proved sufficient to revitalize the *Eclectic*. Parken edited the *Eclectic* from 1806 until 1811, when he handed over the editorship to Theodore Williams in order to take up legal practice. For a period before Parken resigned, the three young men ran the publication almost without other assistance.[6]

James Montgomery, a minor poet of the period, contributed at least thirty-one reviews, mostly in the period before Parken's premature death in 1811.[7] Among other important literary works reviewed by him were *Marmion* and *Rokeby*; *Gertrude of Wyoming*; Crabbe's *Poems*; *Roderick* and the *Life of Nelson*; and Wordsworth's *Poems in Two Volumes*, *Convention of Cintra Tract*, and *The Excursion*.[8] Montgomery was a dissenter, as was his fellow contributor John Foster, the essayist. Foster wrote 184 articles for the *Eclectic*, between 1806 and 1839, among which were reviews of *The Curse of Kehama* and Coleridge's periodical, *The Friend*.[9] It was Foster who helped push the *Eclectic* into the dissenters' camp and who gave the periodical its reputation for liberal political opinions.[10] Other known contributors were, for the most part, nonconformist ministers.[11]

[1] 'Advertisement for the New Series', *EcR*, I 2s (1814), i–ii. J. E. Ryland, *The Life and Correspondence of John Foster*, I, 374–76, 377–78.

[2] See 'Advertisement' in previous note, and John Holland and James Everett, *Memoirs of the Life and Writings of James Montgomery*, III, 21–22.

[3] John Foster, *Contributions . . . to the Eclectic Review*, I, iv.

[4] Holland and Everett, II, 89. J. Conder, p. 48; Mineka, p. 68; Foster, I, iii. See also *Evangelical Magazine*, XX (Oct., 1812), 373–79 (Obit. of D. Parken).

[5] John Styles, *Early Blossoms*, p. 164.

[6] Holland and Everett, II, 88; see also II, 301, where Theodore Williams is identified as 'a son of a Divinity tutor at the Dissenters' Academy, near Rotherham'. *EcR*, XVI, 3s (Dec., 1836), 550.

[7] Holland and Everett, II, 89; III, 21.

[8] *Ibid.*, II, 183, 193, 234; III, 20, 48, 64, 65.

[9] Ryland, II, 580–86.

[10] *Ibid.*, I, 375, 339. See also Warter, III, 275; and W. W. Everts, *John Foster*, p. 9.

[11] J. Conder (p. 48) lists as contributors: Olinthus Gregory, Adam Clarke,

Under Parken's editorship there were signs of interference from the 'four supporters' (apparently the proprietors) of the *Eclectic*, and this interference was probably one of the main causes for the *Eclectic*'s decline under Williams; by 1814 the publication was losing money.[1] It was purchased in 1814 by Josiah Conder, a bookseller and evangelical nonconformist, who had in fact occasionally acted as editor before that time. Under his editorship, which lasted until 1836, the *Eclectic* established a reputation for liberal opinion.[2] In 1821, its circulation was estimated at about 3000.[3] Conder was also a diligent reviewer; marked copies of many volumes of the *Eclectic* in the London Library attribute to him nineteen of the reviews dealt with in this study.[4]

The *Eclectic* showed the influence of the *Edinburgh Review* by dropping the very short reviews of its earlier numbers; it gradually took on the appearance of the larger quarterly Reviews. A unique feature was its low price of *2s.* (the other monthlies were *2s. 6d.*), which was explained in the Preface to Volume I as an attempt to reach the widest possible audience.[5]

Two years after the founding of the *Eclectic*, still another Review began, the last monthly to be established for some years. The *Oxford Review* (1807–8) was, according to a contemporary, an infamous ruse set up by Sir Richard Phillips, a London bookseller and publisher of the *Monthly Magazine*, to sell his own wares; William Mavor, one of

John Pye Smith, and John W. Cunningham (the only Evangelical on the list and later editor of the *CO*). Many of the names on this list were also mentioned as contributors in Holland and Everett, II, 87. For a further list of contributors, see Mineka, p. 68n, and *EcR*, XVI 3s (Dec., 1836), 350–51.

1 Ryland, I, 48; J. Conder, p. 48. 'Advertisement' (see p. 48, note 1, above).

2 Ryland, I, 374. Warter, III, 275. E. R. Conder, *Josiah Conder*, p. 125. See also the 'Advertisement' (p. 48, note 1, above), and Mineka, p. 69.

3 Oliphant, I, 499.

4 In view of the marking of all reviews in many of the volumes, it seems likely that they were staff copies. The reviews assigned to Josiah Conder are: *The Corsair; Lara; Hebrew Melodies; The Siege of Corinth* and *Parisina; Poems upon Domestic Circumstances; Childe Harold* (III) and *The Prisoner of Chillon; Manfred; The Lament of Tasso; Childe Harold* (IV); *The Field of Waterloo; Christabel; The White Doe of Rylstone; The Thanksgiving Ode; The Poet's Pilgrimage; The Lay of the Laureate; Alastor; The Round Table;* Keats' *Poems* of 1817. Two reviews (of *The Lord of the Isles* and *Lalla Rookh*) were assigned to 'C.N.', possibly Cornelius Neale, known to be a contributor (*EcR*, XVI 3s [Dec., 1836], 550).

5 Prices of all reviewing periodicals operating in 1807 are given in the *Literary Panorama*, II (1807), 65.

Phillips' assistants, was said to be a major contributor.[1] The ruse, it was claimed, fooled the public at first, but it soon became well known that no Oxford dons were contributing.[2] An advertisement in the *Oxford*, dated May 20, 1807 (that is, six months after it began), made the bold claim that it had a circulation surpassed by only one London Review. With all its chicanery, it expired little more than a year later.

The following year, the *London Review* (1809), the first of the quarterlies to be founded after the *Edinburgh Review*, was begun by Richard Cumberland, a minor dramatist who was then a man in his late seventies. He was himself very sensitive to criticism—Garrick had called him 'a man without a skin'—which helps to account for a novelty which he attempted to introduce into his periodical: every review would be accompanied by the contributor's name. In the Introductory Address, in which Cumberland argues the senselessness of anonymity, he also contends that critics ought to be favorable towards their contemporaries and predicts that a great literary age is at hand.

In addition to this introductory sweet reasonableness, Cumberland showed his shrewdness in being aware of the change of format now necessary for a successful Review; the *London* was a very close imitation of the *Edinburgh*, especially in the length of its reviews. Furthermore, the contributors he managed to assemble were of some note; among others were Henry Crabb Robinson, who reviewed Wordsworth's *Convention of Cintra* Pamphlet; Henry James Pye, the Poet Laureate, who reviewed Scott's edition of Dryden; and Horace Twiss, a lawyer and politician, who reviewed *Marmion* and *Gertrude of Wyoming*, and later contributed to the *Quarterly*. Horace and James Smith, who were soon to become famous for their *Rejected Addresses*, also contributed to the publication. Reasonableness and talent, how-

[1] J. Conder, p. 45.

[2] *Ibid.*, pp. 45–47. Conder quotes from 'a reputable French Journal: "Les Archives Littéraires de l'Europe, ou Mélange de Litérature, d'Histoire, et de Philosophie" '. Another indication of how well known the ruse was can be obtained by reading the transcripts of a trial in which Phillips was a witness (Anon., *Libel. Sir John Carr against Hood and Sharpe*). The Attorney General, in summing up (p. 24), asks, 'Now, Gentlemen, is Sir Richard Phillips that pure immaculate character which he states himself to be?—I put it to you, thus—do you believe he swears truly when he swears, that he became the publisher of the Oxford Review, merely for the purpose of giving to the public one honest review in this kingdom? Do you believe he swears truly when he swears that?' The verdict went against Phillips' side.

ever, are not always enough to ensure success, and the *London Review* expired after only four numbers.[1]

A year later, another quarterly came on the scene, the *British Review* (1811–25). Begun by John Weyland, a lawyer and social writer, the *British* was edited by him for one or two numbers and then handed over to William Roberts, another lawyer, who edited it until 1822.[2] It was published for most of its existence by John Hatchard, the publisher of the *Christian Observer*. Like that earlier monthly, it was an Evangelical periodical. The *British*, however, did review a wider selection of books: Hannah More, the Evangelical bluestocking, praised the *British* not so much for its criticisms of religious works, as for reviewing 'secular works in a Christian spirit'.[3] Among its contributors were John M. Good, an Evangelical, physician, and neighbor of Roberts, and others connected with 'the Church or University'.[4]

In an article in the March number of 1821, Roberts boasted that 'no man of any party of the state contributes to our pages. . . .' This was apparently not entirely a matter of policy, because the government seems to have been indifferent to the *British*, at least as regards direct support.[5] This indifference was a bit ungrateful, since, according to his son, Roberts 'took many opportunities in the "Review", of advocating the measures of the Government'.[6] In any event, the *British* was in serious trouble as early as 1814, when it was suspended for a year and a half. Publication was resumed when 'a leading member of the administration' requested Roberts to do so. By 1817 its reputation was on the rise, even if its sales were not.[7]

The *British* probably more than any other journal of the period was the work of one man—William Roberts, the editor. According to his son, Roberts wrote most of the leading articles and often four or five reviews in a number (i.e., almost half), not to mention extensive revision of articles contributed by others.[8] In 1823, when he was no longer editor, Roberts told a correspondent that the spirit of the *British* was 'peculiarly my own', as it must have been.[9]

[1] At the end of 1809, Samuel Tipper, the *London Review*'s publisher, went bankrupt. There were various references at the time to the *London*'s inferiority. See, for example, Robberds, II, 274.

[2] Arthur Roberts, *The Life, Letters, and Opinions of William Roberts*, pp. 37–38.

[3] *Ibid.*, p. 65n.

[4] Gregory (see p. 43, note 2 above), p. 108; Roberts, p. 40.

[5] *BR*, XVII (1821), 2. Roberts, pp. 82–83.

[6] Roberts, p. 40.

[7] *Ibid.*, pp. 41, 81.

[8] *Ibid.*, p. 40.

[9] *Ibid.*, p. 73.

All of the reviews of Byron's works were attributed to Roberts by his son; these, probably as much as any lack of Government support, indirectly brought about the end of the *British.*[1] The quarrel between Byron and 'my Grandmother's Review, the British' is undoubtedly the best known part of the history of the *British*, so it needs no retelling here.[2] Roberts' incredible gullibility helped Byron's nickname to stick, and the *British* must have become a source of embarrassment to those whom it so actively supported. Roberts' editorship ended in 1822; he was offered a Police Magistracy, which seems to have been the standard reward for pro-ministry editors (John Gifford of the *Antijacobin Review* had been given one), but he declined. In 1823 there was a complete change in administrators, who announced a new emphasis on religion, which is reflected in the almost total exclusion of reviews of secular works for the last two years of the *British*'s existence.[3]

The one Review remaining for discussion was neither a monthly nor a quarterly. The *Annual Review* (1802–8), which began in the same year as the *Edinburgh*, was another nonconformist (Unitarian) periodical. It was published by Longman's, who were also the proprietors, and it had a reputation for liberal, even radical, opinions. In view of the number of similar publications current at its founding, it is at first difficult to imagine why the *Annual Review*, with its ponderous yearly volumes, some running to almost 1000 pages, should have been founded at all.[4] Yet it was quite popular, in spite of its uneven quality.[5] The reason why is told in one contributor's letter written years later: 'The work had a great sale in the colonies, and there was always a hurry to get it out for the spring fleet to India.'[6] Homesick colonials must have been eager to receive a one-volume periodical which, in brief (one to ten double-column pages) reviews, allowed them to keep up with not only the major publications of the previous year, but with most of the minor works as well.[7]

[1] Roberts., pp. 43, 45. Roberts also reviewed *Christabel* (*ibid.*, pp. 53, 56).

[2] For a short account of the quarrel, see W. S. Ward, 'Lord Byron and "My Grandmother's Review" '.

[3] See the Preface to Volume XXI (1823). It is curious that Roberts' son and biographer seems to think that the *BR* ceased after his father's editorship (Roberts, p. 38).

[4] J. Conder, p. 47.

[5] Warter, I, 251, 298.

[6] P. H. Le Breton, *Memoirs, Miscellanies, and Letters of the Late Lucy Aikin*, p. 163 (letter from Lucy Aikin to Mr. Mallet, July 4, [1850?]).

[7] In the Preface to Volume II (1804), the editor claims that 'out of nearly five

The *Annual* was largely a family concern. Arthur Aikin, a writer of scientific works, was the editor of six of the seven volumes published. Among the contributors were his father, Dr. John Aikin, literary editor at this time of the *Monthly Magazine*; his aunt, Mrs. Barbauld, a well-known bluestocking; and his sister, Lucy Aikin. The *Annual* was arranged by categories; Mrs. Barbauld wrote for the Belles-Lettres section in the early volumes, reviewing Scott's *Lay of the Last Minstrel* among other works; her niece, Lucy Aikin, reviewed Byron's *Hours of Idleness* and Wordsworth's *Poems in Two Volumes*.[1] Two other contributors were Charles Wellbeloved and William Wood, both Unitarian ministers.[2]

But the main contributors were those intrepid reviewers for the *Monthly* and the *Critical* at this time, Robert Southey and William Taylor. Southey, who often referred to the editor as 'King Arthur', called Taylor and himself 'the Lancelot and Tristram, the men of proof'.[3] Southey contributed during the entire life of the *Annual*, but mostly in the first four years. Travels and biographies were his special department, but he also reviewed Scott's edition of *Sir Tristrem* and Moore's *Epistles, Odes, and Other Poems*.[4] Taylor, who contributed to all but the last volume, wrote almost a fifth of the entire volume for many years; his special department was 'History, Politics, and Statistics', but he also reviewed Southey's *Metrical Tales* and *Madoc*.[5]

In 1808 Arthur Aikin was dismissed as editor probably because of lateness in publication, and Thomas Rees edited the seventh and last volume.[6] It stopped without warning in the summer of 1809.[7] The

Hundred Articles, which compose the present volume, not one-third have made their appearance in any other Review of Books'.

[1] Le Breton, pp. 163–64. Morley, p. 143. Mrs. Barbauld was thought by many at the time to have reviewed Lamb's *John Woodvile*, but she is on record as having denied authorship (Morley, p. 69).

[2] Rees, p. 54. For other contributors, see Mineka, p. 84.

[3] Robberds, II, 102.

[4] Kenneth Curry, 'Southey's Contributions to the Annual Review'. Southey's contributions to the first four volumes of the *Annual Review* are listed in C. C. Southey, *Life and Correspondence of* Robert *Southey*, VI, 398–99. See also Robberds, II, 265, and Kenneth Curry (ed.), *New Letters of* Robert *Southey*, *passim*.

[5] Robberds, II, 42, 54, 151, 159.

[6] Warter, II, 17. Rees, p. 54. Lucy Aikin claimed her brother quit the editorship of the *Annual Review* when he found 'the office of whipper in to an ill-disciplined literary pack' intolerable (Le Breton, p. 164).

[7] Warter, II, 155.

uneven quality of the *Annual*, noted by Southey and other contemporaries, can be largely attributed to its low rate of payment; Southey wrote Taylor, shortly after its demise, 'If the coroner's inquest should sit upon its body, they may find that it was starved to death. Peace be with it! I served a seven years' apprenticeship to it at low wages, and must have *struck* had it continued longer.'[1]

In 1811, Josiah Conder, commenting on the monthly magazines then current, wrote, 'A periodical work must now-a-days contain a Review, to give it a chance of taking. . . .'[2] The rage for reviews by the early nineteenth century was so great that almost every magazine had a regular reviewing section, or at least an occasional review.

Magazines at that time tended to fall into two categories. The first and most important may be typified by the *Gentleman's Magazine*: a periodical of from 96 to 120 octavo, double-column pages, containing various articles, correspondence, and a chronicle, which would include obituaries, stock report, an account of parliamentary proceedings, and so on. Many such magazines would also carry original essays or even fiction, and almost all had original poetry. Out of this form were to evolve the three most important magazines of the first quarter of the nineteenth century—*Blackwood's*, the *London*, and the *New Monthly* magazines.

The other type of magazine was more ephemeral, what could be described as 'fashionable'. Such magazines were shorter, usually from fifty-six to seventy-two octavo pages, and often appealed to the fair sex with special articles on current fashions; drama criticism also was usually a prominent feature. Chronicles were not included, and reviews were generally confined to the belles-lettres. Among such magazines were the *Ladies' Monthly Museum* (1798–1828), *La Belle Assemblée* (1806–32) and its imitator *Le Beau Monde* (1806–10), the *Cabinet* (1807–9), the *New Bon Ton Magazine* (1818–21), and the *Literary Speculum* (1821–22).[3] Not much is known of these 'fashionable' magazines, their editors or contributors,

Most magazines of both categories had substantial reviewing departments often occupying a third or more of their pages. They were not mere after-thoughts, as can be ascertained by a look at almost any introductory preface, where reviewing policies are often

[1] Robberds, II, 283. [2] J. Conder, p. 44.

[3] *Le Beau Monde* was published in quarto, and the *Literary Speculum* in duodecimo.

set forth in some detail. But even with this decided emphasis on their reviews, the magazines never assumed much importance or influence as reviewing periodicals—with the exception of *Blackwood's*, the *New Monthly*, and the *London Magazine*, later in the period. There are few contemporary references, for example, to the reviews in the *Gentleman's* or the *Monthly Magazine*. As a result, very little is known of the magazine reviewers, again with the exception of *Blackwood's* and the *London Magazine*.

There are two important differences between the reviews in the monthly magazines and in the monthly Reviews. In the magazines the reviews were on the whole shorter, especially early in the period. But a more important difference is one of policy: there was in the magazines almost no attempt made to maintain a consistent opinion.[1] George Griffiths, writing to his troublesome contributor, William Taylor (December 4, 1820), draws the distinction clearly:

> The Review ought to be always consistent; and one writer should not advance opinions on established points which he may deem just, but which others are not prepared to maintain, and may even be disposed to contradict; while in a Magazine there is no necessity for homogeneity, and each writer may *sport* what he pleases, without reference to other papers, past, present, or future.[2]

The magazine reviewers, then, had the latitude of the quarterly reviewers, with generally less space than the monthly reviewers in which to apply it, but possessed the importance and influence of neither.

The oldest magazine to survive the eighteenth century was the venerable *Gentleman's Magazine* (1731–1868). Its editorial pseudonym, 'Sylvanus Urban', hid the name of John Nichols, himself a survivor of the eighteenth-century literary world, from 1792 until his death in 1826. His son, John Bowyer Nichols, probably helped edit the *Gentleman's* shortly before 1826 and became the proprietor in 1833. The *Gentleman's* had a regular 'Review of New Publications', which criticized a substantial part of the latest literary productions. As with so many of the magazines, almost all the reviewers are unknown.[3]

[1] The *London Magazine* was an exception. See Josephine Bauer, *The London Magazine 1820–29*, p. 73.

[2] Robberds, II, 492.

[3] In the Preface (pp. lxxiv–lxxviii) to Volume III of *The General Index to the Gentleman's Magazine 1787–1818* (London, 1821), there is a list of some of the contributors to the *GM*.

George Dyer, a minor author and friend of Charles Lamb, reviewed Lamb's *Works* in 1819.[1]

Another time-proven magazine, started only a few years after the *Gentleman's*, was the *Scots Magazine* (1739–1826). It was acquired in 1801 by Archibald Constable, the publisher of the *Edinburgh Review*, and was edited successively in 1802 by Dr. John Leyden, the poet, and Alexander Murray.[2] A later editor was Dr. Morehead; and Pringle and Cleghorn, the first editors of Blackwood's abortive *Edinburgh Monthly Magazine* in 1817, became editors of the *Scots* in that year.[3]

According to Henry Curwen, in his *History of Booksellers*, the *Scots* had a reputation for criticism of 'some importance', but this must have been later in the period, probably about 1818, when William Hazlitt and J. H. Reynolds contributed essays to the *Scots*.[4] In fact, from 1802 to 1804 there were only occasional reviews; the 'Scottish Review', a feature which began in 1805, concentrated on works by Scottish authors, although it did contain some reviews of Byron's poetry.

Up to 1817, the *Scots* was an unimportant, provincial publication, with an average size of only eighty pages. In that year, faced with the competition of *Blackwood's*, the *Scots* began a new series, increasing in size from ninety-six to 120 pages. Its title changed to the *Edinburgh Magazine*, and the title of its reviewing section became 'Review of New Publications'. In 1819, the *Edinburgh Magazine* followed the lead of *Blackwood's* in having no specific review section, interspersing its reviews with the other articles.

The *European Magazine and London Review* (1782–1826) was established by James Perry, who was later proprietor of the *Morning Chronicle*. Until 1806, it announced itself as written 'By the Philological Society of London', and was edited after 1807 by Stephen Jones, more notable as a newspaper editor of the period, and by Edward Dubois, a lawyer, probably before that date.[5] Isaac Reed,

[1] George Dyer, *The Privileges of the University of Cambridge*, Postscript to Volume II.

[2] Thomas Constable, *Archibald Constable and His Literary Correspondents*, I, 202, 221.

[3] *Ibid.*, II, 448. Oliphant, I, 105.

[4] Henry Curwen, *History of Booksellers*, p. 113. P. P. Howe, *The Life of William Hazlitt*, p. 241; Herschel Baker, *William Hazlitt*, pp. 202, 255n; *EdM*, I 2s (Sept., 1817), p. 102. Leonidas M. Jones, 'The Essays and Critical Writing of John Hamilton Reynolds', p. 5.

[5] John Bates Dibdin may have had something to do with editing the *EM* (E. V. Lucas, *The Life of Charles Lamb*, p. 622).

a lawyer and editor of Shakespeare and other poets, was for a time one of the proprietors. The *European* had the usual magazine miscellany, but there was a special attempt 'to unite in one periodical work the distinct qualities of the Magazine and Review'.[1] This resulted in longer reviews (average about five double-column pages), but in 1822 the format changed to more and shorter reviews, with fewer quotations and smaller print. G. F. Mathews initialed his reviews of Keats' *Poems* of 1817 and Coleridge's *Christabel* volume in the *European*.

Thirteen years after the founding of the *European*, the *Monthly Mirror* (1795–1811) came on the periodical scene. Thomas Bellamy, a minor writer, was the founder. Thomas Hill, a book-collector and patron of 'the Smith and Theodore Hook Squad', was one of the proprietors, probably shortly after Bellamy's death in 1800.[2] Edward Dubois was editor at one time, most likely from the beginning of the new series in 1808.[3] The *Monthly Mirror* was shorter than most of the other magazines, ranging from seventy to eighty pages; this, as well as its emphasis on dramatic criticism, would place it more in the category of the 'fashionable' magazine. And yet, in spite of its original intention to review only popular works, with the definite exclusion of works of 'profound literature', it usually had a large reviewing department and criticized most of the important literary works published during its existence.[4] After the change in administration in 1807, the *Monthly Mirror*, according to a contemporary, suffered a decline and finally expired early in 1811.[5]

In 1796, the most radical of all the reviewing periodicals, the *Monthly Magazine* (1796–1826), was founded. Said to have been suggested and planned by the well-known radical, Dr. Priestley, it was founded by Sir Richard Phillips and owned by him until 1824.[6] Phillips, himself a radical and later proprietor of the *Oxford Review*,

[1] Quoted in the Introduction to Volume II, p. iii.

[2] See William G. Lane, 'Keats and "The Smith and Theodore Hook Squad"', p. 22. In *N & Q*, XII 2s (1861), 222, there is a letter to Hill as 'Editor of the Monthly Mirror' from Joseph Ritson, Feb. 17, 1803.

[3] There was a new editor about that time (see 'The Editor to the Public', IX n.s. [1811], 83), and Dubois was probably replaced by Stephen Jones as editor of the *European Magazine* in 1807. At least the dates fit.

[4] Preface to Volume I (1795), xi. James Smith was a contributor between 1807 and 1810 (A. H. Beavan, *James and Horace Smith*, p. 208).

[5] J. Conder, p. 45.

[6] Anon., *Memoirs of . . . Sir Richard Phillips*, p. 68.

seems to have been something of a rogue.[1] Dr. John Aikin, father of Arthur Aikin of the *Annual Review*, was literary editor of the *Monthly* from 1796 to 1806, when he quarreled with Phillips over a business deal.[2] He was replaced by George Gregory, one of Phillips' many business assistants, who died in 1808. His immediate successor is unknown, but according to one source, Dr. George Croly was editor, Laman Blanchard sub-editor, in the 1820's.[3]

While Dr. Aikin was editor, many of his dissenting friends and relatives contributed, among whom were Dr. Enfield and Mrs. Barbauld; 'a Mr. Norgate of Norwich' was usually the critic in the supplements.[4] Another contributor whom Aikin introduced was that pillar of Romantic periodicals, William Taylor, who contributed at least 764 articles between 1796 and 1824.[5] Among them was the only important literary review in the *Monthly Magazine* which can now be identified, a review of Southey's *Madoc*.[6] Other famous contributors were Malthus, Godwin, Hazlitt, and Southey.[7]

In addition to the usual magazine features, the *Monthly Magazine* contained 'proceedings of Learned Societies' and showed a special interest in foreign studies and philosophy. The literary reviews were generally very short, often only part of a page. From 1802 to 1811, they were found in a 'Half-Yearly Retrospect', which was contained in supplementary numbers. These changed in 1811 to mere excerpts from literary works with no criticism whatsoever. The Retrospect ended in 1816, and a section called 'Critical Notices of Books' began. This section was supplemented early in 1821 by a series of longer reviews which had the caption 'News from Parnassus'.

The *Monthly Magazine* was popular with the Dissenters, and in 1811 it was still successful, if Sir Richard Phillips can be believed.[8] But by 1824, its chief rival, the *New Monthly Magazine* was even more successful, and Phillips sold out.[9]

[1] See A. Boyle, 'The Publisher—Sir Richard Phillips'. See also Warter, II, 83, for a comment on Phillips by Southey, and p. 50, note 2 above.

[2] Anon., *Memoirs of . . . Sir Richard Phillips*, pp. 71–80. On p. 82, the anonymous author claims that Dr. Aikin was the sole editor of the *MM*. But Lucy Aikin said that her father was only the literary editor, with Phillips handling the other editorial duties (*Memoir of John Aikin, M.D.*, I, 188).

[3] Felix Sper, *The Periodical Press of London, 1800–1830*, p. 29.

[4] Rees, p. 80 (see also Aikin, I, 307). Curry, *New Letters*, I, 391–92

[5] Robberds, I, 126. The articles by Taylor are listed in footnotes by Robberds.

[6] *Ibid.*, II, 146n.

[7] Geoffrey Carnall, 'The Monthly Magazine', p. 158.

[8] Robberds, II, 394. Carnall, p. 158.

[9] Carnall, p. 162.

Of all the regular magazines published in the period, the next to be founded, the *Literary Panorama* (1806–19), was surely the least important or influential. Copies of it are scarce, and references to it by contemporaries are rare.[1] Its great novelty was its size: 112 double-column pages in quarto. Its literary reviewing was curiously selective, but a greater number of important works were included in its later issues. It finally merged with the *New Monthly Magazine* in 1819, claiming at the point of merger to share that magazine's views, which were then still conservative.[2]

In 1814, the real beginning of the later rivalry between the three most important magazines of the period took place with the founding of the *New Monthly Magazine* (1814–36). Begun by Henry Colburn, the publisher, and Frederick Shoberl, the *New Monthly* was edited by a Dr. Watkins until some time in 1818, when Alaric Watts, then only twenty-two years old, took over the editorship. He held it until June, 1819, when he quarreled with Colburn.[3]

The *New Monthly* was professedly founded to counteract the radical politics of Phillips and his *Monthly Magazine*, especially its favorable attitude toward Napoleon.[4] But otherwise the *New Monthly* was an imitation of the old; the 'Address to the Public' in the first volume makes an obvious appeal to the encyclopaedically inclined, who had been the mainstays of the *Monthly Magazine* for almost eighteen years. The *New Monthly*, however, was not particularly distinguished at first, having all the standard magazine features but little vitality. The reviews were likewise mostly insignificant, mainly short remarks contained in a 'List of New Publications', which began in Volume II.

Then in 1818, probably about the time that Watts took over as editor, longer reviews were also placed before the list. By that time there was a competitor, *Blackwood's Magazine*. After Watts resigned, the *New Monthly* had no official editor; the copy was merely given to the printer with the articles in a certain order.[5] And yet the magazine continued to improve, probably because of the new contributions of Thomas Talfourd and Cyrus Redding, which began 'about 1820'.[6] In that year, the influence exerted by *Blackwood's* was revealed in the

[1] J. Conder mentions it in passing (p. 44).

[2] 'Address' (dated July 1, 1819), IX 2s (1819), 3.

[3] Alaric Alfred Watts, *Alaric Watts*, I, 57, 61.

[4] See 'Address to the Public', at the beginning of Vol. I (1814).

[5] Cyrus Redding, *Fifty Years Recollections . . .*, II, 168.

[6] *Ibid.*

New Monthly's more up-to-date layout; correspondence was replaced by essays, the lengthier reviews were scattered through each number, and shorter ones continued in the list.

But the really significant date in the history of the *New Monthly* was 1821. In January of that year, Thomas Campbell, the poet, became editor. Colburn had to pay well for the 'name'—five hundred pounds a year—and had to provide a subeditor.[1] The first, Edward Dubois, a friend of Campbell and previously editor of the *European Magazine* and the *Monthly Mirror*, lasted only one number; he left after a quarrel with Campbell.[2] Dubois was replaced by Cyrus Redding, who, according to his version at least, ended up doing almost all of the editing.[3] The *New Monthly*, in any case, received a face-lift, including new type styling and a new name: the *New Monthly Magazine and Literary Journal*.

The *New Monthly* attracted new contributors as well. Besides Campbell, who was required to contribute twelve articles annually in verse and prose, there were Horace Smith, P. G. Patmore, and William Hazlitt.[4] Both Talfourd and Redding also continued to contribute.[5] The longer reviews were scattered throughout the first two volumes of 'Original Papers'; their authorship is unknown. Shorter critical remarks continued in the third volume; some of these were written by Redding, but most were 'by a hand paid for the contribution. . . .'[6]

The politics of the *New Monthly* had also changed by this time. The original anti-Jacobinism had dissipated from lack of support and from diffuseness; by 1820, the magazine's political position was indeterminate.[7] Under the influence of Redding, the *New Monthly* became liberal; Walter Scott, for example, refused to contribute.[8] Only Colburn, the publisher and proprietor, kept it from becoming even more boldly liberal.[9]

It is necessary to go back a few years to date the most important event in the history of the magazines during this period. It was

[1] William Beattie, *The Life and Letters of Thomas Campbell*, II, 357.

[2] Redding, II, 172.

[3] *Ibid.*, II, 185–86, 230.

[4] Beattie, II, 357. Olive M. Taylor, 'John Taylor', p. 264. Redding, II, 298.

[5] Redding, II, 169. Redding lists other contributors (II, 169–70).

[6] *Ibid.*, p. 169. The *New Monthly* was apparently published monthly with pagination set up to fit the three yearly volumes, the first two entitled 'Original Papers' and the third 'Historical Register'.

[7] *Ibid.*, p. 168. [8] *Ibid.*, pp. 230–31 [9] *Ibid.*, p. 298.

October, 1817, which saw the first issue of *Blackwood's Edinburgh Magazine* (1817–). William Blackwood had started the *Edinburgh Monthly Magazine* earlier that year to rival Constable's *Edinburgh Magazine*, but both of these had much the same appearance as the *Gentleman's* and the other regular magazines. Now *Blackwood's* brought a change in layout of articles which was to set the pattern for other magazines: the formal departments were all dropped, and the correspondence and other articles were intermingled. The reviews, usually at least several pages long, were likewise scattered throughout *Blackwood's*.

The *Edinburgh Monthly Magazine* was doing well but was not yet paying its way when it was discontinued.[1] Its circulation was under 2500, pointing up the success of *Blackwood's*, its successor, which in 1818 was printing 6000 copies of an issue.[2] Part of the reason for this phenomenal rise in circulation was the famous 'Chaldee MS' in the first number, which brought libel suits in its wake, but which also made *Blackwood's* the most talked-about periodical of the day.[3] And its popularity increased, as well it might with such contributors as Sir Walter Scott, S. T. Coleridge, James Hogg, and William Maginn.[4]

But the two most important contributors to *Blackwood's* before 1825 were John Wilson and John Gibson Lockhart, who between them contributed almost all of the imporant literary reviews between 1817 and 1825.[5] Wilson, a young lawyer and poet in 1817, and later professor of moral philosophy at the University of Edinburgh, wrote most of the reviews of the works of Byron, Moore, Lamb; and Wordsworth, as well as of the *Biographia Literaria* and Crabbe's *Tales of the Hall*. Lockhart, also a lawyer and writer, and later editor of the *Quarterly Review*, reviewed most of the instalments of Byron's *Don Juan*, as well as his *Sardanapalus*, and most of the works of Shelley. What remained was done by Eyre Evans Crowe, an historical writer, who reviewed Hazlitt's *Table Talk* and Moore's *Irish Melodies*,

1 Oliphant, I, 105–6.
2 *Ibid.*, pp. 99, 191.
3 *Ibid.*, pp. 117, 129, 130–32. See also R. P. Gillies, *Memoirs of a Literary Veteran*, II, 233–34.
4 For a list of all contributors to *Blackwood's* 1817–25, see A. L. Strout, *A Bibliography of Articles in Blackwood's Magazine 1817–25*, pp. 139–87. All attributions of reviews in *Blackwood's* which follow are from Strout.
5 Strout (p. 15) says, 'Of the critical pieces in these early years Wilson and Lockhart very probably wrote the majority and a gambler could safely assign almost any single review to one or the other, and probably be right half the time.'

and by George Croly, a Churchman and very minor poet, who reviewed *Adonais*.

The editorship of *Blackwood's* during the early years is very difficult to ascertain, the main contenders being Lockhart, Wilson, and William Blackwood, the publisher. Alan Strout, the foremost scholar to deal with *Blackwood's*, hazarded a guess

> that for at least two years, August, 1818, to August, 1820, Lockhart and Wilson were literary editors, with Blackwood having always the veto power over his violently aggressive coadjutors. The uneasy triumvirate had probably begun in the summer of 1817; and probably continued until Lockhart left for London to become editor of the *Quarterly Review* at the end of 1825, with Blackwood taking over, more and more, the duties of his periodical in the later years.[1]

Even the literary editorship changed from issue to issue, and a constant attempt was made to confuse the public as to just who was responsible.[2]

Or rather, as far as the reviewing in general went, who was irresponsible; for *Blackwood's* has the worst record of all the major periodicals in this respect. It was not merely the political partisanship (*Blackwood's* was ultra-Tory) of some of the articles, such as the infamous series, 'On the Cockney School of Poetry', but it was *Blackwood's* policy as a whole.[3] True, most magazines made little attempt at critical consistency, yet there is on record no other example comparable to the indifference of Wilson and Lockhart toward reviewing ethics. A poet was damned and praised and damned again in successive numbers by the same hand.[4] This critical chicanery is most blatant in a review of Roger's *Italy* (possibly by Lockhart). Since *Italy* was published anonymously, and since the reviewer wished to praise it in spite of suspicions of Cockney authorship, he playfully remarked that if his suspicions materialized, the author could be attacked in the review of his next work 'if we see fit',

[1] Strout, p. 3. For Mrs. Oliphant's conjecture on the early editorship of *Blackwood's*, see her *Annals of a Publishing House*, I, 150 n, 185–86.

[2] Strout, p. 6. Oliphant, I, 136, 150, 154, 155, 161. See also Gillies, II, 235–36.

[3] For a good example of *Blackwood's* political bias, see the Preface to Volume XI (1822).

[4] For example, Wilson vacillated wildly in early criticisms of Wordsworth; see *BM*, I (June, 1817), 261–66; II (Oct., 1817), 65–73; and II (Nov., 1817), 201–4.

or 'we can get some clever correspondent to attack us lustily, for having bestowed on it any commendation, and drive us out of the field by an elaborate proof of its utter worthlessness'.[1] Needless to say, the 'correspondent' would most likely be either himself or one of the regular contributors.

It was just this critical irresponsibility which brought about the first actual tragedy in the pen-and-ink war between the various periodicals: the death of John Scott, the first editor of the *London Magazine* (1820–29). The *London* was the third of the trio of most important magazines of the early nineteenth century, *Blackwood's* and the *New Monthly* being the other two; and the *London*, like the *New Monthly*, was greatly influenced by *Blackwood's*, especially in arrangement of articles and in general design.

Published first by Robert Baldwin, the *London* was edited by John Scott (who had previously edited the *Champion*, a weekly) from its first issue until his death in a duel with Christie, a friend of Lockhart, in February, 1821.[2] Under Scott, the *London* was at its best, for he gave to the magazine an *esprit de corps*, much like that enjoyed by *Blackwood's* contributors.[3] But even so, the *London* was not a success. For several months after Scott's death, it was edited by Robert Baldwin with the assistance of J. H. Reynolds and others; and then the *London* was sold to the firm of Taylor and Hessey, the publishers of Keats, who began publishing it in July, 1821.[4] After considering several candidates for the editorship, John Taylor decided to take on the job himself, and with the assistance of Hessey, his partner, edited the *London* until December of 1824.[5] Thomas Hood, the poet, acted (in his own words) 'as a sort of subeditor' from June, 1821, until approximately June, 1823, when he was replaced by C. W. Dilke and others.[6]

The contributors during the first five years include an impressive array of literary talent. It would suffice to mention that Lamb contributed to the *London* his *Essays of Elia*; Hazlitt his *Table Talk*; and DeQuincey his *Confessions of an English Opium Eater;* but even the second-string talent was very strong: John Clare, J. H. Reynolds,

[1] *BM*, XI (Mar., 1822), 280.

[2] For the most detailed account of the duel, see Bauer, pp. 75–80.

[3] *Ibid.*, p. 67.

[4] *Ibid.*, pp. 81–82. Edmund Blunden, *Keats's Publisher*, p. 123.

[5] Peter F. Morgan, 'Taylor and Hessey; Aspects of Their Conduct of the *London Magazine*', pp. 62–63.

[6] Walter Jerrold, *Thomas Hood*, p. 93. Bauer, p. 87. Taylor, p. 262.

Horace Smith, B. W. Proctor, T. N. Talfourd, and Alan Cunningham—all substantial secondary literary men of the age. Many of these were connected with the Cockney School and this led Cyrus Redding to go so far as to call the *London* 'a *coterie* periodical'.[1]

The important literary reviews, which after the ninth number were interspersed with other articles in the manner of *Blackwood's*, were not on the whole assigned to the less talented contributors.[2] John Scott wrote reviews of four Waverley novels, Hazlitt's *Lectures Chiefly on the Dramatic Literature of the Age of Elizabeth*, Keats' *Lamia* Volume, and Shelley's *The Cenci*; and Hazlitt reviewed two other Waverley novels, Byron's *Letter to [John Murray]*, and *Marino Faliero*. T. N. Talfourd, who also contributed to the *Edinburgh Review* and the *New Monthly*, wrote a review of *Table Talk* and probably one of *Sardanapalus*. P. G. Patmore, a contributor to many other journals, reviewed Hunt's *Hero and Leander* and Keats' *Endymion*. Scott's *Halidon Hill* was probably criticized by Alan Cunningham, a minor author; and J. H. Reynolds reviewed Moore's *Loves of the Angels*.[3]

With all the talent at its beck and call, the *London Magazine* should have been a success, but strangely such was not the case. If the circulation was inadequate under Scott's editorship, it was even more so under John Taylor. Its circulation was approximately 1600 early in 1821, increasing by one hundred by August of that year; it was reported not doing well in 1822; and the next figure available is 1600 again in June, 1825.[4] This failure can be attributed in part to Taylor's editorial incompetence; but since most of the original

[1] Redding, III, 314.

[2] All attributions of *London* articles, unless otherwise noted, are from T. Rowland Hughes, 'The London Magazine'. Hughes makes the attributions pertinent to this study on the following bases: the reviewers of the *Cenci*, *Hero and Leander*, *Endymion*, and *Lamia* were identified by MS. notes written by John Taylor on his copy of the magazine (for the *Cenci*, see also Shelley's letter to the Olliers, Jan. 20, 1821). For the review of Hazlitt's *Lectures on the Age of Elizabeth*, see P. P. Howe, *The Life of William Hazlitt*, p. 265. For the reviews of Byron's *Letter to [John Murray]* and *Marino Faliero*, see P. P. Howe (ed.), *The Complete Works of William Hazlitt*, XIX, 340. For the review of *Table Talk*, see S. Butterworth, 'The Old "London Magazine" ', p. 16. The review of *Sardanapalus* was identified solely on the basis of style, and that of *Halidon Hill* on the basis both of style and the initial 'C.'.

[3] H. Rollins (ed.), *The Keats' Circle* (Cambridge, Mass.: Harvard University Press, 1948), II, 429.

[4] Morgan, pp. 61–62. Taylor, p. 264.

contributors remained for several years after Scott's death, the decline of such a talent-laden magazine is difficult to understand.[1]

The *London*'s political opinions were probably not involved in its failure, at least while Scott was editor. His many conservative preconceptions were balanced by many progressive opinions, leaving the *London* in something of an independent political position.[2] Under Baldwin's short interregnum as editor, the *London Magazine* was more or less neutral.[3] It was John Taylor who gave it a more distinctly liberal tone, but it never became what could be called radical while under his control.[4]

In its first year and a half, the *London* was known as 'Baldwin's *London Magazine*', in order to distinguish it from another magazine also begun in January, 1820; *The London Magazine and Monthly Critical and Dramatic Review* (1820–21).[5] This magazine was published by Joyce Gold; nothing is now known of its editor or contributors.[6] It was amalgamated with Baldwin's *London Magazine* in July, 1821.[7]

The early 1820's saw a spate of a new type of periodical—the quarterly magazine. These ran from 200 to 240 octavo, single-column pages and had the usual magazine features, including reviews. Such was the *Investigator* (1820–24), with the names of its editors on its title page: the Rev. William Collyer, the Rev. Thomas Raffles, and James B. Brown, a writer and lawyer. Having two ministers on its staff, the *Investigator* naturally took a religious tone, which was reflected in its literary reviews.[8] The *Album* (1822–25) was edited by Francis St. Leger, a minor novelist. Like the *Investigator* it contained the usual miscellany, but after its third volume was given over completely to essays. *Knight's Quarterly Magazine* (1823–24) was similar to the other two, except that it carried only one review in its

[1] Bauer, p. 82. Blunden, *Keats's Publisher*, p. 130.

[2] Bauer, p. 122. See also pp. 92–118.

[3] *Ibid.*, pp. 119–21.

[4] *Ibid.*, p. 122.

[5] The name of this periodical in fact changed to *Gold's London Magazine and Theatrical Inquisitor* in Feb., 1821.

[6] It was published by 'Gold and Northhouse' in 1820 and by 'Gold and Co.' in 1821.

[7] Blunden, *Keats's Publisher*, p. 123.

[8] The *Investigator*'s Prospectus (quoted in T. S. Raffles, *Memoirs of Dr. Thomas Raffles*, p. 184) states the magazine's intentions as 'to elucidate and establish the agreement and connexion between genuine philosophy and scriptural piety, between sound literature and true religion'.

short life (of *Quentin Durward*). It attempted to copy *Blackwood's* vivacity by creating a similar cast of pseudonyms, but lasted little more than a year.

The final category of reviewing periodical to be considered is the weekly. This category can be divided into (1) Weekly Literary Reviews and (2) Sunday Papers, as done in the *Cambridge Bibliography of English Literature*; but the difference between the two subdivisions is negligible. All weeklies had about the same amount of print, whether published as eight-page folio or as sixteen-page quarto periodicals. The *Champion* in fact changed from the one to the other a few years after its founding. Those not published on Sunday were published on Saturday, while a few had two editions printed on either day—one for London readers and one for rural subscribers. Almost all had regular weekly departments, including Politics, the Fine Arts, Drama, Original Poetry, a Gazette, Reviews, and some chronicles. Literary reviews generally ran from one to two quarto pages, assuming more or less importance depending on the periodical; but except for the *Literary Gazette* and its imitators, there was no attempt to review all major literature published.

The *Examiner* (1808–81) was the first important weekly of the period. A sixteen-page Sunday paper begun jointly by John and Leigh Hunt in January, 1808, it was published by John Hunt, the elder brother, and edited solely by Leigh Hunt until his nephew, Henry Leigh Hunt, joined him in the editorship in 1819.[1] The *Examiner*, begun as a non-partisan paper, soon came out for Reform and other liberal movements; it began quickly to encounter opposition in the form of actions for libel, which culminated in the imprisonment of the Hunt brothers, co-proprietors, from February, 1813, to February, 1815, on a charge of libeling the Prince Regent. Leigh Hunt continued to edit the paper in prison; but in order to eliminate any future chance of having the editor imprisoned, Leigh Hunt ceased to be a proprietor by 1819.[2]

The *Examiner* was successful from the start. The circulation by November, 1808, was 2200; in 1812 Jeremy Bentham wrote James Mill that of the weeklies the *Examiner* 'especially among the high

[1] George D. Stout, 'The Political History of Leigh Hunt's Examiner . . .', p. 37; Louis Landré, *Leigh Hunt*, I, 49, 138.

[2] Edmund Blunden, *Leigh Hunt's 'Examiner' Examined*, pp. 36, 89; Landré, I, 90.

political men, is the one most in vogue'.[1] He added that the circulation was 'between 7000 and 8000', which, if correct, must have signified that the paper was enjoying its heyday—the circulation having dropped to about 4000 by 1817 and 1818.[2] In 1819, the trend continued downward to 3200, a decline which Leigh Hunt later ascribed to political causes.[3] There was a brief rise in 1820 caused by the interest in the trial of the Queen. This did not last long, and in October, 1820, Leigh Hunt ceased to edit the paper, apparently leaving it in the hands of his nephew.[4] Leigh Hunt left for Italy in November, 1821, and John Hunt was imprisoned in that same year for another libel.[5] The paper was sold to Dr. Fellowes after Leigh Hunt left for Italy, but for a time was edited by Henry Leigh Hunt, perhaps until 1830.[6] The *Examiner* suffered accordingly, in quality if not also in circulation.[7]

The 1810's saw the peak of the *Examiner*'s greatness. Many of its articles were written by Leigh Hunt, but other talented men also contributed, including William Hazlitt, Charles Lamb, Thomas Barnes, Benjamin Robert Haydon, Horace Smith, and Barron Field.[8] In addition, the *Examiner* had an enviable list of poetical contributors: among others, Byron, Wordsworth, Keats, and Shelley.[9]

The *Examiner* was not primarily a reviewing periodical; in fact, there was only one review (Hazlitt's 1814 review of the *Excursion*) before 1816. In June of that year began the 'Literary Notices', a regular reviewing department. William Hazlitt wrote most of the important literary reviews before June, 1817, when he stopped contributing to the *Examiner* for several years.[10] He reviewed Coleridge's *Christabel*, the second *Lay Sermon*, and *Statesman's Manual*, as well as Southey's *Lay of the Laureate*, *Wat Tyler*, and *Letter to William Smith*.[11] From June, 1817, to March, 1820, the important literary reviews

[1] Thornton Hunt (ed.), *The Correspondence of Leigh Hunt*, I, 40; Alexander Bain, *James Mill*, p. 123.

[2] Stout, p. 37.

[3] *Ibid.* Leigh Hunt, *Autobiography*, p. 280.

[4] Stout, pp. 37–38; Landré, I, 86.

[5] Blunden, *Examiner*, pp. 108–9.

[6] E. B. De Fonblanque, *Life and Labour of Albany Fonblanque*, pp. 25, 27.

[7] Blunden, *Examiner*, p. 112.

[8] *Ibid.*, p. 93.

[9] *Ibid.*, pp. 55, 57, 60, 67, 68, 82.

[10] P. P. Howe, *The Life of William Hazlitt*, p. 211; Landré, I, 92, 119; Herschel Baker, *William Hazlitt*, p. 203.

[11] Howe, *Life*, pp. 183, 187, 202, 204; Blunden, *Examiner*, pp. 58, 59; Baker, p. 202.

were written by Leigh Hunt. They include reviews of Keats' *Poems* of 1817; Lamb's *Works*; *The Revolt of Islam*, *Rosalind and Helen*, and *The Cenci; Peter Bell; Monody on the Death of Sheridan* and *Don Juan* (I and II); and four of Hazlitt's works.[1] In 1820, there were also two reprints of reviews: of Keats' *Lamia* Volume by Lamb (from the *New Times*) and of *Endymion* by J. H. Reynolds (from *Alfred*).[2] Then, from 1821 to 1825, most of the reviews were signed 'Q'. Among these are reviews of most of Byron's later works; the *Liberal* (I and II); *Liber Amoris*; *The Loves of the Angels* and *The Fables for the Holy Alliance*; Shelley's *Posthumous Poems*; and *A Vision of Judgement*. Since one of these (the review of *Liber Amoris*) has been attributed to Albany Fonblanque, later editor of the *Examiner*, all of them are possibly by that same hand.[3]

With Hazlitt and Leigh Hunt writing most of the reviews before 1820, and both Keats and Hunt contributing poetry, it is not surprising to find the *Examiner* described as the chief organ of the Cockney School before the *London Magazine* assumed that function in 1820.[4]

John Scott, later editor of the *London Magazine*, was the first editor, publisher, and proprietor of the *Champion* (1814–22).[5] As might be expected from Scott's successive editorships, the *Champion* shared with the *Examiner* the honor of being an organ of the Cockney School, just as it shared in its early years most of the *Examiner*'s contributors, including Hazlitt, Lamb, Thomas Barnes, and Benjamin Robert Haydon. Its 'Cockneyism' was increased by the additional support of J. H. Reynolds and Thomas N. Talfourd.[6]

Begun as an eight-page Sunday paper of folio size, the *Champion* was mainly written by John Scott and Hazlitt late in 1814 and early 1815, before Hazlitt transferred his efforts to the *Examiner* in March, 1815.[7] For the next few months, Scott did almost all of the writing

[1] Blunden, *Examiner*, pp. 68, 74, 83, 89, 91, 92–93, 103; Howe, p. 252; Landré, II, 177, 182, 183, 184, 187, 188, 191.

[2] George L. Marsh, 'The Writings of Keats's Friend Reynolds', p. 496.

[3] Howe, *Life*, p. 326. No authority is given for the attribution. Fonblanque was writing for the *Examiner* between 1820 and 1830 (De Fonblanque, pp. 12–13, 14).

[4] Stout, p. 38.

[5] Horace Smith was part proprietor and a principal contributor. See his 'A Graybeard's Gossip', pp. 415–16.

[6] For mention of contributors (with the exception of T. N. Talfourd), see T. Rowland Hughes, 'John Scott: Editor, Author, and Critic'.

[7] *Ibid.*, p. 520.

for the *Champion*. In the summer of 1815, he visited Paris, leaving the paper in the hands of George Soane until the following October, as he left it again (in unknown hands) in the fall of 1816.[1] The *Champion* continued to carry Scott's name as publisher until July, 1817, when R. D. Richards became publisher.[2] Hazlitt was again a contributor in this year.[3] In January, 1818, the *Champion* became a sixteen-page quarto; in September Richards' name was replaced by the uninformative 'Published at the Champion Office'. John Thelwall assumed the editorship in January, 1819, and became the editor, proprietor, and publisher in January, 1820.[4] He performed these duties until 1822, when the *Champion* ran through three publishers in short order, signaling its impending death. The name was changed in June, 1822, to the *Investigator*, which lasted only one month.

The *Champion*'s political position under Scott is difficult to describe exactly, as was that of the later *London Magazine* when under his control. Jacob Zeitlin, in an article on Scott, claims that Scott's *Champion* held to the middle of the road, and had both strong conservative and liberal tendencies.[5] But the *Champion* under Thelwall was explicitly Reformist, with the statement in its 1819 motto, 'Our object is Reform....' On one issue (September 30, 1821), there is an indication of Utilitarian influence with the change of motto to 'The Greatest Happiness of the Greatest Number'.

The *Champion* contained a regular review department from the beginning, reflecting one of the main interests in its subtitle, 'A

[1] *Ibid.*, pp. 520, 522–23. L. M. Jones (p. 56, note 4, above), p. 11n. Scott was apparently trying to sell the *Champion* in 1816 (see *The Letters of William and Dorothy Wordsworth, The Middle Years*, ed. E. De Selincourt (Oxford: Clarendon Press, 1937), II, 746.

[2] In 1816, the *Champion* was sold to 'Mr J. Clayton Jennings, who had been Fiscal at Demerara and Essequibo', according to Horace Smith (see p. 68, note 5, above), p. 416. There is, however, no indication of this change in the listing of the management at the end of each issue.

[3] Howe, *Life*, pp. 216, 225; Baker, p. 203.

[4] See the Editorial, *Champion*, Jan. 3, 1819, pp. 1–2, for Thelwall's assumption of editorship in 1819. Circulation figures for the *Champion* estimated on the yearly amount of stamps purchased are: 1817, 1225; 1818, 575; 1819, 475; 1820, 700 (*Journals of the House of Commons*, LXXVI [Apr. 19, 1821], 943–45); 1821, 575 (LXXVII [May 1, 1822], 930–31).

[5] Jacob Zeitlin, 'The Editor of the *London Magazine*', pp. 328–40. But Cyrus Redding (in *Fifty Years Recollections*, II, 226) says that John Scott 'had for a long period supported ultra-liberal doctrines', switching political allegiance after the fall of Napoleon in 1815. L. M. Jones (p. 10) claims that Scott was 'moderately liberal in his political views'.

Weekly Political and Literary Journal'. This literary preoccupation continued to be displayed in some form or other of its subtitle (which changed frequently) until January, 1820, when no subtitle appeared. The number of reviews then diminished so that there were none of importance after 1820.

Unlike those of the *Examiner*, the *Champion*'s reviewers are difficult to identify. Almost the only source of information is the initials sometimes given with a review. Thus, 'S*' and 'ed.' identify John Scott's reviews of *The Descent of Liberty*, *The White Doe of Rylstone*, and *Roderick*.[1] 'R', the reviewer of *The Characters of Shakespear's Plays*, is probably J. H. Reynolds, known to be a contributor at the time the review appeared; Reynolds also reviewed Keats' *Poems* of 1817.[2] Reviews of *Tom Crib's Memorial* and of *Don Juan* (I and II) were written by 'T.' (and the continuation of the latter review in the following issue by 'J. T.'), undoubtedly the initials of John Thelwall, editor at the time they were printed. 'T.N.T.', the reviewer of Lamb's *Works*, was Thomas N. Talfourd, later a biographer of Lamb.

In January, 1817, Henry Colburn, publisher of the *New Monthly Magazine*, began what was soon to become the most important literary weekly, the *Literary Gazette* (1817–62). This sixteen-page Saturday paper was published by Colburn until November, 1819. Either at the beginning or shortly thereafter he shared the proprietorship with Pinnoch and Maunder, booksellers, who also began to publish the *Gazette* in July, 1817.[3] The first editorship is difficult to ascertain, but apparently it was shared by H. E. Lloyd, a civil servant and philologist, and a 'Miss Ross'.[4] Then, in July, 1817, William Jerdan, former editor of the *Sun* and other periodicals, became part proprietor and editor and was to conduct the paper for over thirty years, assisted in the earlier period by Lloyd, Alaric Watts, and others.[5]

[1] See W. M. Parker and D. Hudson, 'Thomas Barnes and "The Champion"'. See also Zeitlin, p. 340n.

[2] Hughes, p. 522. See also George L. Marsh, 'The Writings of Keats's Friend Reynolds', p. 495. For the review of Keats' *Poems*, see J. M. Turnbull, 'Keats, Reynolds, and *The Champion*'; and Hyder E. Rollins, 'Keats's Elgin Marbles Sonnets'.

[3] William Jerdan, *Autobiography*, II, 182. From July, 1817, to Nov., 1819, the *Literary Gazette* was published jointly by Colburn, Pinnoch and Maunder, and John Bell.

[4] Curwen, p. 281. See also Jerdan, II, 178.

[5] Jerdan, II, 177, 179, 182, 236; IV, 5.

The *Literary Gazette* was not immediately successful. By the end of the first year, the circulation was only about 1250; although rising steadily, according to Jerdan, the paper did not show enough profit in its first three years to support the editor.[1] In November of 1819, William Chalk became sole publisher, and Pinnoch and Maunder resigned their co-proprietorship with Colburn and Jerdan.[2] Then early in 1820, W. A. Scripps, former publisher of the *Sun*, began to publish the *Literary Gazette*; Colburn and Jerdan were joined in that year by Longmans, forming a 'Tripartite partnership'.[3] With this additional support, the *Literary Gazette* became more successful; circulation was estimated at about 3000 by December, 1821. The Address in the 1822 volume printed on the back of the title page (written at the end of the year) claims a circulation in England second only to the *Edinburgh Review* and the *Quarterly Review*.[4] The Address on the first page of the volume for 1824 (January 3, 1824) boasts that the paper has a 'circulation more extensive than any literary work in Europe', but this may well be an exaggeration. In any case, it was successful enough to provoke many imitators.[5]

Although the *Literary Gazette* could claim some talented contributors, they were generally inferior to those of the *Examiner* and *Champion*. Among them were William Maginn, who wrote also for *Blackwood's*, and Theodore Hook, editor of *John Bull*.[6] Alaric Watts, who had been editor of the *New Monthly*, contributed for about three years beginning in early 1819.[7] The poetical contributors included B. W. Proctor and George Croly, who also wrote for *Blackwood's*, as well as Crabbe, Southey, and Moore.[8]

With such contributors—especially those connected with *Blackwood's* and *John Bull*—the political bias of the *Literary Gazette* should be obvious enough. Add to this the facts that William Jerdan was a friend of both John Gifford, editor of the *Antijacobin Review*, and William Gifford, editor of the *Quarterly Review*, and that the Prince

[1] *Ibid.*, II, 195, 297. Circulation figures for the *Literary Gazette* estimated on the yearly amount of stamps purchased are: 1817, 1025; 1818, 600; 1819, 950; 1820, 800 (*Journals of the House of Commons*, LXXVI [Apr. 19, 1821], 943–45).

[2] Jerdan, III, 62.

[3] *Ibid.*, pp. 62, 64–65.

[4] Oliphant, I, 498.

[5] Jerdan, III, 210.

[6] *Ibid.*, p. 78. For mention of other contributors to the *Literary Gazette*, see *ibid.*, II, 188, 190, 234; III, 60, 282–83.

[7] Watts, I, 107.

[8] Jerdan, II, 235–36; III, 58, 62. For other poetical contributors, see *ibid.*, II, 235–36.

Regent was the paper's first subscriber, and it is unmistakably a Tory periodical.[1] Jerdan later claimed the *Literary Gazette* had maintained political neutrality. Alaric A. Watts, however, in the biography of his father, after testifying to the *Literary Gazette*'s generally liberal principles, mentions that

> there was a powerful clerical pen affected to its service in these days much concerned with the interests of 'the Throne and the Altar' and very severe in consequence, occasionally, upon 'radicals' and 'atheists'.[2]

The *Literary Gazette*, as its title would seem to warrant, placed a greater emphasis on literature than did either the *Examiner* or *Champion*. This is reflected in the reviewing section, which became the lead article in September, 1817, and remained so throughout the period under study. Also, unlike previous weeklies, the *Literary Gazette* wished to become 'a complete and authentic Chronological Literary Record for general reference'; although it did not review every literary work published, it missed very few.[3] Unfortunately, the author of not one review between 1817 and 1825 has been identified; but Jerdan, in his autobiography, mysteriously describes the literary reviewer in early 1817 as 'a correspondent of no mean discrimination and talent', and states that he himself wrote reviews while editor.[4]

Two close imitations of the *Literary Gazette* followed in the next few years, the *Literary Chronicle and Weekly Review* (1819–29) and the *Literary Register* (1822–23). Like their prototype, both were sixteen-page papers published on Saturday, each with a special country edition; and both were very clearly literary periodicals, with usually a half of every issue given over to reviews. The only important difference between the two was that the reviews in the *Literary Chronicle* were largely taken up with quotations, with very little comment.[5] Nothing is known of the editors or contributors of either paper.

One of the *idées reçues* concerning the reviewers in the lesser Romantic periodicals is that they were political and critical reaction-

[1] Jerdan, III, pp. 176, 232.
[2] *Ibid.*, pp. 178–79. Watts, I, 108.
[3] *Jerdan*, II, 176.
[4] *Ibid.*, pp. 178, 179; III, 66.
[5] The *Literary Chronicle* had a definite policy of giving what amounted to little more than an abstract. See the 'Address to the Public', Jan. 6, 1821, p. 1.

aries, who, either subsidized by the government or acting from their own political or literary prejudices, were attempting to stifle the new literature of their age. This is not always explicit, but the suggestion is almost inevitably present when the subject is discussed.[1] Based on the foregoing study of the publishers, editors, contributors, and the reviewing practices of the secondary journals, it should be obvious that this attitude toward the reviewers is unjustified.

Two points should stand out from all the data presented. One of these concerns the political backgrounds of the most important of the lesser reviewing periodicals. Especially in the case of the monthly Reviews in the early part of the period, the religious and political attitudes of the Reviews were very closely related, with a majority of them run by Dissenters, who, for various reasons, held liberal views. Opposed to these—the *Monthly Review*, the *Critical Review*, the *Annual Review*, and the *Eclectic Review*—there were only two important reactionary monthlies, largely supported by members of the Established Church: the *British Critic* and the *Antijacobin Review*, which were later joined by the quarterly *British Review*. None of the latter appears to have been considered very important by its contemporaries; and such evidence as there is seems to indicate that the *Antijacobin Review* and the *British Review* received little government support.

Except for the fact that religious affiliation did not play much of a role in their administration, the same situation held true with the monthly magazines of critical importance. The *New Monthly* did begin as a reactionary magazine, but at a time when its critical influence was negligible; later on it became at once more influential and more liberal. The *London Magazine* passed through an early neutral stage to become a liberal publication. Only *Blackwood's* was politically reactionary, and its politics were quite strictly partisan in nature. However, the partisanship was so obvious and mixed with so much frivolousness and inconsistency, that it would be difficult to call *Blackwood's* a reactionary publication pure and simple.

The important weeklies present a similar situation. The *Examiner* was radical, and the *Champion* early moved from a neutral to a more radical position. The *Literary Gazette*, a Tory publication with possibly some liberal tendencies, was the only important reviewing weekly to oppose them.

[1] For the most explicit presentation, see William S. Ward, 'Some Aspects of the Conservative Attitude toward Poetry in English Criticism, 1798–1820'.

Because the political life of the period was so thoroughly engrossed in the political theories behind the French Revolution—and all the dangers and opportunities they presented for England—it is a simple matter to translate this concern into overemphasis of the role politics played in the lives of individuals. Granted that politics is always an important human consideration and that in the early nineteenth century it was unusually important, it is surely unnecessary to regard most periodical contributors as men who must have been blinded by political prejudices—unless they were merely hired hacks, rather than intelligent, well-educated men of their time.

That they were the latter is the second point which should now be clear. Other contributors to the reviewing periodicals aside, those known to have reviewed important literary works were either writers themselves or professional men, or both. There were at least fifteen men of letters involved, including William Hazlitt, William Taylor of Norwich, Robert Southey, Leigh Hunt, James Montgomery, John Foster, Francis Hodgson, Alan Cunningham, J. H. Reynolds, and John Scott. All were writers of considerable reputation in the period. The professional men were somewhat more numerous. The largest group were lawyers, among whom were John Gibson Lockhart, John Wilson, Henry Crabb Robinson, William Roberts, Thomas N. Talfourd, Thomas Denman, Horace Twiss, and Francis Jeffrey. Others were physicians, ministers, journalists, and university professors. All were respected and often highly successful members of their professions.

The early years of the nineteenth century saw the beginnings of both a literary revival and of a new, broader reading public desirous of critical assistance. Thus was created an unprecedented challenge to periodical criticism too large to be met by the *Edinburgh Review* and the *Quarterly Review* alone. Fortunately, in an age which was undergoing a revolution in political and social thinking, many of the secondary reviewing periodicals were liberal, both politically and (a usual correlative) intellectually, and were supported by some of the most talented men of the time. And, as might be expected of such men when also confronted with a literary revolution, with all the turmoil and disorderliness which the metaphor implies, the Romantic reviewers overwhelmingly favored the new literature of their age, although they had serious critical reservations, as well they might. Taken all in all, they were equal to the challenge.

Part II

The Reviews and Schools

Authors are just as much public characters as secretaries of state are; if they voluntarily come forward upon the stage of public life, under pretence of being able to enlighten, or in any other way to benefit the community at large, of course they must expect that their pretensions will be canvassed; that their opinions and principles will become a subject of discussion; misrepresentation and misconception, unreasonable censure and blind admiration—these are matters of course—the penalty paid in all cases for publicity. . . .

The *British Critic* (review of *Biographia Literaria*)

3

The Lake School

Literature written in the first quarter of the nineteenth century is most often divided into two groups: the five major poets—Wordsworth, Coleridge, Byron, Shelley, and Keats—and the numerous minor writers. This hierarchical approach is both necessary and useful, but it was not the way in which contemporary reviewers categorized the same writers. While they tended to classify their authors by the comparative merits of their talents as they saw them, there was nevertheless a substantial range of disagreement as to any definite hierarchy of literary merit.

Classification is a useful, time-saving device; the human mind, in fact, seems to demand it, even at the risk of forcing disparate entities into the same category. The reviewers, lacking the hierarchical division provided by the passage of time, fell upon the idea of schools. The names of some of these schools, such as the Lake School and the Cockney School, pertain to the locale in which the writers lived, as well as shared peculiarities of content or style; another, the Satanic School, was concerned only with the morality of the works produced by its members. Still others, which were created to cope with the motley literary output of the period and which emphasized some one peculiar aspect of the style of its members, have by now lost all significance. One such would be the Flemish School. None of the schools is a specific category, and many reviewers, as well as the writers themselves, attacked them as misleading and absurd. But some of the school titles stuck and were widely used; and since what follows is an examination of the critical evaluations at the time of their currency, nothing would reflect the over-all attitudes of the Romantic reviewers so well as a treatment by schools.

William Wordsworth

For reviews of what was later considered the first important production of the Lake School, we must go back four years before the founding of the *Edinburgh Review*. The *Lyrical Ballads* was published in September, 1798, and reviews of this joint production of Wordsworth and Coleridge began in the following month.[1]

It is one of the ironies of the history of Wordsworth's relationship with the reviewers that he received one of his first unfavorable reviews from a fellow Laker, Robert Southey.[2] Only when compared with the favorable reviews of the volume that were to follow, however, does his criticism in the *Critical Review* seem so adverse. Southey is fairly severe when dealing with 'The Rime of the Ancient Mariner' and the ballad pieces, but he praises 'Tintern Abbey' highly. In this article there is also an attack on Wordsworth's lowly subject-matter, which would be picked up in later reviews.

Other reviews of the volume were on the whole favorable, some of them laudatory; the work was even welcomed by a few as a relief from the Darwinian and Della Cruscan styles of poetry. But dislike of 'The Rime of the Ancient Mariner' was prevalent; and charges of babyism and social withdrawal, later to be echoed by some of the Reviews, were made by Dr. Charles Burney in the *Monthly Review*.[3] Considering the sentiments of social discontent present in some of the ballads, the first edition of the *Lyrical Ballads* received very good support, even from the *Antijacobin Review*.[4]

[1] For chronological lists of reviews of the works mentioned in the text, see Appendix II.

[2] For identification of Southey as reviewer, see Jack Simmons, *Southey*, p. 78.

[3] For identification of Dr. Burney as reviewer, see B. C. Nangle, *The Monthly Review, Second Series*.

[4] Examples of potentially offensive ballads are 'The Female Vagrant', 'The Last of the Flock', and 'The Dungeon'. Robert Mayo, however, in 'The Contemporaneity of the *Lyrical Ballads*', *PMLA*, LXIX (1954), 503–6, claims that social criticism of this kind was a convention of the magazine poetry of the period. According to the staff copy in the British Museum, the review in the *AjR* was by the Rev. William Heath.

The second edition, published in two volumes with additional poems in 1800, was likewise well received by the three periodicals that reviewed it.[1] The *Monthly Mirror* makes the first reference to the existence of a school of which Wordsworth is the head, and mentions the gloominess of some of the poems, as well as the influence of Cowper—all of which topics were to recur in later reviews.

Whether or not the Reviews were responsible for the success of the *Lyrical Ballads*—they can scarcely have been a hindrance—the two volumes went into a fourth edition in 1805. Since, however, the Reviews had a policy of ignoring new editions of works without significant additions or changes, none of the new editions was reviewed.[2]

Nevertheless, in 1802 Wordsworth received some attention from Francis Jeffrey in a critique in the *Edinburgh Review* of Southey's *Thalaba*. This gratuitous onslaught on Wordsworth was part of a general criticism of the Lake School, now called such by name. The review opens with the dictum so often quoted as proof positive of Jeffrey's neoclassical dogmatism: 'Poetry has this much, at least, in common with religion, that its standards were fixed long ago, by certain inspired writers, whose authority it is no longer lawful to call in question. . . .'[3] The phrasing here is misleadingly forceful since the sentence begins a long, witty conceit comparing literature and religion. In any case, Jeffrey's real reason for attacking the Lakers comes on the following page: 'They constitute, at present, the most formidable conspiracy that has lately been formed against sound judgment in matters poetical. . . .'

The 'conspiracy' is criticized on three counts, all aimed more specifically at Wordsworth: diction, subject-matter, and social attitudes. On the matter of diction, Jeffrey makes it clear that he is not attacking Wordsworth's 'rejection of glaring or superfluous ornament', but rather 'the bold use of those rude and negligent expressions, which would be banished by a little discrimination'.[4] He

[1] Elsie Smith, in *An Estimate of William Wordsworth by His Contemporaries 1793–1822*, p. 45, tentatively attributes the review in the *BC* to Francis Wrangham. I have been unable to discover any indication, much less proof, that this attribution is correct. For attribution of articles after 1802, see Chaps. 1 and 2, above, under the appropriate periodical.

[2] Elsie Smith (p. 63) was apparently unaware of this policy, for she claims that the Preface caused the third edition to be ignored.

[3] *ER*, I (Oct., 1802), 63.

[4] *Ibid.*, p. 65.

also attacks Wordsworth's argument, in the Preface to the *Lyrical Ballads*, for using the language of the lower classes:

> The language of the higher and more cultivated orders may fairly be presumed to be better than that of their inferiors; at any rate, it has all those associations in its favour, by means of which a style can ever appear beautiful or exalted, and is adapted to the purposes of poetry, by having been long consecrated to its use. The language of the vulgar, on the other hand, has all the opposite associations to contend with; and must seem unfit for poetry, (if there were no other reason,) merely because it has scarcely ever been employed in it. A great genius may indeed overcome these disadvantages; but we scarcely conceive that he should court them.[1]

This argument Jeffrey follows with a distinction, which Coleridge was later to make in the *Biographia Literaria* (Chapter XVII): that if there be any phrases that are not used in good society, they will appear as blemishes in the composition . . .' and 'if there be no such phrases, the style cannot be characteristic' of the lower orders.[2]

After such a forceful rebuttal of Wordsworth's theory of diction, Jeffrey then completely misses the point with regard to the representation of the sentiments of the lower classes. Or perhaps it would be more correct to say that Jeffrey and Wordsworth are talking about two different types of lower classes. To Jeffrey, the vulgar are represented by 'a clown, a tradesman or a market-wench', whereas, if he had read the review of the *Lyrical Ballads* of 1800 in the *British Critic*, he would have come across the fact that the shepherd-farmers of Cumberland and Westmorland, of whom Wordsworth was talking, were of a different kind of lower order than that Jeffrey had in mind.[3] This point was later taken up in reviews of the *Excursion* and also used in Coleridge's discussion of the subject in the *Biographia Literaria* (Chapter XVII).[4]

Jeffrey also made a surprising accusation, in view of his Whiggish interest in social reforms, against what he called 'a splenetic and idle discontent with the existing institutions of society', which he saw 'at the bottom of all their serious and peculiar sentiments'.[5] It is remarkable, as mentioned above, that the reactionary periodicals had not seen fit to notice this in reviews of the *Lyrical Ballads*.

[1] *ER*, I (Oct., 1802), 66.

[2] *Ibid.*, p. 67. See S. T. Coleridge, *Biographia Literaria*, ed. J. Shawcross (Oxford: Clarendon Press, 1965), II, 38–39.

[3] *ER*, I (Oct., 1802), 66; *BC*, XVII (Feb., 1801), 126n.

[4] Coleridge, II, 31.

[5] *ER*, I (Oct., 1802), 71.

Jeffrey had other criticisms to make of the Lake School in this review, but they are mostly of a minor nature. Two others, however, are worth remarking upon briefly: a charge of 'perpetual exaggeration of thought', which is something like the 'mental bombast' defined in the *Biographia Literaria* (Chapter XXII), and of a form of verbal bombast—to make 'a very ordinary conception' striking, they use several contrivances, one of which is 'to wrap it up in a veil of mysterious and unintelligible language, which flows past with so much solemnity, that it is difficult to believe it conveys nothing of any value'.[1] But all of these criticisms, coming as they did in remarks on the Lake School as a whole, were general observations with no evidence to substantiate them.

Wordsworth's first new production after the founding of the *Edinburgh Review*, *Poems in Two Volumes* of 1807, was met by reviews in an impressive array of ten reviewing periodicals, seven of which were not in existence in 1800, and by notices in several others, which are not, strictly speaking, reviews. And probably because of the new impetus and example provided by the *Edinburgh Review*, the reviews of the *Poems in Two Volumes* show a new trend toward more detailed and theoretical criticism.

This new trend is unfortunate in a way, especially if one is developing a respect for the reviewers; for the critical reception of this work is one of the most disgraceful in the annals of reviewing. Not that the theorizing, where it occurs, is generally bad—some of it is quite intelligent and appropriate; nor that the reviewers simply dismiss Wordsworth—although the majority of them are unfavorable toward the *Poems in Two Volumes*. Most of them see the work as a decline from the *Lyrical Ballads*, which receives a good deal of praise. It is not even that this claim of a falling-off is indefensible—there are a number of the new poems that deserve the criticism received, especially the charge of childishness, another charge levelled in most of the reviews.[2] The failure of the reviewers comes instead from not recognizing the truly great poems in the volumes, such

[1] *Ibid.*, pp. 69, 70. See Coleridge, II, 109.

[2] Barbara Garlitz, in 'The Baby's Debut: The Contemporary Reaction to Wordsworth's Poetry of Childhood', claims that some of Wordsworth's poems did in fact resemble contemporary children's poetry and were selected for volumes of verse for children. As examples of peculiarly childish poems, I make reference to 'The Kitten and the Falling Leaves', 'The Redbreast and the Butterfly', and 'To a Butterfly'.

as the 'Ode: Intimations of Immortality', 'Resolution and Independence', 'Elegiac Stanzas', 'The Solitary Reaper', 'I wandered lonely as a cloud', and 'My heart leaps up'. Only the sonnets received much praise.

The first review set the tone. Lord Byron, in *Monthly Literary Recreations*, praised the *Lyrical Ballads* and Wordsworth's great poetic talents, but saw the *Poems in Two Volumes* as a decline. Besides regretting the waste of Wordsworth's genius on 'trifling subjects', Byron remarks: 'When Mr. W. ceases to please, it is by "abandoning" his mind to the most common-place ideas, at the same time clothing them in language not simple, but puerile. . . .'[1] The review in the following month in the *Critical Review* likewise laments the misuse of Wordsworth's powers, but places the guilt on the 'tribe' to which he belongs, as well as on his egotism.[2]

In October, 1807, two of the most severe and indefensible reviews appeared. The reviewer in *Le Beau Monde*, after praising the *Lyrical Ballads* in general terms, pointed out that even there, Wordsworth 'had a knack of feeling about subjects with which feeling had no proper concern. . . .'[3] Almost all of the poems in the new volumes were dismissed as either unintelligible or puerile.

The other October review was by Jeffrey in the *Edinburgh Review*. As did previous reviewers of the volumes, he begins by praising the *Lyrical Ballads*, although with considerable reservations, and maintains that his previous remarks about Wordsworth have been justified. Jeffrey again emphasizes the idea of a school and claims that the defects of diction in the volumes are included 'upon principle and system', adding that what may have begun as an attempt to use natural diction has become itself a mannerism.[4] After first making clear that he is not defending 'the hackneyed common-places of ordinary versemen', he makes the exaggerated claim that Wordsworth's 'diction has no where any pretensions to elegance or dignity; and he has scarcely ever condescended to give the grace of correctness or melody to his versification'.[5] As before, Jeffrey also attacked Wordsworth's subject-matter:

It is possible enough, we allow, that the sight of a friend's garden-spade, or a sparrow's nest, or a man gathering leeches, might really have suggested to such a mind a train of powerful impressions and interesting

[1] *Monthly Literary Recreations*, III (July, 1807), 66.

[2] *CR*, XI (Aug., 1807), 400.

[3] *LeBM*, II (Oct., 1807), 138.

[4] *ER*, XI (Oct., 1807), 217.

[5] *Ibid.*

reflections; but it is certain, that, to most minds, such associations will always appear forced, strained, and unnatural. . . .[1]

It is unfortunate that Jeffrey included the example of the leech gatherer, for the inapplicability of that one example tends to vitiate an argument that is perhaps not easily dismissed; it is one, in fact, that is brought forward by Coleridge in the *Biographia Literaria* (Chapter XXII).[2] Only if one can conceive of a serious poem being written on a chamber pot can Jeffrey's argument be dismissed on principle.

Jeffrey's specific criticism of individual poems is something else again. Amidst some defensible censure of inferior poems is mingled ridicule of such poems as 'Resolution and Independence' and 'My heart leaps up', all of which abuse culminates in Jeffrey's obtuseness about the 'Ode: Intimations of Immortality': 'This is, beyond all doubt, the most illegible and unintelligible part of the publication.'[3] Jeffrey stops short at the sonnets and claims that because 'all English writers of sonnets have imitated Milton', Wordsworth has here escaped from his system, and that, therefore, the sonnets are 'much superior to the greater part of his other poems. . . .'[4] One possible explanation for Jeffrey's general critical obtuseness in dealing with these poems is that the charge he brings against Wordsworth is true of himself: he had previously created a 'system' of critical attitudes with regard to Wordsworth and must stick with it regardless of the quality of poetry that confronts him.

The abuse continued in the following month in the *Satirist.* But besides the remarks made in the pattern of the other periodicals, the reviewer had several novel criticisms to make. Anticipating a comment in the *Biographia Literaria* (Chapter XVII) on the apparent applicability to all poetry of Wordsworth's remarks on poetic diction in the 1800 Preface, he says:

Of this grand system of poetry, which was thus first discovered by Mr. William Wordsworth, about the year of our Lord 1800, and was of course

[1] *Ibid.*, p. 218. [2] Coleridge, II, 109.

[3] *ER*, XI (Oct., 1807), 227.

[4] *Ibid.*, p. 230. It is worth noting in connection with the 'Ode: Intimations' that in the *Poems in Two Volumes* it was entitled simply 'Ode' and carried no motto poem. The full name and motto poem were added in the collected edition of 1815—see Herbert Hartman, 'The "Intimations" of Wordsworth's "Ode" ', *RES*, VI (1930), 145n.

altogether unknown to Homer, Virgil, Shakspeare, Milton, and Dryden, the grand principle was, that nature could only be represented with fidelity by a close imitation of the language, and a constant adoption of the phrases made use of by persons in the lowest stages of life: as if language were not entirely factitious and arbitrary; as if men of all ranks and situations were not the creatures of habit; as if the expressions of the meanest individuals were not the result of the education which they receive, while those of the higher orders are rendered natural by long usage to the well-informed and accomplished part of mankind.[1]

The *Satirist*, moreover, was the first to criticize Wordsworth's rhymes:

With all his high pretensions to a pure and unsophisticated phraseology, his sacrifices of sense to sound are numerous and inhuman. The *Small* Celandine is said to be as lively as a *leveret!* that the corresponding line may end with 'nature's favourite'.[2]

James Montgomery gives a more sympathetic criticism of the volumes in the January, 1808, issue of the *Eclectic Review*, but he repeats most of the judgments made by the other periodicals. Wordsworth's theory of diction he particularly disagrees with. Deceptively he begins by agreeing with Wordsworth that the poet is above ordinary men, especially in his feelings; and then the reason for the agreement becomes obvious: 'Will such a man array the most pure, sublime, and perfect conceptions of his superior mind in its highest fervour, only with "the real language of men in a state of vivid excitement"?'[3] To ensure a negative answer to this rhetorical question, reference is then made to Milton, Thomson, Young, and Shakespeare, as well as to 'The Old Cumberland Beggar' and 'Tintern Abbey', where Wordsworth himself 'has attired his thoughts in diction of transcendent beauty'.[4] But Montgomery does grant that in the ballad pieces, such as 'Goody Blake and Harry Gill', ' "the real language of men" may be employed with pleasing effect'. And, in spite of a great deal of adverse criticism, Montgomery manages to make the following observation:

In Mr. Wordsworth's poetry, more perhaps than in that of any other man,

[1] *Sat*, I (Nov., 1807), 188–89 (see Coleridge, II, 29–30).

[2] *Sat*, I, 190. The poem in which the rhyme occurs is 'To the Daisy', but the error does not affect the criticism.

[3] *EcR*, IV i (Jan., 1808), 36.

[4] *Ibid.*, p. 37.

we frequently find images and sentiments, which we have seen and felt a thousand times, without particularly *reflecting* on them, and which, when presented by him, flash upon us with all the delight and surprize of novelty.[1]

If there is any palliation possible for Jeffrey's review of the *Poems in Two Volumes*, it would be that Montgomery, who is very sympathetic to Wordsworth, agreed in general with Jeffrey, even on the unintelligibility of the 'Ode: Intimations of Immortality'.

Reviews of the *Poems in Two Volumes* continued into 1808. In the *Annual Review* for 1807 (published in 1808), Lucy Aikin launches into a long discussion of Wordsworth's poetic system. After remarking the obscurity and the jargon of the Preface of 1800, she adds a new twist to Wordsworth's argument that meter makes pathetic passages endurable: 'Is not Mr. W. aware that these very arguments might equally be urged in favour of that poetic diction which he is so anxious to banish from his pages, and that the same instances might be adduced in its support that he here brings in favour of metre?'[2] She also quarrels with Wordsworth's definition of a poet: 'It is only that of a person of strong sympathies, who possesses in an unusual degree the power of imagining and describing the feelings of other human beings. A good novel writer must be all this—a descriptive or lyric poet, though perfect in his kind, need not.'[3] No, a poet must have something more, a something that is difficult to describe: a 'kind of fancy, akin to wit', which selects, creates, and organizes. But Wordsworth's major error is his failure to distinguish 'between rhetorical and poetical diction'. It is the former, 'this spirit of paraphrase and periphrasis, this idle parade of fine words, that is the bane of modern verse writing. . . .'[4] The criticism of Wordsworth's poems that follows points up their prolixity, bad rhymes, and what appeared to be capricious associations of unusual feelings with common subject-matter.

The remaining reviews of the volumes continue in the same strain. The *Cabinet* is noteworthy, having perhaps the most virulent review of the lot, and the review in the *British Critic* represents the most complete reversal of those earlier favorable reviews of the *Lyrical Ballads*. The review in the *Poetical Register* for 1806–7 (published in 1811) comes too late to be considered a review as such, but it shows

[1] *Ibid.*, p. 41.
[2] *AR*, VI (1808), 522–23.
[3] *Ibid.*, p. 523.
[4] *Ibid.*, p. 524.

that unfavorable opinion of the work was probably still in vogue four years after publication.

Compared with the *Poems in Two Volumes*, Wordsworth's tract on the *Convention of Cintra*, published in May, 1809, caused very little stir among the reviewers. The review in the *Eclectic Review* by James Montgomery, that in the *British Critic*, and that in the *London Review* by Henry Crabb Robinson all agreed in praising the work, which was, however, censured for some obscurity and prolixity, and for some of the sentiments. And, as might be expected of a political work that censured the government's role in the Cintra affair, there was some disagreement with Wordsworth's views in the *British Critic*.

The next major chapter in the history of Wordsworth and the reviewers, the reception of the *Excursion*, displays a considerable change in attitude from the reviews of the *Poems in Two Volumes*. Of the two principal Reviews, the *Quarterly Review*'s criticism, written by Charles Lamb (and heavily edited by William Gifford), was very favorable, while the *Edinburgh Review*'s judgment, delivered by Jeffrey, was generally unfavorable. The attitude of the secondary reviewing periodicals was also split: the *Augustan Review*, the *Examiner* review by William Hazlitt, and the review in the *Monthly Review* by John H. Merivale were on the whole unfavorable; the critique in the *Eclectic Review* by James Montgomery, and those in the *British Critic*, the *British Review*, and *La Belle Assemblée* were favorable; and very brief reviews in the *Monthly Magazine* and the *New Monthly Magazine* took extreme positions on either side (the former for and the latter against the volume). But in spite of the virtual split down the middle, the attitude as a whole toward the work was more favorable, since most of those who praised the work did so wholeheartedly, while those who were adverse also had a great deal to say of a positive nature. Jeffrey, for example, began his review with the famous 'This will never do', but ended by wishing to rescind his judgment.

The critical reversal has been seen as a victory for Wordsworth, which indeed it was in a way.[1] But, then, what does this reversal say for the quality of the reviewing? It is commonplace today to say that Wordsworth wrote his greatest poetry before 1807, and even that the *Excursion*, mostly written after that date, is as a whole a

[1] Such is the tone of William S. Ward's 'Wordsworth, the Lake Poets, and Their Contemporary Magazine Critics, 1798–1820', p. 98.

failure. Thus we are confronted in the Reviews not with an advance in critical perceptiveness, but with a set-back. Would many today, for example, agree with James Montgomery when he summed up his attitude toward the poem: 'Mr. Wordsworth did not miscalculate his powers, when he began to compose this "literary work";—it *will* live . . .'?[1]

And yet, in the process of giving their judgments of the *Excursion*, the reviewers had a great deal to say that is to some extent valid and is certainly provocative. And most of them agreed in praising the best parts of the poem: the Solitary's own story, the tales of Ellen and of the Whig and the Jacobin, and, especially, the tale of Margaret.

Those who praised the volume spent much of their time defending Wordsworth's 'philosophy', ignoring for the most part matters of style and construction. Most of them emphasized the difficulty for insensitive or worldly readers of understanding the poet's views of things; the emphasis points to the existence of a cult. The criticism in the *British Review*, indeed, would warm the cockles of any Wordsworthian's heart, containing as it does an elaborate defense of the *Lyrical Ballads*, as well as an attack on those critics who had already attacked the *Excursion*, with a particular reference to Jeffrey:

> To this poem it is necessary that the reader should bring a portion of the same meditative disposition, innocent tastes, calm affections, reverential feelings, philosophic habits, which characterize the poet himself; for readers of another kind we greatly fear, (and we deeply sympathize in the author's shame and mortification,) that this poem 'will never do'.[2]

This review also contains what is one of the first statements of the charge brought against the reviewers, that they expect contemporary poets to conform 'to some arbitrary classic model of the age that was past'.[3]

The reviewer in the *British Critic* attempted to set forth Wordsworth's principles: 'that whatsoever material or temporary exists before our senses, is capable of being associated, in our minds, with something spiritual and eternal; that such associations tend to ennoble and purify the heart . . .'; but the reviewer did not consider the principles to be confined to metaphysics, but rather to be behind

[1] *EcR*, III 2s (Jan., 1815), 39.

[2] *BR*, VI (Aug., 1815), 51.

[3] *Ibid.*, p. 53.

'every page of true poetry', and 'the end of descriptive verse' as a whole.[1] He also added that Wordsworth 'has not sufficiently distinguished between the common feelings of mankind and the wanderings of his own solitary spirit. He is too familiar with his art to see where the beginner finds difficulty.'[2]

Adverse criticisms of the volume were forced to run into new channels. Charles Lamb, in his favorable review in the *Quarterly Review*, pointed out that the *Excursion* had few of the qualities that had given so much offense in Wordsworth's earlier poems. This is, of course, true; there is none of the simple diction and little of the puerile subject-matter of the earlier ballads. Some of the reviewers, however, found enough else to criticize; quite pertinently they censured the wordiness and uninteresting 'plot', as well as the generally faulty construction of the poem. Hazlitt, in the *Examiner*, especially attacked the dialogue construction, claiming that all the characters were in fact embodiments of the poet, and also censured the lack of apparent connection between the tales and the truths they were to communicate. Both of these faults he blamed on Wordsworth's egotism, 'a systematic unwillingness to share the palm with his subject'.[3] Jeffrey, in the *Edinburgh Review*, emphasized the 'rapturous mysticism which eludes all comprehension', and, like John H. Merivale in the *Monthly Review*, he considered the ideas that were not unintelligible to be quite commonplace.[4] Merivale, however, praised Wordsworth's blank verse as 'one of the nearest approaches that has yet been made to the majesty of Milton'.[5]

But one of the main controversies concerned characterization, more specifically the use of a peddler as a central figure in a philosophic poem. Those who criticized the Wanderer did so on grounds of the improbability of a peddler having either such thoughts or such articulation as Wordsworth gave him. The defenders insisted on the background which the poet attributed to the Wanderer and stressed the fact that intellectual qualifications are not the result only of higher education. The *Philanthropist* also pointed out the Pedlar's

[1] *BC*, III 2s (May, 1815), 451. In a letter from Dorothy Wordsworth to Catherine Clarkson (June 28, 1815), the reviewer was identified cryptically as 'a friend of the Coleridges' (Ernest De Selincourt [ed.], *Letters of William and Dorothy Wordsworth, The Middle Years* [Oxford: Clarendon Press, 1937], II, 674).

[2] *BC*, III 2s (May, 1815), 465.

[3] *Exam*, Aug. 21, 1814, p. 556.

[4] *ER*, XXIV (Nov., 1814), 10.

[5] *MR*, LXXVI (Feb., 1815), 136.

peculiar fitness for his role as a guide, while Lamb, in the *Quarterly Review*, skirted the problem of improbability of characterization by pointing out that 'it might be answered that Mr. Wordsworth's plan required a character in humble life to be the organ of his philosophy. It was in harmony with the system and scenery of his poem.'[1] Lamb further made reference to *Piers Plowman*, in which 'the lowness of the teacher seems to add a simple dignity to the doctrine', adding that, if the name *'pedlar'* was offensive, it could be replaced by *'Pilgrim' or 'Palmer'*.[2]

Several periodicals made the defense, used earlier by the *British Critic* on the *Lyrical Ballads*, that Northern rustics were of a different breed from the lower orders to the South; but Hazlitt, in the *Examiner*, referring to personal experience, entered a protest: 'If the inhabitants of the mountainous districts, described by Mr. Wordsworth, are less gross and sensual than others, they are more selfish.'[3] (It is ironic that Hazlitt, soon to be ridiculed as a 'Cockney', objected to the Pedlar as 'low company'.)[4] James Montgomery, in the *Eclectic Review*, offered a more abstract argument; having said that the character is successful, he explains that 'if this paragon have no prototype in individual man, it has perfect ideal existence, and therefore poetical reality'.[5] The *British Review* added to its arguments in favor of the Pedlar an astonishingly anticritical remark: 'It is an arrogant ignorance of the nature of the human mind that ventures thus to prescribe to the poet his probabilities of character.'[6]

While the Reviews were still dealing with the *Excursion*, Wordsworth published, in May, 1815, *The White Doe of Rylstone*. Written in 1807 and 1808, the poem was mainly in tetrameter couplets and had something like a ballad style, and so came in for some of the criticism leveled earlier at the *Poems in Two Volumes*. The weight of the Reviews, indeed, was against the poem, with both the *Quarterly Review* and *Edinburgh Review*, joined by the *Monthly Review*, the *Champion*, the *Theatrical Inquisitor*, and the *New Monthly Magazine*, all in an adverse position, confronted only by the *British Review*, the *Augustan Review*, and the *Eclectic Review*, and the *Gentleman's*, the *European*, and the *British Lady's Magazine*. And yet, while there was some criticism of the unfitness of the diction, there was nonetheless a

[1] *QR*, XII (Oct., 1814), 111.
[2] *Ibid.*
[3] *Exam.* Oct. 2, 1814, p. 638.
[4] *Ibid.*, p. 636.
[5] *EcR*, III 2s (Jan., 1815), 29.
[6] *BR*, VI (Aug., 1815), 58.

great deal of praise and defense of Wordsworth in the reviews that were unfavorable. The criticisms were largely aimed at the construction of the poem, its length, and the handling of the narrative.

But if criticisms of Wordsworth's unrefined diction abated, a new charge against his choice of words was brought forward by William Lyall in the *Quarterly Review*. Beginning with the statement 'that mere simplicity of language is no merit at all, if it be purchased at the expense of perspicuity; and this is a price which our author is continually paying for it', Lyall gives several examples that are either laboriously prolix or 'absolutely devoid of meaning'.[1] An example of the latter is (the italics were added by the reviewer):

> For *deepest sorrows* that *aspire*
> Go *high*, no *transport* ever higher.

Lyall continues:

> He seems to think that if words only have a good character, and mean something pleasant when by themselves, whether they have any relation to one another in a sentence is a matter of no great importance. Hence it is, for we can no otherwise account for it, that Emily is always called the 'consecrated Emily', and that every pleasant thought is a 'dream' a 'vision', or a 'phantom', just as it happens.[2]

The criticisms of the poem itself are on the whole neither detailed nor especially interesting, but some more general remarks on Wordsworth are worth noting. John Scott, writing of Wordsworth for the first time in the *Champion*, went back to defend the *Lyrical Ballads* against the charge of undignified diction. After doing so at some length, Scott then makes an acute observation:

> We do not, however, mean to conceal our opinion, that Mr. Wordsworth often most unguardedly and unnecessarily exposes himself to the enemy. A stricter principle of selection than this author chooses to exercise, seems to us essential to Poetry. We would suggest that a Poet should discriminate between all that he feels, and what he can successfully convey; and, with deference, we would say, that Mr. Wordsworth often neglects to do this. He has told us that to him
>
> —'the meanest flower that blows can give
> Thoughts, that do often lie too deep for tears;'—

[1] *QR*, XIV (Oct., 1815), 223, 224.

[2] *Ibid.*, p. 225.

but if there are narrower limits to language than to his thoughts, he should, in his publications, stop within the former,—for otherwise what takes place? That which is rich and dignified in its original existence, is rendered mean and poor in the process by which it is brought forward to challenge admiration.[1]

Another mixed attitude toward Wordsworth's poetry is found in the article in the *Eclectic Review* by Josiah Conder:

From a character with which ordinary persons cannot sympathize, of the inner springs of which they can know little—and such a character, judging from his productions, we must conceive Mr. Wordsworth's to be—we may naturally expect a degree of singularity in its productions, which ill deserves to be submitted to the flippancy of opinion, but which must, nevertheless, interfere with the impression that their excellencies are adapted to produce.[2]

The remark about flippancy is undoubtedly a reference to Jeffrey's article in the *Edinburgh Review*, which is one of the worst in this regard, and in general exaggerates the faults of the poem. And yet Jeffrey's flippant opening—'This, we think, has the merit of being the very worst poem we ever saw imprinted in a quarto volume . . .' —must be understood to be to some extent a part of the contemporary attack on the 'bookmaking' of the period—in this instance, publication of a poem only in an expensive edition.[3] The reviewer in the *Eclectic Review* also repeated, in this connection, Jeffrey's contention that the *White Doe* would have been more successful in a shorter ballad form.

In 1815, the same year in which the *White Doe* appeared, Wordsworth published a collected edition of his poetry, with a preface, supplementary essay, and a new system of categorizing the poems. According to standard reviewing policies, this work should not have been reviewed at all, but the *Quarterly Review*, the *Augustan Review*, and the *Monthly Review* passed judgment on it. The *Monthly Review* censured the publication, as it had the *Excursion*: the new preface was attacked for lack of humility and clarity, the categorization for being meaningless, and the poetry for being nine-tenths of it unsatisfactory

[1] *Champ*, June 25, 1815, p. 206.

[2] *EcR*, V 2s (Jan., 1816), 37.

[3] *ER*, XXV (Oct., 1815), 355. Elsie Smith (p. 225) quotes Jeffrey as thinking the poem 'to be "the very worst poem ever seen in print . . ." '.

(as if that, considering the number of poems, were a condemnation). William Lyall, with a joint review in the *Quarterly Review* of the volume and the *White Doe*, limited himself to the new preface and essay. He considered the preface well written, but not always commonsensical, and he censured Wordsworth's belligerence: the poet should remember that the public and the critics

> have at least as much right to dislike *his* poetical taste, as he has to dislike *theirs*. If he voluntarily steps forward to make an attack upon the latter, the burthen of proof rests clearly upon him: to be in an ill temper merely because his opponents will not at once surrender at discretion, is surely most unreasonable.[1]

Lyall then begins a full-scale attack upon Wordsworth's theories about poetic diction and subject-matter, basing his argument on a simple criterion of pleasure. When he abandons that argument, he makes more sense, as with these remarks on diction: 'the most convenient language, either for a poet or any other man to make use of, is that by which he can with most precision make himself understood by those to whom he addresses himself.' Now, since Wordsworth is not writing for the lower orders and confesses himself the dangers of wrong connotations, he 'is paying to mere sounds (be they ever so philosophical) an homage which we can never be brought to believe that they deserve'.[2] But he agrees with Wordsworth in disliking poetical diction; periphrasis, for example, is indirect, 'is not the language of present feeling', and therefore is especially out of place in poetry dealing with present scenes and objects 'as they relate immediately to our feelings'. Moreover, the exclusion of such language 'need not interfere with the utmost degree of strength, nor the most refined harmony and elegance of language', as some of Wordsworth's poetry proves.[3]

Lyall also enters into the problem of Wordsworth's peculiar associations: Wordsworth's living habits and his 'habits of mind' differ from those of other people.

> When we are called upon to feel *emotions which lie too deep for tears even with respect to the meanest flower that blows*, to *cry for nothing, like Diana in the fountain*, over every ordinary object and every common-place occurrence

[1] *QR*, XIV (Oct., 1815), 202–3.
[2] *Ibid.*, p. 205.
[3] *Ibid.*, pp. 206, 207.

that may happen to cross our way, all communion of feeling between the poet and those who know no more of poetry than their own experience and an acquaintance with the best models will bestow, is necessarily broken off.[1]

If the poet must use language as used by other men, he must '*feel* as other men feel'. A poet

must, of course, consult his own feelings; it is, however, only so far as he knows them to be in unison with those of mankind at large, that he can safely trust himself to their direction; because, if they preserve not the same relative subordination and the same proportions among each other that they possess in the minds of people in general, it is plain that his compositions must appear to the greater part of his readers like pictures constructed upon false principles of perspective, and whatever resemblance they may bear to objects as they appeared to his own mind, may bear no more resemblance to objects as they appear in nature than the fantastical devices of an Indian screen.[2]

And Wordsworth's intimation that it takes a superior mind to understand his poetry is considered to be invalid,

upon a supposition at least, that his poetry really is what it professes to be: because, when a poet's avowed object is merely to trace in the plain and intelligible language of every-day life, those 'great and simple affections', those 'elementary feelings' and 'essential passions' which are assumed, by definition, to be common to all men alike,—it would seem but reasonable to expect that it would find readers in every class of society.[3]

Wordsworth's pamphlet published in 1816, entitled *A Letter to a Friend of Robert Burns*, elicited another slight critical reversal in Wordsworth's favor. The *Monthly Review*, which since its review of the first edition of the *Lyrical Ballads* had not had much good to say about Wordsworth's productions, professed to be 'delighted' with the pamphlet, both as to sentiment and expression. The *Critical Review* was likewise favorable. Only *Blackwood's*, in the person of John Wilson, was unfavorable, and Wilson was wholeheartedly so: Wordsworth was impertinent, incompetent, and egotistical in writing the *Letter*. The extent to which Wilson was willing to go can be seen

[1] *Ibid.*, p. 208.
[2] *Ibid.*, p. 209.
[3] *Ibid.*

in his defense of the *Edinburgh Review*, which Wordsworth had attacked: the poet

> with the voice and countenance of a maniac, fixes his teeth in the blue cover of the Edinburgh. He growls over it—shakes it violently to and fro—and at last, wearied out with vain efforts at mastication, leaves it covered over with the drivelling slaver of his impotent rage.[1]

Wilson followed this review with two anonymous letters, the first reversing this position and the second reverting to it.[2]

Wordsworth's *Thanksgiving Ode*, published that same year, received enthusiastic reviews in the *British Critic* and the *Champion*, which indicate how far Wordsworth's admirers were willing to go, for the poem is uninspired, to say the least. The *Champion*, usually more sensible, went as far out as possible:

> Whatever his subject may be, the soul and imagination of the poet make the all in all of the performance. Every thing that proceeds from him is an emanation of himself:—he creates it in his own image,—and, without meaning to suggest any improper analogy, we would say, that *he* it is who sees that it is good.[3]

The most level-headed review of the work was in the *Eclectic Review*, in which Josiah Conder praised Wordsworth, but not this particular publication. The reviewer in the *Monthly Review* admitted his dislike of poems on contemporary events, before dismissing the work.

In 1819, Wordsworth published for the first time two poems written much earlier, *Peter Bell* (1798) and *The Waggoner* (1805). As might be expected by the dates of composition, suggesting as they do Wordsworth's earlier style and subject-matter, both poems encountered considerable resistance.

And yet the first to be published, *Peter Bell*, occasioned a reversal of judgment in only one periodical favorable to the *Excursion*, the *Monthly Magazine*. Otherwise (apart from the *Edinburgh Review* and the *Quarterly Review*, which did not review the poem) the reviewers remained more or less constant: the *British Critic* and the *Eclectic Review* gave favorable appraisals of the poem, and were joined by very

[1] *BM*, I (June, 1817), 265.

[2] For a more detailed discussion of these articles by Wilson, see Alan L. Strout, 'John Wilson, "Champion" of Wordsworth'.

[3] *Champ*, Oct. 20, 1816, p. 334.

favorable reviews in the *Gentleman's*, *Blackwood's*, and the *European Magazine*; the *Examiner*, with Leigh Hunt as reviewer, and the *Monthly Review* continued their stand against Wordsworth, with the support of periodicals new to the dispute—the *Edinburgh Magazine*, the *Literary Gazette*, the *Literary Chronicle*, and three other minor periodicals.

There was some agreement on both sides as to the most successful parts of the poem: the gradual reformation of Peter Bell and the ending of the poem, especially the description of the widow's grief. The faults most often noted, which were generally ridiculed with great glee, were the puerile diction and subject-matter—the same faults with which Wordsworth was charged in reviews of the *Poems in Two Volumes*. One passage in particular came in for considerable censure:

> ''Tis come then to a pretty pass'
> Said Peter to the groaning ass,
> 'But I will *bang* your bones.'

This passage was deleted in editions after 1820.

Two other objections (made by more than one reviewer) concerned the didactic mysticism of the poem and the humor in the Prologue. Concerning the former, the *Theatrical Inquisitor*, after quoting the following lines,

> [In vain, through every changeful year,
> Did Nature lead him as before;]
> A primrose by a river's brim
> A yellow primrose was to him,
> And it was nothing more,

admitted a similar guilt: 'for we have never been able to discover, any more than Peter, any thing more, in "*a yellow primrose*", than a yellow primrose itself'.[1]

As for the humor in the Prologue, the *Eclectic Review* made the most sympathetic remonstration: Wordsworth

> cannot be comic, and it is well known to what ungraceful expedients persons devoid of native humour are seduced to resort by a misdirected

[1] *TI*, XIV (May, 1819), 371.

> ambition. To see a man trying to be playful and sportive, to whose rigidity of form, and unelastic tread, and solemnity of voice, the tones and attitudes of humour or of grace are incapable of being communicated, is a spectacle which only the malicious can take delight in.[1]

The best review of *Peter Bell*, however, was in the *British Critic*. Notable for its intelligence and objectivity, the review would be difficult, I think, to surpass as a sympathetic appraisal of the poem or as an explanation of Wordsworth's relations with his contemporary critics—so attention will be given to it as an example of reviewing at its best.

After a very high estimate of Wordsworth's talents, the reviewer expressed considerable concern for the poet's future fame. Wordsworth, to be sure, would always have his admirers, 'but we are much in error if in any age the ablest of those admirers will be able satisfactorily to answer the objections urged against him by candid and feeling readers of a different persuasion. . . .' For

> We scarcely ever met with a single person, whose opinion on the subject we valued, and who was open to express it, that could say he had read any whole poem of Wordsworth's composition, longer than a mere sonnet, without being obliged to get over, and subdue, in some part of it, offensive and disturbing feelings; to forget something that shocked his taste, and checked that full current of admiration, which the remainder excited; the latter feeling perhaps after all predominated, yet the mind was left in a state of incomplete satisfaction.[2]

Then, after repeating the explanation of the principles of material-spiritual association behind Wordsworth's poetry noted above in the *British Critic*'s review of the *Excursion*, he warned that with poetry written on such principles 'there is always danger of writing in a way which may seem mystical to many readers; we would earnestly desire to avoid this except at the expence of truth'.[3] And, although Wordsworth's principles are correct, he has, in their application, fallen into 'the excesses, from which no manliness or strength of mind seems able to guard the reviver of an old, or the inventor of a new system'.[4] Wordsworth has formed the principles into a system and has forgotten 'that poetry is a communicative art, that the state of the

[1] *EcR*, XII 2s (July, 1819), 64.
[2] *BC*, XI 2s (June, 1819), 585.
[3] *Ibid.*, p. 586.
[4] *Ibid.*, p. 587.

recipient is to be considered, as well as that of the communicant; that it is little to have mixed up all the essential ingredients of poetic pleasure if they are to be neutralized or overpowered by certain accompanying feelings of disgust or ridicule'.[1] Poetry may exist in the mind uncommunicated, but once communication has taken place, then a poet's audience must be considered. Now then,

all objects or appearances in nature are intrinsically capable of that speculation and association which are the basis of poetical pleasure; a large class of them, however, from other circumstances, apparently permanent in their nature, and from inveterate counter-associations, whether reasonable or not, are either esteemed by the mass of men as trifling, or felt to be disgusting; when these, therefore, are made the subjects of grave or delicate speculation, the poet's associations and the reader's are at direct variance; and even if the powers of the former, with the intrinsic justice of his thoughts, should prevail over the mere habits and feelings of the latter, it is evident that a victory obtained by a struggle does not and cannot impart that full and perfect pleasure which it is the business of poetry to bestow. This we take to be a just account of the dispute between Wordsworth and the mass of his readers. . . .[2]

There follows a very fair detailed criticism of the poem with both flaws and beauties pointed out. The reviewer then admits that on first reading he was prepared to damn the poem, and urges a second reading on his readers with the following *caveat*:

Wordsworth demands from his readers, not only the sacrifice of many prejudices, and the conquest of some reasonable dispositions to laughter, or mortification, but also an open heart, and a patient exercise of his intellect. People may doubt, whether a poet has a right to demand all these, but of this we are certain, that he who can, and will grant them, will derive from Wordsworth nearly as high gratification as any poet is capable of bestowing.[3]

That, I submit, is one of the best short defenses of Wordsworth ever written.

The Waggoner was published one month after *Peter Bell* and got much the same kind of reception. But there was enough difference in the tone of the two poems to occasion several critical reversals. The *Eclectic Review* and the *European Magazine* were, for a change,

[1] *Ibid.*, p. 588. [2] *Ibid.*, p. 591. [3] *Ibid.*, p. 603.

unfavorable, while the *Monthly Review*, after a long history of censure, confessed that it considered *The Waggoner* 'to be one of the best and most ingenious of *all* Mr. Wordsworth's poems'.[1] The remainder of those journals which criticized both poems remained constant in their positions.

There was likewise the same general agreement about the most successful passages of *The Waggoner*, namely the tavern scene and the description of the storm; the criticism of the undignified subject-matter and diction continued. The *Literary Gazette* also reiterated its own criticism of Wordsworth's diction made before in its review of *Peter Bell*: there are 'improper words adopted for rhymes' sake, expletives to eke out the measure, or expressions which do not convey the meaning of the writer'.[2] As examples of the latter, lines 7 and 8 are criticized: ' "Soft darkness" is hard to understand; "confiding glow-worms" with their "earth-born light", still more unintelligible. . . .'

And yet some of the reviewers managed to overcome their feelings about the 'vulgarity' of the subject-matter and were able to appreciate what is surely one of Wordsworth's most gleeful and humane poems and perhaps his nearest approach to the Chaucerian spirit. The *Monthly Review* gave the best account of this tone in *The Waggoner*:

> a sly covert sort of irony, an *under-tone* of playfulness, smiling at the mock heroics of the author; and preserving that difficult but exact spirit of bombast, which betrays a consciousness of misapplied sublimity, without rendering it quite gross and ridiculous.[3]

The *British Critic* also detected the playfulness, as well as a

> moral sympathy and human fellow-feeling, that emotion of benevolent regard which a writer excites in the minds of his readers, either towards himself or his characters, by the amiable and good-natured thoughts, or actions, or remarks, which he indicates as habitual to himself, or makes to seem so in them.[4]

Becoming more specific, the reviewer adds:

> The Waggoner himself is a strong exemplification of these remarks; a great part of the charm of the poem, and the friendly regret which we feel at the close, is to be found in the amiableness of his character, his patience

[1] *MR*, XC (Sept., 1819), 37.
[2] *LG*, June 12, 1819, p. 370.
[3] *MR*, XC (Sept., 1819), 37.
[4] *BC*, XII 2s (Nov., 1819), 469.

with, and care of his horses, his feelings for the poor woman and her child in the storm . . .,[1]

and even his horses' affection for him.

Another general remark on Wordsworth's poetry in the *Eclectic Review* ought not to go unnoticed here—being somewhat prophetic. The reviewer contends that 'Mr. Wordsworth has one chance of being read by posterity', which is to have a friend collect his best pieces into one volume: 'some of his early lyrics, a few of his odes, his noble sonnets, all his landscape sketches, and the best parts of the Excursion. . . .'[2]

In 1820, the uneven course of the critical reception accorded Wordsworth's writings took another violent turn in reviews of his *River Duddon* volume. Besides the sonnets in the series, composed between 1806 and 1820, there were other miscellaneous poems, chief of which was 'Vaudracour and Julia', probably composed in 1804. Eight of the periodicals which had reviewed *The Waggoner* praised the new volume (four of them reversing their disfavor), and were joined in that praise by Gold's *London Magazine*, the *Literary Chronicle*, the *Ladies' Monthly Museum*, and the *British Review*. Only one very minor periodical, the *Literary and Statistical Magazine for Scotland*, continued its adverse criticism of Wordsworth. (The *Edinburgh Review* and *Quarterly Review*, apparently too busy to comment on this fourth volume since their last reviews of Wordsworth, remained silent.)

The reason behind this drastic change of sentiment is stated in many of the reviews themselves. After the 'set-back' of *Peter Bell* and *The Waggoner*, with their lowly subject-matter and style, the *River Duddon* volume offered very little in that way to upset the reviewers. After a bit of crowing, the *Monthly Review* summed up a feeling that is present in many of the reviews: 'In serious truth, we view the major portion of the present volume as a practical recantation, as a distinct palinodia, sung in his best style, of all Mr. Wordsworth's poetical theories, or rather heresies, concerning the identity of the language of prose and verse, &c. &c.'[3]

There was also a consensus about the best parts of the volume: the *River Duddon* (especially the use of the river as a frame for the sonnets), 'Vaudracour and Julia', 'Dion', and 'The Lament of Mary

[1] *Ibid.*, p. 470.
[2] *EcR*, XII 2s (July, 1819), 74.
[3] *MR*, XCIII (Oct., 1820), 133.

Queen of Scots'. Several prose items in the volume—a long note on Rev. Robert Walker and the appended *Topographical Description of the Country of the Lakes*—also came in for a large share of praise.

But the criticism of the volume is in general disappointing. The praise is largely overdone and what there is of censure is concerned mainly with minor defects of diction. There are, however, several more lengthy attempts to estimate the general worth of Wordsworth's poetry. Since Gold's *London Magazine* was reviewing Wordsworth for the first time, it went back through his career and tried to describe his peculiar poetic qualities, one of which was 'the accurate and minute manner in which he places his description before the mind's-eye of his readers'.[1] There were other general remarks in the *Eclectic Review* and *British Review*, but nothing as extensive as those in the *British Critic*, which devoted over twenty pages to an estimate of Wordsworth. High but discriminating praise is given Wordsworth's ability to discover intuitive truths, his powers of reasoning, his observation and description of nature, and his powers as a metrist, especially in blank verse.

The second collected edition of Wordsworth's poetry, in four volumes, appeared later in 1820 and received what amounted to only a description and recommendation in the *Literary Gazette*.

The next new productions after the *River Duddon* were the *Ecclesiastical Sketches* and the *Memorials of a Tour on the Continent*, published separately in the spring of 1822. The reviewers had apparently recovered from their surprised admiration for the *River Duddon* volume, for their critical position took another turn toward disfavor. But, then, both of the volumes are, I believe, poetically inferior to their predecessor, and so the reversal can be viewed as critically valid.

The first to be published, the *Ecclesiastical Sketches*, was, like the *River Duddon*, a sonnet series. Unfortunately, as most of the reviewers pointed out, it did not hang together so well; besides having generally uninteresting subject-matter, the poetry itself was uninspired. Even the *British Critic*, which had long been intelligently defending Wordsworth, concurred in this verdict. Only John Wilson, in *Blackwood's*, was favorable, but his criticism was so indiscriminate and enthusiastic as to be eliminated from serious consideration. A short quotation from his introductory remarks will give an idea of its tone: 'Indeed, his poetry is to him religion; and we venture to say, that it

[1] Gold's *LM*, I (June, 1820), 623.

has been felt to be so by thousands. It would be absolute profanity to speak one word against many of his finest breathings.'[1] It was not just his enemies that Wordsworth had to fear.

The *Memorials of a Tour on the Continent*, a collection of sonnets and other short poems on subjects indicated by the title of the volume, received a slightly better reception. The *Literary Gazette*, however, had twitted the 'great leading Reviews' for avoiding 'authors with whom they do not wish to come in collision', and Jeffrey finally reviewed Wordsworth after six years of silence.[2] He quickly made up for lost time by summing up Wordsworth's last three volumes as 'a sort of prosy, solemn, obscure, feeble kind of mouthing,—sadly garnished with shreds of phrases from Milton and the Bible—but without nature and without passion,—and with a plentiful lack of meaning, compensated only by a large allowance of affectation and egotism'.[3] The review continues in that tone of ridicule, which obscures a certain amount of valid criticism.

In any event, the *Edinburgh Review* was joined in its disapproval by only three weeklies, while the *British Critic*, the *British Review*, *Blackwood's*, the *Literary Museum*, and the *Monthly Magazine* were generally favorable, although with some qualifications. For example, the *Literary Museum* remarked:

> This volume does not contain any elaborate efforts of our poet's muse, but is really what it pretends to be and nothing more—a collection of such sonnets and poems as he occasionally wrote during his excursion, for the amusement of himself and the gratification of his fellow travellers. These are not the grander flights of his imagination. . . .[4]

Political prejudices, if they had anything to do with the critical reception of Wordsworth's poetry, had at least been unspoken before 1822, but in reviews of the two volumes published in that year, such prejudices became overt. They cropped up on both sides: the *Edinburgh Review* and the *Literary Chronicle* mentioned disparagingly his admiration for and connections with the ministry; the *British Review* thanked Wordsworth for bringing back his *Memorials* from the Continent instead of the usual 'seeds of revolutionary mischief'.[5]

[1] *BM*, XII (Aug., 1822), 175.
[2] *LG*, Apr. 6, 1822, p. 212.
[3] *ER*, XXXVII (Nov., 1822), 450.
[4] *LitMus*, May 18, 1822, p. 52.
[5] *BR*, XX (Dec., 1822), 466.

In 1822 a separate publication of *A Description of the Scenery of the Lakes* received one review—a favorable one in the *New European Magazine*; but Wordsworth's productive life was for all practical purposes at an end. What, then, can now be said of the critical reception given Wordsworth's works by the reviewing periodicals of his time?

One of the first points to present itself from the above sketch is the uneven course of the critical appraisal of Wordsworth. A favorable acceptance of the *Lyrical Ballads* was reversed in reviews of the *Poems in Two Volumes*, which was reversed in the general acceptance of the *Excursion*, which was reversed in reviews of the *White Doe*, and so on. Possibilities of political, religious, and personal prejudices aside for the present, such reversals can be understood in terms of valid literary assessments, that is, in terms of the unevenness of Wordsworth's poetry itself.

With this in mind, one of the main defects of the assessments is clear. Time has a way of straightening out the comparative worth of a poet's productions: we can now check what has in fact 'lived' with what the reviewers predicted would do so. Their most serious blunders occurred in judgments, both positive and negative—a critical obtuseness in rejecting the *Poems in Two Volumes* and a too ready acceptance of the *Excursion* and the *River Duddon* volume. Posterity has reversed all three of these judgments in its turn.

Another defect of the criticism as a whole, closely connected with the first, is that many of the reviewers seem often to have been more concerned with Wordsworth's reputation than with the particular work under review. In many cases this resulted in extreme positions, both for and against, often without intelligent discrimination. Extravagant ridicule was met with extravagant praise.

The extent and asperity of some of the ridicule of Wordsworth and his productions cannot be fully comprehended from the terms 'favorable' and 'unfavorable' in the sketch above. Even considering the more permissive attitude at the time toward ridicule of authors, which to our more fastidious age appears much more serious than it actually was, there was a good deal too much of it in the reviews of Wordsworth. Wordsworth, to be sure, was notoriously egotistical, and this led to provocatively vain remarks and even scorn for the reviewers in some of his prefaces and in the *Letter to a Friend of Burns*. In short, he asked for a certain amount of abuse, but the reviewers overindulged themselves.

And yet all of these defects should not obscure the positive achievement of Wordsworth's reviewers. They managed to present the public with a good deal of intelligent criticism of Wordsworth's theories and practices, and almost every volume received some discriminating judgments at their hands. In this regard, the *Eclectic Review* and the *British Critic* are particularly noteworthy. And if the extent of ridicule has been necessarily obscured because of limits of space, such also is the case with the very high estimates of Wordsworth's genius set forth by both hostile and friendly reviewers. From as early as reviews of the *Excursion* to the latest reviews of his last two volumes in 1822, phrases such as 'true poet' and 'real genius' are not uncommon. These high estimates came, too, from critics who did not have masses of scholarly and critical studies of Wordsworth to fall back on and who were reviewing not the works selected by the passage of time, but entire volumes, some of which later underwent extensive revisions. And these critics had never seen the *Prelude*, upon which, as Herbert Read has justly remarked, 'We base the claim of Wordsworth to be considered as one of our major poets.'[1]

Samuel Taylor Coleridge

With the exception of the third edition of his *Poems*, which received several favorable reviews, almost ten years passed after the founding of the *Edinburgh Review* before Coleridge published any works. Even then, the publication in 1812 of *The Friend*, a series of essays taken from his weekly periodical (1809–10) of the same name, received no reviews. There was, however, in October, 1811, a review in the *Eclectic Review* by John Foster of *The Friend* in its periodical form—reviews of periodicals were a not unusual occurrence with the Reviews. Foster, an essayist himself, suggested that among the reasons for the failure of the periodical was the heavy subject matter, poorly suited to a weekly publication and requiring a great deal more revision than was possible in a weekly. In addition there was considerable indecision in choice of subjects, with consequent confusion and lack of continuity. There is also in this review a long and intelligent discussion of the qualities of Coleridge's mind.

But the first publication after 1802 to receive full-scale critical

[1] *Wordsworth*, 2d ed. (London: Faber and Faber, 1949), p. 21.

treatment was Coleridge's play, *Remorse*, published in 1813. The play received more adverse than favorable criticism, but the more influential reviews were in the latter category: the *Quarterly Review*, with its review written by Coleridge's nephew, John Taylor Coleridge, was joined by the *Monthly Review* (Francis Hodgson reviewing) and the *Christian Observer* in general approval of the play. Against these were the *British Review* and the *Critical Review*, as well as the *Satirist* and the *Theatrical Inquisitor*. There are, besides the disagreement in the general assessments, a great many violently contradictory judgments concerning the sentiments, the style, and especially the characterization—more contradiction in fact than is warranted by the unevenness of the play itself. Just how far the contradictions went can be seen by placing the judgment of the *Christian Observer* that the play was more successful when read, alongside the judgment of the *British Review* that as a closet drama it was a failure.

The next publication after *Remorse* resulted in an appreciable turn for the worse in Coleridge's contemporary reputation. The volume in question contained three early poems published in 1816 for the first time—'Christabel', 'Kubla Khan', and 'The Pains of Sleep'. Considering that the first of these poems was a fragment and the second professedly composed during sleep, this volume posed perhaps the most difficult challenge that the reviewers in the period had to face. Reviewers in the *Edinburgh Review*, the *Monthly Review*, the *Antijacobin Review*, the *Augustan Review*, and the *British Review* (William Roberts reviewing), as well as the *Champion*, the *Examiner* (Hazlitt reviewing), and the *British Lady's Magazine*, decided to reject the volume in general while admitting Coleridge's genius and lamenting its waste.

These were hardly counterbalanced by the enthusiastic approbation in the *Critical Review* and the *European Magazine*, joined by somewhat qualified approval in the *Literary Panorama* and the *Eclectic Review* (Josiah Conder reviewing). But the lengths to which the two enthusiastic reviewers had to go in defense of the volume indicates the difficulty of contemporary acceptance. The reviewer in the *Critical Review* spends some time attacking the critics of the age and their 'diseased appetite' and states boldly (and somewhat questionably) that 'it is more advantageous to point out one beauty than to discover ten deformities'.[1] Later he offers more acceptable advice

[1] *CR*, III 5s (May, 1816), 505.

by admonishing readers not to be put off if they encounter early passages in 'Christabel' 'not exactly according with their pre-conceived notions of excellence'.[1] The reviewer in the *European Magazine*, George Felton Mathew, stresses the originality of 'Christabel' and concludes that 'it is not, therefore, to be judged of by comparison, but by those effects which it produces upon the hearts and imaginations of its readers'.[2]

The adverse reviews of the volume should not be judged by the well-known attack in the *Edinburgh Review*, which is easily the worst review of the lot. Two of the criticisms advanced, which pertain to the obscurity and the meter, were, however, the principal preoccupations of the other periodicals; for reviews of this volume were not as contradictory as those of *Remorse*. And yet various methods and reasonings can be used in making the same basic judgments, and the other reviewers were on the whole less snide and flippant than the reviewer in the *Edinburgh Review*.

The *Champion* review is one of the best, and its handling of the two main criticisms is at least well taken. Of the obscurity, the reviewer says:

> To Persons who, on the principle that fiction should be as opposite to fact as possible, think a slice of unintelligibility by no means a fault in a Poem,—the obscurity and undiscoverable drift of the story, may appear a means of heightening its sublimity: but Mr. Coleridge is not in truth entitled to this indulgence. The principle of producing effect by means of obscurity, is very admissible, and has been advantageously used by the greatest Poets in the subordinate and incidental points and circumstances in the progress of a story:—but here the line must be drawn, and the license must never be applied to the main thread of the narrative. It must not be made an excuse for the utter absence of perspicuity and connection in the main fable, or of the definiteness in the characters, the passions, and the situations.[3]

As for the meter, he says further on:

> His verse professedly runs on accents instead of feet—so that there is scarcely any variety of ballad metre that comes within the limits of four accents, which he has not introduced;—and to keep pace with the accents in long lines, we are sometimes obliged to gallop along, like choristers in a long verse in the Psalms.

[1] *Ibid.*, p. 510. [2] *EM*, LXX (Nov., 1816), 434–35.
[3] *Champ*, May 26, 1816, p. 167.

Summing up his objections, he says:

> In diction, in numbers, in thought, in short in every thing appertaining to the Poem, Mr. Coleridge's licentiousness out-Herods Herod. Assuredly we are far from wishing to see our poetry again subjugated to those inexorable canons of propriety which, like every species of despotism, effectually repress the transcendant efforts of genius. We do not want our Poets servilely to imitate Addison or Pope. But the opposite extreme, which appears to be the besetting sin of the poetry of the day, is not less to be guarded against.—In our zeal for natural feeling and natural expression we should be cautious how we admit under these denominations every crude, and puerile familiarity which perverse, or indolent, or weak writers may palm upon us under the sanction of that much perverted word '*nature*'.—There is no greater mistake than to suppose that every thing that is in nature may be hooked into Poetry:—much of what is *natural* in language and in sentiment, is essentially flat, ordinary, and prosaic. There are weeds as well as flowers—a poet must exercise some selection, some discrimination. . . .[1]

Compared with 'Christabel', 'Kubla Khan' received very little attention. Coleridge said in a short preface to the poem that it was published 'as far as the Author's own opinions are concerned, rather as a psychological curiosity, than on the ground of any supposed *poetic* merits', and the reviewers on the whole agreed with this opinion, except that there was considerable liking for, if not approval of, the poem. Hazlitt, in the *Examiner*, for example, after calling it '*nonsense* verses', decided that, in fact, it was 'not a poem, but a musical composition'. And of a quotation, he admitted that 'we could repeat these lines to ourselves not the less often for not knowing the meaning of them'.[2]

An interesting reaction to the psychological circumstance of the composition of 'Kubla Khan' was the claim in several reviews that composition during sleep was not unusual with poets. The *Monthly Review*, on the other hand, questioned Coleridge's testimony, asking if it was 'not rather the effect of rapid and instant composition after he was awake, than of memory immediately recording that which he dreamt when asleep? By what process of consciousness could he distinguish between such composition and such reminiscence?'[3]

[1] *Champ*, May 26, 1816, p. 167. [2] *Exam*, June 2, 1816, p. 349.

[3] *MR*, LXXXII (Jan., 1817), 24. Elisabeth Schneider, (*Coleridge, Opium, and Kubla Khan* [Chicago: University of Chicago Press, 1953], pp. 16–17) points out that some later critics have thought Coleridge's account incredible.

Criticism of Coleridge continued adverse in the few reviews of his two Lay Sermons, the *Statesman's Manual* in late 1816 and *Blessed Are Ye That Sow* early in 1817. Of the three reviews of the former, one was a short unfavorable notice in the *Monthly Magazine*, and the other two were written by Hazlitt, in the *Edinburgh Review* and in the *Examiner* respectively. Both of Hazlitt's criticisms followed in general the light tone he set in a still earlier spoof review in the *Examiner* of an advertisement of the work: 'We see no sort of difference between his published and his unpublished compositions. It is just as impossible to get at the meaning of the one as the other. No man ever yet gave Mr. Coleridge "a penny for his thoughts". His are all maiden ideas, immaculate conceptions.'[1] There was, however, some serious criticism interwoven, especially in his genuine *Examiner* review, where he points out many of the inconsistencies and the general inconclusiveness of Coleridge's arguments. His critique in the *Edinburgh Review* was much more concerned with Coleridge's politics.

The second Lay Sermon, *Blessed Are Ye That Sow*, received one favorable review from the *Critical Review*, which had earlier praised his *Christabel* volume. A 'review' in the *Monthly Repository* was concerned solely with censuring Coleridge's attacks on the Unitarians.

The year 1817 saw the separate publication of the second Lay Sermon (already discussed), *Sibylline Leaves*, the *Biographia Literaria*, and *Zapolya*, a drama.

The *Biographia Literaria* is a unique work, a mixture of autobiography, metaphysics, creative theory, and literary criticism; and as such, it posed another major challenge to the reviewers. Their verdict, as set forth by Hazlitt in the *Edinburgh Review*, John Wilson in *Blackwood's* and by critics in the *Literary Gazette*, the *Monthly Review*, and the *Monthly* and the *New Monthly Magazine*, was unfavorable toward the work as a whole. The one dissenting opinion, voiced in the *British Critic*, was itself qualified: it is an 'able, and, notwithstanding our author's endless and bottomless discussions on metaphysical matters, upon the whole, an entertaining performance'.[2]

Even though there was a difference in the ultimate verdict, all of the longer criticisms made similar distinctions between various parts of the work; and, like the *British Critic*, they all dismissed the philosophical sections as unintelligible. But the autobiographical portions received a great deal of praise, especially the accounts of the

[1] *Exam.* Sept. 8, 1816, p. 571.

[2] *BC*, VIII 2s (Nov., 1817), 463.

Watchman and of the government spy. Along with the praise, however, there was some disparagement of Coleridge's political change, but it was such as arose naturally from the discussion of an autobiography, and was confined chiefly to Hazlitt's review in the *Edinburgh Review* and Wilson's maverick review in *Blackwood's*. Hazlitt, for example, points out the inconsistency of Coleridge's apology for Southey's personal virtues when the only attack ever made upon them came from writers on the staff of the *Anti-Jacobin; or Weekly Examiner*—'the Cannings, the Giffords, and the Freres', with whom he and Southey were now allied.[1]

Coleridge's criticisms of Wordsworth's poetry and poetic theory also met with a great deal of approval, which is not surprising, since, as we have seen, so much of that criticism had been made previously by the reviewers themselves. The *Monthly Review* noted that Coleridge, in spite of his adverse criticism of Wordsworth, retained his consistency in calling him a great poet by his further claim that the theoretical defects he pointed out are rarely seen in Wordsworth's practice; significantly, the reviewer did not quarrel with Coleridge's principles, but only with the infrequency with which Coleridge claimed the defects occurred. Hazlitt, in the *Edinburgh Review*, took the opportunity of Coleridge's remarks on Wordsworth to set forth a defense of artificial diction in certain types of 'descriptive and fanciful poetry'.[2]

As for the literary qualities of the *Biographia Literaria*, most of the reviewers were content to mention the confusion and inconclusiveness of construction. Coleridge's build-up to Chapter XIII ('On the Imagination, or Esemplastic Power') and his subsequent omission of the discussion altogether were not overlooked. But only the *British Critic* saw fit to comment on the style of the work: 'it is certainly expressive, but it does not seem to be constructed upon any settled principles of composition, farther than are implied in an apparent preference of our early writers . . .', that is, of sixteenth- and seventeenth-century English prose writers.[3] He continues:

To say that our author has succeeded in reminding us of the models whom he appears desirous of emulating, is not saying much in his praise. It is just as easy to put into one sentence what ought properly to form three, as to put into three, what ought properly to form only one; nor is

[1] *ER*, XXVIII (Aug., 1817), 492. [2] *Ibid.*, p. 513.
[3] *BC*, VIII 2s (Nov., 1817), 463.

it a matter of much greater difficulty to sprinkle our manner of speaking with learned phrases and obsolete forms of expression.

And yet there is 'an air of truth and simplicity, which is plainly natural to him; and his language, though sometimes pedantic, and often by no means free from that philosophical jargon which is almost the characteristical affectation of the present race of writers, is nevertheless, that of a scholar. . . .'[1]

The *Sibylline Leaves*, a volume of poetry originally intended as a companion volume to the *Biographia Literaria* but published separately at about the same time, was in fact the fourth collected edition of Coleridge's poems with but few additions. As such, in accordance with standard reviewing policies the volume should not have been reviewed, but it received two fairly lengthy reviews in the *Edinburgh Magazine* and in the *Monthly Review*, as well as shorter reviews in three other periodicals. Only the *Edinburgh Magazine* was favorable.

Except for the remarks that arose naturally in discussing the *Biographia Literaria*, Coleridge had comparatively seldom been linked adversely with the Lake School, but the *Edinburgh Magazine* (as well as two other periodicals) now made the connection. Coleridge is said to display the typical sentimentality, choice of trifling subjects, and use of vulgar expressions that are shared by all the Lakers. The reviewer continues:

However, it cannot be denied, that there are other qualities of Mr. Coleridge's poetry which entitle it to a place among the finest productions of modern times. There is, in particular, a wildness of narrative, and a picturesque grouping of qualities and objects, which are in fine contrast to the tameness and placidity of ordinary poetry;—a freshness of colouring and a delicacy of shading, which mark the hand of a great master.[2]

Coleridge also 'possesses, in no ordinary perfection, the power of presenting to the imagination of his readers a correct idea of natural scenery'.[3] But the descriptions are not always given as a faithful representation, but rather often in order

to aid him in communicating, with more perfect success, the vivid emotion which was present to his mind; and which, while it adds prodigiously to

[1] *Ibid.*, p. 464.
[2] *EdM*, I 2s (Oct., 1817), 245.
[3] *Ibid.*, p. 246.

the effect of his scenes, throws often around them an aerial dimness, that seems to take something away from their merely material nature.[1]

The first thirty-eight lines of 'Hymn before Sun-Rise in the Vale of Chamouni' are quoted to exemplify the last comments.

The *Monthly Review* took the occasion of its review of the volume to attack both Wordsworth and the taste of the 'light and frivolous generation of readers' by facetiously attempting to explain Coleridge's lack of popularity.[2] Coleridge, of course, gets caught in the bombardment, but the reviewer manages to praise parts of the 'Ancient Mariner', 'Fears in Solitude', 'Love', 'The Hymn before Sun-Rise', and 'This Lime-Tree Bower'. The long 'Apologetic Preface' to 'Fire, Famine, and Slaughter', however, brought about some political animadversions, which are also present in the short notice in the *Monthly Magazine*.

The last original production published by Coleridge in the period under study was *Zapolya*, a drama (or rather, melodrama). The quarterlies were again silent, and the monthlies and weeklies that reviewed the play were on the whole unfavorable. The bantering tone of ridicule, however, is completely absent, probably because the play is not sufficiently distinguished by any peculiarities and has a number of beautiful passages that were noticed, at least in part, by most of the reviewers. The adverse criticism, in any case, centered mostly on the characterization. The *Edinburgh Magazine* offered the most intelligent single criticism of the play:

> Our author's idea of passion is by far too *elementary*. He wants *adaptation*. Much of the most striking parts of his story is related, and not acted. He has always before him, as it were, a good map of the chief lines and figures of passion, but then he does not enforce these with the exact sentiment which is to body them forth to the reader or hearer, and to serve also, in pushing on the story, that purpose of dramatic action for which they were copied or sketched out,—both at once, and in the quickest possible manner. But this is what a dramatic writer must do.[3]

A three-volume second edition of *The Friend* in 1818 was Coleridge's last publication to be reviewed before 1825. It received only one review—in the *European Magazine*—and that was highly favorable. The essays were said to be interesting, informative, and enter-

[1] *EdM*, I 2s (Oct., 1817), 247.
[2] *MR*, LXXXVIII (Jan., 1819), 24.
[3] *EdM*, I 2s (Dec., 1817), 457.

taining. There also occurs a brief prophecy that affords a pleasing note with which to conclude this brief history: both Coleridge's poetry and prose are 'destined to form, in after ages, a bold specimen of the literature of the nineteenth century'.[1]

For the most part, evaluations of Coleridge's publications, as we have seen, would not have led one to expect such a prophecy, yet there are many recognitions of Coleridge's genius in the reviews of his works, and, especially in the unfavorable ones, usually expressions of regret at his failure to make proper use of that genius. With this attitude posterity can agree.

But posterity has not agreed with all of the assessments of the individual works. *Remorse* received the most favorable judgments, and most of them would now seem exaggerated; there were, however, almost equally loud voices of dissent. The *Christabel* volume, on the other hand, was on the whole rejected; yet given all the problems that the volume presented, this disagreement with posterity is, I think, understandable. The *Biographia Literaria* was, as a total work of literature, quite rightly rejected, and the autobiographical and critical chapters—that is, the ones that have survived for general readers—were accepted.

Compared with Wordsworth's relationship with the reviewers, that enjoyed by Coleridge was certainly less stormy, even though almost all of his publications met with general disapproval. There were, of course, fewer works—fewer great, wholly satisfactory works—to cause the kind of unevenness that typifies Wordsworth's contemporary reputation. There was also less material of a provocative nature in Coleridge's publications; he seldom was treated as flippantly as Wordsworth, and seldom attacked as a member of the Lake School. But Coleridge, like Wordsworth, received a good deal of intelligent criticism, especially from reviewers in the *Champion* and the *Edinburgh Magazine*, and though his debt to the reviewers was not so great as Wordsworth's, he owed them something nonetheless.

Robert Southey

The works of Robert Southey, the third member of the Lakish triumvirate, are not read much today. This, however, was not the case during the period under study, for between 1802 and 1824

[1] *EM*, LXXV (Feb., 1819), 141.

Southey produced an average of one work a year, most of which received a good deal of critical attention. Besides being uncommonly prolific, he was also extremely versatile in his writings, producing not only poetry in great quantity, but biographies, prose translations, histories, and editions of past and contemporary poetry as well. Since these works are for the most part little known and since, in any case, there is scarcely any interest in the year-by-year history of their critical reception, chronological arrangement will be abandoned in favor of separate discussion of each type of work Southey produced.

His poetic output can be separated easily into works written before and after he received the laureateship in 1813. The pre-laureateship poems include his four major narratives, which are, in order of publication, *Thalaba* (1801), *Madoc* (1805), *The Curse of Kehama* (1810), and *Roderick* (1814), as well as the *Metrical Tales and Other Poems* (1805), a collection of ballads, sonnets, and humorous verse.

This last volume encountered a mixed reception, with censure of the subject matter and diction preponderant in the unfavorable reviews. Several reviewers pointed out the incongruity of the ballad style used as a vehicle for complex tales and conceits. There was, however, considerable praise for the burlesque 'Love Elegies of Abel Shufflebottom', praise that was continued in the otherwise unfavorable review in the *Monthly Review* of *The Minor Poems of Robert Southey*, published in 1815.

Southey's longer poems, especially the first three, posed far greater problems for the reviewers. The roots of most of the problems lay in the subject-matter itself. This is particularly true of *Thalaba*, which was based on Arabian myths and information dredged up from books about the Near East, and of *The Curse of Kehama*, which drew most of its characters and machinery from Hindu mythology. *Madoc*, with its account of the semi-historical voyage of the Welsh to the New World in the twelfth century (which account was, however, based on later accounts of Columbus and Cortes), presented problems of a different kind.

As might be anticipated from the choice of such subject-matter, the treatment it received was not much less daring, and both manner and matter were heavily criticized. In *Thalaba* and *The Curse of Kehama*, the mythology and supernatural machinery were censured for the obscurity consequent to their strangeness, for lack of interest owing to the same cause and to faulty construction that often led nowhere, and for various incongruities and inconsistencies arising from Southey's ineptitude. *Madoc*, with its freedom from supernatural machinery, was criticized for incongruities of a natural kind—such as the ease with which Madoc sailed back and forth from Wales to the New World without a compass—and for natural marvels, like earthquakes, occurring at just the right time. *Madoc* was also criticized for its peculiar structure: it was divided into two sections (one on Wales, the other on Aztland) with little connection between them. Plot summaries of all three poems were often given facetiously; in fact, so fantastic are the plots that it was with some difficulty that more sympathetic reviewers managed serious versions.

The characterization also suffered from the fantastic subject matter. *Thalaba* and *The Curse of Kehama* were criticized for having few human characters in the first place, and then for allowing little pathos or sympathy because of the inhuman situations and the constant interventions of the gods. Typical of such censure are the following remarks of the *Monthly Mirror* on *The Curse of Kehama*:

> The pathetic has no place, for there is no room for pity, nor is it possible to shed a tear for those with whom we have nothing in common, and cannot sympathize. Their predicament we can never stand in, and, although it is good that innocence and fortitude should always triumph, no one can refrain from smiling, to see the sufferers protected by gods, who cannot protect themselves.[1]

Madoc had only humans in its cast, but they were censured for being too generalized and too refined for the period in which they lived. Moreover, Madoc was several times said to be too perfect a hero.

The versification was of a piece with the peculiar contents of the poems. Both *Thalaba* and *The Curse of Kehama* were metrical experiments mainly built on iambic measure, but with various line lengths and some mixture of other meters. The generally prosaic result, as well as the dissatisfaction caused by the irregularity and metrical mixture, were pointed out by many reviewers. *Madoc*, written in blank verse, escaped such censure; but Jeffrey, reviewing the poem in the *Edinburgh Review*, thought Southey's versification had something to do with his verbosity:

> We really fear that the great easiness of that loose and colloquial blank

[1] *MonMir*, IX 2s (Feb., 1811), 134.

verse, in which Mr. Southey has chosen to compose, will one day be the ruin of him. It leads him on insensibly from line to line, and from page to page, without let or obstruction, and carries him smoothly through every sort of illustration or exposition that occurs to him. . . .[1]

A similar facility in diction, Jeffrey continued, also led to problems in Southey's poetry: 'As he has always plenty of good words, he never pauses to look for exquisite ones. . . .' This censure of his diction, however, was not the most common one made by the reviewers. It was more usual to select his neologisms, such as 'deathiness' and 'bluey', noted in *Thalaba*, or his compounds, such as 'the-for-ever-one', noted in *Madoc*. Babyisms, such as 'Dearest Dear' in *The Curse of Kehama*, were also pointed out. The proper names in *Madoc* presented a difficulty all their own; as the reviewer in the *Monthly Review* put it, 'How could we swallow *Yuhidthiton*, *Coanocotzin*, and, above all, the yawning jaw-dislocating *Ayayaca*?'[2] It is little wonder that the reviewers sometimes considered themselves a linguistic police force.

A great deal less was found to complain of in *Roderick*, although criticism of verbosity and bad diction continued. And, indeed, *Roderick* is much the best of the epics, with superior plot, incidents, characterization, and moral tone, all of which received considerable, though qualified, praise. One of the most important flaws, discovered by John H. Merivale in the *Monthly Review*, was Southey's extenuation of Roderick's guilt with respect to the crime that sets off most of the action of the story. Such extenuation caused much of the motivation of the central characters to seem disproportionate.

And yet with all the adverse criticisms of Southey's epics, it is a mistake to suppose that either they or the poet were rejected. On the contrary, there were many favorable reviews of all of the long poems; and, although reviews of *Thalaba* were on the whole adverse, reviews of *Madoc* were more generally favorable, those of *The Curse of Kehama* divided (with the quarterlies for and the monthlies against), and those of *Roderick*, as might be expected, very favorable. And almost every review contains some testimony to Southey's genius.

There are several reasons for this apparent inconsistency. One is that a number of reviews were written by Southey's friends. William Taylor, for example, wrote one favorable review of *Thalaba* in the

[1] *ER*, VII (Oct., 1805), 4.

[2] *MR*, XLVIII (Oct., 1805), 115.

Critical Review and two of *Madoc*, in the *Monthly Magazine* and in the *Annual Review* respectively. Walter Scott and Grosvenor Bedford also put the *Quarterly Review* to Southey's defense. And even those who criticized the poems heavily were for some reason more level-headed than in their dealings with the other Lake poets; this is especially true of Jeffrey in the *Edinburgh Review*, who went out of his way to underline the merits of the poems.

Those prejudiced in Southey's favor made some attempt to apologize for the weakness of the poems, but the apologies were usually feeble and eminently at the expense of critical discrimination. The friendly reviewers, in any event, concentrated on very real virtues: the occasional beautiful passage and Southey's talent for descriptive verse. In the praise of both of these, they were seconded by the otherwise hostile reviewers.

Reading and estimation of past English literature at the present time takes its cue from university courses in English literature; the emphasis for the most part is placed on easily teachable poems, that is, on short lyric pieces. Coming as Southey's poems do in a period replete with great poetry, especially short lyric pieces, and being, as they are, marred by so many defects, it is not surprising that most of his poems, particularly his best, longer works, have been almost wholly by-passed. This is, however, unfortunate; for there are sections of Southey's epics that are far from contemptible.

The reviewers, at least, considered Southey's descriptive powers peculiarly praiseworthy. John T. Coleridge, in his review of *Roderick* in the *British Critic*, praises Southey's 'power of representing, by a very few words, any incident or situation as perfectly as could be done by the most correct or animated of painters'.[1] One example he gives to substantiate his remarks is Roderick's memories of Florinda (whom he had raped) 'with her abhorrent hands'. John Foster's review of *The Curse of Kehama* in the *Eclectic Review* goes into even more detail on this point.

As for individual passages selected for beauties of a general nature, it is difficult to quote them out of the context of the narrative. One or two, however, need nothing outside themselves for complete intelligibility; and it would not be a waste of space, I think, to give them at length. John T. Coleridge, in the review referred to above, selected the following philosophical passage from *Roderick*

[1] *BC*, III 2s (Apr., 1815), 358.

(Section XXI) as 'after the best manner of Mr. Wordsworth, praise of no common value in our estimation':[1]

Here we see
The water at its well-head; clear it is,
Not more transpicuous the invisible air;
Pure as an infant's thoughts; and here to life
And good directed all its uses serve.
The herb grows greener on its brink; sweet flowers
Bend o'er the stream that feeds their freshened roots;
The red-breast loves it for his wintry haunts;
And when the buds begin to open forth,
Builds near it with his mate their brooding nest;
The thirsty stag with widening nostrils there
Invigorated draws his copious draught;
And there amid its flags the wild-boar stands,
Nor suffering wrong nor meditating hurt.
Through woodlands wild and solitary fields
Unsullied thus it holds its bounteous course;
But when it reaches the resorts of men,
The service of the city there defiles
The tainted stream; corrupt and foul it flows
Through loathsome banks and o'er a bed impure,
Till in the sea, the appointed end to which
Through all its way it hastens, 'tis received,
And, losing all pollution, mingles there
In the wide world of waters. So is it
With the great stream of things, if all were seen;
Good the beginning, good the end shall be,
And transitory evil only make
The good end happier. Ages pass away,
Thrones fall, and nations disappear, and worlds
Grow old and go to wreck; the soul alone
Endures, and what she chuseth for herself,
The arbiter of her own destiny,
That only shall be permanent.

Francis Jeffrey, in his review of *Madoc* in the *Edinburgh*, chose the following 'Lay of Love' (Part I, Section XIV) for praise:

I have harnessed thee, my steed of shining grey,
And thou shalt bear me to the dear white walls.

[1] *BC.*, III 2s (Apr., 1815), 381.

I love the white walls by the verdant bank,
That glitter in the sun, where Bashfulness
Watches the silver sea-mew sail along.
I love the glittering dwelling, where we hear
The ever-sounding waves; for there she dwells,
The shapely maid, fair as the ocean spray,
Her cheek as lovely as the apple-flower,
Or evening's summer glow. I pine for her;
In crowded halls my spirit is with her;
Through the long sleepless night I think on her;
And happiness is gone, and health is lost,
And fled the flush of youth, and I am pale
As the pale ocean on a sunless morn.
I pine away for her, yet pity her,
That she should spurn a love so true as mine.

After his *Roderick*, Southey's poetical productions took the form of works about public events, most of them written in his capacity of Poet Laureate. With the exception of *The Poet's Pilgrimage to Waterloo*, these productions received on the whole very adverse criticism, especially when compared with the reception given to *Roderick*, most recent of the epics. Jeffrey, who had been attempting to give Southey his due in reviews of the epics in the *Edinburgh Review*, was probably his reviewer once more; if so, he was annoyed at the obvious decline in quality in the first Laureate ode, the *Carmen Triumphale* (1814): 'We cannot help owing him a little grudge . . . for putting us so unmercifully in the wrong, as he has done by this publication.'[1] This ode was attacked by most reviewers for its meter, imagery, diction, and a certain affectation; and the poet-laureateship itself came in for a good deal of ridicule. The *Congratulatory Odes*, also published in 1814, received little criticism—most of that favorable.

In 1816, Southey published two poems written in stanza form that contained allegorical visions: *The Poet's Pilgrimage to Waterloo* and the *Carmen Nuptiale*. The former received a fair amount of praise, as well it might; for it is the only one of the later poems that rises above the category of occasional verse. It was censured for the long-winded details in the first section, as well as for the overall failure of the allegory in the second; but Southey's approach to the great victory through a philosophic visit to the scene of battle was

[1] *ER*, XXII (Jan., 1814), 447.

seen as an improvement upon the usual attempt to describe the battle itself. The simple but touching domestic scene with which the poem opens also received much praise. The second poem, the *Carmen Nuptiale*, in honor of the marriage of Princess Charlotte, was likewise censured for defects of allegory; and a central flaw—a failure in tone—was well described by the reviewer in the *Champion*: the poem 'is more like an old gentleman's admonition to a school-girl, than a Poet's song on the Nuptials of his Sovereign'.[1] It received on the whole unfavorable reviews.

But the most damning reception given to any of Southey's poems in the period was reserved for the last, *A Vision of Judgement* (1821) —only one periodical, the *Antijacobin Review*, had nerve enough to defend it. Known now only for inspiring Byron's comic masterpiece of the same name, it was also the occasion for great merriment in the Reviews. The *Literary Gazette*, for example, commented: 'Mr. Southey has indeed indulged in a *Vision*, but in the *Judgment* part of the matter he has been lamentably deficient.'[2]

The poem nevertheless received serious attention, which took the form of attack upon the hexameters used by Southey and upon the blasphemy and intolerance discovered in the vision. Of the first, most of the reviewers were content to state that hexameters simply did not work in English. Jeffrey, in his review in the *Edinburgh Review*, however, devoted over ten pages to an explanation of just why they did not work. It is an involved and carefully worked out discussion, the gist of which is that classical meters were not only quantitative, but also demanded equal duration of pronunciation to one long syllable as to two short ones, while English is accentual and each syllable receives pronunciation of relatively equal duration. Thus, in spite of the differing amount of syllables in the opening feet of a classical hexameter line, there is regularity in point of duration of pronunciation; in an English hexameter line, on the other hand, the uneven number of syllables in the opening feet have not that regularity, and a sound indistinguishable from prose is the result.

As for the blasphemy found in the vision, the reviewer in the *Examiner* (probably Albany Fonblanque) remarked that Southey 'draws the curtain from before the judgment seat, and coolly delivers sentence for him who sits thereon. The whole heavenly host is made

[1] *Champ*, June 30, 1816, p. 206.
[2] *LG*, Mar. 17, 1821, p. 161.

to aid and assist in a piece of official servility. Talk of blasphemy truly!'[1] The *Eclectic Review*, in a joint review of Byron's *Cain* and Southey's *Vision*, pronounced Byron's poem, which was violently attacked by many for profaneness, to be free from that vice, but not Southey's, if by profaneness is meant 'an irreverent use of sacred names and things'.[2] And 'Profaneness', the reviewer added,

> is certainly more intolerable, if not more criminal, in proportion to its vulgarity. Now there is much in the Vision of Judgment that is positively vulgar—vulgar in the conception, vulgar in the political feeling which inspired it, vulgar in the bungling machinery, the stage clouds and canvas heavens of the performance, vulgar in the Laureate's hired and fulsome loyalty.[3]

Posterity has not treated Southey's poetry as seriously as his contemporaries did, when posterity has seen fit to deal with it at all. But Southey's prose is another matter; he has often been hailed as a master of prose. This was the critical estimation at the time his prose works were published.

Southey's biographies, his *Life of Nelson* (1813) and his *Life of Wesley* (1820), were especially esteemed in this respect. The *Life of Nelson* received unanimous approval, with particular praise of its style and its objectivity. The main qualification of the approval concerned Southey's statement that the work might serve as a manual for young sailors; the reviewers quite rightly pointed out that Nelson's affair with Lady Hamilton and his repeated disobedience of orders, even though followed by success, were not exactly proper patterns of behavior for naval youth to model their lives upon. The *Life of Wesley*, as might be expected at a time when religious feelings ran high, received some unfavorable criticism from the Dissenting periodicals; it was said to show bias, ignorance of religious issues and doctrine, and a certain amount of skepticism. As fate would have it, the Evangelical *British Review* attacked Southey for his mistaken dismissal of Wesley's religious views, which were in fact doctrines held by his own Church of England.

In addition to the biographies, Southey published several miscellaneous prose works in the period under study. The first of these, the *Letters from England by Don Manuel Alvarez Espriella*, published

[1] *Exam*, Apr. 29, 1821, p. 258.
[2] *EcR*, XVII 2s (May, 1822), 419.
[3] *Ibid.*, p. 421.

anonymously in 1807, was purportedly a translation of a series of letters, by which English manners and institutions were subjected to satire, much in the way of Montesquieu's *Les Lettres Persanes*. The ruse fooled no reviewer completely, although the *Oxford Review* treated it as an authentic document except for a short coda that expressed some skepticism; the *Critical Review* reacted to the ruse with bad humor, refusing to review it because they simplemindedly considered it to be a fraud. Otherwise, its reception was on the whole very favorable.

The next miscellaneous prose production was the *Omniana*, a sort of commonplace book which was put together jointly by Southey and Coleridge and published in 1812. It received relatively few reviews, though all of them were favorable.

In 1817 Southey published *A Letter to William Smith, Esq., M.P.*, the last of his miscellaneous prose works before 1825. This letter was concerned with the pirated publication of *Wat Tyler*, a jacobinical play which Southey had written more than twenty years before and which Smith had brought forward in the House of Commons, along with a recent article in the *Quarterly Review* also reputed to be by Southey, as evidence of the extremes to which political writers were liable.[1] Both the play and the letter received many reviews. *Wat Tyler* was on the whole merely dismissed as a youthful production, notable mainly for lack of literary merit and for extravagant political views; there were even many attacks made on the dastardly publishers. But the *Letter to William Smith* was another matter, for in it Southey not only praised himself at great length but also attempted to defend the play, saying that he would not alter it much except to add to it. Furthermore, as many of the reviewers pointed out, Southey defended his change of politics but not the virulence of his attack upon those who held his former beliefs, which was the object of Smith's attack.

The issues were, of course, basically political, and it is remarkable how much political objectivity was shown by the pro-ministry periodicals, although the absurdity of both the play and the letter would be difficult to defend. Only the *New Monthly Magazine* could bring itself to defend either production, and this was done in very short notices. The *British Critic*, which was a champion of the

[1] For a detailed account of the affair, see Frank T. Hoadley, 'The Controversy over Southey's *Wat Tyler*'.

ministry, made some sympathetic remarks, but nevertheless commented on Southey's political reversal as follows:

> Something at least was due to the common sense of the people, who are warmly alive to every thing like an interested desertion of old opinions; and who knowing that Mr. Southey was once imbued with democratical principles, and yet seeing him now the most vehement supporter of establishments and constituted authorities, would naturally, without entering into a minute examination of all palliating circumstances, accuse him of dishonourable apostacy.[1]

This is followed by an attack on the language 'which he generally employs, and which is at once so intolerant, so self-satisfied, and so intemperate'. An amusing antidote to Southey's virulence came from the other side, in a review of the *Letter* by Hazlitt in the *Examiner*: 'A decent mixture of the pleasurable and the sensual might relieve the morbid acrimony of his temper, and a little more indulgence of his appetites might make him a little less tenacious of his opinions.'[2]

It remains now only to speak of Southey's prose translations, his editions of poetry, and his histories. The translations of *Amadis of Gaul* (1803), *Palmerin of England* (1807), and the *Chronicle of the Cid* (1808) met with general approval, with special praise for the early English style and the scriptural diction, for the abridgments and compilations. Mixed in were some disagreements with the judgments made in the prefaces and some criticism of Southey's coinages. The editions of Chatterton (1803) and of Henry Kirke White (Vols. I and II, 1807, and Vol. III, 1822) likewise received over-all approval, but Southey's *Specimens of the Later English Poets* (1807) was criticized severely for unsatisfactory selections and useless introductory notices. Southey's edition of the *Morte d'Arthur* (1817) received only one review, and it was favorable.

Southey's historical efforts came later, beginning with *The History of Brazil* in three volumes (1810, 1817, 1819), followed by *The Expedition of Orsua* (1821), the *History of the Peninsular War*, Vol. I (1823), and *The Book of the Church* (1824). Reviews of these histories were generally favorable, and there is a great deal of praise of Southey's talents as historiographer, as well as some serious qualification of that praise. The central flaw found in *The History of Brazil* is a serious one: that Southey merely presents facts without

[1] *BC*, VII 2s (May, 1817), 444.

[2] *Exam*, May 18, 1817, p. 316.

giving either a comprehensive view of the subject or any interpretations. When he began to give interpretations in the *History of the Peninsular War* and *The Book of the Church*, however, he was soundly criticized for political and religious bias respectively, although he was exonerated from any charge of distorting the facts themselves. The reviewer of the *History of the Peninsular War* in the *Literary Chronicle*, after remarking Southey's political tergiversation, commented sagely that 'those who can forgive, but not forget it, may still read his works to advantage'.[1] The same reviewer suspected that Southey would be remembered for his histories and biographies, when his poetry had been forgotten.

The biographies at least have been remembered, especially the *Life of Nelson*, and the poetry has been forgotten. The reviewers have shared with posterity a high esteem for Southey's great talents as a prose writer; and if they paid more attention to his poetry than has been the case ever since, it is, I believe, posterity that has been the loser. The poetry has something to recommend it, and Southey is badly in need of a highly selective edition.

But the reviewers were by no means taken in by Southey's poetic short-comings; there is a great deal of sensible, discriminating criticism of both his epics and his laureate odes. One of the most remarkable points, in fact, about Southey's relations with his reviewers is the restraint which they showed in the face of great provocation. For Southey, even more than his fellow Lakers, was obtrusively egotistical, and, as was the case with them, his egotism led him to taunt his critics with claims of indifference and with abuse, which can be found in many of his prefaces and in the *Letter to William Smith*. For some reason—perhaps Southey's ingenuousness disarmed them or his intemperance provided them with an immediate example to avoid—the reviewers most often met such provocation with amused detachment. Jeffrey in the *Edinburgh Review*, for example, was much more tolerant when dealing with Southey than with Wordsworth, and consequently delivered much more intelligent and acceptable judgments.

As a category, the 'Lake School' was artificial; and the Lakish 'heresies' were attributable mainly to Wordsworth, who received the brunt of the attack on the School. Coleridge received less abuse in this respect; and Southey, probably because both his matter and

[1] *LC*, Dec. 21, 1822, p. 801.

manner were so egregiously individual, was seldom attacked as a Laker. It is fortunate that such was the case; for though all three poets owed the reviewers a debt for some intelligent critical discussion of their works, Wordsworth's and Coleridge's works have received a great deal of critical attention since that time and could afford whatever biased contemporary criticism they met with. The reviewers' criticisms of Southey's works, which have only been sketched out here, are all the more valuable, since such post-contemporary critical treatment has not been his lot.

4

The Satanic School

The Satanic School was a title originated by Robert Southey in the preface to *A Vision of Judgement*. It was applied vaguely to what Southey considered a group of licentious writers. Although no names were mentioned, Byron assumed himself to be the main writer in question and answered Southey in an appendix to *The Two Foscari*. Unlike the Lake School and the Cockney School, the Satanic School never gained much currency with the reviewers; it was, in fact, only used with reference to Byron, and then mostly to ridicule its application.

Since the title 'Satanic' implies only moral considerations, there should be no difficulty in connecting Byron and Shelley with that title, since both poets published works which were subject to moral condemnation in an age during which literary criticism was concerned with moral issues. There may be some difficulty, however, in accepting Scott in this category—no doubt the reviewers themselves would have been at least mildly surprised to hear that Scott was a member of a Satanic School. And yet Scott was more than a mere literary precursor of Byron in the verse romance form; his works also occasioned a good deal of moral controversy, chiefly centered on the problem of his vicious heroes—controversy in which Byron was later to become involved. I am including Scott in the Satanic School merely to emphasize this aspect of the critical reception of his poetry; his novels were another matter, but they are not to be dealt with in this study.

There is a further resemblance in the critical reception accorded the three poets which has no direct bearing on moral issues. All were attacked constantly for elementary defects in the composition of their poems. With Scott and Byron it was said to be a matter of carelessness and indifference; Shelley's stylistic shortcomings, on the other hand, were thought to be due to perverse literary principles and methods. But, whatever the reasons assigned, even in this matter of faulty composition there were occasional charges of a moral nature—that the poets were instrumental in corrupting the language and literature of their country.

Sir Walter Scott

Before his composition of the long verse romances which were to make him one of the most popular poets of the period, Scott made use of his antiquarian knowledge in several editions of early British poetry. The most important of these was the *Minstrelsy of the Scottish Border*, published in three volumes (1802–3). Most of the reviews of this edition of ballads were favorable, with praise for Scott's research, as shown in the introduction, notes, and the selections, as well as for the ballad imitations included, written by Scott and his friends. Lockhart Muirhead in the *Monthly Review*, however, had many reservations on most of these points. He also was the only reviewer to withhold full praise from *Sir Tristrem*, a medieval romance edited by Scott and published in 1804. There were, nevertheless, many objections raised in the other reviews concerning the price of the limited edition—the beginning of an attack on 'bookmaking', a note to be struck frequently in reviews of Scott.

After editing these works, Scott produced in 1805 a verse romance of his own, *The Lay of the Last Minstrel.* The poem found the reviewers in a good humor; in spite of weighty objections to the story and Scott's handling of it, as well as to the diction, the versification, and the characterization, most of the Reviews praised the poem as a whole. Jeffrey, in the *Edinburgh Review*, can in fact be suspected of bias for his friend Scott, inasmuch as he dismisses the story as highly defective and then claims that this does not, as it turns out, really affect the quality of the poem, since 'a poem is intended to please by the images it suggests, and the feelings it inspires. . . .'[1] A story has no effect on these, and Scott, Jeffrey contended, was successful in imagery and sentiment. Such critical equivocations were also to be

[1] *ER*, VI (Apr., 1805), 6.

found in articles in both the *Monthly Review* by Lockhart Muirhead (which is in fact modeled on Jeffrey's review) and in the *Critical Review*.

In a hostile critique of the volume in the *Imperial Review* came the first sign of censure of Scott on moral grounds, a position which was to be taken up, although in a different manner, in criticism of his next romance, *Marmion*. Here the culprits were the notes, which Scott had loaded with antiquarian lore on the rapacious Borderers:

> We should seriously advise these hunters after human weakness and folly, to question themselves respecting the *cui bono* of their pursuits before they continue them; or, at least, if they are determined themselves to follow them, not to vitiate or disgust the public taste, by committing the result of their researches to the press. We do not see any possible good that can be derived from knowing the exact extent, and all the minute particulars, of the cruelty, robbery, and superstition of our ancestors: but we do see many injurious consequences that necessarily will be produced. The authors of German plays, and German novels, and the herd of their imitators in this country, have been justly censured for feeding the minds of the public with scenes of cruelty, and horror, and for working upon, and thus recalling and strengthening, those superstitious notions, which were beginning to wear out, even among the vulgar of most nations.[1]

Hostility toward Scott's 'bookmaking', which subsided but was still present in reviews of the *Lay*, became a predominant note in articles on his next publication, the *Ballads and Lyrical Pieces* (1806). This collection of pieces published previously in magazines and anthologies, although it received on the whole favorable reviews (with special praise of 'Cadyow Castle' and 'Glenfinlas'), was seen as a fraud on the reading public. The *Critical Review* remarked in this regard: 'We conceive that country gentlemen, of some taste but of limited incomes, no great collectors of books, having already two copies of these poems in their possessions, will thank us for saving them the expense of a third.'[2] The poems were also attacked for faulty diction and versification, as well as for the tone of horror present in so many of them. *Le Beau Monde* put the matter bluntly: 'Mr. Scott seems a kind of poetical Godwin, and calls upon the

[1] *IR*, IV (Jan., 1805), 102.
[2] *CR*, IX 3s (Dec., 1806), 343.

public to submit to a state of barbarism, by way of arriving at perfection.'[1]

Scott's second verse romance, *Marmion* (1808), did not meet with the tolerance accorded the *Lay*. The critical reception was not wholly unfavorable, and yet it met with enthusiastic approbation from only a small number of minor periodicals. Although almost all of the seventeen periodicals which reviewed the poem praised the scenes of the trial of Constance (Canto II) and of the battle (Canto VI), and recognized the great popularity *Marmion* was enjoying, most had serious objections to make, even if they were willing to recommend the poem. Others damned most aspects of the poem in great detail.

It was almost too easy, for *Marmion* in both manner and matter almost forces critical disapproval regardless of standards or even lack of them. The versification received its fair share: the *Critical* thought the poem appeared 'to have been written by an engagement binding the writer to furnish so many yards of verse, within a certain period, at so much per yard'.[2] Thus, Scott selected tetrameter as the most appropriately facile meter, but even his attempts to achieve some elevation by varying that meter failed: 'It is not . . . in change of meter, but in judicious change of cadence under the direction of an ear fine in itself, and attuned by long practice, that true and pure harmony consists.'[3]

La Belle Assemblée made a special attack on the rhyme and grammar:

Mr. Scott seems to think that, for the sake of a rhyme, a poet may take any liberties he pleases with the participles of verbs. This inference we are at least justified in drawing from such instances as the following:—Hast wove—were tore—had broke—hath swore—were chose—and many others of the like kind.

Other examples of bad rhyme were 'broad'/'showed', 'one'/'man', and 'executioner'/'there'. The reviewer continued:

Violations of grammar are not uncommon. From any person who has had the education of a gentleman, we should scarcely have expected such gross faults as these:

By four deep gaps *are* entrance given

. . . .

[1] *LeBM*, I (Feb., 1807), 206.

[2] *CR*, XIII 3s (Apr., 1808). 397.

[3] *Ibid.*, p. 400.

> Scarce by the pale moon-light *was* seen
> The foldings of his mantle green.
>
> . . . .
>
> Even such weak minister as *me*
> May the oppressor bruise.[1]

Scott, in the Introduction to Canto III, offered an excuse for such carelessness ('Flow forth, flow unrestrain'd, my Tale!'), and the reviewer in *Le Beau Monde* commented: 'When petty poets write ill, they do no harm but to their publishers; but when Mr. Scott writes ill, he does harm to our language.'[2]

The story itself and the conduct of the narrative came in for even more adverse criticism. Scott, it was said, had made just about every mistake possible: he not only looked to his own ease by threading together gross impossibilities and coincidences and created incidents as mere vehicles for descriptions—incidents which often did not forward the plot at all—but, in spite of the facility, the story is almost completely unintelligible on first reading. Horace Twiss in the *London Review* turned the knife: Scott succeeds at keeping readers in the dark, 'but while it is true that they cannot know, it is no less true that they have no reason to care'.[3]

Moreover, the charge of 'bookmaking' is again leveled by many reviewers. Not only the 136 quarto pages of notes and the exorbitant price (£1 11*s.* 6*d.*), but also the dedicatory stanzas, which introduced each canto even though unconnected with the story, were censured in this respect. The dedications 'are not however without their use', remarked the *Critical Review* ironically, 'and we recommend them strongly to those who scrupulously abstain from writing verses on the score of having nothing to say'.[4]

The characterization was also censured heavily, especially the insignificance of De Wilton, the 'hero' of the piece, when compared with Marmion. Constance is said to be unnecessarily vicious, and Clare is, according to Jeffrey in the *Edinburgh Review*, 'like a great miss from a boarding school. . . .'[5] But the predominant censure was reserved for Marmion, the real hero of the poem, whose viciousness—he is a seducer and a forger—was considered inconsistent with his knightly virtues. This point is made here more in terms of loss

[1] *LaBA*, IV (Apr., 1808), 183.
[2] *LeBM*, III (June, 1808), 320.
[3] *LR*, I (Feb., 1809), 98.
[4] *CR*, XIII 3s (Apr., 1808), 393.
[5] *ER*, XII (Apr., 1808), 12.

of sympathy or as a defect in poetic justice, but it would soon become the subject of a more involved moral discussion, especially in reviews of Byron.

Scott's next verse romance, *The Lady of the Lake* (1810), occasioned a considerable shift towards critical approbation. It is in fact a much more satisfactory poem than *Marmion;* improvements in the conduct of the story, in versification and diction, and in characterization were noted by many reviewers, even though a number of them also remarked that the general carelessness was not likely to ensure its immortality. Francis Hodgson in the *Monthly Review*, after noting Scott's taunts at his critics in both the prologue and epilogue of the poem, commented that Scott's 'carelessness in composition is, we conceive, making a rapid progress in barbarizing our language and corrupting our taste', through his own works and those of his imitators.[1] Moreover, the large proportion of notes to text (143 pp. as compared to 290 pp.) brought further charges of 'bookmaking'; the *Eclectic Review* called Scott 'the very Midas of literature'.[2]

There was only one adverse moral criticism of the characterization in the poem—an ironic remark in the *Eclectic Review* that the work was 'free from any taint of Christian principle'.[3] On the positive side, Jeffrey in the *Edinburgh Review* made an acute observation on Scott's aristocratic characters: he has given them a 'tone of good society'—'that air of gaiety and playfulness in which persons of high rank seem, from time immemorial, to have thought it necessary to array, not their courtesy only, but their generosity and hostility'. He has thus circumvented 'the monotony of that tragic solemnity which ordinary writers appear to think indispensable to the dignity of poetical heroes and heroines'.[4]

There was a reversion to hostility in reviews of Scott's next work, *The Vision of Don Roderick* (1811). Even though it was a charitable production, the proceeds from which were to go to the victims of the war in Portugal, the reviewers for the most part treated it as just another poem. It was noted that more care had been taken with the execution of the Spenserian stanzas in which the poem was written, and there was the usual praise of Scott's descriptive powers; but the characteristic flaws were pointed out. Francis Hodgson in the *Monthly Review* ended his criticism with a cry from the soul: 'Why

[1] *MR*, LXII (June, 1810), 178.
[2] *EcR*, VI ii (July, 1810), 577.
[3] *Ibid.*, p. 578.
[4] *ER*, XVI (Aug., 1810), 273.

must we be compelled to condemn errors, and instances of idleness, which might so easily be avoided?'[1]

There were political objections to Scott's partisan selection of British heroes to be praised for their part in the Peninsular campaign. The *Eclectic Review* combined its political criticism with a moral concern for the militarism in Scott's poems:

Almost their only moral effect is, to inspire a passion for strife and violence, inducing a contempt for the insipid comforts of peaceful and civilized society, and a secret but decided preference for the times of lawless and sanguinary adventure. Here, however, he is not only a martial poet, but a ministerial partizan. The present poem is in effect a political declamation, inflammatory and antigallican; dealing out invective against our enemies and compliment to ourselves, with a liberality not inferior to the Morning Post.[2]

After the setback occasioned by the *Vision*, Scott's critical reputation rose again in reviews of *Rokeby* (1813), the fourth verse romance. Although most of the reviewers were favorable towards the poem, few reviews were enthusiastic; several judged it merely as 'creditable to Scott's reputation', and the censure of Scott's poetic techniques continued. The *Scourge* blamed his bad diction on the use of tetrameter couplets:

The melody of the eight line verses, depending chiefly on their concatenation with each other, and admitting the 'slur' of many words in a line, confines the poet to little scrupulosity of diction: Mr. Scott has many passages, therefore, that are beautiful in their general effect, and that excite the feelings with uncontrolable [*sic*] power, but yield but little delight on a minute investigation. We can seldom assert of any of his verbs or epithets, that they are the very best that could have been adopted to express the particular mode of action and existence, or the particular object, that they were meant to designate.[3]

The reviewer ended by saying that if Scott continued to write as he had 'he will not long be regarded as any thing better than a *haberdasher* of romances. . . .'[4]

There was, nevertheless, considerable praise in some reviews for the descriptions, the conduct of the plot, and the characterization.

[1] *MR*, LXV (July, 1811), 306.
[2] *EcR*, VII ii (Aug., 1811), 673.
[3] *Scourge*, V (Feb., 1813), 156. [4] *Ibid.*, p. 162.

Bertram and Wilfrid were singled out for special approbation; and the opening scene in which the villainous Oswald is teased by the haughty Bertram into asking directly about the result of a commissioned assassination, was highly praised for dramatic handling.

Bertram, another of Scott's vicious heroes, was censured once on moral grounds: Francis Hodgson in the *Monthly Review* remarked that 'something must be wrong where poetical effect and moral approbation are so much at variance'.[1] The *British Critic*, on the other hand, attempted to refute charges against Scott's vicious heroes: 'From the very nature of virtue and vice, of a good or a bad character, the lineaments of one must be necessarily more striking than those of the other.'[2]

In the same year as *Rokeby*, Scott published the first of his anonymous verse romances, *The Bridal of Triermain*. By a piece of chicanery—the poem was offered as the extension of a parody of Scott (one of three parodies previously published in the *Edinburgh Annual Register*)—Scott fooled all of the reviewers, who gave the poem favorable reviews, although it is clear that tolerance toward a new writer is involved. Most thought it a very good imitation, while a few even preferred it in some respects to Scott's signed publications. Francis Hodgson in the *Monthly Review* was not sure that it was not Scott's work; but, he remarked, if it was, 'he writes anonymously with much more correctness and with much less spirit than he displays *in propria persona*'.[3]

After enjoying this respite afforded by anonymity, Scott published *The Lord of the Isles* (1815), the last verse romance to carry his name. Scott had by this time begun his career as a novelist, after seeing his poetic popularity wane in favor of Byron's; and the reviewers now moved in to give his poetic career the *coup de grâce*. Although several monthlies, particularly the magazines, continued to support Scott, both of the great quarterlies, as well as most of the other monthlies, were hostile.

The stylistic flaws continued unabated in the poem, and Francis Hodgson in the *Monthly Review* threw up his hands: 'We really believe that he *cannot* write correct English; and we therefore dismiss him as an *incurable* . . .', adding that Scott 'has indeed largely contributed to humble and to corrupt our national taste in poetry'.[4] George Ellis,

[1] *MR*, LXX (Mar., 1813), 233.
[2] *BC*, XLII (Aug., 1813), 120.
[3] *MR*, LXXIII (Mar., 1814), 239.
[4] *MR*, LXXVI (Mar., 1815), 267, 268.

who had begun reviewing Scott's romances in the *Quarterly Review* in 1810 by disdainfully attacking Jeffrey's objections in the *Edinburgh Review*, now completely reversed his stand: 'let the essence of poetry be defined as it may, still it is plain that whatever tends to give grace and delicacy to the pleasure which it imparts, cannot be without importance.' In *The Lord of the Isles*, 'this feeling [of pleasure] is more frequently counteracted by others of an opposite description . . . than even the licence of popular taste can reasonably be expected to sanction.'[1]

That Scott's critics had lost all patience with his careless writing is further evidenced by the hostile reception given *The Field of Waterloo* (1815), another of Scott's charitable publications. The contribution of the proceeds to the Waterloo Subscription was not even mentioned in most of the reviews, and the technical flaws in diction, grammar, logic, and versification were unmercifully dealt with. Scott was also roundly censured for accusing Napoleon of cowardice; the *Critical Review* considered it 'mean, and wholly unworthy of British candour'.[2]

Scott's second anonymous verse romance and final publication in this genre, *Harold the Dauntless* (1817), met likewise with a cold reception. It was announced as by the author of *The Bridal of Triermain*, and, as was the case with that romance, no one attributed it to Scott's authorship, although the reviewer in *Blackwood's* suspected the ruse from external evidence. But just as the reviewers had become impatient with poems carrying Scott's name, so now most of the reviewers were no longer willing to be tolerant toward this unknown author, and attacked what they thought his second verse romance rather savagely. The *Monthly Review* put the matter bluntly: 'Criticism can no longer endure protracted tales of terror, or diluted mixtures of nursery-nonsense and antiquarian pedantry, offered to an insulted public in a vehicle of nondescript verse, or rather of fantastical Prose.'[3]

Both the reviewers and the public seem to have tired of verse romance by 1817, and Scott's last poetic production in the period, *Halidon Hill; a Dramatic Sketch* (1822), met with a mixed reception, with many reviewers very favorable and many extremely hostile. This short dramatic work thus was at least sufficiently well executed

[1] *QR*, XIII (July, 1815), 288, 289.
[2] *CR*, II 5s (Nov., 1815), 459.
[3] *MR*, LXXXIV (Sept., 1817), 11.

to cause violent disagreement. It is, in my estimation, one of Scott's best poetic publications from the standpoints of characterization and poetic execution, whatever its merits as a drama. Although the customary carelessness as well as structural problems arise from its composition as an incomplete 'dramatic sketch', the criticisms of the hostile reviewers seem to me to be ill-considered judgments, especially as regards the probability of the characters. *Halidon Hill* is perhaps best described by the reviewer in the *Literary Register*: 'the last two acts of a tragedy written very hastily by a man of considerable dramatic talent'.[1]

Besides poetry and fiction, Scott also published several editions both of literature and of historical documents. His edition of Dryden (1808) and his Introductory Life to *The State Papers and Letters of Sir Ralph Sadler* (1809) provoked a great deal of criticism of the kind with which he was by that time familiar in reviews of his own poetry, that is, censure of his careless style and of his 'bookmaking'. Added to this customary censure were attacks on his historical inaccuracies. But some of the less discriminating reviewers gave those two publications favorable treatment; and Scott's thirteen-volume edition of *Sommer's Collection of Tracts* (1809–12), *Miss Seward's Life and Poetical Works* (1810), his *Life and Works of Jonathan Swift* (1814), his introduction to the *Border Antiquities* (1817), his *The Provincial Antiquities* (1818), and his edition of Patrick Carey's *Trivial Poems and Triolets* (1819) received scattered and on the whole favorable reviews.

Scott's early literary career was very similar to Southey's in many respects; there was the same succession of long narrative poems with copious notes, the same collections of original ballad pieces, the same editing of poetry, and even a poem by each on Roderick and on the Battle of Waterloo. The critical reception accorded the works of the two professional men of letters was likewise similar. On the positive side, there was the same praise of individual passages and of descriptive powers. As was the case with Southey's poetry, much of this praise, I believe, was warranted. There are some good scenes and fine descriptive passages in Scott's longer poems; but Scott's poetry, unlike Southey's, is greatly marred by very facile versification and by incredible carelessness and lack of polish. In fact, the praise of Scott's poetry expressed in the reviewing periodicals, especially in

[1] *LitReg*, July 6, 1822, p. 6.

the *British Critic* and in the lesser magazines, often goes far beyond the poetry's merits.

This exorbitant praise is not difficult to account for, inasmuch as Scott was by far the most popular poet during the years in which he published his verse romances. His popularity was in all likelihood simply too overpowering for many of the more fashionable magazines to withstand, even had they wished to do so. Some of the more powerful periodicals did attempt to stem the tide of Scott's popularity—or perhaps it would be more correct to say that in their desire to influence Scott to compose more carefully they sought to qualify public approbation until that desire was achieved. Some even attempted to account for the inconsistency involved in Scott's popularity and their strictures against him by disquisitions on theories of taste; many merely attacked the taste of the age as frivolous.

Scott's technical shortcomings, his easy versification, imprecise diction, faulty construction, incorrect grammar, and so on, were too obvious to be overlooked even by his more sympathetic reviewers. Be it said in defense of his critics, many, such as Francis Hodgson in the *Monthly Review*, took a firm stand against what they considered a corrupting influence on the language and literature of England. Posterity has repaid Scott's indifference and bad writing by ignoring in the main his verse publications—just the fate many of the reviewers predicted for them. Francis Jeffrey in his review of *Marmion* in the *Edinburgh* warned: 'He who writes for immortality should not be sparing of time; and if it be true, that in every thing which has a principle of life, the period of gestation and growth bears some proportion to that of the whole future existence, the author now before us should tremble when he looks back on the miracles of his own facility.'[1]

Lord Byron

Byron's relations with his reviewers began on a fairly favorable note. His *Hours of Idleness* (1807), which contained poems and translations written before he was twenty, was well received by all of the reviewing periodicals with the exception of the *Satirist*, the *Monthly Mirror*, and, of course, the *Edinburgh Review*. Most of the reviewers praised the taste and sentiments evinced by the poems, even though in many

[1] ER, XII (Apr., 1808), 34.

reviews there was an undertone of dissatisfaction with the carelessness and improprieties—a hint of what were to become major criticisms in a few years.[1]

Part of this favorable reception was explicitly due to leniency evoked by Byron's age and by what many saw as his 'modest' preface. It was, however, the preface, with its immature and out-of-date pose of the *amateur*, that the hostile reviewers ridiculed with great glee. Henry Brougham in the *Edinburgh Review*, for example, ended his facetious review of the poems by referring to Byron's cavalier statement that he would not likely 'ever obtrude [himself] a second time on the public . . .':

> Therefore, let us take what we get and be thankful. What right have we poor devils to be nice? We are well off to have got so much from a man of this Lord's station, who does not live in a garret, but 'has the sway' of Newstead Abbey. Again, we say, let us be thankful; and, with honest Sancho, bid God bless the giver, nor look the gift horse in the mouth.[2]

John Higgs Hunt in the *Critical Review* noticed a satiric bent in some of the poems, which although unsuccessful, showed that 'he has enough within him to constitute a keen and successful sportsman'.[3] Within two years, Byron turned the insight into a prophecy by hunting down his critical adversaries in the satiric *English Bards and Scotch Reviewers*, published anonymously in 1809. Both Jeffrey whom Byron mistakenly supposed to be the author of the offensive *Edinburgh Review* article, and Hewson Clarke, the reviewer in the *Satirist*, were attacked by name.

Neither of these periodicals reviewed the satire, nor did the *Monthly Mirror*, the other periodical hostile to the earlier volume. But most of the other journals did, the reception of the poem being unanimously favorable. There was, however, considerable questioning of the justice of Byron's critical dispensations. The *Critical Review*, which had earlier noticed Byron's latent satiric powers, now gave the most discriminating judgment on their employment. The reviewer noted an immaturity in the promiscuous and disconnected flourishes; while agreeing with Byron's principles and praising the poetic execution, he found too little modification and discrimination

[1] Among the favorable reviews, it should be noted, was one in the *MLR*, which had the same publisher as the volume under review.

[2] *ER*, *XI* (Jan., 1808), 289.

[3] *CR*, XII 3s (Sept., 1807), 50.

in the censure, adding by way of another prophecy that proved true: we 'fear that he may repent too late in his maturer years of having inflicted some wounds where they were not deserved, and driven into the ranks of his foes, some persons whom he might have been proud to embrace as his friends'.[1]

Byron left on a tour of the Near East in 1809 and on his return published the first two cantos of *Childe Harold* (1812). Both the poet and his poem were a success overnight with the reading public, and the literary success was given critical sanction by both of the major quarterlies as well as most of the monthlies. The critical approbation was, however, qualified. Most of the reviewers remarked upon the total lack of plot and consequent lack of an important source of interest, the general carelessness in the verse, the incongruous attempts at humor, and the obsolete diction. Many also noted the difficulty in distinguishing the poet from his hero; Harold himself was adversely criticized as an unnecessary appendage to the poem. There were also objections to his bringing with him inconsistencies (his apathy ill-consorted with his sensibility) and incongruities (what was a medieval knight doing at the Battle of Talavera?).

The unorthodox views expressed in the poem were, however, more important in provoking unfavorable reviews. Byron's dismissal of all religions and his skepticism concerning an afterlife caused a good deal of adverse criticism. George Ellis in the *Quarterly Review* made perhaps the wisest objection to such views on the grounds of taste: 'The common courtesy of society has, we think, very justly proscribed the intrusive introduction of such topics as these into conversation. . . .'[2] The Childe's melancholy, misanthropy, and animadversions on the fair sex were also widely censured; William Roberts in the *British Review*, for example, remarked:

> No man has a right to be angry with the world because he has been outwitted by it in a contest of iniquity; because prostitutes have jilted him; and the promises of sensuality have proved false and treacherous. There is no dignity in the melancholy or misanthropy of such a man.[3]

Roberts' review of the poem is one of the best despite some rather obtuse moral objections. Like almost all of the other reviewers, he praises the descriptions. But Roberts goes into more detail on the

[1] *CR*, XVII 3s (May, 1809), 85.
[2] *QR*, VII (Mar., 1812), 198.
[3] *BR*, III (June, 1812), 285.

technical aspects of Byron's handling of the Spenserian stanza. The poet

> has managed the stanza with poetical skill; and in the distribution of the pauses, and particularly in the cadence of the closing line, has given the expanded melody, of which the verse is susceptible, without the monotony to which it is liable. The caesura which is generally placed on the sixth syllable of the last line, is varied in the other parts of the stanza with considerable delicacy of ear; and upon the whole, we cannot but think that the rhythm of the stanza has received some improvement under his lordship's hands.[1]

Earlier in the review, however, he noted that in descriptive poetry stanzas have to deal with one thought or suffer awkward transitions. '... The effect of this necessity of filling out the stanza by the amplification of a single thought', he continued, 'is often to dilute its strength; which accounts for the frequent occurrence of nerveless expletory lines in the midst of an otherwise energetic stanza.' The need for unity of idea combined with the difficulty of the rhyme scheme also means often 'sacrificing compression of thought, and propriety of language'.[2]

Childe Harold was succeeded swiftly by *Waltz* (1813), a short anonymous satire, which was favorably reviewed without Byron's authorship being suspected, and by three Eastern Tales, *The Giaour* (1813), *The Bride of Abydos* (1813), *The Corsair* (1814), as well as *Lara* (1814), an anonymous sequel to the last. These Tales were extremely popular, and they were received on the whole favorably, with the decided approbation of the *Edinburgh Review* and the *Quarterly Review* and some of the more influential monthlies. There was, nevertheless, considerable dissent from this favorable verdict by many monthlies, and the quarterly *British Review* was hostile throughout.

As was the case in the reviews of the verse narratives of Southey and Scott, the approbation fell mainly on Byron's descriptive powers and on individual passages; the butterfly simile in *The Giaour*, for example, received almost unanimous, though sometimes qualified, praise. These aspects of the Tales were considered in fact sufficiently praiseworthy to compensate for the defects noted, numerous though they were.

Scott's popularity was by his own admission dislodged by Byron's,

[1] *Ibid.*, p. 298. [2] *Ibid.*, pp. 286–87.

and the adverse criticisms made of Scott's poems were inherited by his successor; there were even specific references to Scott's bad influence on Byron in reviews of the first two Tales. Objections in the same vein as those made against Scott were raised against Byron's carelessness in diction and grammar, his bad choice of subjects, and his use of pedantic terminology (in Byron's case it was Turkish). The censure of faulty construction and consequent obscurity was even more severe because of the fragmentary construction of *The Giaour* and the mystery surrounding the past history and future fate of Conrad (in *The Corsair*) and of Lara. Byron's peculiar lazy use of the dash was also censured; the *British Critic* in its review of *The Corsair* expressed a wish 'that the Noble Lord would omit these linear conjunctions; and resort to those more intelligible connections which language and grammar afford'.[1]

The objections to Scott's tetrameters were also duplicated in criticisms of *The Bride of Abydos*. William Roberts in the *British Review* remarked with what difficulty such meter could sustain a dignified tone. The reviewer in the *British Critic* went into more detail on the shortcomings:

> The length of the line but ill corresponds with the expansion of idea, and each sentence means something more than its words can express. Hence we too often find the most animated descriptions labouring under the distortions of a forced conciseness, and the most eloquent addresses assuming a sort of pertness and petulance. The frequent omission of necessary particles diminishes also that perspicuity which is the very soul of poetry; and the inversions of grammatical position give the whole an air of harsh and rugged obscurity.[2]

Furthermore, the poet, 'by way of balancing accounts with the understanding, is seduced into a flat and meagre affectation of simplicity, and an uninteresting relation of those trifling circumstances, which are best expressed in the measure of the verse'.

Byron, possibly because of these strictures, changed to heroic couplets in *The Corsair* and *Lara*; and Jeffrey in the *Edinburgh* commented in a review of the former poem that Byron had proven that heroic couplets 'could be accommodated to the variations of a tale of passion . . .' and had displayed their flexibility. ' . . . We cer-

[1] *BC*, I 2s (Mar., 1814), 288.
[2] *BC*, I 2s (Jan., 1814), 46.

tainly never read so many ten-syllable couplets together before', he continued, 'with so little feeling of heaviness or monotony.'[1]

Byron's characterizations, like Scott's, were censured strongly, with a special emphasis on the sameness in his heroes, who would in a later age be denominated 'Byronic'. From as early as the critique in the *Eclectic Review* of *The Giaour*, in which a similarity of the hero to Childe Harold is noted, there were many adverse criticisms of the repetitious, brooding figure. In its review of *Lara*, the *British Critic* observed: 'We have heard of a tribe of Indians, who were extremely ingenious in sculpture, but the only image which they could carve, was that of the devil. Thus is it with our noble author, "Mungo here, Mungo there, Mungo every where." '[2] George Ellis, reviewing *The Corsair* in the *Quarterly*, took a different view of the matter by way of an interesting theory

> that the Giaour, Conrad, and Lara may, very probably, have been intended by the author to be identical with Childe Harold; or, in other words, that the materials, of which Lord Byron's later tales have been composed, were originally collected for the purpose of being wrought into a series of adventures, tending to illustrate and develop the whimsical character of that Childe.[3]

But the major objection to the characters was concerned with their moral makeup, more specifically the confusing mixture of vice and virtue which they display. This was not so simpleminded as it may sound, and such criticisms were usually prefaced by remarks on the improbability or even the impossibility of such characters as Byron portrayed. The *Critical Review*, for example, made the following comment on *The Corsair*:

> By no means of the solemn tribe, who would clip the wings of imagination, and restrain the more eccentric flights of mind, we yet would have an accordance of parts; an agreement of one thing with another—we would not have the same individual a merciless and unhuman plunderer, a delicate and adoring lover, a high-minded soldier, who will not save himself from impalement, by the assassination of his direst foe. We can conceive enchantment, supernatural agency, and occult operation. If wonderful, they are not contradictory: but man, with such opposite qualities like physical impossibility, never can be conceived. Lord Byron

[1] *ER*, XXIII (Apr., 1814), 206.
[2] *BC*, II 2s (Oct., 1814), 408.
[3] *QR*, XI (July, 1814), 453.

may suppose his Corsair to be *one* character, but he is really three. . . . Mental superiority and ungovernable passion, are the poetical order of the day; but setting ambition aside, how seldom are they found in union. We are therefore becoming weary of Marmions, and Roderick Dhus, and Bertrands, and Kehamas, (if the last are any body) and sincerely hope, that high souled villainy, will shortly become as vulgar, as spiritless virtue.[1]

William Roberts, in his criticism of the same poem in the *British Review*, combined a charge of immorality with that of improbability:

We must once more declare ourselves hard to be reconciled to these pictures of character which give to the fierce and sanguinary what belongs only to the gentle and generous. For the want of a sound moral it is scarcely compensation enough to be merely natural; but to violate the consistencies of morality without any charter from nature is a gratuitous injury to the cause of virtue. . . .[2]

Specific moral objections to the mixed characterization of the heroes were that they 'inculcate the dangerous error that vice does *not* degrade the mind' (*Eclectic Review* on *The Giaour*), and that they 'confound the relations of conduct and sentiment, and exhibit virtue as the fortuitous offspring of vagrant feelings rather than as the fair daughter of truth and conscience' (*British Review* on *The Bride of Abydos*).[3] The *European Magazine*, however, overlooking these objections, struck a pragmatic note in its review of *The Corsair*: 'Though it concludes with no general moral, it is impossible to read it without delighting in virtue; and, as we do not think that there is much fear of any of its readers becoming Corsairs, we think it will, in general, be productive of moral good.'[4]

Among the minor poems published along with *The Corsair* was the short 'Lines on a Lady Weeping', which was an attack on the Prince Regent; and according to Samuel Chew's account of Byron's contemporary fame, the poem caused a decline in Byron's popularity.[5] This decline, however, was not reflected immediately, if at all, in the reviews. The three periodicals which censured the offending poem—the *British Critic*, the *Antijacobin Review*, and the *Satirist*—

[1] *CR*, V 4s (Feb., 1814), 154–55.
[2] *BR*, V (Feb., 1814), 510–11.
[3] *EcR*, IX ii (Nov., 1813), 531; *BR*, V (Feb., 1814), 393.
[4] *EM*, LXV (Feb., 1814), 135.
[5] *Byron in England*, p. 15.

did give adverse reviews to *The Corsair* as well, but they had been hostile to the previously published poem, *The Bride*. And the following publication, the *Ode to Napoleon* (1814) met with a favorable reception on the whole.

In 1815 Byron married, and his only publication during that year was the *Hebrew Melodies*. This volume of songs was in general badly received by the reviewers, with even some anti-semitism intermixed —the *British Critic* thought Byron could 'now be considered as poet laureat [*sic*] to the synagogue'.[1] And yet much of the criticism was well taken, with special notice of the incongruity between the more serious subjects and the light, tripping meter in which they were set forth, as well as the scarcity of anything specifically religious, or Hebrew, or Near Eastern in the poems.

Byron's standing with the critics was still fairly low in reviews of the joint publication of *The Siege of Corinth* and *Parisina*, which came out early in 1816. The former of these short narrative poems was censured as the previous Tales had been, with emphasis on the meagre story, incidents, and characters, and on the careless style. *Parisina* received some commendation for improvement in style, but its theme of incest brought down moral censure on Byron's head. The *British Critic* objected to the theme of incest *per se*, but more particularly to Byron's holding up 'both the offenders and the offence . . . as objects more of commiseration than of disgust. . . .'[2] This is not an untrue statement of Byron's handling of the theme, and moral objections are not out of order. William Roberts in the *British Review*, however, made the moral strictures seem ridiculous by the extravagance of his position: we object 'because we have sons and daughters: but this is but a partial reason; let us add—because Britannia has sons and daughters, and in the duration of their characteristic virtue and modesty we behold the best pledge of our superiority over faithless France and prostrate Italy, and of the continuance of our happiness and greatness'.[3] 'We solemnly proscribe this poem,' Roberts ends by announcing, 'from the English fireside. . . .'[4]

After confronting such overblown indignation, it is refreshing to take up the *Champion's* review of the volume, certainly one of the best on Byron's early works. It begins by taking the poet to task

[1] *BC*, III 2s (June, 1815), 603.
[2] *BC*, V 2s (Apr., 1816), 436.
[3] *BR*, VII (May, 1816), 456.
[4] *Ibid.*, p. 463.

for his vow to stop publishing and the anonymous publications which followed that vow:

> He will and he won't: he regrets having written at all, and anon he writes again: he will not write for some years, and he cannot hold for a few weeks. Poetry is no toy of the moment, to be lightly taken up, and scornfully laid down. . . . We speak thus severely, because we see that the moment has arrived when Lord Byron must either lose part of his popularity, or it must continue at the expense of public discernment. The pamphlet before us . . . is neither more nor less than another of those brief, mannered, indistinct sketches, which deserved and received the highest praise as the first exercises of a masterly spirit, supposed to be preparing itself for productions of sound meaning and fine and finished arrangement.[1]

Such productions, he continued, have not been forthcoming; in fact, Byron's poems have become progressively worse. But as for the moral charges brought against Byron's poetry by others:

> We are prepared to maintain, that the delineation of the bad passions, and of their effects, as subjects of human interest, fall honestly within the province of Art. Nor do we hold it necessary to couple every sin with its proper caution in poetical description. Our charge against Lord Byron is, that, in a temper of restless and indecent disdain, he presumes on his popularity to become a downright scribbler. . . . He does not even affect the slightest respect for the public taste, or care for its quality. . . .[2]

The reviewer then brings forward another serious moral charge of his own:

> Criticism can scarcely be accused of captiousness, if it protests strongly against this perversion of poetical talent, this corruption of feeling, and arrogant disregard of what is due to consciousness and obligation. The great mischief is, that those fiery applications destroy the healthy tone of the public's sensibility: they lead it to cherish that fatal fondness for quick and forced excitement, which utterly kills in the mind the capacity of serious enjoyment of natural sentiment;—the niceties of genuine character and situation are deemed feeble and tedious after these seductions of exaggeration and artifice. Lord Byron's readers are led to mistake hurry-skurry for noble rapidity,—and there is a proneness in the common

[1] *Champ.*, Feb. 11, 1816, p. 45.
[2] *Ibid.*, p. 46.

taste to this mistake, which renders him who administers to it, very reprehensible.

In the spring of 1816, with such moral criticisms already hanging over his head, Byron went through the public scandal of a separation and exiled himself from England. And, as if this were not enough, he privately published several poems on the affair—'Fare thee well' and 'A Sketch'—which were pirated in the *Champion* and then in book form. Needless to say, the scattered reviews of the volume were anything but favorable. Some of them were even malicious; the *New Monthly Magazine*, in its attack on 'A Sketch', instead of merely finding the personal abuse of Lady Byron's servant unmanly, made a reference to Byron's own physical defect and to the skeletons in the Byron family closet.

As for the remaining works published in 1816, there is no noticeable decline in the critical estimate made by the reviewers. Byron's next work, the *Monody on the Death of Sheridan*, received scattered, partly favorable reviews; and the third Canto of *Childe Harold* and *The Prisoner of Chillon* volume were on the whole well received. As usual, their favorable reception was due largely to the presence of admired passages; this is especially true of *Childe Harold*.

But there were a good many references in reviews of *Childe Harold* III to Byron's domestic scandal; it would be remarkable if there were not, with the poet making references to it himself in the poem. When the attitude toward the affair was not one of sheer disgust, there was usually a comment on the injustice of making accusations that his wife had no way of answering.

Political issues were raised for the first time in any large way in reviews of Canto III, and again it would have been surprising if such had not been the case in view of the potentially offensive passages. Walter Scott, in his review of the poem in the *Quarterly Review*, found Byron's adverse feelings about the Battle of Waterloo the result of his immaturity and his passionate, poetic nature. Byron's paean to Napoleon also brought about much hostility; Roberts in the *British Review* remarked ironically that 'the Christian precept commands us to love our enemies, but not out of spite to our friends'.[1]

Moreover, the moral strictures made on the Tales continued in reviews of *Childe Harold* III. Jeffrey's review in the *Edinburgh*

[1] *BR*, IX (Feb., 1817), 10.

Review contained a long argument on this aspect of Byron's poetry, and though it was more or less a summary of what had been said before by himself and by other reviewers, it is remarkable for the persuasiveness of its forensic construction, with possible concessions followed and undercut by more powerful arguments. Jeffrey also noted in the third Canto a point made by almost every periodical: the poet and his hero were even more difficult to tell apart than in earlier cantos.

Josiah Conder in the *Eclectic Review* took this opportunity to present a psychological analysis of the factors evident in Byron's characterizations. First of all, Byron's particular brand of egotism

> appears less like the display of his own feelings, than the effect of their perpetually haunting him, intercepting and colouring his view of every other object, and rendering it impossible for him to forget
>
> 'the weary dream
> Of selfish grief or gladness'.[1]

Furthermore, he questioned if 'any of Lord Byron's characters are strictly fictitious', for they all have 'the same combination of morbid feelings and phrensied passions, aggravated into various degrees of guilt. . . .' Indeed, 'they are only shadowy outlines which serve to express, in the symbolic language of poetry, the objects of passionate emotions and of remembrances not unreal.' Of this form of poetic transfer, he concludes:

> On this one image, thus multiplied in the fantastic reflections of thought, it seems to be the highest intellectual solace for the Author to fix the intent gaze of his imagination; not like Narcissus, enamoured of the reflection of himself, but losing in the contemplation of that social shadow, the conscious wretchedness of the original.[2]

Byron's Spenserian stanzas received another round of applause from Roberts in the *British Review*, but the general carelessness of grammar and versification, especially in *The Prisoner of Chillon*, received customary censure. It is amusing, however, to read Walter Scott's defense in the *Quarterly* of Byron's careless style; he was, of course, defending himself. But the most important remarks on the style of the two volumes concern the discovery of the influence of the Lake poets on Byron's attitude toward nature, his pathos, and

[1] *EcR*, VII 2s (Mar., 1817), 293.

[2] *Ibid.*, p. 294.

his diction, cited in eight separate reviews.[1] This influence was seen as beneficial on the whole; but Byron, it was said in the *Critical Review*'s notice of *The Prisoner of Chillon*, sometimes went to an extreme, as in copying Wordsworth's babyisms: 'thus, who can read without laughter the lines in which Lord Byron supposes a *sunbeam to have lost its way*, and to have *fallen down* (faint and weary, probably) into the dungeon through the cleft. . . .'[2]

The year 1817 saw a fall and then a rise in Byron's reputation with the critics, in reviews of his two publications, *Manfred* and *The Lament of Tasso*. The decline evidenced in reviews of the former poem would have been more severe, had not Jeffrey come out in its favor in the *Edinburgh Review;* for most of the monthlies were decidedly hostile. Jeffrey's review itself was far from enthusiastic; he in fact obviously went out of his way to be as favorable as possible, even at the expense of some questionable consideration of Byron's intentions:

> If we were to consider it as a proper drama, or even as a finished poem, we should be obliged to add, that it is far too indistinct and unsatisfactory. But this we take to be according to the design and conception of the author. He contemplated but a dim and magnificent sketch of a subject which did not admit of more accurate drawing, or more brilliant colouring. Its obscurity is a part of its grandeur. . . .[3]

Most of the other journals were not so prone to indulgence. Although they did not miss the forceful writing and beautiful passages, these were for once not considered sufficient to compensate for flaws, as more or less summed up by Josiah Conder in the *Eclectic Review*:

> There is absolutely nothing of novelty in this poem, except the mysticism and immaterial machinery; and the latter, although invested with all

[1] For more information on this point, see Edwin M. Everett, 'Lord Byron's Lakist Interlude', *SP*, LV (1958), 62–75. The reviews in which the Lakist influence is noted are as follows: *CR*, IV 5s (Nov., 1816), 495–506, (Dec., 1816), 367–81; *Portfolio*, Nov. 23, 1816, pp. 73–77, Nov. 30, 1816, pp. 97–102, Dec. 7, 1816, pp. 125–28; *Champ*, Nov. 24, 1816, p. 374, Dec. 1, 1816, pp. 382–83; *ER*, XXVII (Dec., 1816), 277–310; *EcR*, VII 2s (Mar., 1817), 292–304; *QR*, XVI (Oct., 1816), 172–208; *MR*, LXXVIII (June, 1817), 177–201; *BM*, III (May 1818), 216–18*.

[2] *CR*, IV 5s (Dec., 1816), 573.

[3] *ER*, XXVIII (Aug., 1817), 430.

> the charms of song, is of too flimsy and shadowy a nature to interest. The drama is without plot and without purpose; Manfred is one of those unintelligible and impossible beings which we meet with only in the regions of sentimental romance; a most interesting and amiable wicked rascal....[1]

The hints at incest were duly noted by most of the reviewers, with, however, little comment; but Roberts in the *British Review* restated his objections to the mixture of vice and virtue in the Byronic hero.

The short *Lament of Tasso*, which followed *Manfred*, was praised more than it deserved, probably because of the reviewers' avowed relief at finding no egotism or skepticism to speak of. Only the *British Critic* was unfavorable, but since its review of *The Giaour* it had become increasingly hostile, until by 1816 its criticisms of Byron's works had turned largely into abuse.

Beppo, a comic precursor of *Don Juan*, was published anonymously early in 1818. Most of the reviewers identified the poem as Byron's, and most, including the *British Critic*, were favorable—some even enthusiastic. But the anonymity allowed several reviewers to discover signs of parodies of Byron's Eastern Tales, as well as take-offs of other poets; most of these detections were, however, rather far-fetched.

The reception was on the whole what one would have hoped for; there is a great deal of praise of the style and tone, and admiration for the humor of the peace. Jeffrey's review in the *Edinburgh Review* was one of his best; *Beppo*, he remarked, 'affords a very curious and complete specimen of a kind of diction and composition of which our English literature has hitherto afforded very few examples'.[2] 'The great charm', he explained, 'is in the simplicity and naturalness of the language—the free but guarded use of all polite idioms, and even of all phrases of temporary currency that have the stamp of good company upon them,—with the exclusion of all scholastic or ambitious eloquence, all profound views, and all deep emotions.'[3]

There were, nevertheless, some moral strictures on *Beppo*; Roberts in the *British Review* was most severe in this respect. If questions of morality could be put aside, he admitted, the poem was 'a production of great humour and unquestionable excellence'. But he did not put moral questions aside: 'We are [not] quite sure that many a maiden and many a mother, British-born and British-bred', will

[1] *EcR*, VIII 2s (July, 1817), 62.
[2] *ER*, XXIX (Feb., 1818), 302.
[3] *Ibid.*, p. 303.

not finish 'this light and sportive raillery on the marriage vow, with many troublesome prejudices removed, an encreased dread of being righteous overmuch, and a resolution, in spite of a prying and censorious world, to live in charity with her neighbours of the other sex, though it should be called facility or levity'.[1] In spite of the pompous manner in which this objection is expressed, the position can, I think, be argued. Admiration for Roberts' previous remarks on the handling of Spenserian stanzas in *Childe Harold*, however, loses some of its force, when in this review he confuses the *ottava rima* with the other form.

The fourth Canto of *Childe Harold* followed *Beppo* later in 1818 and likewise had a generally favorable reception, although there was a good deal of disagreement about its comparative merit in relation to the earlier cantos. The customary praise of the descriptions and of individual passages increased, with recognition also of a new mellowness in the reflections of the poet-hero. Nevertheless, the usual censure of the style and objections to Byron's obtrusive egotism and to the questionable morality of the reflections, mellowed or not, continued. Many of the reviewers took the opportunity of reviewing what was professedly the last canto to make some observations on the whole poem. One of the best of these summaries appeared in the *Monthly Review*, which observed of Byron's expressions of higher sentiments:

> The remark made on Collins may be applied, we think, with great justice to Lord Byron, that sublimity is rather the character of his inclination than of his genius. On many grand occasions, he exhibits a great restlessness and gasping; a struggle, as it were, towards some higher range of thought, which often ends in a repetition of the same idea in different terms, or in mere bombast and tumour of phrase.[2]

In the spring of 1819, *Mazeppa*, the last-but-one of Byron's Tales, was published. The reception was on the whole favorable, with the quarterlies silent, most of the monthlies well disposed toward the poem, and most of the weeklies hostile. Shorter than most of the Tales, it was nevertheless better constructed and without the usual gloominess and the oppressively Byronic hero; but these points were scarcely raised by the reviewers, who seem to have by this time

[1] *BR*, XI (May, 1818), 329.
[2] *MR*, LXXXVII (Nov., 1818), 297.

become accustomed only to pointing out fine descriptions and passages. The adverse criticism likewise ran in its normal channels, with censure aimed at stylistic defects and moral shortcomings. Objections to the latter, however, had the novelty of being directed for once at the admiration of violence engendered by Byron's writings. The *Edinburgh Magazine* considered this new taste for 'violent excitement' to be caused by both the late wars and by the poet's Tales: 'we are not at all sure that we shall turn with the same disgust from the murderous cruelties that we could not endure in our earlier days, now that a series of dreadful realities has been succeeded by gloomy fictions decked out in terrible graces, or clothed in beautiful imagery by genius of unexampled potency[1].' But some of the moral criticism hit at a different aspect of the poem—'Adultery, Adultery, Adultery is the Cuckoo strain from beginning to end . . .', remarked the *Champion*.[2] The scene was now set for the appearance of *Don Juan*.

'Juan was my Moscow . . .', said Byron later in the poem (Canto XI, Stanza LVI) after calling himself 'the grand Napoleon of the realms of rhyme'; and the first two cantos of *Don Juan* (1819) did cause a considerable stir in the reviewing periodicals when the anonymous work was published. The two major quarterlies did not review the volume, but the quarterly *British Review*, the monthlies, and the weeklies thrashed the poem about, some affording it a favorable reception, some a hostile one. A majority praised it as a composition, usually very highly, though censuring it for certain moral shortcomings. The anonymity fooled no one.

The construction and style of the poem received many testimonies of enthusiastic approbation. The reviewer in *Blackwood's*, probably Lockhart, called it 'by far the most admirable specimen of the mixture of ease, strength, gayety, and seriousness extant in the whole body of English poetry. . . .'[3] 'The flexibility of the English language', reported the *Monthly Magazine*, 'was never exhibited so perfectly before; in pliability it now appears equal to the cartilaginous suppleness of the Italian, and, in agility, turns all the skipping graces of the French into shrugs and dislocations.'[4] 'The noble author has shown an absolute control over his means . . .', observed the *Literary Gazette*.[5] Yet several reviewers, it should be added, were so caught

[1] *EdM*, V 2s (Aug., 1819), 145.
[2] *Champ*, July 25, 1819, p. 471.
[3] *BM*, V (Aug., 1819), 512.
[4] *MM*, *XLVIII* (Aug., 1819), 56.
[5] *LG*, July 24, 1819, p. 471.

up by their moral indignation that they could only see 'doggrel' and 'jargon'.

Some of the reviewers were decidedly morally indignant. The *British Critic*, which had managed to give a favorable review of *Beppo*, now indulged in such phrases as 'degrading debauchery' and 'shameless indecency', working up to their pronouncement:

> Upon the indecency, and the blasphemy which this volume contains, a very few words will suffice. The adventures which it recounts are of such a nature, and described in such language, as to forbid its entrance within the doors of any modest woman, or decent man. Nor is it a history only, but a manual of profligacy.[1]

But this review in the *British Critic* was the most enraged, even though a few others refused to sully their pages with extracts; and there were a few attempts to defend the morality of *Don Juan*, notably in the *Examiner*. Leigh Hunt, the reviewer, remarked upon the account of Juan and Donna Julia:

> This, it is said, has tendency to corrupt the minds of 'us youth', and to make us *think* lightly of breaking the matrimonial contract. But if to do this be immoral, we can only say that Nature is immoral. Lord Byron does no more than relate the consequences of certain absurdities. If he speaks slightingly of the ties between a girl and a husband old enough for her father, it is because the ties themselves *are* slight. He does not ridicule the bonds of marriage generally, or where they are formed as they should be: he merely shows the folly and wickedness of setting forms and opinions against nature.[2]

Then, Hunt pointed out, there is the additional fact that Julia suffers. But, sound as these arguments are, his further attempt to defend the affair between Juan and Haideé on the grounds of, among other things, the uniqueness of their situation outside social bonds, is not so convincing.

Another criticism, often made a moral issue, concerns the mixture of sentiment and raillery, the abrupt transitions from pathos to comedy. Apparently unaware of this aspect of the genre, almost every periodical, including the *Examiner*, censures this trifling with human feelings, whether or not they are otherwise concerned with the morality of the poem.[3]

[1] *BC*, XII 2s (Aug., 1809), 202. [2] *Exam.*, Oct. 31, 1819, p. 701.
[3] See Samuel Chew, *Byron in England*, p. 79n.

In 1820 Byron published nothing at all, but the following year he produced a variety of works. One of these was the *Letter to [John Murray]* on the Bowles controversy, in which Byron claims ethical poetry to be the highest literary form and Pope to be the greatest of ethical poets (although Shakespeare and Milton were somehow greater poets). The volume received a majority of unfavorable reviews—a surprising fact to anyone who believes that the reviewers of the period were neoclassical admirers of didactic poetry. But Byron's major publications of 1821 were his four dramas, *Marino Faliero* (published with the non-dramatic *Prophecy of Dante*), and *Sardanapalus*, *The Two Foscari*, and *Cain*, published later in the year in one volume.

> But Juan was my Moscow, and Faliero
> My Leipsic, and my Mont Saint Jean seems Cain . . . ,

and so, in the metaphor of Napoleon's successive defeats, went the critical reception of the first and last of these dramas: *Marino Faliero* and *Cain* received mostly unfavorable reviews. The same fate was shared by *The Two Foscari*, but *Sardanapalus*, although it met with a good deal of hostility, was generally made an exception to the critical rejection of Byron's dramas.

That Byron was a failure as a dramatic writer was a common note in these reviews, even in those of *Sardanapalus*, which was esteemed as a dramatic poem, not as a poetic drama. There were several attempts to explain the failure. Hazlitt in his review of *Marino Faliero* in the *London Magazine* attributed it to Byron's fundamental incapacity to sympathize with characters who were not involved in a situation similar to his own. Jeffrey in his review of the *Sardanapalus* volume in the *Edinburgh Review* made a similar point, but gave more emphasis to the problem of Byron's egotism, offering Shakespeare as a model for him to emulate. And several other reviewers observed that all of the characters in the dramas were really Byron in disguise. Still another theory was presented by Roberts in his *British Review* article on *Marino Faliero*, who thought that the meditative, discursive quality of the characters, whose long-winded dialogues killed so much of the dramatic effect, was caused in turn by Byron's misanthropy: 'A poesy so interwoven with a dark and discouraging philosophy, must necessarily assume a casuistic form,—for casuistry is generally employed in contradicting and negativing the external appearances of things.'[1]

A very likely source of dramatic failure was Byron's adherence to the unities, which he defended with much arrogance in the preface to *Sardanapalus*. Almost every reviewer ridiculed Byron's defense, and not one reviewer agreed with him. The arguments against the unities are too diverse to be listed here, but anyone who thinks of the Romantic reviewers as rule-bound neoclassical rationalists (as typified by Thomas Rymer) would do well to read reviews of *Sardanapalus*. In fact, Richard Heber in his review of *Marino Faliero* in the *Quarterly Review* and Jeffrey in his review of *The Two Foscari* in the *Edinburgh Review* each made the point that in the plays being reviewed some singular implausibility of motivation could have been avoided by employing previous scenes as a build-up, letting the unities go to the devil. And Roberts, reviewing *Sardanapalus* in the *British Review*, criticized Byron for sinning against the unity of time 'in the only way in which it could be sinned against', that is, by writing a drama, such as *Sardanapalus*, 'where the time in which the drama itself supposes the events to have happened, is such as can by no possible effort of imagination be made to square with their accomplishment'.[2]

In the preface to *Sardanapalus*, Byron reiterated his statement made in the preface to *Marino Faliero* that his dramas were not intended for the stage, and the inconsistency of these remarks with his fuss about the unities was mentioned by more than one reviewer. Some also pointed out that whether a play was written for the stage or not, it must be 'dramatic'. Roberts in his review of *Marino Faliero* in the *British Review*, for example, observed: 'Such is the habitual force of association in our minds, that a play, even in private perusal, undergoes a sort of scenic exhibition. We image to ourselves the agents and personages of the scene.'[3]

But it was not merely the dramatic aspects of the plays which were seen to have failed; the blank verse was also heavily censured, although there were, to be sure, many passages in all the plays selected for high praise. The *Edinburgh Magazine* began its review of the *Sardanapalus* volume by referring to Byron's hasty composition: 'We wish much that Lord Byron's imagination had had power and honesty

[1] *BR*, XVII (June, 1821), 441.
[2] *BR*, XIX (Mar., 1822), 77–78.
[3] *BR*, XVII (June, 1821), 442.

enough to have represented to him the looks and feelings of the fastidious bard of Twickenham, enduring a rehearsal of his Lordship's tragedies, before he thrust them upon public observation.'[1] Jeffrey, in his review in the *Edinburgh Review* of the same volume, thought the plays, on the contrary, not too careless, but 'very elaborate and hard-wrought compositions', lacking in the 'passion and energy' of his earlier writings; and these signs of labor he thought attributable to Byron's aversion to criticism.[2] This was perhaps unkind of Jeffrey, but probably true; for Byron's sensitivity to censure is apparent even in the arrogance of his prefaces.

Whatever the cause, there was a serious flaw in the blank verse of the plays noticed by many reviewers—the termination of lines in an insignificant monosyllable, which gave a prosaic effect to the verse. Roberts in the *British Review* summed up the problem in his review of *Sardanapalus:* 'The poet has a most merciless habit of cutting in twain the sense by the division of his lines. Thus the preposition frequently ends a line, the next beginning with the noun it governs; and the same divorce between the adjective and substantive is perpetually occurring; never was syntax made obsequious to the wants of a rhythm that deserved so little sacrifice.'[3] Roberts gives seven short examples, one of which is as follows:

When we know
All that can come, and how to meet it, our
Resolves, if firm, may merit a more noble
Word. . . .

He then continues:

The copulative 'and' often ends a line, and even words of still less poetical dignity, as 'if', 'no', 'such', 'which', 'with', 'ay', 'both', 'is', 'his', ''tis', 'has', which, it is not too much to say, are such favourites with this poet, as to be stationed in the place where they must necessarily rest upon the ear, and acquire distinction from their very situation.

Besides these general objections to the plays, there were problems posed by each play, usually involving the characterization. In *Marino Faliero*, most reviewers observed that the anger of the Doge

1 *EdM*, X 2s (Jan., 1822), 102.
2 *ER*, XXXVI (Feb., 1822), 419.
3 *BR*, XIX (Mar., 1822), 81–82.

which led him to conspire to wipe out the entire Venetian aristocracy, was disproportionate to the offence against him, and therefore all sympathy was precluded. As for any defense based on the authen ticity of the event, Richard Heber in the *Quarterly Review* reminded Byron that 'a thing may be true without being probable. . . .'[1]

Another issue raised in reviews of *Marino Faliero*, the plot and characters of which were the same as those of Otway's *Venice Preserved*, was plagiarism. The *Literary Gazette* was particularly keen at rooting out verbal resemblances to Otway, as well as to Shakespeare, but other periodicals also noted them. But as with most charges of literary plagiarism, the resemblances were largely far-fetched and such as would naturally occur. As the *Monthly Review* put it: 'it is difficult to say how far the unavoidable recollections of a poetical mind *will* create apparent imitations, or indeed how far minds of kindred bent and import *must* think of the same subject in a similar way, and express their thoughts in parallel language'.[2] It is ironic too that the *European Magazine* plagiarized the charge of plagiarism from the *Literary Gazette*.

In *Sardanapalus* and *The Two Foscari*, the main problems concerned the characterization. In the first, it is the unnatural mixture of vice and virtue contained in the hero. This was not always pointed out, in fact the *Edinburgh Review* and the *Quarterly Review* praised the conception of *Sardanapalus*; but many reviewers did resurrect the old issue. The *Edinburgh Magazine*, for example, observed:

> An indolent man may be roused to great exertion: a diffident man to desperate resolution; a luxurious man to valiant daring: but the lazy, torpid sensualist, was ever yet selfish, ungenerous, cruel. The passion for effeminate enjoyments was never found in company with the love of humankind, or with reluctance to occasion human misery. . . . Tiberius, Caligula, Nero, Henry the Eighth, Charles the Second, and many others, amply illustrate the remark.[3]

Byron, of course, might have answered that he had 'a friend', who combined just such disparate elements, but then it is not merely possibility at issue in the reviewers' judgment, but probability. In *The Two Foscari*, the reviewers objected to the unnatural character

[1] *QR*, XXVII (July, 1822), 488.
[2] *MR*, XCV (May, 1821), 49.
[3] *EdM*, X 2s (Jan., 1822), 105.

of the younger Foscari, whose extravagant patriotism led him to prefer torture to exile.

In reviews of *Cain*, it was not a concern with characterization as such that brought down so much hostile criticism, although Heber in the *Quarterly Review* remarked, what the others missed, that the catastrophe of the murder of Abel was defective in being almost an accident, and not, as more dramatically represented in Scripture, the result of envy. What so many of the reviewers did find offensive was the blasphemy and impiety put into the mouths of Cain and, especially, of Lucifer, who calls God a tyrant who created only to torture. As might be expected, some of the more religious periodicals resorted to high-pitched indignation; one reviewer even suggested that the Devil had had a hand in the composition. Byron's prefatory remarks came in for a great deal of comment on their own, occasioning many unfavorable comparisons with *Paradise Lost* and Milton's proper handling of the character of Lucifer.

Many reviewers, on the other hand, remained level-headed in the face of so much impiety and such a stir of indignation. Even among those who censured the play strongly were some who saw little danger in its publication. Jeffrey, in the *Edinburgh Review*, regretted that it had been published on the ground that it 'will give great scandal and offence to pious persons in general. . . .'[1] And, like others, he saw that the arguments which Byron forwarded against a benevolent God were left unrefuted, and furthermore, that those arguments were presented with bias and 'without the responsibility or the liability to answer that would attach to a philosophical disputant'.[2]

In 1821, before the publication of the *Sardanapalus* volume, Cantos III–V of *Don Juan* were given to the world. The critical world, certainly the British critical world, now saw fit to reject *Don Juan*. Most of the reviewers, now that they knew what to expect, were less morally enraged than they had been before; but the *Investigator* compared Byron to the Earl of Rochester, and the *British Critic* indulged in some colorful imagery: slimy, creepy things give birth in hiding; 'the Poem before us is one of these hole and corner deposits; not only begotten but spawned in filth and darkness. Every accoucheur of literature has refused his obstetric aid to the obscure and ditch-delivered foundling. . . .'[3] Most of the critics, however, found

[1] *ER*, XXXVI (Feb., 1822), 437.
[2] *Ibid.*, p. 438.
[3] *BC*, XVI 2s (Sept., 1821), 252.

in the new cantos an improvement in morals over the old; and there is, of course, nothing as risqué as the Donna Julia affair in these cantos. Roberts in the *British Review* thought the indecencies of the poem to be in any case a less serious mischief than the 'constant jesting . . . kept up with God's ordinances, and man's relations and duties'.[1] This objection showed a certain short-sightedness and lack of humor, but it is good to remember that the moral issues involved were not wholly concerned with sexual morality.

In any event, the reviewers were not entirely hostile; Roberts, for example, thought 'the genius of the writer . . . unquestionable', and, as did most of the others, he found passages 'of considerable merit both in thought and expression. . . .'[2] Many reviewers, nonetheless, claimed to have detected a falling-off of literary merit in the new cantos; and this observation is, I think, critically valid. As for the moral issues, there were attempts at defense, notably in the *Monthly Magazine*. Marriage, the ridicule of which was objected to by others, was quite rightly defended as 'time out of mind . . . a legitimate butt. . . .'[3] Byron's ridicule of humanity was defended, more questionably, as much less serious than that of Swift—'a dignitary of the church, and of unimpeached character'.[4] And, most important, the reviewer in summing up makes the long overdue reference to the genre of the poem:

> Of the sarcastic wit and poetical talents of this composition, there can be no question; and we must bear in mind that it is framed upon a model, which in all languages has been allowed considerable latitude of subject and expression. Whether the noble author has acted wisely in reviving this style of writing is another matter; but those who are acquainted with the labours of his predecessors in this vineyard, will be inclined to think that he has not exercised his privileges in a very outrageous manner.[5]

In 1822, with the indignation of his critics still ringing in his ears on the score of the objectionable *Don Juan* and *Cain*, Byron joined with Leigh Hunt and Shelley in producing the *Liberal*, a quarterly journal which ran for four numbers. All four were reviewed, mostly by the weeklies, and the journal was attacked very strongly, with much questioning of its right to the title 'liberal'. Overtones of the

[1] *BR*, XVIII (Dec., 1821), 253.
[2] *Ibid.*, p. 263.
[3] *MM*, LII (Sept., 1821), 125.
[4] *Ibid.*, p. 126.
[5] *Ibid.*, p. 129.

abuse leveled at the Cockney School, with which the Satanic School was now allied, were another feature of many reviews.

In the first issue was a burlesque of Southey's *A Vision of Judgement* by Byron. The criticism of Byron's poem, which is surely a comic masterpiece, was very poor, amounting on the whole to cries of impiety and blasphemy, with, however, enough slighting comments on the absurdity of Southey's original to make political bias at least a questionable motive. What seems instead to have been the cause of the reviewers' inability to appreciate the comic genius displayed was the abuse of the late king, the ridicule of his blindness and insanity. Perhaps it takes an effort of the historical imagination to appreciate their indignation; but if an effort is made, their reaction is not, I think, surprising. With heavy irony, the *Literary Gazette* summed up its objections on this score:

> The *feeling* allusion to the infirmities of a body worn out with many years, and a mind visited by the deepest affliction to which humanity is liable, proclaims the taste, the philanthropy, the loyalty, the patriotism, and the tenderness of the illustrious writer. That the venerable man thus ridiculed was a king, and allowed by the Noble Lord himself to be gifted with every private virtue, adds an indescribable zest to the brilliant stroke, which is crowned by the simple fact that he had also descended into the grave.[1]

The second number of the *Liberal* (1823) had a better reception. Byron's drama, *Heaven and Earth*, Part I, received a good deal of praise for descriptions, for particular passages, and, especially, for containing nothing objectionable; but the irregular line lengths occasioned some criticism. Some of the praise, notably in the *Edinburgh Review* and in the *Monthly Magazine*, was in fact excessive. The third and fourth issues of the *Liberal*, also published in 1823, contained little by Byron; and probably because the attraction which his work had afforded was missing, they received fewer reviews, and most of those were hostile.

During 1823, while publication of the *Liberal* was being terminated, and early in 1824, the four last installments of *Don Juan* were published. They were reviewed mainly by the weeklies, with only a few monthlies bothering to criticize the one-shilling pamphlets, and the criticism was on the whole unsatisfactory. The *Literary Examiner* was the only periodical consistently to support the poem, and the

[1] *LG*, Oct. 19, 1822, p. 656.

close family connection between the proprietors of that journal and the publisher of *Don Juan* made the reviewer reluctant to give much more than a preliminary notice. The first two installments, which included the harem scene and the amour with Catherine the Great, not to mention any number of offensive digressions irreligious and skeptical, came in for a great deal of moral and religious chastisement. The reviewer for the *Literary Gazette* could scarcely contain himself: say that the installment containing Cantos VI–VIII is the work of a nobleman, 'instead of being, as it is, the gloating brutality of a wretched debauchee; and then, we would ask, what *man* would choose to wallow in the sty of his own luxury, in words and in description, like a drivelling dotard . . .?'[1] 'Moral vomit' was another expression used. And in its review of the next installment, the same periodical asked if Byron could be sane and answered itself negatively.

None of the other reviewers was quite so hysterical; most contented themselves with congratulating the world at the falling-off in interest and poetry in the later cantos. This observation of deterioration in the poem is valid; there are only brief passages as good as most of the first two cantos. However, it is no credit to some of the periodicals, especially the *British Critic*, that they admitted the very high worth of the early cantos only now and merely gloated at the falling-off.

The hostility, however, diminished with the reviews of Cantos XII–XIV, and something like fair criticism was tendered, now that Byron had almost completely eliminated offensive passages. Moreover, there were a few sensible reviews of the poem before that time, particularly in the *Monthly Magazine* and *Blackwood's*. The best of these was by John Gibson Lockhart, reviewing Cantos IX–XI in the latter periodical. He accuses *Blackwood's* (for the review is in the form of a letter) of falling 'into the crying sin of the age—*humbug*', in its remarks upon the poem, which it had called dull. 'Good heavens!' Lockhart protested, 'Do you imagine that people will believe three cantos of DON JUAN to be unredeemedly and uniformly DULL, merely upon your saying so, without proving what you say by quotation?'[2] With that matter taken care of, he turned to the positive side:

> I maintain, and have always maintained, that Don Juan is, without exception, the first of Lord Byron's works. It is by far the most original in

[1] *LG*, July 19, 1823, p. 451.

[2] *BM*, XIV (Sept., 1823), 282.

point of *conception*. It is decidedly original in point of *tone*. . . . It contains the finest specimens of serious poetry he has ever written; and it contains the finest specimens of ludicrous poetry that our age has witnessed. . . . No, sir; Don Juan, say the canting world what it will, is destined to hold a permanent rank in the literature of our country. It will always be referred to as furnishing the most powerful picture of that vein of thought, (no matter how false and bad,) which distinguishes *a great portion of the thinking people of our time*.[1]

And as for the morality of the poem:

Say the worst of Don Juan, that can with fairness be said of it, what does the thing amount to? Is it *more* obscene than Tom Jones?—Is it *more* blasphemous than Voltaire's novels? In point of fact, it is not within fifty miles of either of them: and as to obscenity, there is more of that in the pious Richardson's pious Pamela, than in all the novels and poems that have been written since.[2]

This review by itself almost compensates for the stupid and mean criticism in which *Blackwood's* so often dealt.

Two other elements are also present in these reviews in a much more substantial form than was customary in reviews of Byron's works. One of these was political bias, overt and unmistakable, not just on the reactionary side, such as can be seen in the censure of attacks on Castlereagh, but on the liberal also, as in the praise of Byron's attacks on tyranny. The other element, closely connected with the first, was the ridicule aimed at Byron's late relationship with the Cockneys—'the Riminists, or Cocknico-Carbonari', as the *British Critic* phrased it in its review of Cantos IX–XI.[3]

In the last two years of his life, Byron published, besides the later installments of *Don Juan* and the four issues of the *Liberal*, a motley description of minor poems: *Werner* (1822), a drama; *The Age of Bronze* (1823), an anonymous satire; *The Island* (1823), a verse narrative; and the first two parts of *The Deformed Transformed* (1824), a drama. The intimation, given by the diffuseness of the genres, of some sort of deterioration—a feeling that the poet was madly searching for some form of expression which he had lost—is substantiated by the low quality of the poems themselves. The reviewers in the weeklies and monthlies (the quarterlies did not bother to review the

[1] *BM*, XIV (Sept., 1823), 282–83.
[2] *Ibid.*, p. 283.
[3] *BC*, XX 2s (Nov., 1823), 524.

poems) noted a decided decline in Byron's powers; and three of the poems received unfavorable reviews. The exception, *The Age of Bronze*, was a political satire with a liberal bias; and since most of the periodicals reviewing the poem were liberal, the reception was naturally more favorable than otherwise.

Even that reception by friendly critics was not entirely favorable; for all four publications received a considerable amount of the sort of criticism to which Byron had been accustomed from the beginning of his career. Characterization was censured for being inconsistent and the heroes of two of the poems for displaying the usual Byronic mixture of vice and virtue. The dramas were reproached for being unstageable, as well as for being prosaic because of the monosyllabic line endings of the blank verse. And, of course, the usual censure of Byron's careless poetic execution was meted out by many reviewers; the criticism of *Werner* in the *Monthly Review* is interesting in this respect for bringing together at this late date the names of Byron and Scott as corruptors of the language.

The only unusual criticism made of any of these poems had to do with Byron's very extensive borrowing of the plot, characters, incidents, and even a considerable part of the dialogue of *Werner*, from a published tale. In a preface, Byron referred readers to that tale to see how much he had borrowed; and many reviewers, after following the poet's instructions, returned the verdict that the play could scarcely be considered Byron's at all. The *British Critic* announced: 'The originality of Lord Byron consists in this, that whereas others have usually translated verse into prose, or prose into verse, his Lordship hath conceived and successfully realized his conception of the possibility of translating prose into prose.'[1]

One final review deserves to be mentioned, not for being unusual, but for being one of the best of its kind; John Wilson's article on *The Age of Bronze* in *Blackwood's* is a masterpiece of abuse. To be fair, within the article Wilson disclaims honestly any intention of a review, as he should for suggesting the following extra-literary punishment for the anonymous author: 'Suppose him stripped naked to the very want of shirt, and tarred and feathered. Up Hampstead Hill he goes, with his downy posteriors, like one of Mr. Moore's angels, to recover himself, to a crowing fit on his own dunghill.'[2] After

[1] *BC*, XIX 2s (Mar., 1823), 245.
[2] *BM*, XIII (Apr., 1823), 458.

thus warming up, he proceeds to the following *tour de force* of scurrility:

> Who would spit upon a toad crawling in its unwieldy and freckled putrefaction? It is enough to see the reptile drag itself in slime away into some common sewer—to be washed down by the mingled mud of kennels, along with every stinking thing, into a subterranean receptacle of filth, there to rot among the hidden abominations.[1]

On April 19, 1824, Byron died, and the critical commotion soon ceased. The reviewers had followed Byron through an immensely prolific career, which lasted for seventeen years and included the appearance of thirty-eight separate publications. Each publication received some attention; many received judgments at the hands of almost every reviewing periodical in circulation at the time.

At first glance, the estimates of Byron's works seem incorrect, and the final conclusions given concerning many of the poems were, I believe, erroneous. This is especially true of the favorable receptions accorded the earlier works—the Tales and Cantos I and II of *Childe Harold*. The reviewers were here confronted with poems the popularity of which was second to none at the time, or perhaps at any time; and as was the case with their appraisal of Scott's verse, they were probably influenced by the overwhelming public acceptance. But it should not be forgotten that the reviewers returned favorable verdicts based on the descriptions and passages that they admired and *in spite of* many shortcomings in both form and content. Posterity has not disagreed about the shortcomings; it has merely rejected the judgment that the merits provide adequate compensation.

With regard to the later publications (excluding the comic poems), the reviewers were not far wrong in their estimates. The dramas were generally regarded as failures, and for the most part posterity has not reversed that verdict. The comic poems are another matter. It is far more difficult to be indulgent toward the reviewers' low estimate of *Don Juan* and *The Vision of Judgement* than toward their high estimate of Byron's earlier works. Yet *Beppo* was well received, and *Don Juan* met with considerable acclaim for its literary merits. *The Vision of Judgement*, as has been pointed out, had to contend with contemporary sympathy toward the late king; and sympathetic involvement, as Bergson once observed, precludes any appreciation of humor.

[1] *BM*, XIII (Apr., 1823), 460.

Byron's reputation has always suffered from the disproportionate attention paid to his private life; in emphasizing the biographical, later generations have been more guilty than the critics of the time. Not that the reviewers were uninterested in Byron's personal life; there were even reviewers concerned about his religious salvation; but in view of the large number of personal allusions in his poems, they showed remarkable reserve. When a reference to his personal history was considered unavoidable, as in reviews of *Childe Harold*, it was most often prefaced by remarks on the reviewer's policy of criticizing the works and not the man.

And if Byron was not reluctant to bring himself and his problems before the public, he was still less hesitant about offending his British readers' religious, patriotic, and political opinions and prejudices. When such offenses occurred, the reviewers who disagreed quite naturally attacked his positions. Political and doctrinal issues, however, were only raised when Byron raised them—political prejudice undoubtedly sometimes affecting in a large way the reviewers' estimates of his works. At times, for example, the *British Critic* ceased to operate as a critical organ and dealt only in abuse. And yet it would be difficult to prove, I think, very many instances of politically influenced judgments; for in most cases legitimate critical issues were brought forward and illustrated by examples.

Byron's reviewers were for the most part serious critics; right or wrong in their verdicts, they provided a valuable service in their attempts to persuade Byron to correct his literary shortcomings. It is a matter of no small regret that they were on the whole unsuccessful.

Percy Bysshe Shelley

Percy Bysshe Shelley, the last poet to be discussed as a member of the Satanic School, was, in fact, never referred to as such, but was instead occasionally attacked as a Cockney because of his relations with Leigh Hunt. And yet Shelley seldom shared the charge of vulgarity levelled at the principal Cockneys, while he did have the honor of once being thrown into an unnamed school by a reviewer who referred to the co-residence of Byron and Shelley on Lake Geneva, and it was several times crudely suggested that he was a devil in disguise. In any case, the discussion of his works in the Reviews was closely connected with the kind of criticism found in reviews of Scott and Byron, so he will be treated here as a member of their school.

Shelley, like Wordsworth, has been fortunate in having the reviews of his works collected into one volume.[1] Professor White, who edited the collection, arranged the reviews chronologically, and the availability of this arrangement will make a chronological discussion here unnecessary. General moral, religious, political, and stylistic issues raised by the reviewers will be discussed instead.

Another reason for discarding chronology is that the reviews of Shelley showed little of the vacillation of reputation notable in the careers of other poets: the great majority of reviews of all of his works were unfavorable. The *Examiner*, *Blackwood's*, and Gold's *London Magazine* fairly consistently passed favorable judgments and were joined occasionally by other periodicals; there were also many divided judgments on the works published in 1819–21, with hostility toward the theories set forth mixed with esteem for the poetry. Nevertheless, the over-all reception of Shelley's works was decidedly hostile.

Some of this hostility can be attributed to 'personality' on the part of the reviewers. This is particularly true of John Taylor Coleridge's review of *The Revolt of Islam* in the *Quarterly Review*, which ends with a nasty hint at some disgrace in Shelley's life, something that *could* be told but isn't. A review of *Queen Mab* in the *Literary Gazette* is more forthright; it mentions the suicide of Shelley's first wife and the loss of his children through Chancery proceedings. But such personal references are rare.[2]

Partisan politics could also account for some of the animosity in the reviews, but the presence of a very large admixture of partisan prejudice would be difficult to prove; the only explicit remarks of this nature—and they were few—were largely confined to ridicule of Shelley's connection with Leigh Hunt. The unlikelihood of simple partisan prejudice could more easily be argued: Tory *Blackwood's* was sympathetic to Shelley while the radical *Monthly Magazine* was hostile. And then there is Hazlitt, a Cockney and radical in his own right, who nevertheless returned an unfavorable verdict in his review of the *Posthumous Poems* in the *Edinburgh Review*. Hazlitt

[1] N. I. White, *The Unextinguished Hearth.*

[2] N. I. White, (p. 20) came to the same general conclusion: 'The treatment he received was not . . . particularly personal.' White, however, was not loath to accuse the reviewers of political, religious, and moral bigotry (pp. 15–16).

in fact considered Shelley's extreme radical positions to be disadvantageous to the liberal cause: Shelley 'gave great encouragement to those who believe in all received absurdities, and are wedded to all existing abuses: his extravagance seeming to sanction their grossness and selfishness, as theirs were a full justification of his folly and eccentricity'.[1] The *Monthly Magazine* also had its doubts. After remarking that the notes to *Queen Mab* came out 'in favour of Atheism, the equalization of property, and the unrestrained intercourse of the sexes', it cut short its review of that poem: 'Advocates, as we are, for a very extended freedom of the press, we fear commenting further on this work, lest we should, unintentionally, assist in that *powerful* criticism, to which, we fear, it will soon be subjected.'[2] As far as partisan prejudice goes, the most suspect periodical was the *Examiner*, in which all of Shelley's works were reviewed favorably—after *The Revolt of Islam* with indiscriminate praise. But, since Shelley and Leigh Hunt were friends, such favorable reception in Hunt's *Examiner* could be ascribed merely to personal bias.

Shelley's political and social philosophy was an altogether different matter; his theories provoked a great deal of hostility. Purely political bias of the kind a Reformist might encounter, however, hardly enters the question; for Shelley was no mere Reformist, but rather his philosophy, as expounded in *The Revolt of Islam*, *Rosalind and Helen*, and *Queen Mab*, proposed as a necessary prelude to human happiness the eradication of, among other things, monarchies and matrimony. Almost all of the reviewers attacked such theories, as they quite naturally should; but most were content to forward strong objections.

John Taylor Coleridge in his review of *The Revolt of Islam* in the *Quarterly Review* went further. After giving a summary of Shelley's philosophy, he proceeds to point out that the political argument as given in the poem is loaded in Shelley's favor by the selection of a tyrant and a corrupt Turkish court as a model of the monarchical system. Later on, he considers the outcome of such a philosophy:

> This indeed is a serious question; but, as in most schemes of reform, it is easier to say what is to be removed, and destroyed, than what is to be put in its place. Mr. Shelley would abrogate our laws—this would put an end to felonies and misdemeanours at a blow; he would abolish the rights of property, of course there could thenceforward be no violations of them,

[1] *ER*, XL (July, 1824), 497.

[2] *MM*, LI (June, 1821), 460–61.

no heart-burnings between the poor and the rich, no disputed wills, no litigated inheritances, no food in short for sophistical judges, or hireling lawyers; he would overthrow the constitution, and then we should have no expensive court, no pensions or sinecures, no silken lords or corrupt commoners, no slavish and enslaving army or navy. . . . This is at least intelligible; but it is not so easy to describe the structure, which Mr. Shelley would build upon this vast heap of ruins. 'Love', he says, 'is to be the sole law which shall govern the moral world'; but Love is a wide word with many significations, and we are at a loss as to which of them he would have it now bear.[1]

William Hazlitt in his review of the *Posthumous Poems* in the *Edinburgh Review* attempted to explain Shelley's extravagant philosophy, partly by his too great dependence on reason and partly by his rage for novelty. Of the latter, Hazlitt observed:

We wish to speak of the errors of a man of genius with tenderness. His nature was kind, and his sentiments noble; but in him the rage of free inquiry and private judgment amounted to a species of madness. Whatever was new, untried, unheard of, unauthorized, exerted a kind of fascination over his mind. The examples of the world, the opinions of others, instead of acting as a check upon him, served but to impel him forward with double velocity in his wild and hazardous career. Spurning the world of realities, he rushed into the world of nonentities and contingencies, like air into a *vacuum*. If a thing was old and established, this was with him a certain proof of its having no solid foundation to rest upon: if it was new, it was good and right. Every paradox was to him a self-evident truth; every prejudice an undoubted absurdity. The weight of authority, the sanction of ages, the common consent of mankind, were vouchers only for ignorance, error, and imposture. Whatever shocked the feelings of others, conciliated his regard; whatever was light, extravagant, and vain, was to him a proportionable relief from the dulness and stupidity of established opinions.[2]

Thus wrote a contemporary who was both a personal acquaintance of Shelley and a radical.

The religious objections Shelley encountered were very similar to those occasioned by his political and social theories. The objections were neither narrowly sectarian nor doctrinal; for, as in the case of the political and social theories with which they were always connected, Shelley's religious theories went beyond the point where

[1] *QR*, XXI (Apr., 1819), 468.

[2] *ER*, XL (July, 1824), 497.

limited issues could be raised. Not satisfied with frequent ridicule of orthodox belief in God, he made constant attacks on both priests in general and basic Christian beliefs in particular. These things were done without delicacy; and Shelley was at least culpable of bad taste in directing his diatribes against an almost wholly Christian audience. Some respect is due to the opinions even of the majority.

Some of the reviewers cried, 'Blasphemy!'; some were more level-headed and merely remonstrated or asked him to grow up; but W. S. Walker in his review in the *Quarterly Review* of *Prometheus Unbound*, decided to take issue with the poet. After noting Shelley's attacks on Christianity in *Prometheus Unbound* and in the *Ode to Liberty*, he argued:

If any one, after a serious investigation of the truth of Christianity, still doubts or disbelieves, he is to be pitied and pardoned; if he is a good man, he will himself lament that he has not come to a different conclusion; for even the enemies of our faith admit, that it is precious for the restraints which it imposes on human vices, and for the consolations which it furnishes under the evils of life. But what is to be said of a man, who, like Mr. Shelley, wantonly and unnecessarily goes out of his way, not to reason against, but to revile Christianity and its author? Let him adduce his arguments against our religion, and we shall tell him where to find them answered: but let him not presume to insult the world, and to profane the language in which he writes, by rhyming invectives against a faith of which he knows nothing but the name.[1]

The over-confident tone which comes from writing to a Christian audience should not obscure what I believe is a reasonable objection.

Besides political and religious bias, Shelley's reviewers are also liable to the accusation of moral bigotry. Some of them admittedly were more narrowly moral in the puritanical sense. What is perhaps an example of this is contained in criticism of *Rosalind and Helen* in the *Monthly Review*:

We can overlook a few general sallies of a thoughtless nature: but, when a man comes to such a degree of perverseness, as to represent the vicious union of two individuals of different sexes as equally sacred with the nuptial tie, we really should be wanting in our duty not to reprobate so gross an immorality.[2]

[1] *QR*, XXVI (Oct., 1821), 178–79.
[2] *MR*, XC (Oct., 1819), 207.

But most of the moral criticism is of a more general nature. Josiah Conder, reviewing *Alastor* in the *Eclectic Review*, charges Shelley with 'intellectual luxury' for having no moral purpose in the poem. *Alastor* has only 'glitter without warmth, succession without progress, excitement without purpose, and a search which terminates in annihilation'.[1] Lockhart, in a generally favorable review of *Rosalind and Helen* in *Blackwood's*, makes a similar objection:

One seeks, in vain, through his poetry, fine as it often is, for any principles of action in the characters who move before us. They are at all times fighting against the law of the world, the law of nature, and the law of God—there is nothing satisfactory in their happiness, and always something wilful in their misery.[2]

'. . . He is ever an obscure and cheerless moralist', Lockhart concludes.

But it was the subject-matter of *The Cenci* which brought about the most prolonged moral discussions. Censure of subject-matter was concerned not merely with the incest, but also with the parricide and the crimes of Count Cenci, who, in the words of the *Literary Gazette*, 'transforms a Richard III., an Iago, a Sir Giles Overreach, comparatively into angels of light'.[3] There were several exceptions to this moral censure, however: Leigh Hunt in the *Examiner* called the plot 'a most terrific family story' and emphasized the amiable tone which he claimed Shelley gave to the play; and the reviewer in the *Theatrical Inquisitor* not only did not object to the story, but obviously enjoyed the passage following the incest: 'We see the victim of *Cenci*'s destructive hatred, rushing from his serpent coil, her veins swoln with the venom of his infectious guilt, and her heart bruised in her very bosom by his merciless pressure.'[4]

Most of the moral censure of the play was concerned with the effect such a story would most likely have on its readers. The *New Monthly Magazine* gave what is perhaps the best statement of the position:

The narrative, we believe, is 'extant in choice Italian'; but this is no excuse for making its awful circumstances the groundwork of a tragedy. If such things have been, it is the part of a wise moralist decently to cover

[1] *EcR*, VI 2s (Oct., 1816), 392.
[2] *BM*, V (June, 1819), 273.
[3] *LG*, Apr. 1, 1820, p. 209.
[4] *Exam*, Mar. 19, 1820, p. 190; *TI*, XVI (Apr., 1820), 214.

them. There is nothing in the circumstance of a tale being true which renders it fit for the general ear. The exposure of a crime too often pollutes the very soul which shudders at its recital, and destroys that unconsciousness of ill which most safely preserves its sanctities.[1]

The reviewer then goes on to mention how newspapers play up crime to the point where people are no longer shocked. Furthermore, 'there is no small encouragement to vice in gazing into the dark pits of fathomless infamy. The ordinary wicked regard themselves as on a pinnacle of virtue, while they look into the fearful depth beneath them.'[2]

A slightly different attitude, insofar as it takes a more extreme position, was to be found in the *British Review*:

They who can find dramatic poetry in such representations of human life must excuse us for wondering of what materials their minds are composed. Delineations like these are worse than unpoetical; they are unholy and immoral. But 'they are as lights', if we believe Mr. Shelley, 'to make apparent some of the most dark and secret caverns of the human heart'. No, no; they teach nothing; and, if they did, knowledge must not be bought at too high a price. There is a knowledge which is death and pollution. Is knowledge any compensation for the injury sustained by being made familiar with that which ought to be to us all as if it were not? If such feelings, such ideas, exist in the world, (we cannot believe they do, for the Cenci of the Roman tradition is very different from the Cenci of Mr. Shelley) let them remain concealed.[3]

If the reference to newspapers, mentioned in the *New Monthly Magazine*'s review, brings to mind the modern tabloid's lurid accounts of crimes and atrocities and the present concern over the exploitation of sex and violence in all mass media, the general premise

[1] *NMM*, XIII (May, 1820), 551.

[2] The reviewer also quotes from the last chapter of Sir Thomas Browne's *Enquiries into Vulgar Errors*, as follows: 'For of sins heteroclital, and such as want either name or precedent, there is oft-times a sin even in their histories. We desire no records of such enormities: sins should be accounted new, that so [*sic*] they may be esteemed monstrous. The pens of men may sufficiently expatiate without these singularities of villainy; for as they encrease the hatred of vice in some, so do they enlarge the theory of wickedness in all. And this is one thing that may make latter ages worse than the former; for the vicious examples of ages past, poison the curiosity of these present, affording a hint of sin unto seduceable spirits, and soliciting those unto the imitation of them, whose heads were never so perversely principled as to invent them.'

[3] *BR*, XVII (June, 1821), 385–86.

underlying these objections may not seem unreasonable, however well or badly they may be thought to fit the particular content and conduct of Shelley's play. Present concern with such issues in serious literature is negligible, presumably because so few readers are involved.

It is possible that all the objections discussed so far—the philosophical, religious and moral questions—can be dismissed as invalid or out of place in criticism of literary works. Putting such considerations aside for the moment, the reviews of Shelley's works almost always contain considerable criticism of their purely literary aspects. This criticism not only deserves serious consideration, but should also act as a restraint against dismissing the reviews *in toto* as merely bigoted.

One of the best of these criticisms of Shelley's poetic worth is W. S. Walker's review of *Prometheus Unbound* in the *Quarterly Review*. Many objections had been raised in previous reviews of *Alastor* and *The Revolt of Islam*—even in the *Examiner*—to the unintelligibility and obscurity (less sympathetic critics called it 'nonsense') in the poems. Walker attempted to describe this defect at greater length:

> In Mr. Shelley's poetry all is brilliance, vacuity, and confusion. We are dazzled by the multitude of words which sound as if they denoted something very grand or splendid: fragments of images pass in crowds before us; but when the procession has gone by, and the tumult of it is over, not a trace of it remains upon the memory. The mind, fatigued and perplexed, is mortified by the consciousness that its labour has not been rewarded by the acquisition of a single distinct conception. . . .[1]

Having thus described what he considers the general effect of the poetry, he continues:

> Far be it from us to call for strict reasoning, or the precision of logical deductions, in poetry; but we have a right to demand clear, distinct conceptions. The colouring of the pictures may be brighter or more variegated than that of reality; elements may be combined which do not in fact exist in a state of union; but there must be no confusion in the forms presented to us. Upon a question of mere beauty, there may be a difference of taste. . . . But the question of meaning, or no meaning, is a matter of fact on which common sense, with common attention, is adequate to decide; and the decision to which we may come will not be impugned, whatever be

[1] *QR*, XXVI (Oct., 1821), 169.

the want of taste, or insensibility to poetical excellence, which it may please Mr. Shelley, or any of his coterie, to impute to us. . . . If, however, we should completely establish this charge [of want of meaning], we look upon the question of Mr. Shelley's poetical merits as at an end; for he who has the trick of writing very showy verses without ideas, or without coherent ideas, can contribute to the instruction of none, and can please only those who have learned to read without having ever learned to think.[1]

The first example Walker gives is from *Prometheus Unbound* (III, iii, 49–56):

'Lovely apparitions, dim at first,
Then radiant, as the mind, arising bright
From the embrace of beauty, whence the forms
Of which these are the phantoms, cast on them
The gathered rays which are reality,
Shall visit us, the immortal progeny
Of painting, sculpture, and wrapt poesy,
And arts, tho' unimagined, yet to be.'—p. 105.

The verses are very sonorous; and so many fine words are played off upon us, such as, *painting, sculpture, poesy, phantoms, radiance, the embrace of beauty, immortal progeny*, &c. that a careless reader, influenced by his habit of associating such phrases with lofty or agreeable ideas, may possibly have his fancy tickled into a transient feeling of satisfaction.[2]

Later, Walker elaborates on this point:

Poetry like that of Mr. Shelley presents every where glittering constellations of words, which taken separately have a meaning, and either communicate some activity to the imagination, or dazzle it by their brilliance. Many of them relate to beautiful or interesting objects, and are therefore capable of imparting pleasure to us by the associations attached to them. The reader is conscious that his mind is raised from a state of stagnation, and he is willing to believe, that he is astounded and bewildered, not by the absurdity, but by the originality and sublimity of the author.

It appears to us much more surprizing, that any man of education should write such poetry as that of 'Prometheus Unbound', than, that when written, it should find admirers. It is easy to read without attention; but it is difficult to conceive how an author, unless his intellectual habits are thoroughly depraved, should not take the trouble to observe whether his imagination has definite forms before it, or is gazing in stupid wonder on assemblages of brilliant words.[3]

[1] *Ibid.*, pp. 169–70. [2] *Ibid.*, p. 170. [3] *Ibid.*, p. 176.

Then, shortly after the above passage, Walker makes a final onslaught:

But it is often said, that though the poems are bad, they at least show poetical power. Poetical power can be shown only by writing good poetry, and this Mr. Shelley has not yet done. The proofs of Mr. Shelley's genius, which his admirers allege, are the very exaggeration, copiousness of verbiage, and incoherence of ideas which we complain of as intolerable. They argue in criticism, as those men do in morals, who think debauchery and dissipation an excellent proof of a good heart. The want of meaning is called sublimity, absurdity becomes venerable under the name of originality, the jumble of metaphor is the richness of imagination, and even the rough, clumsy, confused structure of the style, with not unfrequent violations of the rules of grammar, is, forsooth, the sign and effect of a bold overflowing genius, that disdains to walk in common trammels.[1]

The review of the same poem in the *Literary Gazette* likewise censured its obscurity, but was more successful in showing the role of the imagery in contributing to it. After remarking that Prometheus 'is "*nailed*" by *chains* of "*burning cold*" ', the reviewer quotes lines 62–64 and 66–69 of Act I (italics added by the reviewer):

Ye icy Springs, *stagnant* with wrinkling frost,
Which *vibrated* to hear me: and then *crept*
Shuddering through India.
And ye, *swift* Whirlwinds, who, on *poised* wings
Hung *mute* and *moveless* o'er yon hushed abyss,
As thunder, *louder* than your own, made rock
The orbed world.

The reviewer commented:

The chief secret of Mr. Shelley's poetry . . . is merely opposition of words, phrases, and sentiments, so violent as to be utter nonsense: *ex. gr.* the vibration of stagnant springs, and their creeping shuddering;—the swift moveless (*i.e.* motionless) whirlwinds, on poised wings, which hung mute over a hushed abyss as thunder louder than their own!! In the same strain, Prometheus, who ought to have been called Sphinx, when answered in a *whisper*, says,

'Tis scarce like sound: it tingles thro' the frame
As lightning tingles, *hovering ere it strike.*

[1] *QR*, XXVI (Oct., 1821), 177.

Common bards would have thought the tingling was felt when it struck, and not before,—when it was hovering too, of all things for lightning to be guilty of![1]

These are by no means the only adverse criticisms of Shelley's style, but they will suffice as examples of the kind of objections which the reviewers were constantly making.

But less frequent were the sustained discussions of Shelley's poetic techniques and principles. W. S. Walker's treatment I have already quoted at some length, but another, the review of the *Posthumous Poems* by William Hazlitt in the *Edinburgh Review* deserves notice in this regard, not only because it has intrinsic merits of its own, but also because Hazlitt's reputation as a critic and the sympathy so notable in his approach to Shelley's poetry defend it from the charge of bigotry. Since this review is not contained in Professor White's collection and since it seems to have attracted little attention, some lengthy extracts are called for.

He begins:

Mr. Shelley's style is to poetry what astrology is to natural science—a passionate dream, a straining after impossibilities, a record of fond conjectures, a confused embodying of vague abstractions,—a fever of the soul, thirsting and craving after what it cannot have, indulging its love of power and novelty at the expense of truth and nature, associating ideas by contraries, and wasting great powers by their application to unattainable objects.

Poetry, we grant, creates a world of its own; but it creates it out of existing materials. Mr. Shelley is the maker of his own poetry—out of nothing. Not that he is deficient in the true sources of strength and beauty, if he had given himself fair play (the volume before us, as well as his other productions, contains many proofs to the contrary): But, in him, fancy, will, caprice, predominated over and absorbed the natural influences of things; and he had no respect for any poetry that did not strain the intellect as well as fire the imagination—and was not sublimed into a high spirit of metaphysical philosophy. Instead of giving a language to thought, or lending the heart a tongue, he utters dark sayings, and deals in allegories and riddles. His Muse offers her services to clothe shadowy doubts and inscrutable difficulties in a robe of glittering words, and to turn nature into a brilliant paradox. We thank him—but we must be excused.[2]

[1] *LG*, Sept. 9, 1820, p. 580.

[2] *ER*, XL (July, 1824), 494.

Hazlitt further observed:

He ransacked his brain for incongruities, and believed in whatever was incredible. Almost all is effort, almost all is extravagant, almost all is quaint, incomprehensible, and abortive, from aiming to be more than it is. Epithets are applied, because they do not fit: subjects are chosen, because they are repulsive: the colours of his style, for their gaudy, changeful, startling effect, resemble the display of fireworks in the dark, and, like them, have neither durability, nor keeping, nor discriminate form. Yet Mr. Shelley, with all his faults, was a man of genius; and we lament that uncontrollable violence of temperament which gave it a forced and false direction. He has single thoughts of great depth and force, single images of rare beauty, detached passages of extreme tenderness; and, in his smaller pieces, where he has attempted little, he has done most. If some casual and interesting idea touched his feelings or struck his fancy, he expressed it in pleasing and unaffected verse: but give him a larger subject, and time to reflect, and he was sure to get entangled in a system. The fumes of vanity rolled volumes of smoke, mixed with sparkles of fire, from the cloudy tabernacle of his thought. The success of his writings is therefore in general in the inverse ratio of the extent of his undertakings; inasmuch as his desire to teach, his ambition to excel, as soon as it was brought into play, encroached upon, and outstripped his powers of execution.[1]

Julian and Maddalo was apparently one of the more successful minor poems Hazlitt had in mind. Despite some obscurity and indistinctness,

This poem is . . . in Mr. Shelley's best and *least mannered* manner. If it has less brilliancy, it has less extravagance and confusion. It is in his stanza-poetry, that his Muse chiefly runs riot, and baffles all pursuit of common comprehension or critical acumen. The *Witch of Atlas*, the *Triumph of Life*, and *Marianne's Dream*, are rhapsodies or allegories of this description; full of fancy and of fire, with glowing allusions and wild machinery, but which it is difficult to read through, from the disjointedness of the materials, the incongruous metaphors and violent transitions, and of which, after reading them through, it is impossible, in most instances, to guess the drift or the moral.[2]

To these poems he preferred the *Letter to Maria Gisborne*, *Prince Athanase*, and the *Ode to Naples*, the last of which 'though somewhat turbid and overloaded in the diction, we regard as a fair specimen of

[1] *ER*. XL (July, 1824), 495.

[2] *Ibid*., p. 502.

Mr. Shelley's highest powers—whose eager animation wanted only a greater sternness and solidity to be sublime.'[1]

The critical issues involved in reviews of Shelley's poetry were much the same as those found in contemporary criticisms of Scott and Byron. There is the same concern over the details of composition, although in the case of Shelley there are few references to carelessness, and the same moral and (in reviews of Byron and Shelley) the same religious and political objections.

As far as the latter objections are concerned, Shelley had even less to complain of in the treatment accorded him by the critics than did Byron, since a good many of Shelley's poems contain much more extravagant political and religious theories.[2] What I have attempted to show is that they were sufficiently extreme as to exclude any question of sectarian or partisan bigotry in the objections put forward. It might be argued, of course, that such issues as were raised are altogether out of place in the criticism of literature; but if this is true (and I do not think it is), such issues are just as surely out of place in the literary works themselves. Furthermore, it goes without saying that bigotry is not confined to the forces of reaction: if the contemporary critics were bigots for remonstrating with Shelley just as inescapably was the poet a bigot for obtruding his theories into his poetry without substantiating them.

But if most of the reviews were not infected with bigotry, many of them are nevertheless unsatisfactory as pieces of criticism. Some of the reviewers, in the first place, were a good deal too abusive, too ready to resort to highly colored terminology—to say 'nonsensical' or 'absurd' where they meant 'obscure' or 'unintelligible'. This is especially true of the *Literary Gazette*, which in fact went so far as to suggest diabolism; but other periodicals were occasionally culpable. The reviewers seem to have been inflamed by the extravagance of the political and religious theories; to have found an easy mark for their irritation in the poetic defects; and so, to have been, at that point, unable to restrain themselves.

On the other hand, there is too much uncritical praise in some of the reviews, too much critical indulgence at the expense of critical

[1] *Ibid.*, pp. 507–8. The conclusions of Donald Davie, in his chapter on Shelley in *The Purity of Diction in English Verse* (London: Chatto and Windus, 1952), are remarkably like many of those arrived at by Hazlitt, especially the preference for minor poems in the familiar style.

[2] See White, p. 21.

rigor. Lockhart in *Blackwood's*, for example, found *Alastor* 'a magnificent pilgrimage no doubt, and not the less so on account of its being rather unintelligible'; and the reviewer in the *Edinburgh Magazine* remarked of Shelley's poetry in the *Posthumous Poems* that 'every word he uses, even though the idea he labours to express be vague, or exaggerated, or unnatural, is intensely poetical'.[1] This sort of critical juggling is no doubt merely the other extreme of the abuse mentioned above: it must be difficult for a sympathetic critic, when faced with the work of an unpopular poet, to set limits to his tolerance.

Fortunately, however, a good many critics managed to deliver level-headed judgments of Shelley's poetry; the *Monthly Review* and the *Monthly Magazine* are notable in this respect. As for the worth of the adverse criticisms of Shelley's style, I am aware that for the past few decades a controversy has been raging over Shelley's poetic methods. This is scarcely the place to engage in that controversy, but some opinion on the validity of the hostile contemporary judgments is, I think, rightly to be expected. Although I would not wish to endorse all of those judgments, I do believe that the critical position on which they are based is in general legitimate and correct.

Such a critical position is at least respectable. In line with William Hazlitt and many of the reviewers, Matthew Arnold and T. S. Eliot have delivered unfavorable judgments of Shelley's poetry.[2] Still others who have taken a similar stand are F. R. Leavis, Douglas Bush, Donald Davie, and Stephen Spender.[3] These comprise a formidable group, but I would prefer to let an unknown reviewer (in the *Literary Register*) have the last word:

The objections we have directed against [the poetry], may be visited on our incapacity to comprehend the sublime or profound; or upon our

[1] *BM*, VI (Nov., 1819), 149; *EdM*, XV 2s (July, 1824), 13.

[2] For Arnold's position see especially incidental remarks in 'The Study of Poetry', 'The Function of Criticism', 'Byron', and 'Maurice de Guerin', in *Essays in Criticism* (New York: A. L. Burt, n.d.). For Eliot's position see 'Shelley and Keats', in *The Use of Poetry and the Use of Criticism* (Cambridge, Mass.: Harvard University Press, 1933).

[3] See relevant chapters in F. R. Leavis, *Revaluation* (New York: G. W. Stewart, 1947), Douglas Bush, *Mythology and the Romantic Tradition in English Poetry* (Cambridge, Mass.: Harvard University Press, 1937), Donald Davie, *Purity of Diction in English Verse* (London: Chatto and Windus, 1952), and Stephen Spender, *Shelley* (London: Longmans, Green, 1952).

readiness to mistake the one for obscurity, and the other for utter darkness. The pervading intelligence of Mr. Shelley's poetry may be as completely hidden from our eyes, as the pervading essence of God—we almost shudder at the parallel—in a tree, a pool of water, or a lump of clay. Taste for the former perception, may depend on capability for the latter; and estimation for his poetical beauties may be entombed in the opacity of mind with which we resist the influence of his metaphysical theories. Be it so, if it be so.[1]

[1] *LitReg*, Sept. 28, 1822, p. 194.

5

The Cockney School

The idea of a 'Cockney School of Poetry' was originated by John Gibson Lockhart in *Blackwood's Magazine* in a scurrilous series of articles begun in October, 1817. In the same month, the *Edinburgh Magazine* recognized a literary group which included the same writers, Leigh Hunt, John Keats, and William Hazlitt. Thus it is evident that the grouping by *Blackwood's* is not ascribable solely to a desire for lumping together offensive writers for ease of attack, as was largely the case with Southey's vaguely descriptive 'Satanic School'.

The Cockney School was, in fact, the nearest approach to a literary school of any so denominated by the reviewers. The members lived in the London area and they were friends. More important, they shared certain attitudes toward life and literature, as well as certain peculiarities of style and sentiment. Ironically, Hazlitt's writings had the least of the vulgarity which the title 'Cockney' was meant to designate, but he was more often than Hunt or Keats attacked as a 'Cockney'.

Much of the abuse discharged at the Cockneys was, of course, political. With Leigh Hunt, who was in many ways the center of the group, editing the radical *Examiner* during most of the period, this should surprise no one. What is remarkable, however, was the extent to which their political affiliations were more an asset than a liability, as we shall see.

Leigh Hunt

In the light of Leigh Hunt's well-known skirmishes with *Blackwood's Magazine*, the relations of the 'King of the Cockneys' with his reviewers would most likely be thought to have been hostile, but such is not the case. The 'On the Cockney School of Poetry' series in that periodical, it is true, deal mainly with Hunt, but most of the articles are not reviews but invective of the lowest order. In any case, *Blackwood's* did not reflect the opinion of the reviewers as a whole, who rendered favorable judgments on most of Hunt's publications.

The first of these, the *Critical Essays on the Performers of the London Theatres* (1807), contained selections of Hunt's dramatic criticism as published in the *News*. It was in general well received, with particular approbation given to his judgment, impartiality, and taste. Qualifications took the form of censure of stylistic blemishes, such as quaint diction (for example, 'close wideness'), evident immaturity in thinking, and unsuccessful attempts at humor. Hunt's only other extensive prose publication in the period under study, *An Attempt to Shew the Folly and Danger of Methodism* (1809), was likewise a collection of articles published previously, this time in the *Examiner*. It received only two reviews, both favorable.

Discounting Hunt's verses in the *Examiner*, which received a gratuitous hostile review in the *Satirist*, his first poetic publication after 1802 was *The Feast of the Poets* (1814). As with the prose pieces, this satiric poem met with a majority of favorable verdicts though there was a good deal of adverse criticism of the slovenliness and vulgarity of the style. Hunt's vanity also came under good-humored fire in the *Critical Review*, which commented on Hunt's statement of reluctance, as a critic himself, to publish verse:

> There is a constitutional quality in this gentleman which operates so undisguisedly—a frankness of assumption, which proves him to be on such excellent terms with himself, that we hear of his perplexity with a most satisfied persuasion of its philosophical endurance. . . . [And yet] a little solemn coxcombry, when united to ability and good intention is pardonable enough; and possibly not the less palatable for a slight perception of the ridiculous which attends our regard of it.[1]

[1] *CR*, V 4s (Mar., 1814), 293–94.

The *Critical Review* also observed that Hunt went too far in taking his attacks on the poets into their private lives; and the *Monthly Review* remarked: 'He plays the part of a critic with less mercy than the most merciless of reviewers. . . .'[1] A fit time for the *Satirist* to prefigure *Blackwood's* bitter, personal abuse: Hunt is 'in politics, a drivelling man-milliner; and in literature, an empty coxcomb'.[2]

In the following year, Hunt published *The Descent of Liberty*, an attempt to revive the form of the masque. Again the reception was more favorable than otherwise, but critical opposition was gaining momentum (with, however, only the monthlies and one weekly concerned). There was good reason for the increased hostility; for unlike the light-hearted satire which preceded it, the masque was a serious attempt to succeed with a difficult form and was a failure on many counts. Even John Scott in the *Champion*, who praised the poet and his work to the skies, had to condemn Hunt's affectation and familiarity, and, a more important failing, his allowance of 'a too licentious indulgence of the shadowy gleamings of his fancy, by permitting them to escape him in language like themselves, half-formed, new coined, and unsanctioned'.[3] Scott explained:

> The difficulty of finding words to represent all that passes within the poet's mind, is, in many respects, salutary;—it drives him to the necessity of selecting with some reference to the understandings, tastes, and habits of his readers; it forces him to define what he would otherwise leave vague,—and, in short, forms his and the public's best security, against his being seduced to outpour upon them the egotism, wildness, crudity, and rawness of his secret breast, instead of presenting a refined and assorted collection of what is truly valuable, suitable, and pleasing.

The best criticism of the masque, however, was delivered by the *Theatrical Inquisitor*. After praising Hunt's integrity and independence and censuring his egotism and over-confidence, the reviewer attacks the allegory, 'a species of writing much too abstracted to be entertaining', made even worse here by 'its making an improbable fiction of reality [the political situation on the Continent], and consequently destroying the interest of the tale'.[4] The long-winded, ludicrous stage directions are next ridiculed as they deserved. But the reviewer was just warming up to more serious charges: 'The language is

[1] *MR*, LXXV (Sept., 1814), 100.
[2] *Sat.*, XIV (Apr., 1814), 327.
[3] *Champ*, Mar. 26, 1815, p. 102.
[4] *TI*, VI (Apr., 1815), 290.

often rugged, the metre in many lines is deficient, the ideas trite and quaintly expressed.' One of many stated examples of the latter is a '*Wrapping* looks and *balmy* tongue', and the comment on all the examples was:

Surely no reader of taste or common understanding will accept of these unmeaning phrases as the genuine language of poetry. Even supposing, which is not the case, that the ideas were poetical, the want of just expression would still be felt as a most intolerable defect; for although it must be confessed that words are nothing more than the symbols of ideas, yet the beauty and appropriate use of these symbols form the second great source of the pleasure we receive from poetry.[1]

Then the meaning of passages is questioned: for example, airs 'feel as they were fit for *hearts* and eyes / To *breathe* and sparkle in' (italics added by the reviewer). 'The idea of hearts breathing', he commented, 'has at least the merit of novelty.'[2] Examples of rugged meter ('And summon from their waiting climes / The pleasures that perfect victorious times') and of familiarity ('Phaniel, if your cloud holds two, / I'll come up, and sit with you') were also given. The reviewer observed:

By a strange contradiction of judgment, or of feeling, he has written on two very opposite principles; sometimes he has affected a homeliness of language and ideas, that is almost disgusting; and at other times he has heaped together, without any meaning, a parcel of high-sounding words. . . .[3]

The review ends with the hope that Hunt will abandon poetry and stick to politics: 'In the one he will only lose that credit which he has obtained in the other.'[4]

In the following year (1816), Hunt published what is easily his best original work in verse, *The Story of Rimini*. The reviewers certainly thought it was the best published to that point, and for the first time the quarterlies became involved. Only the *Quarterly Review* and the *New Monthly Magazine* were hostile, although all of those reviewing the poem had reservations of one kind or another.

But the freshness and vigor of the execution received a good deal of praise. Jeffrey (probably drawing upon a MS review by Hazlitt)

[1] *Ibid.*, p. 294. [2] *Ibid.*, p. 295. [3] *Ibid.*, p. 297. [4] *Ibid.*, p. 298.

in the *Edinburgh Review* thought the tone very like Chaucer's, except that Hunt's homeliness and directness often seemed forced. Hunt's vivid descriptions were praised by many reviewers, and Jeffrey noted that the activity being described in the opening account of the procession was reflected in the gaiety and movement of the verse. The progress of the passion of Paulo and Francesca also received favorable comment from many hands.

But then there was the obstacle of Hunt's style, which had, in the words of the *Literary Panorama*, 'imperfections easily pointed out, by men who possess no proportion of his powers'. In this review is also perhaps the best description of the effect of reading the poem:

In this poem he indulges himself in description, and his ideas, his versification, his management are so lively, graceful, and applicable, that the reader shares with him in the delight of his composition, which, perhaps, is as great a compliment as words can utter. Amidst this gratification the reader detects in slovenly affectation of ease, the constraint of Art, a kind of occasional slipshod hitch in the verse. . . .[1]

Another incidental but discerning point was that

In a short poem points of time, or incident, may occur, in which the mind feels the disadvantage resulting from early exhaustion. The mind feels that excessive labour has been bestowed on opening incidents, and to place this labour where it would be more effectual, a part at least of what has been read must be forgot; a new train of ideas, the same, yet not the same, demanded by the imagination, excite a dangerous kind of rivalship, and the poet must forego them, because he has already introduced others so nearly alike, that the most careless reader must detect the resemblance.[2]

The most important defect in the poem, however, was pointed out by Jeffrey in the *Edinburgh Review*: 'The diction of this little poem is among its chief beauties—and yet its greatest blemishes are faults in diction.—It is very English throughout—but often very affectedly negligent, and so extremely familiar as to be absolutely low and vulgar.'[3] Some examples given are 'a scattery light' and 'a clipsome waist'.

In the Preface to the poem, Hunt had echoed Wordsworth's Preface to the *Lyrical Ballads* of 1800: 'The proper language of

[1] *LP*, IV 2s (Sept., 1816), 936.
[2] *Ibid.*, pp. 936–37.
[3] *ER*, XXVI (June, 1816), 491.

poetry is in fact nothing different from that of real life. . . .' And thus the whole controversy in which the reviewers were still engaged at this time with respect to Wordsworth's theories was provoked for the moment in reviews of *The Story of Rimini*. Unfortunately—for those theories—Hunt's poetic practice made only too easy a mark for the opposition. It was so easy, in fact, that the controversy is uninteresting in comparison with the discussion of Wordsworth's theories and practice. John Wilson Croker in the *Quarterly Review* merely quotes from Hunt's Preface, which admits that 'of course mere vulgarisms and fugitive phrases' must be excluded, and comments:

If there be one fault more eminently conspicuous and ridiculous in Mr. Hunt's work than another, it is,—that it is full of *mere vulgarisms* and *fugitive phrases*, and that in every page the language is—not only not *the actual, existing language*, but an ungrammatical, unauthorized, chaotic jargon, such as we believe was never before spoken, much less written.

In what vernacular tongue, for instance, does Mr. Hunt find a lady's waist called *clipsome*, (p. 10.)—or the shout of a mob 'enormous', (p. 9.)—or a fit, *lightsome*;—or that a hero's nose is '*lightsomely* brought down from a forehead of clear-spirited thought', (p. 46.)—or that his back 'drops' *lightsomely in*, (p. 20.).[1]

The question of morality was also raised. The plot of the poem turns on an incestuous liaison; yet it is notable that the reviewers did not object to the mere fact of the incest, although some felt a slight repugnance at the choice of theme. The *British Review* and the *Monthly Review* observed that the story was handled with all possible delicacy; the latter review further remarked, in a sort of inverted defense of the poem, that nevertheless, 'enough occurs to alarm the vigilant and perhaps fastidious supervisors of female reading in the present nice era'.[2] John Gibson Lockhart, on the other hand, in that part of his article on the poem in *Blackwood's* having pretensions to serious criticism, objected strongly to the light-hearted handling of the theme: 'It would fain be the genteel comedy of incest.'[3] And the *Eclectic Review* had its doubts:

We give the Author full credit for the decency of his representations, for the absence of every thing that can disgust, or seduce, or inflame: but still we doubt whether such stories are not likely to do some hurt to the cause

[1] *QR*, XIV (Jan., 1816), 477.
[2] *MR*, LXXX (June, 1816), 138.
[3] *BM*, II (Nov., 1817), 197.

of morality; whether it is possible so to distinguish between the offence and the offender, as to render the one detestable, while the other is represented as so very amiable; and whether indeed this amiableness is not gotten by paring off sundry little portions of the sin; such as selfishness—that unheroic quality, on the part of the seducer; base infidelity on the part of the woman.[1]

The *Literary Panorama* offered a different sort of objection: 'The writer who attributes evils to fate, is not a moral writer.'[2]

Though the reviewers in general were not morally outraged, two hostile reviewers indulged in some vicious personal abuse. The Dedication to Lord Byron was the target; for example, Croker observed:

We never, in so few lines, saw so many clear marks of the vulgar impatience of a low man, conscious and ashamed of his wretched vanity, and labouring, with coarse flippancy, to scramble over the bounds of birth and education, and fidget himself into the *stout-heartedness* of being familiar with a LORD.[3]

The Dedication, like so much of Hunt's writing, is indeed embarrassingly familiar, but such remarks as Croker's are, to say the least, inadmissible.

Faced with the vanity and familiarity of Hunt's dedications and prefaces, and the vulgarity and preciousness of his poetic diction, the reviewers turned more and more to humorous comment. Elements of the comic had been present in some of the earliest reviews of Hunt's works; but it was the totally serious review that was the exception in the criticism of *Foliage* (1818), a collection of original poems (or 'Greenwoods') and translations of classical poetry (or 'Evergreens'). (The *Literary Gazette* remarked on the puns: 'There is much silliness in such doings. . . .')[4] The review in the *Quarterly Review*, possibly by John Wilson Croker, opened on a facetious note:

Winter has at length passed away: spring returns upon us, like a reconciled mistress, with redoubled smiles and graces; and even we poor

[1] *EcR*, V 2s (Apr., 1816), 381.

[2] *LP*, IV 2s (Sept., 1816), 937.

[3] *QR*, XIV (Jan., 1816), 481. Hunt himself later admitted his guilt with regard to this charge. See Leigh Hunt, *Lord Byron and Some of His Contemporaries*, 2d ed. (London, 1828), I, 54–55.

[4] *LG*, Apr. 4, 1818, p. 212.

critics, 'in populous city pent', feel a sort of ungainly inspiration from the starved leaflets and smutty buds in our window-pots; what, then, must be the feelings with which the Arcadian Hunt,

> 'half-stretched on the ground,
> With a *cheek-smoothing air coming taking*
> *him round*,'—p. lxxxi.

must welcome the approach of the 'fair-limbed' goddess to his rural retreat at Hampstead? He owes her indeed especial gratitude; and it would be unpardonable in him to suffer his 'day-sweet' voice, and 'smoothing-on' 'sleeking-up' harp to be mute upon this occasion.[1]

The *Literary Gazette* was a little more serious:

True poetry opens a nobler pursuit than this squirrel-hunting among bushes. . . . Many of our modern writers seem to imagine that poetic genius consists in the fanciful illustration of the most trite objects; that to call a tree leafy, and a bird hoppy, and a cat purry, is genuine nature; that to speak of brutes having '*lamping* eyes', . . . of rills among stones having 'little *whiffling* tones', . . . of 'sleek seas . . .', and similar fooleries, is pure unadulterated inspiration and not silly nonsense. They may be right: we are sceptics.[2]

Fair or not—legitimate critical style or mere abuse—such humorous comment must have been hard to stifle with respect to much of Hunt's verse.

But Hunt's slighting remarks about Christianity, abruptly obtruded into the Preface to the volume, occasioned some serious discussions. The *Eclectic Review* observed that it is very difficult to give oneself to poetry when offensive opinions get in the way—that consequently nothing is more impolitic for a poet than

to obtrude upon his readers those points in his individual character, which relate to differences of religious creed or political opinion, thereby tending to awaken a class of associations opposite to those which it is the business of the poet to excite.

Mr. Leigh Hunt has, in the present volume, been betrayed by his incurable egotism, into this capital error.[3]

[1] *QR*, XVIII (Jan., 1818), 324–25.
[2] *LG*, Apr. 4, 1818, pp. 210–11.
[3] *EcR*, X 2s (Nov., 1818), 484–85.

The *Quarterly* was less circumspect in tendering its objections; Hunt and his associates were branded as Epicureans. And although Hunt is said to avoid in all likelihood the practice which he preaches, he is held accountable for the possible corruption of disciples—those 'who have neither the intellectual pride of a first discovery to compensate them for self-restriction, nor the ardent anxiety for the reputation of an infant sect to support them against their own principle....'[1] This is at least taking Hunt's philosophy more seriously than anyone today would do; but any force the argument might have is invalidated by the vicious, personal attack, which follows, on one of Hunt's associates. It is Shelley, unnamed but unmistakable; and this is in a way ironic; for Shelley is often said to have suffered from his connection with Hunt. In this review, exactly the opposite is the case.

Nevertheless, the *Quarterly Review* in spite of its objections recognized Hunt's merits: 'a general richness of language, and a picturesque imagination; this last indeed, the faculty of placing before us, with considerable warmth of colouring, and truth of drawing, the groups which his fancy assembles, he possesses in an eminent degree....'[2] But perhaps his scenes are a little too picturesque, too like paintings. This last comment, also made in the *Eclectic Review*, is remarkable, inasmuch as the capacity of a poetic scene for graphic transposition was almost always a form of praise used by reviewers.

And yet, the reviewer in the *Quarterly* continues, besides his dangerous philosophy and his stylistic defects Hunt presents, 'though it occurs but seldom, an impurity of both' language and sentiment.

He may amuse or deceive himself with distinctions between voluptuousness and grossness, but will he never learn that things indifferent or innocent in themselves may become dangerous from the weakness or corruption of the recipient? . . . If the thing be practically pernicious, its abstract innocence is but a slight compensation. . . .[3]

What voluptuousness there is occurs mainly in the longest poem of the collection, 'The Nymphs', which received from the reviewers most attention and most praise. The chatty epistles to his friends were not so well received; the *Eclectic Review* briefly described the central problem: 'Mr. Hunt's attempts at playfulness are not graceful.'[4] The *British Critic* likewise summed up the defect in Hunt's

[1] *QR*, XVIII (Jan., 1818), 327.
[2] *Ibid.*, pp. 329–30. [3] *Ibid.*, p. 329. [4] *EcR*, X 2s (Nov., 1818), 492.

exuberant translations: 'We will not call Mr. Hunt a mannerist, but he has the happy faculty of making all the poets whom he translates sing in strains very like his own', often with catastrophic results.[1]

Hunt's next original verse, *Hero and Leander; and Bacchus and Ariadne*, was published in the collected edition of his poetry in 1819. It received only one review, and that one was most strange. P. G. Patmore in the *London Magazine* begins by claiming that Hunt had been badly treated by the reviewers—a claim which can only refer to the reviews of *Foliage*; and yet after indulging in some enthusiastic praise of Hunt's poetry (for example, it is 'all over spots of sunshine'), he defends *The Story of Rimini*, which on the whole had received favorable reviews.[2] Then the strangeness increases as Patmore goes on to enumerate Hunt's stylistic faults, which he maintains are present in that poem as well as in *Hero and Leander*: 'The inveterate mannerism,—the familiarity reaching sometimes to vulgarity,—the recurrence of careless and prosaic lines, and even whole passages,—and the determination to use old and uncommon words in new and uncommon, and sometimes inappropriate and unintelligible senses.' And yet, 'in spite of all this, Hero and Leander in particular, is a very sweet little poem.'[3] It is difficult to understand exactly what caused such inconsistencies and reversals; perhaps the review had been heavily edited or maybe it was just that Patmore was sympathetic in general, becoming confused when faced with Hunt's shortcomings.

Another strange occurrence preceded this: a partly favorable reception in *Blackwood's*, Hunt's most relentless foe, of his annual *Literary Pocket-Book* of 1819 and 1820. The review, possibly by John Wilson, is actually a mixture of attacks on Hunt and Keats, of *Blackwood's* customary cloying, whimsical humor, and of praise and recommendation of the volumes. The *Literary Pocket-Book* of 1821 received a truly favorable review in the *London Magazine*.

Hunt was applauded more loudly by reviewers of his *Amyntas* (1820), a translation of Tasso's *Aminta*. Far and away the best work of Hunt published in the period under study, it received three enthusiastic reviews and only one unfavorable one (in the *Literary Gazette*). The *Monthly Magazine* summed up the general attitude:

> We . . . think this translation superior to any thing of Mr. Hunt's which we have seen: it has more of what is good in his manner, and abounds in

[1] *BC*, X 2s (July, 1818), 95.

[2] *LM*, II (July, 1820), 46.

[3] *Ibid.*, p. 51.

fewer of his faults. It is written, too, quite *con amore*. We perceive our author is in his true element—for the original itself is simple and *affected* throughout.[1]

The reviewer in the *Monthly Review* agreed with this and offered some further observations of a more general nature. He maintained that the 'familiarity and quaintness both of thought and expression', notable in Hunt's previous poems, 'do not arise out of affectation and conceit, as we might first suppose: they are rather the offspring of necessity; of singular and somewhat confined powers both of mind and language. . . .'[2] In fact, 'his success, in the little work before us, is to be chiefly attributed to his want of capacity for greater things'.[3] The reviewer went on to disagree with 'the *dicta* of a modern critic [Hazlitt]: who, with latitudinarian kindness towards the world, maintains that *every thing is poetry*, and that *we are all poets*', by arguing for a more elevated content and form in poetry.[4] But in arguing such points in relation to Hunt's verse, the reviewer has too easy a time and does nothing but set forth his own views, which are not very profound. His remarks on Hunt's merits, after a discussion of his mannerisms, show more thought:

Still this system is not without its use. It has beauties of its own, and of a peculiar kind; and it makes him notice objects that other poets have neglected, and describe them in words which though singular are often happy. There is a freshness of perception about his poetry, and his descriptions of scenery and character are given with ease. The lighter and more transient feelings are likewise under his controul, though the intenseness of the passions is exhibited with little effect.[5]

After years of relatively favorable and for the most part serious criticism, Hunt published *Ultra-Crepidarius* (1823), a satire on William Gifford, editor of the *Quarterly Review*; and the nature of the satire upset the equanimity of the critics. Some of the reviews were favorable and some hostile; but all of them were partisan and therefore uninteresting, except for the extent of their malignity. The reviewer in *Blackwood's*, possibly John Wilson, showed that magazine's usual flair along those lines. In referring to a passage describing the arising of Mercury and Venus from bed, he remarks: 'One

[1] *MM*, L (Aug., 1820), 65.
[2] *MR*, XCIII (Sept., 1820), 18.
[3] *Ibid.*, p. 29. [4] *Ibid.*, p. 19. [5] *Ibid.*, p. 20.

thinks of some aged cur, with mangy back, glazed eyeballs dropping rheum, and with most disconsolate mazzard muzzling among the fleas of his abominable loins, by some accident lying upon the bed where love and beauty are embracing, and embraced.'[1]

Political bias is more obvious in reviews of Hunt's works than in those of most writers dealt with in this study. This should not be surprising in view of Hunt's political career as editor of the *Examiner*. What is remarkable is that the political bias worked largely in Hunt's favor. Periodicals run by Dissenters, such as the *Critical Review* and the *Eclectic Review*, and the liberal journals, such as the *Champion* and the *London Magazine*, gave Hunt critical support, which could scarcely have been offset by the hostility of periodicals of an opposite political persuasion, such as the *British Critic* and the *Literary Gazette*.

And the extent to which the bias affected the literary judgments is, in any case, difficult to determine in view of the unevenness of Hunt's work. His verse is not much esteemed today; there has, in fact, been no edition of his poetry since 1923. It is the incredible unevenness in its quality, I think, that accounts for Hunt's present unpopularity. The poet who could write

> Hallo!—what?—Where? What can it be
> That strikes up so deliciously?
> I never in my life—what? no!
> That little tin-box playing so?

could also pen the following speech of a shepherdess describing her conversion to the ranks of Love (translated from Tasso's *Aminta*):

> I yielded, I confess; and all that conquered me,
> What was it? patience and humility,
> And sighs, and soft laments, and asking pardon.
> Darkness, and one short night, then shewed me more,
> Than the long lustre of a thousand days.

Wordsworth, like Hunt, was dealing with emotions at the point where it becomes difficult to keep from crossing the thin line that separates sentiment from sentimentality—simple emotion from affectation; and Wordsworth sometimes crossed over. Hunt was forever skipping back and forth across that line.

[1] *BM*, XV (Jan., 1824), 87.

Vulgarity, familiarity, bad taste: as terms of critical disapproval these are, I believe, valid and meaningful, although it is not often necessary to call them into use; for the occasion seldom arises when dealing with works of any literary value. When dealing with Hunt's works, some of which are well worth reading, the need for applying such terms is constant. They may at first seem to be mere abuse when encountered in contemporary reviews; but it is difficult to tell a writer he is being vulgar without sounding abusive, just as it is difficult to point out familiarity without resorting to humorous comment. *Blackwood's*, as usual, went too far and indulged in personal abuse, thereby creating a one-sided image of Hunt's contemporary critics. It is significant that the word 'Cockney', applied with such malignity by 'Blackwood's Merry Men', was almost never used by Hunt's reviewers in other periodicals.

John Keats

John Keats' first publication, *Poems* (1817), received a majority of favorable reviews. The volume, in fact, could hardly have had a better reception, considering the evident immaturity of most of the poems and the embarrassingly bad lines and passages. With the exception of *Blackwood's* all reviewers either praised the volume or discovered definite signs of promise. Promise is all that could reasonably have been claimed for the poetry; that more than that was actually claimed is partly attributable to the presence of two close friends on the literary jury: Leigh Hunt was the reviewer for the *Examiner* and John Hamilton Reynolds probably the reviewer for the *Champion*. Another friend, G. F. Mathew, reviewed the volume in the *European Magazine* but was more discriminating in his judgments.[1]

The review in the *Champion* contains such enthusiastic praise (for example, 'The best poets of the day might not blush to own' the volume) that it can scarcely be considered as more than a puff.[2] There is, however, some censure of the meter, the compound epithets, and the over-done descriptions; similar defects are noted by Hunt in the *Examiner*. Both reviewers likewise considered these

[1] J. R. MacGillivray, in his *John Keats, A Bibliography and Reference Guide*, pp. xvii–xviii, suggests that there may have been some bias in Mathew's review.

[2] *Champ*, Mar. 9, 1817, p. 78.

defects to be the result of youth, a verdict arrived at by most of the reviewers. But some of the others included as a contributing factor the deleterious influence of Hunt, to whom the volume is dedicated. In the same month that *Blackwood's* began its series, 'On the Cockney School of Poetry', the *Edinburgh Magazine* observed of Keats:

He seems to have formed his poetical predilections in exactly the same direction as Mr. Hunt; and to write, from personal choice, as well as emulation, at all times, in that strain which can be most recommended to the favour of the general readers of poetry, only by the critical ingenuity and peculiar refinements of Mr. Hazlitt. That style is vivacious, smart, witty, changeful, sparkling, and learned—full of bright points and flashy expressions that strike and even seem to please by a sudden boldness of novelty,—rather abounding in familiarities of conception and oddnesses of manner which shew ingenuity, even though they be perverse, or common, or contemptuous. The writers themselves seem to be persons of considerable taste, and of comfortable pretensions, who really appear as much alive to the socialities and sensual enjoyments of life, as to the contemplative beauties of nature. In addition to their familiarity, though, —they appear to be too full of conceits and sparkling points, ever to excite any thing more than a cold approbation at the long-run—and too fond, even in their favourite descriptions of nature, of a reference to the factitious resemblances of society, ever to touch the heart. Their verse is straggling and uneven, without the lengthened flow of blank verse, or the pointed connection of couplets. They aim laudably enough at force and freshness, but are not so careful of the inlets of vulgarity, nor so self-denying to the temptations of indolence, as to make their force a merit.[1]

Finally, they should be more aware of the 'appalling doom which awaits the faults of mannerism or the ambition of a sickly refinement'. And as for the author under review, 'If Mr. Keats does not forthwith cast off the uncleanness of this school, he will never make his way to the truest strain of poetry in which, taking him by himself, it appears he might succeed.' On the following page of the review, part of the reason for the warning becomes obvious to anyone familiar with Hunt's verse: ' "Leafy luxury", "jaunty streams", "lawny slope", "the moonbeamy air", "a sun-beamy tale"; these, if not namby-pamby, are, at least, the "holiday and lady terms" of those poor affected creatures who write verse "in spite of nature and their stars".'[2]

[1] *EdM*, I 2s (Oct., 1817), 256.

[2] *Ibid.*, p. 257.

But besides stylistic matters, some fundamental discussions about literature were occasioned by the volume. The content of poetry was one of these, as well it might be in view of the scarcity of ideas at work in the verse. Hunt in the *Examiner* put forward a view, seldom found in the criticism of the period but common later in the century, of art-for-art's-sake in his general remarks on Keats: 'here is a young poet giving himself up to his own impressions, and revelling in real poetry for its' [*sic*] own sake'.[1] Josiah Conder in the *Eclectic Review* assumed a position exactly the reverse. After a long discussion of the low intellectual content of the poetry of the age (Wordsworth's poetry was excepted), he asks: 'On what ground, then, does the notion rest, that poetry is a something so sublime, or that so inherent a charm resides in words and syllables arranged in the form of verse, that the value of the composition is in any degree independent of the meaning which links together the sentences?'[2] This is not, it should be noted, a plea for didactic poetry, but rather for a higher estimation of the intellectual content of poetry.

Another issue raised by reviewers concerned Keats' attack on Augustan verse in 'Sleep and Poetry'. John Gibson Lockhart, in what amounts largely to a scurrilous review in *Blackwood's*, nevertheless gave the best answer to this very real impertinence: 'Begging these gentlemens' [*sic*] pardon, although Pope was not a poet of the same high order with some who are now living, yet, to deny his genius, is just about as absurd as to dispute that of Wordsworth, or to believe in that of Hunt.'[3]

Keats' second publication, *Endymion* (1818), also met with a generally favorable reception, and the quarterlies were now involved. Only the reviewer in the *British Critic*, John Wilson Croker in the *Quarterly Review*, and John Gibson Lockhart in *Blackwood's* were hostile; against these were aligned three weeklies, two monthly magazines, and the *Edinburgh Review*. This generally favorable reception for the second volume of a poet long thought by some to have been sent to an early grave by his critics is significant, yet it is by no means true that the friendly reviewers had a monopoly of critical justice on their side. *Endymion* shows improvement over the *Poems* of 1817, but is much closer in poetic merit to that volume than to the one that followed. It is even apparent, when one reads the reviews in the order of their appearance, that the later favorable

[1] *Exam*, July 6, 1817, p. 428.

[2] *EcR*, VIII 2s (Sept., 1817), 267–68.

[3] *BM*, III (Aug. 1818), 520.

reviews of the volume were to some extent a reaction against the hostile criticisms.

The first three reviews of the poem (in May and early June) assumed fairly extreme positions and are therefore not so interesting as the others. The *Literary Journal* did not go so far as the other two, but it did conclude by giving the volume 'most unqualified approbation'.[1] The *British Critic* linked Keats with Hunt and dismissed them both, after a bit of whimsical censure of the diction and story, such as in the following excerpt from its outline of the plot:

> After this Endymion sets out in search of the moon, and meets with a good-natured young woman, whose calling may be easily guessed by the present she offers to make him, of 'all her clear-eyed fish, golden or rainbow-sided, or purplish, vermilion-tail'd, or finn'd with silv'ry gauze', but he stands on 'the pebble bead of doubt', and runs 'into the fearful deep to hide his head from the clear moon, (not very wise when he is in pursuit of her,) the trees, and coming madness. . . .'[2]

This reviewer also called Keats' harmless adolescent eroticism the 'gross slang of voluptuousness'.[3] An enthusiastic review in the *Champion*, possibly by J. H. Reynolds, went to the opposite extreme from the *British Critic* by attempting to forestall censure of the poem by explaining why it was not likely to be popular.

The real onslaught began two months later in an article in the August issue of *Blackwood's* by J. G. Lockhart. In a combined critique of the *Poems* of 1817 and *Endymion*—not strictly a review but the fourth number of 'On the Cockney School of Poetry'—Lockhart treats Keats with less scurrility but with scarcely more respect than Hunt had received in previous numbers of the series. *Endymion* is said to be nothing more than 'calm, settled, imperturbable drivelling idiocy . . .' and Keats himself is said to be 'a still smaller poet' than Hunt and 'only a boy of pretty abilities, which he has done every thing in his power to spoil'.[4] And yet, among all the supercilious remarks, there is some legitimate criticism, as in the italicization of the following ridiculous lines (III, 717–19):

> *O fountain'd hill! Old Homer's Helicon!*
> *That thou wouldst spout a little streamlet o'er*
> *These sorry pages. . . .*

[1] *LJGM*, May 24, 1818, p. 131.
[2] *BC*, IX 2s (June, 1818), 651.
[3] *Ibid.*, p. 652.
[4] *BM*, III (Aug., 1818), 519, 522.

Keats was also censured in *Blackwood's* for an anti-monarchical passage at the beginning of Book III.

The review by John Wilson Croker in the *Quarterly Review* the following month is the most famous review in the history of periodical criticism; it was the one which was held by many then and later to have killed John Keats. The review opens with the statement that it was impossible to get beyond Book I, and much is often made of this in later commentaries. Croker, however, was an industrious man and a thorough scholar, so I think it not unlikely that the statement is merely a rhetorical flourish used for wit and emphasis. In any case, Croker's censure of the obscurity, rhymes, and diction in Book I are valid criticisms of the poem as a whole.

Croker goes on to give Keats some praise: he has 'powers of language, rays of fancy, and gleams of genius'; and later Croker says that he would have spared Keats the pain of censure 'if we had not observed in him a certain degree of talent which deserves to be put in the right way. . . .'[1] This praise may seem niggardly, unless one realizes that almost all the poems for which Keats has always been esteemed had not yet been published.

And then there are the very real flaws in *Endymion*, flaws which Croker exposed with more skill than any other reviewer. The construction of the couplets is first dealt with:

> He seems to us to write a line at random, and then he follows not the thought excited by this line, but that suggested by the *rhyme* with which it concludes. There is hardly a complete couplet inclosing a complete idea in the whole book. He wanders from one subject to another, from the association, not of ideas but of sounds. . . .

As an example, lines 13–21 are quoted:

> 'Such the sun, the moon,
> Trees old and young, sprouting a shady boon
> For simple sheep; and such are daffodils
> With the green world they live in; and clear rills
> That for themselves a cooling covert make
> 'Gainst the hot season; the mid forest brake,
> Rich with a sprinkling of fair musk-rose blooms:
> And such too is the grandeur of the dooms
> We have imagined for the mighty dead; &c. &c.'—pp. 3, 4.

[1] *QR*, XIX (Apr., 1818), 204, 205.

Here it is clear that the word, and not the idea, *moon* produces the simple sheep and their shady *boon*, and that 'the *dooms* of the mighty dead' would never have intruded themselves but for the '*fair musk-rose blooms*'.[1]

Then the versification comes under fire. Seven short examples are given, the longest of which is (I, 965–69):

Endymion! the cave is secreter
Than the isle of Delos. Echo hence shall stir
No sighs but sigh-warm kisses, or light noise
Of thy combing hand, the while it travelling cloys
And trembles through my labyrinthine hair.

Finally, the Huntian diction of the poem is belabored. Some examples are 'turtles passion their voices', the 'honey-feel of bliss', the 'night up-took', 'pantingly', 'refreshfully'.

These criticisms are all valid and are nowadays usually admitted to be so; but Croker was, even at the time and often since, taken to task for giving only one side of the case. This objection is unanswerable: Croker himself found signs of talent and even of genius, and he should have given some notice to them. As it was, the criticism was all too easy and unjust, and smacks of partisan bias. Moreover, the tone of the review is more condescending than necessary, although it is worth remembering that the reviewers as a group were not notable for their sensitivity toward the feelings of writers.

In fact, after reading Lockhart's offensive review, it is difficult to determine why Croker's criticism in the *Quarterly Review* should have been selected instead as the prime cause of Keats' early demise. It is difficult, that is, until one recalls that Shelley, who was largely responsible for creating the myth in his Preface to *Adonais*, had been badly treated by the *Quarterly Review* and well treated by *Blackwood's*.

The remainder of the criticisms of *Endymion* take their cue from the *Quarterly Review*—they all refer disparagingly to Croker's review either directly or by implication, and are all favorable. The condensed reprint in the *Examiner* of J. H. Reynolds' review (published originally in a provincial journal) was enthusiastically favorable to Keats, but unfortunately at the expense of all other contemporary poets. Reynolds also accuses the *Quarterly Review* of

[1] *Ibid.*, p. 206.

political bias in its review. P. G. Patmore's favorable review in the *London Magazine*, on the other hand, praised the *Quarterly Review* while it censured the strictness and injustice of Croker's article. Patmore's own description of *Endymion* is ecstatic, to say the least of it:

It is not *a poem* at all. It is an ecstatic dream of poetry—a flush—a fever—a burning light—an involuntary out-pouring of the spirit of poetry—that will not be controuled. Its movements are the starts and boundings of the young horse before it has felt the bit—the first flights of the young bird. . . . It is the wanderings of the butterfly. . . . It is the May-day of poetry. . . . It is the skylark's hymn to the day-break. . . .[1]

After reading this lyrical outburst, no one is likely to be surprised by the following remarks:

Poetical criticism is, for the most part, a very superfluous and impertinent business; and is to be tolerated at all only when it is written in an unfeigned spirit of admiration and humility. We must therefore do ourselves the justice to disclaim, for once, any intention of writing a regular critique in the present instance. Criticism, like every thing else, is very well in its place; but, like every thing else, it does not always know where that is. Certainly a poet, properly so called, is beyond its jurisdiction;—for *good* and *bad*, when applied to poetry, are words without a meaning. One might as well talk of good and bad virtue. That which *is* poetry must be good. It may differ in kind and in degree, and therefore it may differ in value; but if it *be* poetry, it is a thing about which criticism has no concern, any more than it has with other of the highest productions of Fine Art. . . . These things were given to the world for something better than to be written and talked about. . . .[2]

A dislike of impertinent criticism, shared, I imagine, by everyone, should not obscure the confusion of thought here—the redefinition, for instance, of *poetry* as *good poetry* (and how does one determine what '*is* poetry' without judging it?) in the process of the argument. It is amusing, too, seeing Patmore subsequently in the review censure the plot, the thoughts, and the diction of the poem.

Francis Jeffrey's criticism of *Endymion* in the *Edinburgh Review* was contained in a joint review of that poem and Keats' third volume. Like the others, Jeffrey takes a swipe at Croker's article;

[1] *LM*, I (Apr., 1820), 381. [2] *Ibid.*

although he does not go so far as to mention the *Quarterly Review*, the following remarks are unmistakably aimed in that direction:

There is no work [other than *Endymion*], accordingly, from which a malicious critic could cull more matter for ridicule, or select more obscure, unnatural, or absurd passages. But we do not take *that* to be our office;—and just beg leave, on the contrary, to say, that any one who, on this account, would represent the whole poem as despicable, must either have no notion of poetry, or no regard to truth.[1]

Then, after having pointed out the same defects as had Croker, Jeffrey, apparently to reinforce the above pronouncement, goes on to recommend the 'pure poetry', which he says is more obvious because of those defects. In an obscure style uncharacteristic of Jeffrey and not unlike the sort of hazy discussion by Patmore, he recommends Keats' use of what sounds vaguely like T. S. Eliot's 'objective correlative': the 'fine feeling expressed of those mysterious relations by which visible external things are assimilated with inward thoughts and emotions, and become the images and exponents of all passions and affections'.[2] Further evidence of a certain lack of sincerity in Jeffrey's review is his attentiveness to *Endymion*—the poem attacked by the *Quarterly Review*. Nor does it say much for his judgment (or, it may be, his critical integrity) that Jeffrey, with the much greater poems of the later volume before him, pronounced *Endymion* 'by much the most considerable of his poems'.[3]

The last review of *Endymion*, in the *Edinburgh Magazine*, was likewise published in 1820, late enough to include a review of Keats' last volume. Once more the *Quarterly Review* article is deprecated (under the phrase 'some of the London critics'), and like Jeffrey, the reviewer seems to prefer *Endymion* to the later volume: 'Perhaps the "Endymion", though it contains more positive faults than the last book, ("Lamia",) is more completely in Mr. Keats's own style; and we think that it contains, at least, as many beauties.'[4] And, as occurs in the two previous reviews of *Endymion*, the reviewer makes a statement, which, though neither so extreme as Patmore's nor so vague as Jeffrey's, is nonetheless worth noting because of the others:

[1] *ER*, XXXIV (Aug., 1820), 205.
[2] *Ibid.*, p. 206. [3] *Ibid.*, p. 204.
[4] *EdM*, VII 2s (Aug., 1820), 108.

'after all, poetry is a matter of feeling rather than of argument.' It is as if Keats' defenders, facing on the one side the unfair review in the *Quarterly* which they wished to counteract, and on the other Keats' obvious poetic failings, felt it necessary to resort to obscurantism and equivocation. But there may well be other forces at work: by the end of the century, it is worth recalling, Keats was to be considered a prime example of the 'pure poet'.

In July, 1820, Keats' last volume was published, *Lamia, Isabella, The Eve of St. Agnes, and Other Poems*. Reviewed by a large number of periodicals (the two most obvious absentees being *Blackwood's* and the *Quarterly Review*), it was well received by ten journals, one of which, the *British Critic*, made the rare gesture of apologizing for its bad review of *Endymion*. Only three were hostile: the *Guardian*, the *Eclectic Review*, which was for some reason positively belligerent, and Gold's *London Magazine*, which was antagonistic probably in order to show up Baldwin's *London Magazine*, its rival. The poems were praised for deep thought, originality, imagination, versification, and diction. Although there is little recognition of the greatness which Keats was later acknowledged to possess, there is sufficient praise of individual poems to make it clear that the reviewers were not blind to his achievements.

Probably because of limitations of space, there is not much detailed criticism of any one poem. Most of the criticism is devoted to the opening tales, because their length, use of their titles in the title of the volume, and their placement at the front of the book seem to ask for most attention. As a consequence the remarks on the odes are disappointingly slight. The 'Ode on a Grecian Urn', for example, is mentioned only three times in the reviews, once as the best of the shorter poems and twice disparagingly—the *Monthly Review* considered the idea of 'unheard melodies' being sweeter as an unhappy conceit. 'To Autumn' received three favorable comments; the *Monthly Review* observed that it brings 'the reality of nature more before our eyes than almost any description that we remember'.[1] The 'Ode to a Nightingale' also received several favorable comments, including the judgment in the *Edinburgh Magazine* that it was the best of all the poems. 'We have read this ode over and over again,' the reviewer states, 'and every time with increased delight.'[2] Leigh Hunt in the *Indicator* thought the poem

[1] *MR*, XCII (July, 1820), 309.
[2] *EdM*, VII 2s (Oct., 1820), 315.

offered Keats imaginary relief: 'A poet finds refreshment in his imaginary wine, as other men do in their real. . . .'[1]

Of the longer poems, 'The Eve of St. Agnes' received the fewest comments. Charles Lamb in his review in the *Examiner* (quoted from the daily *New Times*) praises 'the almost Chaucer-like painting, with which this poet illumines every subject he touches. We have scarcely any thing like it in modern description.'[2] Leigh Hunt in the *Indicator* praised the description of Madeline preparing for bed as 'remarkable for its union of extreme richness and good taste. . . . The passage affords a striking specimen of the sudden and strong maturity of the author's genius. When he wrote Endymion he could not have resisted doing too much. To the description before us, it would be a great injury either to add or diminish.'[3] The *New Monthly Magazine* found 'a soft religious light . . . shed over the whole story'.[4] There was enthusiastic praise in several other reviews; only the *British Critic* thought there was not 'much to admire' in the poem.[5]

'Hyperion' was the most popular of the longer poems with the reviewers. The *Monthly Review* considered it 'decidedly the best of Mr. Keats's productions'; the *Monthly Magazine* thought it 'the most powerful'; and John Scott in the *London Magazine* termed it 'one of the most extraordinary creations of any modern imagination'.[6] The opening of the poem in particular was praised highly, as was the description of Hyperion's palace and the abode of the Titans. Leigh Hunt in the *Indicator*, however, objected to the presentation of Apollo at the end of the fragment: 'It strikes us that there is something too effeminate and human in the way in which Apollo receives the exaltation which his wisdom is giving him. He weeps and wonders somewhat too fondly; but his powers gather nobly on him as he proceeds.'[7]

Hunt was also one of the three reviewers to recommend that the fragment be left incomplete. He based his advice on the problem of rendering the superhuman speech of the gods: 'A story which involves passion, almost of necessity involves speech; and though we may well enough describe beings greater than ourselves by comparison, unfortunately we cannot make them speak by comparison.'[8]

[1] *Indic*, Aug. 9, 1820, p. 345.
[2] *Exam.*, July 30, 1820, p. 494.
[3] *Indic*, Aug. 2, 1820, pp. 343–44.
[4] *NMM*, XIV (Sept., 1820), 247.
[5] *BC*, XIV 2s (Sept., 1820), 261.
[6] *MR*, XCII (July, 1820), 306; *MM*, L (Sept., 1820), 166; *LM*, II (Sept. 1820), 319.
[7] *Indic*, Aug. 9, 1820, p. 350.
[8] *Ibid.*, p. 351.

Jeffrey, in the *Edinburgh Review*, had a different reason for suggesting that the poem be laid aside: 'though there are passages of some force and grandeur, it is sufficiently obvious, from the specimen before us, that the subject is too far removed from all the sources of human interest, to be successfully treated by any modern author'.[1] The *British Critic* thought 'Hyperion' contained 'some very beautiful poetry, although the greater part of it appears not to have been executed with much success', and should in any case be left unfinished; 'for it is plainly projected upon principles that would infallibly lead to failure, even supposing the subject were not, which we think it is, somewhat above the pitch of Mr. Keats's peculiar genius, which lies altogether in the region of fancy and description'.[2]

Adverse criticism was reserved mainly for the first two poems in the volume, 'Lamia' and 'Isabella'. This is as it should be; for as several reviewers remarked, 'Lamia' is in the style of *Endymion*, and though there is considerable improvement in the later poem, yet there are vestiges of Keats' earlier shortcomings in 'Lamia', as well as in 'Isabella' and even in others of the poems. The *British Critic* described briefly the sort of faults encountered:

We hear [in 'Lamia'] of 'a clear pool, wherein she *passioned*, to see herself escaped'. P. 14. And likewise of this same person's pacing about 'in a pale contented sort of discontent'. P. 35. In another poem ['Isabella'], we have the following exquisite nonsense to describe a kiss:

> 'So said, his erewhile timid lips grew bold,
> And *poesied* with her's in *dewy rhyme*.' P. 53.

Thus likewise we hear of *pleasuring* a thing, and *mirroring* a thing; of doing a thing *fearingly* and *fairily*; of *leafits*; of walking '*silken* hush'd and *chaste*. . . .'[3]

[1] *ER*, XXXIV (Aug., 1820), 213.

[2] *BC*, XIV 2s (Sept., 1820), 261.

[3] *Ibid.*, p. 264. The presence of *mirroring* in the list indicates that sometimes Keats' coinages became part of the language. The last example in the quotation occurs in stanza XXI of 'The Eve of St. Agnes':

> Safe at last
> Through many a dusky gallery, they gain
> The Maiden's chamber, silken, hush'd and chaste. . . .

The reviewer obviously mistook the last three words to be adverbs modifying the verb *gain*, rather than adjectives modifying the noun *chamber*. The construction of the passage is, however, sufficiently confused (e.g., 'Safe at last . . . they gain') to save the reviewer from the charge of gross stupidity.

John Scott in the *London Magazine* objected to several of Keats' images. One of these (from 'Isabella') was 'these men of cruel clay / Cut Mercy with a sharp knife to the bone.' Scott commented, '. . . We cannot contemplate the *skeleton* of mercy', and this objection, if taken to mean that the personification is too particularized, seems to me valid. He likewise objected to the periphrasis for *breasts* in the same poem, 'Those dainties made to still an infant's cries', calling it 'indeed a very round about way of expression'. In the 'Ode to a Nightingale', Scott took issue with the epithet 'Leaden-eyed' as applied 'to despair, considered as a quality or sentiment'. 'Were it a personification of despair', he commented, 'the compound would be finely applied, as, under the actual circumstances, it is erroneously so.'[1] This objection seems to me valid. Gold's *London Magazine* began its review by ridiculing the extravagant praise given to *Endymion* by its rival, Baldwin's *London Magazine*, thus suggesting a motive for its own elaborate attack on the diction and sense of 'Lamia' and 'Isabella' which followed. Much of the adverse comment is niggling or obtuse or unintelligible, but not all of it. In 'Lamia', for instance, the following lines are ridiculed (italics added by the reviewer):

> So Hermes thought, and a celestial heat
> Burnt from his winged heels to *either ear*.

The clarity of the lines concerning the invisibility of the nymph in the opening scene, 'Pale grew her immortality, for woe / Of all these lovers', is quite rightly, I believe, questioned. Another line in Part II, 'A deadly silence step by step increased', was also censured for misuse of words. Many objectionable compound words were italicized in passages quoted by the reviewer, such as those in the lines, 'Each, as he did please / Might *fancy-fit* his brows, *silk-pillow'd* at his ease.'

And yet, while most reviewers had objections of this sort, some were more tolerant. The *Monthly Review* recognized the courage required in striking out from the beaten paths of poetic diction, as well as the dangers of getting lost—

> Yet, even should this be partially the case, the wild and beautiful scenery, which such an excursion is frequently the means of developing, is a fair

[1] *LM*, II (Sept., 1820), 321.

remuneration for the inequalities and obstructions which he may chance to experience on his ramble. We must add that only by attempts like these can we discover the path of true excellence; and that, in checking such efforts by illiberal and ill-timed discouragement, we shut out the prospect of all improvement. Innovations of every kind, more especially in matters of taste, are at first beheld with dislike and jealousy, and it is only by time and usage that we can appreciate their claims to adoption.[1]

Keats' poetry, he continued, requires thought;

and on this very account, which is perhaps the surest proof of its merit, we are afraid that it will be slighted. Unfortunately, Mr. Keats may blame himself for much of this neglect; since he might have conceded something to established taste, or (if he will) established prejudice, without derogating from his own originality of thought and spirit. . . . [Instead,] he is continually shocking our ideas of poetical decorum, at the very time when we are acknowledging the hand of genius. In thus boldly running counter to old opinions, however, we cannot conceive that Mr. Keats merits either contempt or ridicule; the weapons which are too frequently employed when liberal discussion and argument would be unsuccessful. At all events, let him not be pre-judged without a candid examination of his claims.[2]

John Scott in the *London Magazine* likewise thought Keats asked for some of the hostility he met with. After attacking the *Quarterly Review* article on *Endymion* and Croker by name, Scott, apparently alluding mainly to *Endymion*, admitted:

The author [Keats] provokes opposition . . . : not unfrequently he even suggests angry censure. We cannot help applying the word *insolent*, in a literary sense, to some instances of his neglectfulness, to the random swagger of occasional expressions, to the bravado style of many of his sentiments. But, coupling these great faults with his still greater poetical merits, what a fine, what an interesting subject did he offer for perspicacious, honourable criticism![3]

There were, however, other critical remarks on 'Lamia' and 'Isabella'. The *Monthly Magazine* and the *Eclectic Review* considered 'Lamia' the best of the tales; and though the other reviewers disagreed, there were several instances of favorable comment on parti-

[1] *MR*, XCII (July, 1820), 305.
[2] *Ibid.*, pp. 305–6.
[3] *LM*, II (Sept., 1820), 320–21.

cular passages. Lamb, in the *Examiner* reprint, praised the expression 'the star of Lethe' (I, 81) applied to Hermes: 'one of those prodigal phrases which Mr. Keats abounds in, which are each a poem in a word, and which in this instance lays open to us at once, like a picture, all the dim regions and their inhabitants, and the sudden coming of a celestial among them. . . .'[1] Leigh Hunt in the *Indicator* quoted lines 47–63 of Book I, which describe Lamia in her serpent form, and observed:

The admiration, pity, and horror, to be excited by humanity in a brute shape, were never perhaps called upon by a greater mixture of beauty and deformity than in the picture of this creature. Our pity and suspicions are begged by the first word [*She*]: the profuse and vital beauties with which she is covered seem proportioned to her misery and natural rights; and lest we should lose sight of them in this gorgeousness, the 'woman's mouth' fills us at once with shuddering and compassion.[2]

'Isabella' received special praise for simplicity of pathos and diction. The exhuming of Lorenzo was several times praised in this regard, and more than one reviewer praised the anticipatory epithet 'murdered', as applied to Lorenzo en route to his assassination. Leigh Hunt in the *Indicator* chose a later passage as a model of simple diction: 'The passage about the tone of her voice,—the poor lost-witted coaxing,—the "chuckle", in which she asks after her Pilgrim and her Basil,—is as true and touching an instance of the effect of a happy familiar word, as any in all poetry.'[3] The *Monthly Review*, on the other hand, found evidence to support its thesis of the necessary elevation of poetry above 'the triteness of every-day life':

Why were they proud? again we ask aloud,
Why in the name of Glory were they proud?[4]

But the five stanzas devoted to the abuse of Isabella's brothers brought about the most adverse criticism of the poem. John Scott in the *London Magazine* was most severe: 'Mr. Keats's sensibility is diseased in this respect—that his spirit is impregnated with a flippant impatience, (irritated and justified by a false philosophy) of the great phenomena of society, and the varieties of human nature, which

[1] *Exam*, July 30, 1820, p. 495.
[2] *Indic*, Aug. 2, 1820, p. 338.
[3] *Ibid.*, p. 343.
[4] *MR*, XCII (July, 1820), 308–9.

hurts his poetry quite as much as it corrupts his sentiments. . . .' And (more to the literary point) Keats thus 'repels sympathy by the introduction of caricature. . . .'[1]

J. R. MacGillivray, a recent commentator who has produced the only examination so far which deals with all of the reviews of Keats, found two things wrong with the reviews of Keats' last volume: the censure of his diction and of his use of Greek mythology. MacGillivray's charge against Keats' reviewers was 'that the opulent language of *Hyperion*, *The Eve of St. Agnes*, and the odes was generally thought to be obscure, extravagant, or merely quaint, and that both the choice and the treatment of mythological themes were regretted even by friendly and well-intentioned reviewers of the last volume'.[2] The first part of this statement concerning the censure of the language in the poems mentioned is simply incorrect, if it is taken to mean that direct censure of the kind in question was made against those specific poems. Later on, MacGillivray makes the point that such censure was made 'against the volume as a whole'.[3] In four of the reviews (in the *Eclectic*, the *Literary Chronicle*, the *Monthly Magazine*, and the *London Magazine*), such general censure was delivered, but even in these, the examples of bad diction are taken mostly from the first two tales. The censure of the diction by the *Edinburgh Review* and the *Monthly Review* is vaguely applied and could easily refer mainly to *Endymion*, which the *Edinburgh Review* was reviewing jointly with the later volume, and with which the *Monthly Review* was also concerned since it had not reviewed the earlier poem when published. The two volumes, after all, were published only two years apart. Other reviewers censured the diction only in the tales, where it is in fact often defective; some reviewers did not censure Keats' diction at all.

As for the second objection to the reviews on the question of mythology, there are to begin with few remarks made about Keats' use of mythology. Jeffrey's praise in the *Edinburgh Review* MacGillivray quotes as an exception; but he overlooks similar praise in the *New Monthly Magazine*. On the negative side, the *Monthly Review* remarked that 'though boldly and skilfully sketched, his delineations of the immortals give a faint idea of the nature which the poets of Greece attributed to them'.[4] As a mere statement this is correct;

[1] *LM*, II (Sept., 1820), 316–17.
[2] MacGillivray, p. xii.
[3] *Ibid.*, p. xxviii.
[4] *MR*, XCII (July, 1820), 306.

and even if a disparagement (it is not quite clear in the context), it may refer to *Endymion*, which the reviewer had been discussing. In any event, he goes on to praise 'Hyperion'. There is also a brief comment in Gold's *London Magazine* that Keats' 'knowledge of Greek and mythology seems to mystify him on every occasion', but this occurs in an attempt at total demolition of Keats, whom Gold's rival, Baldwin's *London Magazine*, had praised.[1] The only sustained objection to Keats' use of mythology occurred in the *Eclectic Review* whose reviewer censured *Endymion* and 'Hyperion' for a too realistic, direct presentation of classical deities. Thus, two reviewers praised Keats' 'choice and treatment of classical themes', two or three disparaged them, and eight made no comment on the matter.

Two further comments of MacGillivray are worth quoting as a way of discussing the reviews of Keats' final volume. At one point he remarks, 'No one seems to have found anything astonishing in Keats' poetical development in the three years between the first volume and the third. . . .'[2] As a statement of fact, this remark is erroneous, for Leigh Hunt in the *Indicator* mentioned 'the sudden and strong maturity of the author's genius', and the *New Monthly Magazine* expressed 'wonder at the gigantic stride which he has taken. . . .'[3] The other reviewers, it is true, did not make much of Keats' phenomenally rapid growth as a poet, probably because of the defects remaining in the tales, although most of them did notice a definite improvement. Another of MacGillivray's comments—'Many recognized his rich promise, none his achievement, the gathered harvest of "full ripen'd grain" '—is misleading, inasmuch as the reviewers were aware, as has been shown, of a definite achievement in some of the best poems.[4] As for the 'harvest of "full ripen'd grain" ', why the reviewers should have recognized complete fruition in a poet as young as Keats is not at all clear.

All three of Keats' publications received preponderantly favorable reviews. In fact, at the risk of sounding merely controversial, I should say that the majority of Keats' reviewers, if they sinned at all in their criticism, sinned in the direction of too indulgent, too favorable judgments. Many of his reviewers, such as J. H. Reynolds and Leigh Hunt, were Keats' friends; and the same partisan political

[1] Gold's *LM*, II (Aug., 1820), 161.
[2] MacGillivray, p. xxviii.
[3] *Indic.* Aug. 2, 1820, p. 344; *NMM*, XIV (Sept., 1820), 248.
[4] MacGillivray, p. xxxi.

bias which was responsible at least in part for the hostile reviews in *Blackwood's* and the *Quarterly Review* occasioned other favorable reviews in a process of reaction, even at the cost of critical vagueness. The *Poems* of 1817 and *Endymion* received some enthusiastic praise which they did not deserve; even some of the favorable reviews of the final volume are not as discerning as they might have been. Keats, in fact, had little to complain of; he enjoyed the best critical reception accorded any poet of the period, a much better reception than was given to Wordsworth, who was, I believe, a much greater poet.

William Hazlitt

William Hazlitt, the only writer included in this study whose works are confined to prose, produced mainly familiar essays and literary criticism. Probably because prose in these forms allows for more personal expression than does poetry and because Hazlitt had an assertive personality which took advantage of such an outlet for his highly individualized beliefs and prejudices, his works were much more provocative than were Hunt's, perhaps more than any other writer in the period.

As a controversial thinker, Hazlitt fared better than might have been anticipated. His early works, which have been largely forgotten, were likewise all but overlooked when published and met only a scattered, mixed reception. His later, more important works, however, received their fair proportion of attention. *The Round Table* (1817), the *Lectures on the English Poets* (1818), and *Political Essays* (1819) encountered predominantly unfavorable criticism, but the verdicts were by no means unanimously hostile. *A View of the English Stage* (1818) and *Liber Amoris* (1823), were, however, roundly damned. The *Characters of Shakespear's Plays* (1817), the *Lectures Chiefly on the Dramatic Literature of the Age of Elizabeth* (1820), *Table Talk* (1821–22), and *Characteristics* (1823), on the other hand, enjoyed generally favorable receptions. The grounds on which these judgments were rendered were, as we shall see, almost as numerous as the works themselves.

'Personality' in the reviewing of the period often ran high. Fortunately, however, Hazlitt was a contributor to a number of the reviewing periodicals, including the *Edinburgh Review*, the *Examiner*, the *Champion*, the *Edinburgh Magazine*, and Baldwin's *London Maga-*

zine; as such he had personal prejudice working in his favor. Sometimes, in fact, the friendly critics got out of hand; J. H. Reynolds' remarks in the *Champion* on the *Characters of Shakespear's Plays*, for instance, are scarcely less lyrical than the essay in question: 'The essay on *Romeo and Juliet* is, to our feelings, the best in the volume. The soul of passion is infused into it; and every sentence weighs on the heart like a feeling. The youth of lovers is shed over it. It shakes one like a realized dream of Hope'.[1]

But scurrility was much more the order of the day. The reviewer of *The Round Table* in the *New Monthly Magazine* could have competed successfully with *Blackwood's* in a contest of colorful invective. He suggested that the volume should have been entitled 'the Dunghill', for the essays 'raked together have been gathered from the common sewer of a weekly paper called the Examiner . . .; and they who after that information can have any relish for the feculent garbage of blasphemy and scurrility, may sit down at the Round Table, and enjoy their meal with the same appetite as the negroes in the West Indies eat dirt and filth.'[2] The autobiographical *Liber Amoris*, which can now be read as the tragic account of a man in love with a strumpet against his will and reason, quite understandably amazed Hazlitt's contemporaries and was the occasion of the worst abuse encountered by Hazlitt, or 'Pyg', as he was called by several reviewers playing on the subtitle ('the New Pygmalion').

And yet, in spite of all the 'personality' which Hazlitt encountered, he had little room for complaint, since not only was he a reviewer himself, dealing out just such anonymous attacks (especially on the Lakers), but he abused those poets, as well as any number of politicians and other important figures, throughout his works. This aspect of his writings was often commented upon. In reference to Hazlitt's indignant *Letter to William Gifford*, the reviewer (possibly William Gifford himself) of the *Political Essays* in the *Quarterly Review* calmly commented on Hazlitt's apparent

> belief that it is his prerogative to abuse whom he will, and the privilege of all the world to submit in silence: he lays claim to an autocracy of malediction. . . . There are few characters in England of distinguished eminence whom he has not slandered; and yet he is thrown into a transport of fury

[1] *Champ*, July 26, 1817, p. 237.
[2] *NMM*, VII (July, 1817), 540.

if he is told that he is wrong; if he is reasoned with, laughed at, or reminded of what he is doing and of what he is.[1]

The cause of most of the personal abuse of Hazlitt by his reviewers was, of course, political; but it was not just that Hazlitt was known to be a radical who wrote for the *Examiner* and other liberal periodicals; he was constantly obtruding his political opinions into his works. In the *Political Essays*, such opinions would naturally hold a prominent place, but Hazlitt brought them into his otherwise non-political essays and into his literary criticism, as in his treatment of *Henry VIII* and *Coriolanus*, where monarchy and the nobility are attacked in gross generalizations. As the reviewer (probably T. N. Talfourd) of the *Lectures Chiefly on the Dramatic Literature* in the *Edinburgh Review* put it:

If Mr. Hazlitt has not generally met with impartial justice from his contemporaries, we must say that he has himself partly to blame. Some of the attacks of which he has been the object, have no doubt been purely brutal and malignant; but others have, in a great measure, arisen from feelings of which he has himself set the example. His seeming carelessness of that public opinion which he would influence—his love of startling paradoxes —and his intrusion of political virulence, at seasons when the mind is prepared only for the delicate investigations of taste, have naturally provoked a good deal of asperity, and prevented the due appreciation of his powers.[2]

The *Literary Museum* likewise remarked in its review of *Table Talk*: 'We have nothing to do with Mr. Hazlitt's political opinions; but, as he has taken pretty good care to make the world acquainted with them, (and indeed there are manifest indications of them in the volume before us,) he must expect to meet the common fate of all party men, in the strong censures of many that differ from him on political subjects.' 'Our opinion is', the reviewer commented further, 'that Mr. H. has been fully as much over-rated by one party, as he has been under-rated by the other.'[3]

And so he was. It was not, however, a simple case of Hazlitt's aligning himself with one side and receiving attacks from the other. Many reviewers of the *Political Essays* noted that Hazlitt there attacked the Tories, the Whigs, *and* the Reformers. The *Literary*

[1] *QR*, XXII (July, 1819), 159.
[2] *ER*, XXXIV (Nov., 1820), 438.
[3] *LitMus*, July 13, 1822, p. 177.

Chronicle called him 'a political Ishmaelite, whose pen is against every one . . .', and the *Edinburgh Monthly Review* sourly referred to Hazlitt's independence in attacking all sides as 'the latest and most improved version of the radical creed'.[1] The *Monthly Review* observed that there were so many attacks on everything that it was difficult to take Hazlitt seriously. He even attacked mankind, the reviewer pointed out, and 'yet the welfare of MAN is the object of Mr. Hazlitt's anxious and sleepless solicitude! . . . Mr. H. . . . is like some testy husbands who will suffer nobody to quarrel with their wives but themselves.' And as for Hazlitt's personal attacks: 'An irrepressible vehemence pervades the language of Mr. Hazlitt, which, when applied to *persons*, even in their political capacity as statesmen, orators, or writers, is calculated to alienate and irritate. Reasoning and argument, thus uncourteously *enforced*, lose half their powers of conviction. . . .'[2]

Occasionally a radical periodical objected to Hazlitt's maverick politics; the *Monthly Magazine*, for example, defended Major Cartwright, a Reformer, against Hazlitt's use of him as an example in his essay 'On People with One Idea', in *Table Talk*. But for all Hazlitt's political freethinking, he was obviously on the liberal side; and so the brunt of the attacks he encountered came from reactionary periodicals. The *Quarterly Review* was more politically biased and thus more critically unfair in its dealings with Hazlitt than with any other writer considered in this study. The reviewer of *The Round Table*, possibly James Russell, selected mostly Hunt's contributions to that volume for abuse of Hazlitt, only mentioning at the end of the review that some of the essays were by Hunt but that 'we really have not time to discriminate between the productions of the two gentlemen. . . .'[3] (The authorship of the essays was clearly marked.) The greater proportion of the *Quarterly Review*'s criticism of Hazlitt before 1825, although it does not again sink to the level of injustice of its first review, is patently biased; even the review of the *Lectures on the English Poets* by E. S. Barrett and William Gifford, which is the closest attempt at valid critical judgments, is often niggling.

The reactionary *British Critic* and the *New Monthly Magazine* likewise showed political prejudice in some of their criticism, not to mention, at the other end of the political spectrum, the radical

[1] *LC*, Aug. 21, 1819, p. 209; *EMR*, III (Mar., 1820), 306.

[2] *MR*, XCIII (Nov., 1820), 254–56.

[3] *QR*, XVII (Apr., 1817), 159.

Examiner, the *Champion*, and the *Monthly Magazine*, which at times tended to give Hazlitt indiscriminate praise. But even these periodicals sometimes rendered verdicts independent of political bias; for instance, the *British Critic* favorably reviewed the *Lectures on the English Poets*. And there was a sufficient number of literary issues raised in most of the reviews of Hazlitt to make it difficult to dismiss many of them *in toto* as merely bigoted.

Another subject on which the reviewers raised strong objections was religion. There were few objections to most of Hazlitt's works on moral grounds, except as implied in the censure of his abuse of individuals and of his 'bookmaking' (in reviews of the collections of newspaper articles, *A View of the English Stage* and the *Political Essays*); but Hazlitt's attempt to expand the meaning of 'morality' did cause some consternation, particularly in the critique in the *British Review* of *The Round Table*. It was rather his general attitude towards religion and ministers and his casual use of scriptural language which occasioned the greater hostility. In 'On the Causes of Methodism' (*The Round Table*), Hazlitt began a delimited discussion which soon assumed the form of generalizations, as for instance his assertion that people turn to religion only when dissatisfied with life. In 'On the Clerical Character' (*Political Essays*), he made the further generalization that ministers were hypocrites, gluttons, and ignorant men. Besides being unjustly indiscriminate, such statements were not likely to endear him to reviewers writing for periodicals with religious affiliations. Several reviewers merely censured such remarks as irreligious. The *Literary and Statistical Magazine for Scotland* in its review of *The Round Table* noted 'an undisguised leaning to infidelity in some of the essays', but observed that it was 'a cast of confirmed and careless infidelity, which, when it comes in their way, [Hunt and Hazlitt] do not conceal, rather than any attempt to disseminate its poison'. 'There is in truth', the reviewer continued, however, 'more danger to be dreaded from such compositions, than from irreligious writings of a graver and more philosophical cast.'[1] The *British Review* in its critique of the same volume agreed with the last observation and objected as well to Hazlitt's use of scriptural language:

We must complain not only of the levity with which he treats all received opinions, but that the ignorant perversion of scriptural allusions and expressions in which he indulges has a tendency to diminish the reverence

[1] *LSMS*, I (Nov., 1817), 366–67.

which ought to be inseparably associated with the Word of God. The piety of all ages has agreed to receive certain words in certain acceptations; and where custom has appropriated them to a particular sense or subject, to introduce them in any other manner is, in our opinion, nothing less than profane.[1]

Two of the examples given were ' "His pretensions (Iago's) were not backed by authority, they were not *baptized at the font*, they were not *holy water proof*." (English Stage. p. 78)' and ' "All the proper forms and ceremonies must be complied with before *they two can be made one flesh*." (E.S. p. 284).' The *British Review* was not the only periodical to make this complaint.

Political and religious objections notwithstanding, Hazlitt's writings received a great deal of praise, as might be expected in view of the favorable reception of many of his publications, already mentioned. Much of the praise of both his essays and critical works assumed a more general form, as was usual with the reviewers. Hazlitt's works were said to be versatile, interesting, and acute; and great praise was accorded his originality, independence, and spirit. He was twice compared to Montaigne in the frankness of his essay writing, and the *Literary Chronicle* in a review of *Table Talk* praised his 'honest bluntness, which calls things by their right names'.[2] T. N. Talfourd reviewing the same volume in the *London Magazine* found

the most distinguishing quality of Mr. Hazlitt's essays . . . that which makes them, in a great degree, creations. They have in them a body of feeling and of wisdom, rarely to be found in the works of a professed observer. They do not merely guide us in our estimate of the works of others, or unravel the subtleties of habit, or explain the mysteries of the heart; they give us pieces of sentiment in themselves worthy of a high place in the chambers of memory. He clothes abstract speculations with human thoughts, hopes, and fears.[3]

Gold's *London Magazine* began its review of *Table Talk* as follows:

Mr. Hazlitt is one of the most original and amusing writers of the present day. He is indeed the perfect antipodes of dulness. He possesses the rare faculty of communicating interest to every subject he handles. This he

[1] *BR*, XIII (May, 1819), 337.
[2] *LC*, Apr. 14, 1821, p. 225.
[3] *LM*, III (May, 1821), 545.

appears to do from the earnestness with which he feels, from the directness with which he always comes to the point, and above all from the felicity with which he views and illustrates every topic. By a talent almost peculiar to himself, he can connect every thing, however abstracted, with something of reality; with something that appeals at once to individual feelings and experience, and comes directly home to the business and bosoms of men. . . . There is an off-handed familiarity about him, that creates an immediate intimacy between him and his reader. . . .[1]

That, I think, is a fair description of Hazlitt's peculiar powers as an essayist. As for his critical writings, John Scott in his review of the *Lectures Chiefly on the Dramatic Literature* in the *London Magazine* observed that Hazlitt's 'criticisms have all reference to essential qualities in authors, or their works, or circumstances connected with them;—he considers the fashion of a thing as nothing in the estimate of its value; its absolute substance is alone taken by him into any account'.[2]

These and many other general qualities received due praise at the hands of the reviewers, and although many particular opinions about life and many critical assessments of literature inspired considerable controversy, many were also praised and accepted.

Although Hazlitt's unique style was likewise often approved, it was his style which also was most often censured. Both friendly and hostile reviewers adversely criticized Hazlitt's construction, diction, rhetoric, meaning, and tone. In the review of *The Round Table* in the *Edinburgh Magazine*, possibly written by Hazlitt himself, some of the problems of his construction are set forth in a favorable light: there is not always

harmony and fulness of view, or precision of thought. But there is never any want of directness. He gives a number of extraneous elements and extreme points,—not bound together easily by any common tie, and not very specially designated for their various purposes. . . . We cannot say, on the whole, that they are misplaced; but we may complain that they are not seldom put down with the carelessness of one who sees a certain length and instantly,—but who is more solicitous about the grasp and generality of his idea than about the severe affinity of its relations, or the accuracy of its expression.[3]

[1] Gold's *LM*, III (June, 1821), 618.

[2] *LM*, I (Feb., 1820), 186.

[3] *EdM*, I (Nov., 1817), 353. That Hazlitt was possibly his own reviewer in the

The author, the review continues, comes quickly to judgments and has an 'apparently unconscious gravity', which allows him to dismiss trifles. He never questions the importance of his subject or defends his assertions: 'He throws them out, and leaves the adjustment and harmonizing of them to the taste or caprice of his various readers.'[1] This, the reviewer concludes, is desirable in a guide of public taste.

Other reviewers, noting more or less the same qualities, were less charitable in their estimation of their worth. William Taylor, reviewing *Table Talk* in the *Monthly Review*, complained of

> a want of method, of purpose, and of cohesion in his *matter*: he begins without knowing whither he is going: after having ranged about for some time very pleasantly, he sits down to rest; and the reader feels inclined, like the mathematician, to ask 'what does this prove?' It is not enough to chuse a topic and write 'about it and about it'; there should be drift, intention, end, and aim. 'The Rambler' has an object for every stroll; the present author should be termed *The Saunterer*.[2]

The critic in the *Edinburgh Review* (T. N. Talfourd) of *Lectures Chiefly on the Dramatic Literature* thought the lack of unity to be owing to an absence of principles:

> He has no lack of the deepest feelings, the profoundest sentiments of humanity, or the loftiest aspirations after ideal good. But there are no great leading principles of taste to give singleness to his aims, nor any central points in his mind, around which his feelings may revolve, and his imaginations cluster. There is no sufficient distinction between his intellectual and his imaginative faculties. He confounds the truths of imagination with those of fact—the processes of argument with those of feeling—the immunities of intellect with those of virtue. Hence the seeming inconsistency of many of his doctrines. Hence the want of all continuity in his style. Hence his failure in producing one single, harmonious, and lasting impression on the hearts of his hearers. He never waits to consider whether a sentiment or an image is in place—so it be in itself striking. That keen sense of pleasure in intellectual beauty which is the

---

Edinburgh Magazine was suggested in the *Literary and Statistical Magazine*, III (May, 1819), 208n. Several indications point to this possibility: Hazlitt is known to have been a contributor to the *Edinburgh Magazine*; the review in question was the second critique of *The Round Table* in that periodical; in it there is high praise of Hunt's contributions to the work; and the style is often very like Hazlitt's. See my forthcoming (1969) article—'Hazlitt Reviews Hazlitt?'—in *Modern Language Review*.

[1] *EdM*, I (Nov., 1817), 354.

[2] *MR*, CI (May, 1823), 57.

best charm of his writings, is also his chief deluder. He cannot resist a powerful image, an exquisite quotation, or a pregnant remark, however it may dissipate or even subvert the general feeling which his theme should inspire.[1]

The reviewer further expressed a wish that Hazlitt, 'capable of so lucid and convincing a development of his critical doctrines, would less frequently content himself with giving the mere results of his thought. . . .'[2] This point was also made in the review of *Table Talk* in Gold's *London Magazine*: 'He sets down at once the conclusions of his own judgment, without entering into any arguments for their support, or condescending to inform us of the steps by which he arrived at them.'[3] All of these criticisms, it is worth noting, were made by sympathetic reviewers.

E. S. Barrett and William Gifford, joint-reviewers of the *Lectures on the English Poets* in the *Quarterly Review*, were anything but sympathetic, but at least their review is the only one on Hazlitt in the *Quarterly Review* before 1825 which is entitled to be called literary criticism. Hazlitt's diction was nowhere else censured so severely, although other reviewers observed some vague use of language in this and other of his works. There was, in fact, a good deal of questioning of the meaning of Hazlitt's general definition of poetry in many reviews, even in the sympathetic *Champion*; and the passage in question in the *Lectures on the English Poets* was chosen by the *Quarterly Review* critics for scrutiny.[4] After discussing Hazlitt's use of the words 'sympathy' and 'poetry', they moved on to analyze a shorter passage, more easily quoted here:

As another specimen of his definitions we may take the following. 'Poetry does not define the limits of sense, or analyze the distinctions of the understanding, but signifies the excess of the imagination beyond the actual or ordinary impression of any object or feeling.' Poetry was at the beginning of the book asserted to be an impression; it is now the excess of the imagination beyond an impression: what this excess is we cannot tell, but at least it must be something very unlike an impression. Though the total want of meaning is the weightiest objection to such writing; yet the abuse which it involves of particular words is very remarkable, and

[1] *ER*, XXXIV (Nov., 1820), 440. [2] *Ibid.*, p. 446.

[3] Gold's *LM*, III (June, 1821), 618.

[4] This passage was also selected by George Watson for his attack on Hazlitt's use of language in *The Literary Critics* (Baltimore: Penguin, 1962), p. 137.

will not be overlooked by those who are aware of the inseparable connection between justness of thought and precision of language. What, in strict reasoning, can be meant by the impression of a feeling? How can *actual* and *ordinary* be used as synonymous? Every impression must be an actual impression; and the use of that epithet annihilates the limitations, with which Mr. Hazlitt meant to guard his proposition.[1]

Hazlitt's longer definition of poetry is written in his customary repetitive style, described by the *Champion* as 'one continued eloquence, that leaves the mind little time to pause and be critical'.[2] 'He seems never to be satisfied', the reviewer further observed, '. . . until his subject is exhausted: he fairly runs it down.' Barrett and Gifford in the *Quarterly Review* also attempted to describe this style:

Some vague half-formed notion seems to be floating before his mind; instead of seizing the notion itself, he lays hold of a metaphor, or of an idea connected with it by slight associations: this he expresses; but after he has expressed it, he finds that he has not conveyed his meaning; another metaphor is therefore thrown out, the same course is trodden over and

[1] *QR*, XIX (July, 1818), 428–29. In *A Letter to William Gifford, Esq.* (London, 1819), Hazlitt attempted to answer the *Quarterly Review* criticisms of his works. His answer to the passage quoted in the text went as follows (pp. 62–64): 'Poetry at the beginning of the book was asserted to be not simply an impression "but an impression *by its vividness exciting an involuntary movement of the imagination*": now, you say, it is *the excess of the imagination beyond an impression*; and you bring this as a proof of a contradiction in terms. An impression, by its vividness exciting a movement of the imagination, you discover, must be something very unlike an impression, and as to the imagination itself, you cannot tell what it is; it is an unknown power in your poetical creed. What is most extraordinary is, that you had quoted the very passage which you here represent as a total contradiction to the latter, only two pages before. What, Sir, do you think of your readers? What must they think of you!—"Though the *total want of meaning*", you add, "is the weightiest objection to such writing, yet *the abuse* which it involves of *particular words and phrases*" (in addition to a total want of meaning) "is very remarkable", (it must be so,) "and will not be overlooked by those who are aware of the inseparable connection between justness of thought and precision of language." (You are not aware that there is no precise measure of thought or expression.) "What, in strict reasoning, can be meant by the impression of a feeling?" (The impression which it makes on the mind, as distinct from some other to which it gives birth, is what I meant.) "How can *actual* and *ordinary* be used as synonymous?" (They are not.) "Every impression must be an actual *impression*"; (there is then no such thing as an imaginary impression;) "and the use of that epithet annihilates the limitations which Mr. Hazlitt meant" (in the total want of meaning,) "to guard his proposition." '

[2] *Champ*, May 24, 1818, p. 331.

over again, and half a dozen combinations of phrases are used in vague endeavours to express what ought to have been said directly and concisely in one.[1]

Still another description of Hazlitt's style was attempted in a review of Volume II of *Table Talk* in the *London Magazine*: 'The style of the book is singularly nervous and direct, and seems to aim at mastering its subject by dint of mere hard hitting. There is no such thing as manoeuvering for a blow. The language strikes out, and, if the intention is not fulfilled, the blow is repeated until the subject falls.'[2]

Two other features of Hazlitt's style were defended by Leigh Hunt in his *Examiner* review of the *Lectures on the English Comic Writers*: Hazlitt's 'apparent love of paradox in his zeal to see fair play, and the . . . abrupt and powerful style, which like an oak-tree throws out its branches in short and pithy divisions, often terminating however in a profusion of poetical verdure, and blossoming into floridity'.[3] Both Hazlitt's paradoxes and his florid imagery required defense, for both were often censured by his contemporaries either as profuse enough to be offensive in themselves, or as leading to inconsistencies, or as obscuring his arguments. In a repetitive style not unlike Hazlitt's, the reviewer of *Table Talk* in the *Literary Register* remarked on Hazlitt's paradoxical style:

His book seems written by an ideal character, upon whom an ingenious author would have laboured to fix the curse of a self-conviction of eccentricity, or—which amounts to the same thing—a wish to be thought eccentric. Novel conceptions appear to come rapidly enough to the writer; but they are given out with equal rapidity, and with little allowance for the probable crudeness of a first appearance. He either takes it for granted that a new idea in its generalized form ought to please us as much as it excited him, or he does not trouble himself about the matter, but gives us as much as he allowed himself to get out of it. He does not sufficiently recollect the necessity for a different mode of expression when one thinks to one's self and when one thinks aloud to others. He would appear to confound peculiarity of imagination with originality of imagination, and to believe that to say something that was never said before, is tantamount to saying something which shall delight or convince as well as startle us. He works hard to keep himself at ease, and he lets us see he is so at work. He longs after terseness and briskness, and pines to death for a smart, figurative elucidation.[4]

[1] *QR*, XIX (July, 1818), 425.
[2] *LM*, VII (June, 1823), 689.
[3] *Exam.* Apr. 18, 1819, p. 250.
[4] *LitReg*, July 27, 1822, p. 54.

The reviewer continued:

In a dry metaphysical discussion, when we are just about to rejoice that our author sits at his ease, and looks grave, and speaks plainly as befits his subject, he will anon jump off his feet and throw a poetical summerset; or having first invited us to look at real things, he then applies a metaphorical or rhapsodical lens to our eyes and every object is instantly turned topsy-turvy; beginnings and ends run into each other, and all delineation and outline merges in confusion.

There is admittedly some exaggeration in this description of Hazlitt's style, as there is in much of the criticism of his works. It is as if the reviewers, after reading them, were themselves carried away into making the sort of exaggerations in which Hazlitt often indulged. And yet a good deal of what they said about his writings is pertinent. The *Literary and Statistical Magazine* in its review of the *Lectures on the English Comic Writers* remarked that '. . . to those who know Mr Hazlitt only by his articles in reviews, or by extracts in newspapers, it is impossible to conceive how irksome it is to read one of his volumes from beginning to end.'[1] This, I believe, is true; his rambling construction, repetitious rhetoric, frequent paradoxes and lush imagery, while they also have merits of their own, do become tedious when taken in large doses. It was in such doses, of course, that the reviewers had to take his works.

There is in many of the reviews a tendency to extreme judgments; often no effort at all is required to decide whether a review is predominantly favorable or unfavorable. In view of the controversial nature of much of what he wrote, this is easily understood. Hazlitt, more than Hunt or Keats, paid the price in reviews of his works for his freethinking. He was, more than they, independent in his opinions, and it is ironic that he should have been attacked more often than the two others as a mere member of the Cockney School. And yet, although a portion of the contemporary criticism of Hazlitt must be disregarded as biased in one way or another, there is still a substantial amount that cannot be wisely disregarded—that deserves consideration as valid literary criticism.

[1] *LSMS*, III (May, 1819), 207.

6

Out of School

The three authors brought together in this chapter have little in common. The critics of their own day evidently thought they had equally little in common with any other writers in the period, for they were seldom associated with any of the literary schools invented by the reviewers to suit their own convenience. Thomas Moore and Charles Lamb were suggested as having such connections, the former with the Satanic School and the latter with the Lake and Cockney schools. But these suggestions were not advanced with much conviction, and were even rejected by other reviewers.

What the three writers did share was a degree of popularity with the reading public, as well as a considerable reputation with the critics—the latter usually of a secondary order. Their success, especially with the critics, was doubtless due in part to an absence of morally or politically offensive elements in their works. Even Moore, who upset the reviewers most by his political satires and his voluptuousness, had no dangerous political theories to disseminate, and the moral laxity in his poems was incapable of arousing much indignation.

Most of their writings reviewed in the period have not stimulated interest, let alone controversy, since. Lamb, the least popular at the time, is the one whose works are most widely read today, and those of his works reviewed in the period are principally the ones ignored by posterity. This being the case, it seems most appropriate that the following account of their reception by the critics should be almost entirely descriptive.

Thomas Moore

The works of Thomas Moore published in the period under study were divided between elegant poems about love and political satires in verse and prose. The first two volumes to be dealt with are of the former kind, the pseudonymous *Poetical Works of Thomas Little* (1801) and *Epistles, Odes, and Other Poems* (1806). Both contained a good deal of voluptuous verse, and, together with his earlier translations of the odes of Anacreon, established for Moore the reputation of a licentious poet.

The attitude of the reviewers to Moore's voluptuousness changed considerably between 1801 and 1806. The first volume of original verse, despite the pseudonym of Thomas Little, was known to be the work of Moore. Although there were several remonstrances about the immoral tendency of the tone of the volume, there were three defenses of the poems on moral grounds, and the general reception was favorable. The *Epistles, Odes, and Other Poems*, published five years later, on the other hand, received a majority of unfavorable verdicts, with moral objections much in evidence. It was not, many reviewers pointed out, that the diction was obscene; rather, the total spirit of the work was at fault. The *Literary Journal* observed:

> Without any of the grossness of Lord Rochester, he touches the same strings with no less energy and success. In short, if we were desirous to render a wife unfaithful to her marriage-bed, or to habituate a virgin to listen to the language of seduction: if we were desirous to convey to her the loosest wishes without startling her by corresponding language; and to afford her an excuse to herself for indulging in these emotions, in the apparent purity of what she read, we should certainly put Mr. Moore's amatory poems in her hands.[1]

Regardless of the old-fashioned phrasing, the moral observation underlying the above objection is true, if not a truism.

Jeffrey in the *Edinburgh Review* agreed about the insidiousness of Moore's moral looseness; and, as a result of slightly stronger phrasing in his allusions to the author, he became involved in a duel with Moore, which was stopped in time by the authorities. As for the

[1] *LJ*, I 2s (June, 1806), 647.

technical aspects of the verse of the later volume, there was some praise of the elegance and polish of the diction and versification, but even more censure of the coinages (e.g., 'darkle'), the general carelessness, the repetition of amorous commonplaces, the conceits, and what Jeffrey termed 'the right millinery taste'.[1]

In 1808, Moore began the *Irish Melodies*, a series of collections of songs set to music, which were published every few years—the last in the period under study, the ninth issue, in 1824. These collections were very popular; in the absence of most of Moore's eroticism they received general critical approval, although some decline in quality was noted after the sixth issue (1815). Moore was often said to be easily the best song-writer of the age; extravagant comparisons were even made between Moore and Horace, Anacreon, and Burns. '... It is to his songs', pronounced the *London Magazine* in 1821, 'that Moore must trust for immortality, and immortal he must be as long as English ladies can *love*, or Irish gentlemen can *drink*, which, we take it, is as much of immortality as any modern bard can consider himself equitably entitled to.'[2]

Since the lyrics were written for, and accompanied by, a musical score, their connection with music was often considered, usually with praise of their mutual suitability. E. E. Crowe in *Blackwood's*, however, disagreed, contending that Moore's 'elegant and misplaced sentiments suffer in comparison with the vulgar ideas the tunes naturally excite'.[3] The *British Stage* remarked also that the popularity of the lyrics depended on the popularity of the tunes which accompanied them, and noted one song thus neglected.

The lyrics themselves were censured on several counts. Objections to frequent obtrusions of political themes occurred most often. Horace Twiss in the *Quarterly Review*, for instance, thought that Moore should exclude 'all topics of a local or political nature; topics, which by impartial readers are generally scanned with indifference, and by no small number of zealous partisans with absolute disgust'—yet Twiss admitted that some of the objectionable songs were among the best.[4] As for poetic flaws, Twiss found some songs unintelligible because of Moore's proneness 'to run into strained, incorrect, and remote resemblances', and others he thought namby-pamby.[5] In its criticism of numbers VI and VII, the *Monthly Review* objected to the

[1] *ER*, VIII (July, 1806), 462.
[2] *LM*, III (June, 1821), 659.
[3] *BM*, XI (Jan., 1822), 67.
[4] *QR*, VII (June, 1812), 378.
[5] *Ibid.*

far-fetched similes let off 'like crackers' at the end of many songs.[1] The *British Stage* censured the repetition of amatory paraphernalia: lips, smiles, eyes, sighs, and so on, 'which have rendered Mr. Moore the idol of all silly, sentimental young ladies between Kensington Gravel-Pits and Wapping Wall'.[2] 'The school-boy key on which Moore's love and heroism is always set', was considered by E. E. Crowe in *Blackwood's* to be his 'great defect'.[3]

In the year that saw the first number of the *Irish Melodies*, Moore began, with the publication of *Corruption and Intolerance* (1808), a phase of political and religious satire; also producing *The Sceptic* (1809), *A Letter to the Roman Catholics of Dublin* (1810), and the *Intercepted Letters* (1813). These were all anonymous—necessarily, since they contained, in varying degrees, attacks on the English treatment of Ireland and on anti-Catholic sentiment, as well as ridicule of the Prince Regent and his ministers. C. L. Moody in the *Monthly Review* commented on *Corruption* that, because of his politics, Moore must 'please or displease in the extreme', and this observation holds true for all of these works.[4] They received censure and praise about equally because they were reviewed by about the same number of periodicals having one political slant or the other. Questions of literary merit were scarcely raised, as might have been expected with such volatile subject-matter.

After several years of satiric composition, Moore returned in 1816 to several years of publishing a higher form of verse. In that year he published *Lines on the Death of [Sheridan]* and the first part of *Sacred Songs*. The first of these was reviewed only by the *Theatrical Inquisitore* which gave it favorable mention, while remarking that 'the structurs of the verse is too light and airy for its subject'.[5] Similar objection, were also raised concerning the *Sacred Songs*. Not only the versification was censured as unsuitable, however; to the *Monthly Review* the ideas and language appeared 'painfully *out of keeping*' with the religious subject-matter; it cited as examples the lines 'Its glow by day, *its smile by night*' and 'Thy spirit warms *her fragrant sigh*' (italics added by the reviewer).[6] The *British Review* found too little of the proper tone and attitude expected in religious verse and 'too much of jingle, too much of artifice, and too much of point'; it also predicted

[1] *MR*, LXXXVII (Dec., 1818), 421.
[2] *British Stage*, II (Dec., 1818), 268.
[3] *BM*, XI (Jan., 1822), 64.
[4] *MR*, LVIII (Apr., 1809), 418.
[5] *TI*, XI (Nov., 1817), 364.
[6] *MR*, XC (Dec., 1819), 413, 414.

that these songs would be recited along with Moore's secular numbers, which might prove dangerous 'to a mind of incipient piety and vacillating zeal'.[1] In spite of these objections, however, the *Sacred Songs* received mostly favorable reviews.

Still in a non-political vein, Moore in the following year published *Lalla Rookh*, one of the most popular poems of the period. As such, it received one of the most extensive critical appraisals accorded by the reviewers. The only notable absentee among reviewing periodicals was the *Quarterly Review*, which for some reason saw fit to ignore most of Moore's publications. The reception of the work was generally favorable; the *Edinburgh*, *Blackwood's*, the *Monthly Review*, and most of the magazines were favorably impressed, while most of the monthly reviews and the quarterly *British Review* offered considerable resistance.

Lalla Rookh is actually four poems held together by a prose frame, the poems being recited by a poet who accompanies a princess en route to her marriage. The frame received a good deal of approbation for being interesting in itself; but there was some disagreement on this point, as well as some censure of the prose style. The *Literary Panorama*, moreover, thought there was too much oriental description and that 'things are described, rather than represented'.[2]

Many reviewers also objected to the flippancy of tone in the frame, which, they felt, ill-consorted with the general seriousness of the poems. Most of the flippancy was contained in the characterization of Fadladeen, a pompous chamberlain in the retinue of the princess, who pronounces judgments on the poems recited, in a style obviously parodying contemporary reviewers. For example, he remarks, where the humor is at its broadest:

> Then, as to versification, it was, to say no more of it, execrable: it has neither the copious flow of Ferdosi, the sweetness of Hafez, nor the sententious march of Sadi. . . . [Fadladeen nevertheless concluded,] 'Notwithstanding the observations which I have thought it my duty to make, it is by no means my wish to discourage the young man:—so far from it, indeed, that if he will but totally alter his style of writing and thinking, I have very little doubt that I shall be very pleased with him.'

The response of the reviewers to this parody took several forms, the most frequent of which was the observation that Fadladeen, especi-

[1] *BR*, VIII (Aug., 1816), 167, 165.

[2] *LP*, VI 2s (Sept., 1817), 898.

ally in his criticism of the lushness of the imagery, was quite right—Moore 'should remember the old proverb "many a true word is spoke in jest" ', remarked the *Literary Panorama*.[1] The *Critical Review*, seeing it as an attempt to forestall criticism, commented, 'This might be very fair as a joke, but as a piece of cunning it is unworthy of a man of the reputation of our author.'[2] The *Eclectic Review* made the obvious point that Fadladeen seemed 'a kind of concentration . . . of certain Fadladeens of the North'; and Jeffrey, the head 'Fadladeen' of the *Edinburgh Review*, answered Moore by ignoring the point of the parody: Fadladeen's 'sayings and remarks, we cannot help observing, do not agree very well with the character which is assigned him—being for the most part very smart, snappish, and acute, and by no means solemn, stupid, and pompous, as was to have been expected'.[3]

As for the four poems, the third, 'The Fire Worshippers', was most often chosen as the best, and the fourth, 'The Light of the Haram', as the worst. Of the latter, Jeffrey in the *Edinburgh Review* remarked that it seemed to have been written under the influence of 'intoxicating gas'.[4] The second, 'Paradise and the Peri', received a good deal of approbation, especially as a moral fable. But 'The Veiled Prophet', the first and longest of the poems, received the most comment. The *British Review* objected to Moore's use of decasyllabic couplets in the poem:

> The metre in which this tale is told does not seem suited to Mr. Moore's ear. Many of his lines are very heavy and unharmonious; many very flat and prosaic. This, like the chromatic in music, may, in the more extended compass and variety of blank verse, afford a relief to the ear; but in rhyme, and especially in the couplets of the five feet iambic measure, in which both the sense and cadence is [*sic*] more confined, and each line depends upon its own effect, rather than upon an harmonious arrangement of the verse in general, these liberties are not allowable.[5]

Two examples given were 'With music and with sweets sparkling alive' and 'Is seen glittering at times like the white sail'. The *British Critic* also disliked Moore's versification; but most of the reviewers' censure of the first poem concerned the characterization of Mokanna, the prophet, and Selika, the heroine who becomes one of his harem.

[1] *Ibid.*, p. 908. [2] *CR*, V 5s (June, 1817), 562.
[3] *EcR*, VIII 2s (Oct., 1817), 341; *ER*, XXIX (Nov., 1817), 9.
[4] *ER*, XXIX (Nov., 1817), 30. [5] *BR*, X (Aug., 1817), 40.

The character of Mokanna was considered by many reviewers to be improbable and, what is more, disgusting. Mokanna was also censured, by the *Literary Panorama*, as another example of the vicious hero. Zelika was likewise said by many to be improbable, both in her inexplicable surrender to Mokanna and in her recurrent insanity. Jeffrey's review in the *Edinburgh Review* contains a long discussion of the necessity for characters to partake of '*universal* nature'.[1]

The style of all four poems was often attacked, even though there was also frequent praise of isolated passages. The lushness of the imagery and the general sweetness of the style provoked the chief objections. Jeffrey, who shows some signs of disingenuousness in his review of Moore—his friend and a contributor to the *Edinburgh Review*—nevertheless remarked:

> The effect of the whole is to mingle a certain feeling of disappointment with that of admiration—to excite admiration rather than any warmer sentiment of delight—to dazzle, more than to enchant—and, in the end, more frequently to startle the fancy, and fatigue the attention, with the constant succession of glittering images and high-strained emotions, than to maintain a rising interest, or win a growing sympathy, by a less profuse or more systematic display of attractions.[2]

For, 'no work, consisting of many pages, should have detached and distinguishable beauties in every one of them. No great work, indeed, should have *many* beauties: If it were perfect, it would have but *one*, and that but faintly perceptible, except on a view of the whole', as is the case with a Grecian temple. The *Eclectic Review* and the *British Review* expressed their censure of the cloying aspects of the poem more colorfully: the first said that 'we have been so surfeited with moonlight, that how long it may be before we enjoy a walk in the evening again we cannot venture to say'; and the *British Review* announced that, after reading the poem '[we are] ready almost to wish ourselves in a garden of leeks and onions to relieve our senses. . . .'[3] The *British Review* also complained that the imagery was often meaningless:

> Words and sentences must have definite, clear, and substantial meaning. Poetry has an extensive empire, but not an absolute sway; she must conform, as well as others, to certain rules of eternal authority, founded in

[1] *ER*, XXIX (Nov., 1817), 6. [2] *Ibid.*, p. 2.

[3] *EcR*, VIII 2s (Oct., 1817), 342; *BR*, X (Aug., 1817), 33.

the nature of things, and the constitution of the mind. In a word, there must be good sense and decided meaning to sustain the boldest imagery, and most refined phraseology. To play about the margin of meaning, where the colours of thought are blending into confusion, is a dangerous exercise of the poet's talent. . . .[1]

One example given was:

Who doth not wonder, when, amidst th' acclaim
Of thousands, heralding to heaven his name—
'Mid all those holier harmonies of fame,
Which sound along the path of virtuous souls,
Like music round a planet as it rolls!—
[He turns away. . . .]

Along with this censure of Moore's usual elegant style, many reviewers also observed a new energy and an accompanying carelessness in the verse, often said to be the result of Byron's influence. Byron's recently acquired simplicity of language resulted, according to the *Monthly Review*, in a '*refined simplicity*' when taken over by Moore; and this observation was the occasion for another onslaught by the *Monthly Review* on low diction, the 'vulgar error of the day'.[2] Further indications of Byronic influence noted were the new villainy and melancholy in some of the poems.

Moore was following in Byron's footsteps, too, in using an Eastern setting for the poem. Moore compensated for his lack of first-hand knowledge of the setting by extensive research, reflected in the copious notes, as well as in the descriptions and imagery of the poem. The result received favorable mention from several reviewers; but the *Literary Panorama* contended that the notes are worse than useless since they obstruct the reading, and complained of the extent of Moore's use of his research:

We must protest at once, and entirely, against this writing of large volumes in what may be termed an outlandish jargon. Allusions to foreign customs, and productions are beautiful as ornaments in poetry; but ornaments ought not to be the basis, component parts, and superstructure of a work.[3]

[1] *BR*, X (Aug., 1817), 41.
[2] *MR*, LXXXIII (June, 1817), 183, 184.
[3] *LP*, VI 2s (Sept., 1817), 899.

While the *Asiatic Journal* found 'the costume correctly observed', yet 'the true spirit, the peculiar excellencies of an Oriental Romance, appear to us to be wanting'.[1] Moore, the reviewer explained, is not sufficiently abstracted from reality, and 'does not possess that wave-like flexibility, that power of quick transition, or of various combination, which are indispensible to an Oriental tale'.[2]

Moore's licentiousness, heavily censured in reviews of his earlier volumes, was said to be absent from *Lalla Rookh*; Jeffrey went to some trouble, for example, to give Moore's morals his seal of approval in the *Edinburgh Review*. Yet there still was some protest against Moore's sensual emphasis and his lack of moral purpose. The *British Review*, as usual, had something to say on both of these points: 'We have read a good deal, heard a good deal, and seen a good deal of this world, and having withal, as Critics should have, a sober sort of temperament, we cannot help looking with profane scepticism upon [the] voluptuous detail. . . .'[3] Poetry, the same reviewer remarked on the second point, 'has claims to a nobler use and destination than to the endless whimperings of these turbaned lovers and their silly sultanas.'[4]

Continuing in a non-political vein, Moore began another series of songs the following year—the *National Airs*, the first four numbers of which (1818–24) received scattered, favorable reviews. In that same year, Moore entered another political phase, publishing *The Fudge Family in Paris* (1818) and *Tom Crib's Memorial to Congress* (1819). The reception given these light, political satires was split for the most part along partisan lines, though not entirely so. In its review of the first work, even the *British Critic* made the remarkable statement (considering its habitually partisan criticism of political works) that, providing there is nothing indecent or irreligious involved, 'we should be the last persons in the world, to wrinkle our foreheads into a frown, because a good joke was made at the expense of our politics'.[5]

Political satire was laid aside again in 1823 with the publication of *The Loves of the Angels*. A shorter and less ambitious work than *Lalla Rookh*, it was nevertheless very similar to the earlier production in both style and structure. The critical reception given *The Loves*, on the other hand, differed from that enjoyed by the earlier

[1] *Asiatic Journal*, IV (Nov., 1817), 457.
[2] *Ibid.*, p. 459.
[3] *BR*, X (Aug., 1817), 31.
[4] *Ibid.*, p. 33.
[5] *BC*, IX 2s (May, 1818), 497.

work; it received a majority of hostile reviews. The objections previously set forth by the minority now became majority opinions; the cloying sweetness of the total effect, the obtrusive research in the texts and notes, and the moral laxity of the tone—all were censured.

Some special problems were, however, presented by the work. The three poems of which it is composed all deal with the trysts of angels with women, as suggested by a misinterpreted passage of Scripture. The more serious charge brought against Moore's handling of the accounts was the resultant profanity: 'if there be one way more pernicious than another to make religion a sneer', commented the *Monthly Censor*, 'it is by connecting its solemn and holy records with silly, debasing, and licentious imaginations.'[1] A second, less serious, objection was made against Moore's angels themselves. They were said to be too corporeal, too merely human. 'Not only are they men', remarked John Wilson in *Blackwood's*, 'but they seem as if they were Irishmen; for such furious love was never made out of the land of potatoes.'[2]

Moore's final works in the period were once again political satires, one in verse, *Fables for the Holy Alliance* (1823), and the other in prose, *Memoirs of Captain Rock* (1824). As was customary with reviews of political works in the period, the critical reception of both ran along partisan lines, with the exception of an unfavorable review of the first by the *Monthly Magazine* and a favorable review of the second by the *Literary Gazette*. The probable reason for the occasional crossing of political lines in reviews of Moore's later satires was that they were on the whole lighthearted and free from any dangerous political theories. The lack of satiric bite was mentioned by the *Literary Museum* in its review of the *Fables*: 'Moore indeed has seldom been successful in satire, which, we suspect, demands worse as well as stronger feelings, than any he possesses.'[3]

Moore's critical reception was in many respects like that given the poems of Walter Scott. Both were immensely popular writers; like Scott, Moore occasionally received extravagant praise, especially from the more fashionable magazines. But most of his critics, no matter how friendly, recognized Moore's limitations. He was most often esteemed as a very talented song-writer and as a poet of elegance, not great, but good as far as his abilities extended.

[1] *MC*, II (Mar., 1823), 336.

[2] *BM*, XIII (Jan., 1823), 68.

[3] *LitMus*, May 10, 1823, p. 292.

Charles Lamb

Much of the writing of Charles Lamb published in the period under study appeared in periodicals; consequently reviews of his works are not so numerous as they otherwise might have been. As a result the majority of reviews of Lamb are concerned with only part of his work, that part which has since been largely forgotten.

The first work published in the period was *John Woodvil* (1802), a drama. The critical reception was unanimously unfavorable. The construction was said to lack unity, and Lamb's style was attacked for lack of harmony in the versification and for vulgarity and quaintness in the diction. Several reviewers, in fact, went on from censure of the style to an attack on the unnamed school of which Lamb was for the moment considered to be a member—evidently the Lake School. The sentiments were also attacked with considerable humour as being mawkish, affected, or stilted. Thomas Brown in the *Edinburgh Review* commented waggishly on a passage in Act V, scene ii:

> The artifice with which the poet prepares his audience for the narrative, must be admirably productive of theatrical effect. It introduces, what we believe is a novelty on the stage, a peal of church-bells giving their summons to morning-service.
>
> (*A noise of bells heard.*)
>
> MARGARET
>
> Hark the bells, John.
>
> JOHN
>
> Those are the church bells of St Mary Ottery.
>
> MARGARET
>
> I know it.
>
> JOHN
>
> St Mary Ottery, my native village,
> In the sweet shire of Devon.
> Those are the bells. (p. 100.)
>
> The exactness of John's information is of peculiar use; as Margaret, having been sometime at Nottingham, may be supposed to have forgotten the name of the parish, and perhaps of the sweet shire itself; and the cautious and solemn iteration at the close, in an affair of so much moment, gives an emphasis to the whole, that is almost inimitable.[1]

[1] *ER*, II (Apr., 1803), 92.

Lamb's books for children fared far better with the reviewers. His *Tales from Shakespear* (1807), *Mrs. Leicester's School* (1807), and *Poetry for Children* (1809), all written in collaboration with his sister, as well as his own *The Adventures of Ulysses* (1808), had on the whole a favorable reception. The *Critical Review* compared the *Tales* with *Robinson Crusoe* in their appeal to adults and children alike, and approved highly, as did other periodicals, Lamb's new approach to children's literature. 'In these times of empiricism and system-building', the reviewer remarked, 'the world has been too credulous to the professions of old women of both sexes, who hold the reins of government over the education of children.' The usual sort of moral tale encourages either hypocrisy or a distaste for virtue, whereas the *Tales*, 'in suppressing the bad passions "envy, hatred, and malice" and in humanizing and correcting the heart, . . . will effect more than all the cant' of the old school.[1] *The Adventures of Ulysses* received the most unfavorable reviews, mainly because of an antiquarian quaintness in the style.

In the midst of publishing children's literature, Lamb produced his *Specimens of English Dramatic Poets* (1808). The reviewers were unanimously favorable; some were even enthusiastic about both his plan and his execution, as well as his taste and judgment. There were, however, some objections to the style of his notes, said to be stiff and quaint; and the *Critical Review* disliked the 'castrating and mutilating part' of Lamb's plan, explaining that he should have chosen passages which required no omissions.[2]

Lamb's popularity with the reviewers continued in critiques of the two volumes of *The Works of Charles Lamb* (1818), all of which were favorable. Several reviewers, in fact, could scarcely contain their enthusiasm. T. N. Talfourd, the first editor of Lamb, reviewing the volumes in the *Champion*, praised everything in them, finding two of the pieces 'delicious' and making such comments as, 'His pathos, deep and touching as it is, only draws forth such tears as it is a luxury to shed.'[3] Leigh Hunt in the *Examiner* was more discerning than Talfourd, but did make the confusing pronouncement that 'if we were to make a summary of Mr. Lamb's merits as a writer, we should say that there was not a deeper or more charitable observer existing'.[4]

[1] *CR*, XI 3s (May, 1807), 98.
[2] *CR*, XX 3s (May, 1810), 81.
[3] *Champ*, May 16, 1819, p. 313.
[4] *Exam*, Mar. 28, 1819, p. 206.

Two of the general comments on the volumes, however, are worth extracting as illustrations of a central problem in Lamb's writing. The *British Critic* remarked that for Lamb's

> character and abilities, when properly directed, we entertain an unfeigned respect. But his poems and plays, we think, are decidedly bad. . . . We venture further to predict that such will always be the *general* sentiment concerning them . . . [for] the number of those endowed with such congenial peculiarities of sympathy and feeling, will ever be too minute to have any very sensible weight among the opinions of the generality of readers. . . .[1]

John Wilson in *Blackwood's* got still closer to the problem that even today affects Lamb's critical reputation: 'Mr. Lamb . . . never has been, and we are afraid never will be, a very popular writer. His faults are likely to be very offensive to ordinary readers; while his merits are of so peculiar a kind, that it requires a peculiar taste to feel them justly.'[2] But the consensus of the contemporary reviewers was that on the whole Lamb's feelings, humanity, humor, and style deserved approbation.

The two volumes included, besides poetry, several larger works published previously in book form, *A Tale of Rosamund Gray* and *John Woodvil*, as well as *Mr. H.*, a farce, and critical and familiar essays previously published in periodicals. The poems received a good deal of praise, even though they were often said to be inferior to the prose works. Wilson in *Blackwood's* considered Lamb a good poet within his limits as a poet of the heart. The reviewer in the *Gentleman's Magazine*, Lamb's friend George Dyer, found the poems 'well done, in their way; that is to say, they are poetical, and we are pleased . . .', but wished to reserve his enthusiasm for the remainder of the volume.[3] The *British Critic* thought the poems to be

> written after Mr. Wordsworth's fashion, with much more of his manner than of his genius; bearing, it is true, little trace of his prototype's tendency to metaphysics and mysticism, but with more than enough of his other peculiarities. In a word, they have the air of serious, but awkward and unsuccessful imitations of the lyrical ballads. Equally *natural* with a certain portion of those singular productions; but uninformed by a

[1] *BC*, XI 2s (Feb., 1819), 146–47.
[2] *BM*, III (Aug., 1818), 599.
[3] *GM*, LXXXIX–ii (July, 1819), 49.

particle of that deep feeling and pure poetical spirit which more than redeems all their foibles.[1]

The familiar essays were praised highly, especially his 'Recollections of Christ's Hospital'. Lamb's whimsical humor was a trait singled out in the essays for approval by several reviewers; but John Wilson in *Blackwood's* thought that Lamb's humor 'though always somewhat original, is often very forced and unnatural'.[2] Lamb's critical essays, however, received the most applause. The *British Critic*, as well as others, praised his good taste and knowledge of literature, but expressed wonder that Lamb did not apply such critical ability to his own verse. His 'On the Tragedies of Shakspeare' was the most popular of these critical essays and elicited the most discussion. Lamb's thesis that Shakespeare's tragedies were best read in the closet was approved by the *British Critic* and the *Gentleman's Magazine*. Though both reviewers praised the taste and sense of the essay, neither considered the thesis to be a discovery; and George Dyer in the latter periodical thought that, in spite of Lamb's theory, a good actor 'may often illustrate, and be a sort of running comment to a play. . . .'[3] John Wilson in *Blackwood's* and T. N. Talfourd in the *Champion* agreed in accepting the proposition that Shakespeare loses more by staging than other dramatists, but insisted that his plays still have more beauties that come across in a theatre than others have. Wilson added that Lamb overestimated the fastidiousness of the imagination, and must have been aware of the attraction of his central paradox, 'which is overthrown by the universal consent of mankind'.[4] The *Monthly Review*, on the other hand, disagreed with the whole thesis by rejecting Lamb's premises that many can appreciate 'the more essentially poetical beauties of Shakspeare' or that such beauties are frequent. Shakespeare's 'pervading excellencies . . . are obvious and popular', the reviewer contended, and based his argument, as did Wilson, on experience.[5]

Of the remaining works in the volumes, *A Tale of Rosamund Gray* was most popular; it even managed to evoke considerable mawkish praise. *Mr. H.* was likewise well received, but several reviewers were hostile. Leigh Hunt in the *Examiner* thought that too much interest was built up in the suspense concerning Mr. H.'s

[1] *BC*, XI 2s (Feb., 1819), 141.
[2] *BM*, III (Aug., 1818), 602.
[3] *GM*, LXXXIX–ii (Aug., 1819), 140.
[4] *BM*, III (Aug., 1818), 608.
[5] *MR*, XC (Nov., 1810), 256.

name (Hogsflesh), with disappointment inevitably following its disclosure. *John Woodvil,* in this its second trial before the reviewers, was given some favorable comments; but with the exception of Talfourd's encomium in the *Champion,* it did not fare a great deal better than before.

Lamb's last volume in the period, *Elia: Essays Which Have Appeared under That Signature in the London Magazine* (1823) contains his best-known work. Unfortunately, probably because republished works were usually not reviewed, there were only three reviews, one unfavorable and two favorable. The hostile critique was a very brief one in the *Monthly Magazine,* brief but to the point:

> The pleasure afforded by [the essays] is in a great measure weakened, and sometimes destroyed, by a disagreeable quaintness and affectation. The author's style is founded on the writers of Queen Elizabeth's time, and with many of their beauties he has a still greater proportion of their defects. In some of his papers he will delight the reader by the originality of his subjects, and his pleasant manner of treating them, whilst, in others, he will absolutely disgust, by their revolting indelicacy, and sometimes by their ridiculous puerility.[1]

The critique in the *Monthly Review* was favorable, beginning with praise of 'this flow of original thought, this depth of feeling, this wise and playful humanity, this vein of mixed humour and melancholy running through every line', which together proved the anonymous volume to have been written by Lamb.[2] The *Monthly Review* was particularly interested in Lamb's humor, 'a rich but peculiar fund of drollery; which, though not absolutely amounting to wit, has a fine comic flavor in it that is difficult to resist', further described as 'original humor;—a sort of simple shrewdness and caustic irony, such as we have occasionally known to baffle, in the shape of a simple witness, some keen-set and veteran practitioner of law'.[3] And yet the 'marks of genius' in the essays 'are so whimsically blended with the peculiarities of the author's school, (a school of affected nature and humorous simplicity,) and so dashed with quaintness and conceit, though of a harmless kind, that we cannot resist their influence; and, much as we like their character, we must sometimes indulge a laugh AT as well as WITH the author'.[4] Lamb's

[1] *MM* LV (Feb., 1823), 62–63.
[2] *MR*, CI (June, 1823), 202.
[3] *Ibid.*, pp. 203, 204.
[4] *Ibid.*, p. 203.

serious side, his 'deep vein of pathetic eloquence and powerful appeals both to the heart and the intellect of his readers', was also praised, as was his freedom from dogmatism and virulence.[1] The *Monthly Review* preferred the earlier essays in the volume to the later, such as 'A Dissertation on Roast Pig', and 'Dream Children', which have 'all the peculiarities and excesses, all the metaphysical conjectures and dreamings, of his genius, with not a little of the egotism and quaintness of manner in which he loves to indulge'.[2]

The British Critic was likewise favorable; it considered the essays 'transcendently above the usual level of magazine productions'.[3] The essays were divided into three categories, 'Reminiscences, Extravaganzas, and Essays proper'. Concerning the first category, which included, for example, 'On Some of the Old Actors', Lamb was said to be a 'vivid and accurate recorder'. The reviewer was more qualified in his praise of the second, the 'Extravaganzas': 'All Fool's Day' was 'rather a tame piece of tom-foolery, suited to the occasion', and 'On the Acting of Munden' was too much in the abrupt style of Hazlitt.[4] But 'A Dissertation on Roast Pig' was thought 'a fair and legitimate piece of good fun; intended, perhaps, as a hit at the modern mock-important school of gastronomy, with the sublime Louis Eustache Ude [the author of a popular French cook-book], at its head'. The 'Essays proper', the third category, were said to be the best, with both the 'great humour and liveliness of allusion, as well as happiness of expression' of the essays in the other categories, as well as a frankness, indulgence, and grace of their own.[5] The 'Dream Children' was 'one of the prettiest gems in the volume', and 'The Quaker Meeting, The Praise of Chimney Sweepers, and Modern Gallantry, will be read not only with pleasure, but with benefit to the better feelings.' Lamb was also compared favorably with Washington Irving and Laurence Sterne.

Although Lamb did not publish a great deal in book form compared with other writers in the period 1802 to 1824 he met with a generally more favorable reception than most. This is especially true of his two last, most important publications. There was practically nothing of a controversial nature in his works, no political intrusions to upset the equanimity of his reviewers. Consequently, only literary issues were raised; Lamb's, therefore, was perhaps the

[1] *Ibid.*, p. 204.
[2] *Ibid.*, p. 206.
[3] *BC*, XX 2s (July, 1823), 84.
[4] *Ibid.*, p. 88.
[5] *Ibid.*, p. 91.

best example of the kind of equitable reception which was possible, though rare, in the period.

George Crabbe

George Crabbe, the last writer to be considered in this study, is today one of the most neglected poets of the period—one of the poets with greatest merit and smallest reputation. This circumstance is no doubt partially brought about by his use of heroic couplets, a form very different from that used by most of his contemporaries, and by his realistic treatment of his subject-matter, which also sets him apart from most of his Romantic colleagues. Too careless and loose in his style to be considered an Augustan and too Augustan in much of his view of human nature to be considered a Romantic, Crabbe simply evades treatment in either category and so is often ignored. His poetic career itself overlapped the late Augustan and early Romantic periods. He began to publish in the 1770's and 1780's, and, then, after a fallow period of over twenty years, began his most prolific career in 1807 with his *Poems*, followed by *The Borough* (1810), *Tales in Verse* (1812), and *Tales of the Hall* (1819).

His poems are very similar in form and content, being for the most part collections of tales written in heroic couplets. Reviews of these poems consequently show considerable similarity. The reception given Crabbe's works was almost unanimously favorable, the principal exception being the hostile reviews of *The Borough* by the *Quarterly Review*, the *Eclectic Review*, and the *Monthly Mirror*. It was not, however, the case that Crabbe was received with open arms; his reception by contemporary critics, despite their final approval of the volumes, was in fact stormy. Jeffrey threw the full weight of the *Edinburgh Review* behind Crabbe; and although this promotion was probably not essential to Crabbe's acceptance, the poet's faults, picked apart by all of the reviewers, were considered sufficiently prominent and serious to require extenuation. As Jeffrey put it at the end of his review of the *Tales of the Hall*, 'Mr. Crabbe is so unequal a writer, and at times so unattractive, as to require, more than any other of his degree, some explanation of his system, and some specimens of his powers. . . .'[1]

The most considerable of Crabbe's powers, as far as the reviewers

[1] *ER*, XXXII (Aug., 1819), 148.

were concerned, was that of characterization, his ability to plumb the depths of his characters, his genius in presenting varied but vivid portraits. Several reviewers even remarked that Crabbe undoubtedly had living models for his characters. His talent for portraying madness was especially applauded. For instance, his portrait of the mad hero of 'Sir Eustace Grey' (in the *Poems*) elicited the following comment from the *Universal Magazine*: 'The language is adapted to the subject in a pleasing manner; and the abrupt transitions of Sir Eustace, not wholly incoherent, but preserving an almost evanescent chain of connection, are proofs of Mr. Crabbe's skill. An ordinary poet would have made his hero talk in nothing but interjections.'[1]

Most of Crabbe's characters belonged to the lower orders of society, particularly in the earlier volumes. This aspect of his poems was generally accepted. There was, however, some censure on this point, and the *Monthly Magazine* in its review of *Tales of the Hall* came to Crabbe's defense, showing the influence of new poetic theories in the process: 'let it be considered, that it is not in the drawing-rooms of the great, among the artificial, well-trained sons and daughters of fashion, that human passions, and the genuine impulses of the heart, are best displayed; but among the unsophisticated children of Nature in the humbler walks of life'.[2]

It was not subject-matter, but rather Crabbe's treatment of it, that was disapproved. Applause for the truth and fidelity of Crabbe's representations was, nonetheless, a frequent note in the reviews; Jeffrey's *Edinburgh Review* critique of the *Poems*, for instance, praised Crabbe for exhibiting 'the common people of England pretty much as they are', in contrast to Wordsworth, who presents 'certain whimsical and unheard of beings'.[3] And yet in his review in the *Edinburgh Review* of the next volume, Jeffrey maintained that Crabbe's 'chief fault' was 'his frequent lapse into disgusting representations', and went on to define his terms:

> With regard . . . to human character, action, and feeling, we should be inclined to term every thing disgusting, which represented misery, without making any appeal to our love or our admiration. . . . The only sufferers, then, upon whom we cannot bear to look, are those that excite pain by their wretchedness, while they are too depraved to be the objects of affection, and too weak and insignificant to be the causes of misery to others, or, consequently, of indignation to the spectators.[4]

[1] *UM*, X 2s (Nov., 1808), 128.
[2] *MM*, XLVIII (Sept., 1819), 155.
[3] *ER*, XII (Apr., 1808), 133.
[4] *ER*, XVI (Apr., 1810), 36, 38.

Without propounding any such theories, many other reviewers also objected to some of the tales as disgusting.

'Unpleasant' and 'gloomy' were less forceful terms of disapprobation applied to Crabbe's realistic portrayals. Some, to be sure, attempted to defend Crabbe's realism and morbid view of the world. John Wilson in his review of the *Tales of the Hall* in *Blackwood's* was one such; after admitting that 'the pleasure he excites is almost always a troubled pleasure', Wilson argued that, if in parts the poems were gloomy, this was not the feeling given by the whole.[1] But more reviewers objected to Crabbe's realism. Many did so with no explanation, but several others accepted the truth of Crabbe's pictures of life, and yet insisted that realism had no place in poetry. Robert Grant in his *Quarterly Review* critique of *The Borough* took the escapist theory of poetry as far as it would go: '. . . It is precisely in order to escape from the world as it is, that we fly to poetry.'[2] Most of those who disapproved of Crabbe's morbid realism, however, denied that it did present a realistic view of life, and insisted that it was too extreme, or rather, one-sided. The *British Review* commented on the *Tales in Verse*:

We are not apt to rate our fallen nature too high; but we cannot think the malignancy of conduct and temper which this volume describes so frequent in the present state of humanity, under the influence of religion and education, as to amount to more than exceptions to a rule. . . .[3]

Somewhere between the two positions, the *Critical Review*, in its review of *The Borough*, offered some practical advice:

we recollect that pleasure is a very material, and by most esteemed the chief, end of poetry. Now this pleasure is weakened, and even changed to disgust, by repeated stories of woe: surely, some method might have been found to intermix the cheerful with the mournful, that both the reader's pleasure and instruction might be unabated. We see no reason why all the poor of the Borough, on whose history Mr. Crabbe enlarges, should be either atrociously criminal or heart-rendingly unfortunate. . . .[4]

Further on, the same reviewer observed, 'we fear that men, who have seen much, if they tell what they see, must unfortunately communicate more evil, than good, respecting their species'.[5]

[1] *BM*, V (July, 1819), 472.
[2] *QR*, IV (Nov., 1810), 282.
[3] *BR*, IV (Oct., 1812), 56.
[4] *CR*, XX 3s (July, 1810), 303.
[5] *Ibid.*, p. 305.

Crabbe's power of description, usually considered his second greatest merit, received constant applause for accuracy and vividness, but also occasioned a good deal of censure for being too minute and detailed. This facet of his writing was referred to as 'Chinese accuracy' or, more often—the phrase occurs in almost every review —as 'Dutch minuteness'. Jeffrey, in his *Edinburgh Review* criticism of the *Poems*, admitted that Crabbe's descriptions at times 'enter into details which many readers may pronounce tedious and unnecessary'. 'Yet', Jeffrey added, 'there is a justness and force in the representation which is entitled to something more than indulgence. . . .'[1] Others reviewers were, however, something less than indulgent. Thomas Denman, in his critique of the *Tales in Verse* in the *Monthly Review*, thought the detail unrealistic: '. . . We are disposed to question whether verisimilitude be in truth increased by an enumeration of such particulars, as we are sure would be omitted and overlooked by a person who was relating a series of real facts.'[2] The *Eclectic Review* censured the detailed descriptions in the same work on the grounds that 'the reader of poetry must owe half his pleasure to his own fancies and associations' and that therefore 'to particularize description is most grievously to fetter the imagination'. 'Where every thing is told', he summed up, 'nothing can be added.'[3] In its review of the same volume, the *Critical Review* denied that Crabbe had any right to be compared to the Dutch school of painters, who, besides their minuteness, 'are at least as remarkable for the force, brilliancy, and . . . *terseness* of their execution', while Crabbe, who,

> forgetting this important ingredient, squanders himself away in tedious and flat circumstantiality, may indeed resemble *the school* . . . but will never be ranked by the connoisseur or the critic on the same level with Teniers, Ostade, or Vandevelde. It is not his love of minuteness and detail which ought to be objected to Mr. Crabbe, but his want of taste and discrimination in rendering those qualities subservient to the general effect of his picture.[4]

Besides general praise of his characterizations and descriptions, the reviewers found Crabbe deserving of approval for the morality

[1] *ER*, XII (Apr., 1808), 141.
[2] *MR*, LXIX (Dec., 1812), 353.
[3] *EcR*, VIII ii (Dec., 1812), 1244, 1245.
[4] *CR*, II 4s (Dec., 1812), 576.

in his works, especially for his frequent moral reflections. He was even said several times to be the most moral poet of the age. And yet, as was the case with the other qualities praised, Crabbe was often censured for moral shortcomings. Since Crabbe, besides being a poet, was a minister of the Church of England, it is not to be expected that the strictures concerned lapses of a prurient nature. Nevertheless, he was taken to task by the *Eclectic Review* (on *The Borough*) for too favorable an attitude toward sensual pleasure and by the *Christian Observer* (on the *Tales of the Hall*) for too much emphasis on amatory themes. The moral censure was more often aimed at the absence of any moral purpose in many of the tales; readers, it was objected, were thereby depressed by morbid stories for no good reason.

Other censure of a moral nature likewise turned upon Crabbe's gloomy picture of human nature, which was censured on other grounds as well, as we have seen. The reviewer of the *Tales in Verse* in the *British Review* observed:

> The heart is rather hardened than corrected by these degrading views of its character. A tacit reservation in favour of oneself prevents its operation as a lesson of humility, while it shuts up the fountains of charity and benevolence towards our fellow creatures.[1]

Thomas Denman, reviewing *The Borough* in the *Monthly Review*, objected to a kind of determinism:

> surely a more frequent exhibition of the ability of virtue to triumph over our evil propensities would be but a fair encouragement to frail human nature. To tell us that there are certain temptations under which we cannot fail to yield, as soon as they are adequately presented to us, is in fact to say that we are puppets of an overpowering destiny. . . .[2]

The critic in the *Christian Observer* of Crabbe's last volume likewise noted that Christianity seemed 'a totally insufficient antidote either to the ills or the vices of mankind', and suggested that his works be renamed 'The Triumph of Vice'.[3] Crabbe's participation in one of the popular sports of the period, baiting Methodists, was also censured, even by some who agreed with his point of view, as liable to bring piety in general into contempt.

[1] *BR*, IV (Oct., 1812), 56–57.
[2] *MR*, LXI (Apr., 1810), 398.
[3] *CO*, XVIII (Oct., 1819), 660.

Crabbe's poetic form, as well as content, occasioned a good many mixed judgments. The reviewers often reprimanded Crabbe for his general carelessness, his faulty spelling and punctuation, occasional obscurity, lazy imitations of other poets, and incorrect grammar. The reviewer of the *Poems* in the *Annual Review* urbanely considered these defects to be part of a general coarseness necessarily contracted by 'the *rusticated* portion of our gentry and clergy' living out 'among clowns and cattle'.[1] Some of the grammatical errors were sufficiently glaring to warrant such a remark; examples noted in the same volume by the *Universal Magazine* were 'Where all that's wretched pave the way for death' and 'Some princes had it, or was said to have'.

Crabbe's versification, on the other hand, was often applauded. The *British Critic*, judging *The Borough*, observed that his versification

> is well suited to his subjects; easy and flowing; sometimes apparently negligent; at others pointed and neat. The reader, as he proceeds, is neither fatigued by constant exertion, nor satiated by uniformity of style; he can read the letters with as much ease as if they were prose, with the frequently recurring stimulus of poetical effect, both in the thought and in the expressions.[2]

Other reviewers agreed that the versification was often prosaic, but were not so sure that the negligence was only 'apparent', and censured the verse for frequent harshness. James Montgomery, reviewing the *Poems* in the *Eclectic Review*, however, agreed with the *British Critic* in thinking that the verse was generally fluent, but found it 'exceedingly monotonous; the pause in his heroic measure falling sometimes through ten couplets in a page after the fourth and fifth syllables. . . .' And yet, he continued, Crabbe 'often strikes out single lines of perfect excellence, sententious as proverbs, and pointed like epigrams'.[3] Still others objected to fill-in lines, inversions, and too frequent antithesis—fatiguing in a long poem.

Crabbe's diction met a similar fate, with, on the one hand, praise of the simplicity, copiousness, and energy of his language, and, on the other, censure of occasional harshness, quaintness, and a gossipy familiarity, replete with contractions. Admitting the flaws and Crabbe's unevenness, Jeffrey, in his *Edinburgh Review* critique of

[1] *AR*, VI (1808), 519.

[2] *BC*, XXXVII (Mar., 1811), 238.

[3] *EcR*, V, i (Jan., 1809), 43.

The Borough, nevertheless thought Crabbe's style distinguished 'by great force and compression of diction,—a sort of sententious brevity, once thought essential to poetical composition, but of which he is now the only living example'.[1] The *Monthly Review* considered Crabbe's diction, by the time the final volume was published, to have been so corrupted by the influence of the poetic practice of the age that his verse no longer resembled the Augustans' except as caricature; and the reviewer objected strongly to the 'patches of familiar conversation, interspersed occasionally with high and heart-rending subjects of feeling', which 'have the effect of a pail of dirty water flung into a face which has just begun to be agitated with some heroic emotion!'[2] Many reviewers also censured Crabbe for incorrect rhymes; and the *New Monthly Magazine*, after approving highly of the effect gained by Crabbe's use of triplets 'in the close of an heroic climax', complained that they 'occur as frequently in the middle as in the close of a descriptive period'.[3] Crabbe's puns and plays-on-words were a further source of irritation to several reviewers.

The over-all construction of the poems was censured heavily as well. The frames were considered most often to be either dull in themselves or as providing little unity, with a consequent boredom on the part of the reader. And yet the *Tales in Verse* had no frame whatsoever, and the *British Review* had no objections:

> The manner of relating a story is, without doubt, an important agent in producing its effect upon the hearer, but it looks like a fanciful refinement to consider the reader of a tale as deriving any collateral entertainment from a secret reference in his mind to the supposed character of the narrator.[4]

But the same reviewer thought the absence of suspense and intricacy in the individual tales to be a large draw-back: '. . . In most of the tales simplicity exceeds its proper measure.' 'They want', he continued, 'the necessary stamina of a story, and are incapable of exciting curiosity, or of fixing attention.'[5] The *Eclectic Review*, in its

[1] *ER*, XVI (Apr., 1810), 53.
[2] *MR*, XC (Nov., 1819), 228.
[3] *NMM*, XII (Sept., 1819), 204.
[4] *BR*, IV (Oct., 1812), 55.
[5] *Ibid.*, p. 56.

review of *The Borough*, objected to both the lack of unity in the whole and of interest in the parts:

The admirable descriptions of scenery and sketches of character have scarcely any connection and dependence, either mutual or common; and would lose no interest if detached. There is also a great sameness in the subjects; they are specifically different, but generically alike.[1]

The *Critical Review*, moreover, in its review of the *Tales in Verse* thought that a lack of dramatic skill accompanied Crabbe's genius for portraying 'strong individual traits of character' and that, as a result, most of the tales seemed more like 'characters'.[2]

But, the same reviewer remarked, this same genius was particularly suited for satire; and Crabbe's satiric talents, as well as his humor and his frequent touches of pathos, were still other aspects of his poetry which aroused great admiration. Add to this list the frequent commendation of Crabbe's 'strength', 'force', and 'power of mind', and one arrives at an idea of the reviewers' estimate of Crabbe's poetic range.

Crabbe's reception by his contemporary reviewers was totally unlike that experienced by the other writers dealt with in this study. No other writer was at the same time so bombarded with hostile criticism and yet so praised for having fully compensated for all his faults with still superior merits. The *British Critic* could begin its critique of Crabbe's last volume in the following manner:

We love a Poem which will bear to be outrageously abused: not one, we mean, in which it is impossible to find any thing worth praising; but one which deserves so much praise, and will *have* so much, in spite of all we can say against it, that we may, without compassion, venture to fall foul of every thing that displeases or dissatisfies us. Mr. Crabbe, of all our contemporary Poets, certainly takes most pains to gratify this propensity in us. . . .[3]

All but a few reviewers indulged the propensity, and yet Crabbe almost invariably came away with their commendation.

[1] *EcR*, VI, i (June, 1810), 561.
[2] *CR*, II 4s (Dec., 1812), 562.
[3] *BC*, XII 2s (Sept., 1819), 285.

Part III

Attitudes, Policies, and Practices

Posterity is a severe, and, commonly, an impartial judge; but contemporary criticism, though often the former, is seldom, perhaps never, the latter. A thousand motives, always imperceptible to the world, sometimes to ourselves, and which, if we knew them, we should blush to own, are silently, but effectually operating upon our minds, when we would judge the merits of a living candidate for fame; prejudices, favourable and unfavourable are at work; something we know, or something that we heard; something we see, or something we surmise; a rival or an enemy to oppose; a friend to uphold; good or bad passions to gratify; pride to conciliate that feels humbled in the acknowledgment of genius; and even the pride of maintaining what we have carelessly asserted, as well as the affectation of deviating from established opinion, are among the chief of those obstructions to impartiality in our decisions upon living merit, which the moralists and writers of every age have deplored, but which the wisdom and purity of no age will be able to eradicate.

The *Universal Magazine* (review of *The Lady of the Lake*)

7

Attitudes, Policies, and Practices

Not even in the most expansive moments of generalizing would anyone familiar with the Romantic Reviews imagine that in attempting to ascertain and set forth common policies and practices of the reviewers he was speaking about *all* the Reviews, much less all the reviewers. The difficulties inherent in such a misconception are only too obvious. There are too many Reviews of too many different kinds; and there are too many different reviewers involved, each writing for periodicals which, as individual entities, are often inconsistent in policy and practice. Yet there are patterns of critical thought, policy, and practice that allow for generalizations, mostly in need of qualification but nevertheless valid as far as they go. The following general comments are intended to supply such patterns.

One of the most common attributes of the reviewers is their sense of performing an important function, of being part of a serious endeavor—serious not solemn, for there is too much humor in most of the reviews to pose a question of solemnity. Literature itself was almost always taken seriously. Misuse of diction could lead to corruption of the language; the public taste could also finally be corrupted by bad literature. Literature, in the words of the *British Review*, is 'a powerful engine of moral persuasion . . .', capable of much good or much evil.[1]

Sharing this serious attitude, the reviewers thought their critical

[1] *BR*, IX (Feb., 1817), 21.

function was to influence both the writer and the reader. Duty to the writer was more often mentioned; frequently the poet was to be set straight on certain errors of content or form, and his imitators were often included in the strictures. This corrective influence was most frequently considered to be direct; that is, the reviewer pointed out errors which the writer would, unless incorrigible, take pains to correct. There were even claims put forward occasionally that a particular poet had listened to specific advice (as no doubt must sometimes have happened), but there were also asides, not without at times a tinge of self-pity or frustration, that the poet under review would most probably ignore such advice. A more likely explanation of the effects of their critical pronouncements was given by the *Monthly Review*:

> It would indeed be a satisfaction to the professional critic, and a reward for his long labours, if he could entertain the remotest idea of any *direct* effect being produced by them, on the extravagant mistakes of genius, and on the corruptions of contemporary taste. It might be Utopian to form an expectation of this nature: but it perhaps may not be wholly chimerical to entertain the pleasing hope that an *indirect* effect is, in some distinguished cases, so produced; and that the re-action of literary opinion produces an amendment in style which no individual censor, or body of censors, can accomplish. In this comparatively slow result of criticism, in this good produced by the circuitous diffusion of truth, the critic only shares the common lot of all who work for the improvement of their fellow-men. Especially may he console himself with the reflection, that his superiors in the great council of the nation, who *criticize* on so much ampler a scale, are forced like himself, to wait for this same *round-about* result of their patriotic orations: ministers being quite as incorrigible as authors by any *direct* appeal; and the well-informed of the community—whose judgment needs only to be awakened and recalled to sound principles, whether of government or of literary composition, in order to demand and to secure the necessary changes in practice—being at last the *rational reformers* by whom the prevailing evils are corrected.[1]

And along with this attempt at a corrective influence, individual reviewers frequently made an effort to defend a poet or poem; sometimes they even appealed to the reader to reserve his judgment until he had read a poem several times.

Responsibility to the reading public seems to have been generally

[1] *MR*, XCIII (Oct., 1820), 132–33.

considered secondary to duty to the poet. Since readers turned to Reviews for information about which books were worth buying and reading, this information had to be supplied. On this account, the reviewers waged relentless war against 'bookmaking'. Limited and expensive quarto editions were frequently attacked, as well as collections hastily and poorly thrown together and publications with little substance, eked out and padded with long notes or prefaces. Moreover, the taste of the public, as well as its wallet, had to be protected; and even more important, public morality required careful protection, as will be discussed shortly.

The reviewers realized that in order to fulfill these obligations they must possess certain qualities. Impartiality was considered one of the most important; certainly it was the virtue most often claimed. Critical liberality and flexibility were esteemed to be next in importance, though here there was the recognizable danger of falling into the traps posed by that extreme opposite from dogmatism—critical flabbiness. The *Universal Magazine* voiced what was probably the majority opinion on this matter in its answer to Crabbe's advice to critics ('Spite of truth, let mercy guide your pen'): 'This is specious reasoning: it cloathes error in the form of virtue; and would dignify, sometimes, the vices of the heart with the laurels which should be worn by the uncorrupted, and incorruptible, powers of the mind.—Mercy unrestrained by truth, and unsupported by justice, is a solemn crime against the rights of society.'[1] Humility was not an uncommon element in reviews. Despite the general concept of reviewers as implacable and rule-ridden, they did not generally fill that role in their criticism, even making disarmingly frank admissions of their human fallibility on occasions.

All of their upright attitudes toward literature and criticism and their attempts at virtue were not, however, sufficient to protect the reviewers from the scorn of their contemporaries. The truth is that people do not like criticism, although they may recognize its importance and validity; criticism is in the end always a thankless task. Poets have long been recognized as irritable and peculiarly sensitive to criticism, and the Romantic poets were no exception. At least thirteen separate literary works published in the period contained some sign of disdain for criticism. In addition, ironically, individual reviewers themselves quite often expressed great scorn for their

[1] *UM*, XI 2s (Jan., 1809), 44–45.

colleagues. Cant, bias, insensitivity were only some of the charges leveled at others; in fact, no later commentator, no matter how indignant, could match the reviewers in this regard. When the Romantic reviewers are evaluated, it is only fair to remember some of these irritants they had to endure.

Because attitudes toward literature have undergone such drastic changes since the Romantic period, there are other aspects of reviewing which contemporaries took for granted but which are now obstacles to a just appreciation of the Reviews: the introduction of morality, religion, politics, and 'personality' into literary considerations.

Moral issues would most probably cause the least discomfort now, although there is at least one example of a recent commentator who considered the raising of moral issues as mere bigotry.[1] And the claim that literature is purposeless is not uncommon in critical circles. Art-for-art's-sake is a concept developed during the nineteenth century and probably would not even have been understood by the Romantic reviewers (or the Romantic poets, for that matter).[2] It is worth remarking that all of the great minds in critical theory from Aristotle to Matthew Arnold were of the same mind as the reviewers. The morality of art is, in any case, still an open question.

Literature, as far as the reviewers were concerned, had a moral purpose, variously described but always present either explicitly or implicitly. Most often moral issues were raised in order to censure writers, but this was not always so. A good deal of praise was dispensed, usually of a general nature, in a situation, for example, when a work had the proper overall moral tone.

When the moral concern of the reviewers was censorious the criticism was often quite specific. Matters of sexual morality were conspicuous among such objections, although confined mainly to Byron's *Beppo* and *Don Juan*, Hazlitt's *Liber Amoris*, and many works of Shelley and Moore. Outright examples of prurience in poetry of the times were rare, and many reviewers were aware of this. They often insisted, however, that this only made some works more dan-

[1] William S. Ward, 'Some Aspects of the Conservative Attitude toward Poetry in English Criticism, 1798–1820', pp. 394–95.

[2] For the attitude of the Romantic poets to the morality of literature, see Walter Jackson Bate, *From Classic to Romantic* (New York: Harper, 1946), pp. 168–72; and M. H. Abrams, *The Mirror and the Lamp* (New York: Oxford University Press, 1963), pp. 328–32.

gerous. Natural modesty might lead one to close a pornographic book—and, besides, such could be legislated against—but a work which by sheer poetic enchantment could insinuate a lax attitude toward sexual morality, especially in the young and inexperienced, was extremely dangerous.

That position, reasonable or otherwise, is not, however, an end of the matter. The phrasing of their strictures concerning sexual morality frequently becomes emotional enough to detract from their arguments, and so issues are often confused. Even worse, some reviewers showed signs of an unhealthy puritanical attitude. The *Christian Observer*, usually more sophisticated, announced that although sex and marriage are both God-given, 'We cannot but look forward to that time when, in its grosser sense, "we shall neither marry nor be given in marriage, but shall be as the angels of God in heaven" '.[1] There were also obtuse objections raised to kinds of subject-matter *per se*, particularly themes of incest; while some of the moral strictures took on a ridiculous nationalistic slant, chaste England being compared with indecent France or voluptuous Italy. Works were, moreover, sometimes proscribed only for the fair sex, who were considered often to be innocent and modest, besides being blessed with warm sensibilities which made them especially susceptible to corruptive poetry. The exclusion of dangerous works from the family circle, another form of condemnation, is not easily dismissed, since family readings were a custom of the age; and depending on the volatility of the subject-matter or the scruples and ages of those present, such warnings, at least in theory, could be legitimate.

But sexual morality, although it was raised more often than any other single issue in the reviews, was by no means the only moral issue raised. In fact, other kinds of moral objections in total, amount to more than double those made on the grounds of sexual morality. The sixth commandment had not yet taken over the field.

The dissemination of corrupting sentiments and principles was a frequent moral objection. The sympathetic representation of contempt for law and order met with such censure, as did an overly degrading view of human nature, which might lead to despair. Fatalism and ridicule of virtue were also objected to. The *Eclectic Review* carried on an almost single-handed campaign against the

[1] *CO*, XVIII (Oct., 1819), 666.

glorification of war; and others attacked works which advocated or displayed admiration for cruelty, revenge, or suicide. Presenting vicious heroes was censured on many grounds, chief of which were that vice and virtue were often confused and that dangerous sympathy was evoked for the hero's vices by token of his virtues. Trifling with sentiments, objected to so strongly in reviews of *Don Juan*, was vaguely regarded as immoral, presumably because the trifling led to cynicism.

Since literature was considered moral and since many works published in the period had no ostensible end other than entertainment, lack of moral purpose was a frequent point of censure. The *Anti-jacobin Review* gave what was probably the position of many reviewers: 'An interesting poem, and an amusing novel, are the best channels of instruction to the general class of readers; and he who, having the ability to inform or amend others, neglects to employ [it] for that purpose, does not perform his duty to society.'[1] The Horatian formula that art pleases and instructs was generally accepted, but just how the poet went about instructing his readers is not always clear. The reviewers had little use for strictly didactic poetry, but sometimes the process of instruction is considered to be as direct as is otherwise possible; that is, instruction is conveyed by stories which tell of vice punished and virtue rewarded. And yet references to poetic or dramatic justice in the reviews covered in this study amount to no more than a dozen. There were also occasional statements concerning the moral purpose of poetry which indicate a wider, more acceptable concept. The *Edinburgh Monthly Review*, for example, remarked 'that for sublime and impressive moral *effect*, many pages of Milton and Shakspeare far transcend every thing that has been written by the semi-prosaic school of *direct* moral teachers . . .', and the *Christian Observer* commented that Crabbe instructed by his close delineation of characters, which help us to discriminate in real life, as well as by 'the perpetual recurrence, of inimitable home-strokes', which help us to judge our own minds and motives.[2]

The morality of the reviewers was fundamentally Christian, and the moral strictures were not confined to the periodicals with religious affiliations. Nor was the introduction of more strictly religious

[1] *AjR*, XXXIV (Sept., 1809), 5.
[2] *EMR*, V (May, 1821), 625; *CO*, XVIII (Oct., 1819), 660.

matters into literary criticism, although the religiously oriented periodicals were naturally more concerned with religious issues. Such issues were raised frequently in the criticism of the period; and if the moral insistence of the reviewers is distasteful to some today, the intrusion of religion will be even more so. Some of the objections on religious grounds were indeed obtuse, while others contained intelligent arguments against irreligious theories, themselves intruded into works under review. Unless ideas are considered unimportant, silence on the part of the opposite side would be unnatural; and in any case the reviewers did consider such ideas important. They usually did not go out of their way to introduce religious issues, and it is likely that had there been no provocation, the issues would not have been raised.

The religious battle was often joined on the philosophical level, somewhere beyond particular doctrines and creeds. The pre-existence of the soul, the rejection of an afterlife, and scepticism in general were discussed, sometimes heatedly, sometimes rationally. The latter mode was not always easy; the provocations, for example, in *The Revolt of Islam*, were sometimes wild and irrational themselves. The *Literary Register* observed, 'We think it reasonable that, in a free country, any man shall be allowed to try whatever theoretic voyage he pleases—decently; gravely, or wittily, but still decently: like a philosopher; like a man. . . .' Atheism should be respected if sincere and presented with decency, 'but if it be attempted with sneers and scoffs instead of cool assertion and argument—if our quiet belief—say prejudice—is to be insulted with mockery, and not approached with argument; if we are bandied upon our attributed weakness . . . fie, fie—such a course of proceeding can only arouse our loathing and our chastisement.'[1]

The reviewing periodicals were almost solidly Christian in outlook, but there was sectarian bickering in the reviews, attacks and defenses of Methodists, Unitarians, and Roman Catholics. There was also, nevertheless, a fairly consistent stand taken against profane use of Scripture, blasphemy, levity in the treatment of religious subjects, and anti-clericalism. The principal exception to this solid front was the *Examiner*, in which Leigh Hunt expounded his Universalist views.

Although on all of the above points, both philosophic and more

[1] *LitReg*, Oct. 19, 1822, p. 241.

strictly religious, there were level-headed discussions, not infrequently extreme positions were taken. Often the reviewers, especially in the periodicals with religious affiliations, would indulge in religious comments which were simply impertinent. Byron, for instance, was several times advised to read his Bible, and several writers were referred to as fiends. Such excesses are, of course, indefensible, and lowered the tone of the reviews, at least from a literary point of view. On the other hand, there were many instances of a more sophisticated attitude on religious issues, as well as attacks on the religious excesses, which were usually referred to as 'cant'.

Religion is one topic traditionally proscribed from the drawing room; politics is another. But 'traditionally' must be qualified to mean since sometime after the Romantic period, for politics then pervaded almost every aspect of life. 'Never', recorded William Roberts in the *British Review*, 'has the mind of man been so bent from its natural and ordinary state by the great events of any era as by those of the present day', as by the French Revolution especially.[1] Walter Scott in the *Quarterly Review* referred to politics as 'that extensive gulph whose eddies draw every thing that is British into their vortex'.[2]

The Reviews, some of which were established for specifically political reasons, were at the center of that vortex. Three factions are discernible in the political life of the times and in the Reviews: the Whigs, the Tories, and the Radicals; but since the lines of distinction are often so hazy and since the Whigs and the Radicals often shared liberal attitudes in opposition to the Tories, it is more convenient to speak of the factions as two—liberal and conservative. Most of the reviewing periodicals, despite frequent claims of political independence, were aligned with either one side or the other. They were, in fact, split approximately down the middle, not in numbers—there being more conservative Reviews—but in probable degree of importance and influence. There were also a few, such as the *Literary Museum*, which not only claimed political independence but showed it in their political remarks.

Since, as was the case with religious issues, the writers of the period often obtruded their political views into their publications, political bias was bound sometimes to have influenced the evaluations of their works by the reviewers. It is, however, difficult to decide in most cases whether a reviewer is substituting political for

[1] *BR*, XII (Aug., 1818), 7.

[2] *QR*, XVI (Oct., 1816), 197.

literary values. Reviewers at times made such charges against each other, but in all the reviews covered the *British Critic* is the only Review to admit to having criticized with bias and the *Quarterly Review* is the only one to claim that literary considerations were subordinate to political; in neither case is it clear that reviewing policy is in question.[1] Without such evidence, it is presumptuous to consider a review to be biased merely on the grounds that the author and Review belong to opposite political camps; for literary values are almost always brought forward in the literary assessment. These values must first be proven falsely applied before such an allegation is justified. Furthermore, there are a sufficient number of instances of crossing of political lines in evaluations to make one wary of too easy charges of political bigotry.

The political bias, in any case, did not, of course, all work against the poets. Members of the Cockney School, for example, received more help than hindrance from their reviewers, where prejudice was probably involved. And the existence of political bigotry was not necessarily totally undesirable. The *British Critic* at least found some value in it:

> If one party condemn in excess, another will generally be found to praise in an equal excess; and after the first fermentation of contending opinions has a little subsided, the real truth gradually separates itself from the errors, with which it had been mixed, and becomes perhaps better and more certainly distinguishable, than by almost any other process, to which it could have been subjected. . . . One review is set up by men strongly biassed in favour of one system of principles; another starts in opposition to it by men as warmly favourable to the opposite; both of them, indeed, affect to speak with the authority, that belongs to the judicial office; but they are listened to as judges, only by those of their own party; the public knows well, that they are mere advocates, hired by their prejudices to plead the cause of a particular sect; and by listening to both sides, is much more likely to be put in possession of all the arguments in favour of each, than if it implicitly trusted to the impartiality, with which any single review could state them.[2]

Of the political observations occasioned by political elements in the works under review, some are concerned strictly with partisan politics. Such partisan remarks are usually very brief, since they were

[1] *BC*, XIV 2s Sept., 1820), 257; *QR*, XXI (Apr., 1819), 461.
[2] *BC*, VIII 2s (Nov., 1817), 468.

most often called forth by some slighting treatment of political figures, such as Wellington or Fox. When the work under review was a political satire, more remarks would of course be forthcoming; but if the author was not bitter and kept his satire within partisan limits, as was the case with Moore's *Fudge Family in Paris*, the criticism of the work was on the whole level-headed.

The introduction of dangerous political principles was something else again. Jacobinism, republicanism, attacks on monarchs and monarchy, unpatriotic censure of England or of the British army or navy, and praise of the French Revolution or Napoleon, on one side, and attacks on freedom of the press, on the other, were not strictly partisan issues. Censure of these political extremes was common to both the liberal and conservative periodicals, even though the emphasis differed. And in an age which had seen the aftermath of the French Revolution, it was only natural that concern with political principles and theories should have been intense and the censure heated. In the midst of the furor, an occasional voice could be heard appealing to the poets to exclude politics from their works.

Closely related to political bias was 'personality', or malicious allusions to the private lives of authors. 'Personality' does not, it should be pointed out, include references to an author where the author's personal make-up has in some way affected a work. Such would be a remark upon Hunt's mawkish sensibility, which is within the legitimate limits of the critic's concern. But references to Byron's lameness or to Shelley's marital problems are not.

The reviewers occasionally set forth a policy of reviewing the work and not the man, and many of them did just that. They also berated the writers themselves for unfair allusions to the private lives of fellow writers and political figures—Hazlitt and Byron were especially arraigned for this practice. And there was in fact very little 'personality' in the reviews. It is found mostly in *Blackwood's*, the *Quarterly Review*, and the *Literary Gazette*, all of which belonged to the conservative camp. The poets principally involved—Byron, Shelley, and Keats—were liberal in politics. Political animus is an obvious motive; the *Literary Gazette*, indeed, after mentioning that Shelley's children had been taken from him and that his first wife had committed suicide, admitted that critics should steer clear of a poet's private life, and yet added: 'but when the most horrible doctrines are promulgated with appalling force, it is the duty of every man to expose, in every way, the abominations to which they irresistibly drive their odious professors'.[1] Keats, it is worth noting with regard to 'personality', was not only personally maligned by *Blackwood's*, but had reference made to his 'sickened and shaken body' by Leigh Hunt in the *Indicator*; both personal allusions are equally out of place in criticism.[2]

Attendant on the political and social upheavals of the age, and perhaps to a great extent affected by them, the critical values of the reviewers were neither uniform nor well established. Sir James Macintosh, writing in the *Edinburgh* in 1813, called the age one in which 'the rules of judging and the habits of feeling are unsettled'.[3] The literature of the period has often been called the 'Romantic Revolution'; and the reviewers too sometimes discussed it in such terms. This view certainly is not far from the truth, for even though there was no real break with the past, there was a great deal of experimentation in literary form and content.

Probably in part to diminish feelings of insecurity in the face of so much change, some reviewers had recourse to what were variously referred to as 'established laws', 'rules of composition', 'models of taste', and 'classical authority'. Quite often these phrases occur in passing with little or no explanation. At other times, reviewers went into more detail, explaining that rules of literary criticism were in fact ascertainable from general or universal nature, from the fundamentally unchanging conditions and make-up of human nature itself. In the words of William Roberts in the *British Review*, such rules 'have their foundation in nature, truth, and just sentiment'.[4]

In any case, explicit appeal to rules occurs in a small percentage of the reviews covered in this study. And there are almost as many pronouncements on the insufficiency of criticism which relies too heavily on rules. The *New Monthly Magazine*, for example, remarked that

> it is not enough that the censor be acquainted with those common rules for the discussion of his subject, which have been suggested by the ablest writers of antiquity; he must have a mind pervious to the force of the 'thoughts that breathe and words that burn' of the poet upon whose productions he undertakes to comment—he must be alive to all those recondite excellencies which might escape the notice of an ordinary observer,

[1] *LG*, May 19, 1821, p. 305n.
[2] *Indic*, Aug. 9, 1820, p. 345.
[3] *ER*, XXII (Oct., 1813), 38.
[4] *BR*, VII (May, 1816), 457.

and he must possess, withal, a certain sublime sense of perfection which common readers are strangers to; and which, while it enables him to detect worthlessness and deformity, affords him also equally the means of duly appreciating the beauty of loveliness.[1]

The *Universal Magazine* took the most extreme position: 'The favourite rules of composition, hitherto received, are seldom drawn from any settled principle, or self-evident postulate; neither are they adapted to the natural and invariable constitution of things, but will be found upon examination the arbitrary edicts of legislators, authorized only by themselves. . . .'[2] Furthermore, rejections of arguments based on precedent occur. There are a good number of appeals to experience, both to the personal experience of the reviewer (and sometimes of those with whom he has conversed) on reading a particular work, and, more important, to general experience or observation when appraising the credibility of incidents or characters in a piece of literature. Occasionally, too, readers are merely given quotations and told to judge for themselves the quality of a work.

The charge of dogmatism which has frequently been made against the reviewers most probably originates with a distaste for the over-confident tone of some of them. The reviewers, it is true, for the most part appear to have felt that they knew very well what they were about. This spirit, held within bounds, is, I believe, an asset to a critic. It was not, however, always held within reasonable bounds; Francis Jeffrey in the *Edinburgh Review*, for example, upon the rejection of his previous advice to George Crabbe, began his review of Crabbe's next volume: 'We are very thankful to Mr. Crabbe for these Tales; as we must always be for any thing that comes from his hands. But they are not exactly the tales which we wanted.'[3]

And yet the reviewers' final pronouncements, regardless of the tone of the rest of the review, are almost always qualified. Such words and phrases as 'we think', 'in our opinion', 'perhaps', 'on the whole' are fitted in somewhere in the judgments. Although admittedly they probably often fulfill a rhetorical function in the prose rhythm, there is every reason to suppose that this function is subordinate to that of qualification. That the reviewers were aware of the limitations of their pronouncements is evidenced by their use of qualifications that occasionally result in annoyingly fainthearted

[1] *NMM*, XI (May, 1819), 337.
[2] *UM*, XVI (Aug., 1811), 126.
[3] *ER*, XX (Nov., 1812), 277.

critiques. The *Monitor* summed up its criticism of *Manfred*: 'With respect to the general merit of the poem, as a whole, it is perhaps the most finished of his Lordship's productions. . . .'[1]

With or without strict rules, the reviewers must necessarily have had some general notions about literature, what it is and how it comes into being. Since, however, reviewing is mainly concerned with the description and evaluation of particular works, there are but few, scattered, brief attempts at setting forth esthetic or creative theories. And yet, reviewing being what it is, there are many comments on single aspects of literature occasioned by the works under review; and these comments reveal patterns of literary thought.

There seems, for one thing, to have been a consensus that literature was either concerned directly with humanity or was concerned with nothing. The reviewers had little use for allegory; and poems which leaned far toward the wonderful, such as *The Curse of Kehama* and *Christabel*, called forth protests from the reviewers. Jeffrey in the *Edinburgh Review* was typical in referring to human life as 'the great centre and source of all interest in the works of human beings—to which both verse and prose invariably bring us back, when they succeed in rivetting our attention, or rousing our emotions. . . .'[2]

The criterion of reason and common sense and the demand for more thought content were also shared by most of the reviewers. These common attitudes are not surprising considering the importance which the reviewers attached to both literature and ideas. Some of the reviewers felt that they were fighting a last-ditch battle; the *Monthly Review*, for example, remarked, 'The friends of Reason, we are assured, will stand or fall with her; and if she be quite extinct, why then a cheerful good night to her survivors!'[3] Most were, however, content to demand clarity, or at least intelligibility, of expression and of plot. As for ideas, the reviewers had great disdain for 'mysticism', a term that applies to anything that is inexplicable; and if this disdain is a limitation, at least it kept the reviewers from any fuzzy attempts at explaining the inexplicable.

A few reviewers observed that, of course, good sense is not all there is to poetry, but this qualification was in reality unnecessary. None of the reviewers ever implied that good sense was sufficient; and in view of their decided concern with the role of feelings in

[1] *Monitor*, I (1817), 181.

[2] *ER*, XXXI (Mar., 1819), 325.

[3] *MR*, XCIV (Feb., 1821), 162.

poetry, no one would be likely to mistake their position for an extreme rationalism. The *Literary Chronicle* insisted that 'true poetry . . . speaks to every heart . . .'; and Grosvenor Bedford in the *Quarterly* remarked, 'If poetry has any fundamental rules but those which exhibit the feelings of the human heart, we confess that we are strangers to them.'[1] Many such comments occurred, and sentiments in the works under review were almost always commented upon. Often, too, the reviewers reversed the process by describing the feeling or impression which a poem or a passage seemed to convey. Moreover, although some critics censured poems for mawkish sentiments or affectation, others, especially John Wilson, Thomas N. Talfourd, and P. G. Patmore, were themselves beginning, by the end of the second decade of the nineteenth century, to indulge in mawkish sentiments in their reviews.

Criticisms of description and imagery tended to be concerned more with feeling than with reason. Descriptions were frequently said to be either worthy of a painter's efforts or reminiscent of a particular painter (very often Salvator Rosa). When a description or visual image was considered too detailed, however, comparison was made with the Dutch School of painting, because, like the Dutch artists, the poet by too much detail left nothing for the imagination of the reader to fill in.

Flaws in diction and versification, on the other hand, were dealt with more summarily in terms of reason and experience. Coinages, quaint and obsolete expressions, foreign words, vulgarisms, and compounds, unless no word already existed in current usage to convey the same idea, were considered distractions in a work and potential corrupters of the language. Versification likewise was often censured through its connection with the thought of a poem; tetrameter, it was said, leads to prolixity and lack of thought, just as the Spenserian stanza through its complexity of rhyme leads to confused ideas, unless handled with a great deal of skill. All forms of verse, especially blank verse, were censured for prosiness, harshness, and irregularity. A favorite method of attack was to print an offensive passage as prose, a technique sometimes referred to as 'transprosing'.

The contemporary poets often did not satisfy the critical demands of the reviewers, and yet on the whole the reviewers were favorably disposed to the literature of their times and often openly preferred it

[1] *LC*, July 1, 1820, p. 421; *QR*, XIII (Apr., 1815), 83.

to Augustan poetry. Sometimes the claims made for contemporary poetry even got out of hand, as in the comment of the *European Magazine*:

> The present period is rich in the master-spirits of poetry—perhaps at no time have more brilliant names adorned the poetical annals of our country than in our day—Even the age of Elizabeth, the Augustan aera of our poetry in point of number and excellence, cannot be said to have surpassed our latter times.[1]

Among the more important periodicals, the only exception to this generally favorable attitude was the *Monthly Review*, which seems to have had a fundamental lack of sympathy with the age.

Individually also the poets were well received. Most of them in fact received judgments favorable in excess of their merits, at least as those merits have been sifted by time. This is true of Southey, Scott, Byron, and Moore, as well as of the first two volumes of Keats' poetry. The reviewers did not often err in the other direction. The unfavorable reviews of Wordsworth's poetry represent the most flagrant errors committed by contemporary critics, but the errors are confined principally to critiques of the *Poems in Two Volumes*. Although these errors, particularly the latter, are serious enough, they are not a matter for wonder, I think, considering the problems incident to the criticism of immediately contemporary works. Furthermore, it is a mistake to evaluate such criticism, or any criticism for that matter, only in terms of its validity in the light of ultimate judgments. Criticism performs other functions, not the least of which is the protection and nurture of proper attitudes toward literature in poets and in the reading public. In an age of political and social upheaval and of literary experimentation, this function is all the more important; and the reviewers, I believe, performed it with distinction.

On many counts, the secondary Reviews provided criticism superior to that of the *Edinburgh Review* and the *Quarterly Review*. The *Eclectic Review* and the *British Critic* offered superior criticism of Wordsworth, the *Champion* and the *Edinburgh Magazine* of Coleridge, the *Monthly Review* of Scott and Shelley. Perhaps the two major Reviews were too big and influential, too concerned with their own

[1] *EM*, LXXV (May, 1819), 445.

images. Certainly, the *Quarterly Review* at times indulged in political bias (as in its review of Hazlitt's *Round Table*) and in 'personality' (as in its review of Shelley's *The Revolt of Islam*). The *Edinburgh Review* sinned mostly in the other direction, with Jeffrey's disingenuously favorable reviews of works of his friends: Campbell's *Gertrude of Wyoming* and Moore's *Lalla Rookh. Blackwood's Magazine*, probably the third most influential reviewing periodical of the time, was without question the worst of the critical organs; it had a record of critical irresponsibility, political bias, and personal slander.

With the policies, practices, and attitudes of the reviewers in mind, it is now time to define their place in the tradition of English literary criticism. Such a task has been attempted before, resulting in the viewpoint that the Romantic reviewers were actually eighteenth-century reactionaries, born fifty years too late and anxious to turn back the clock. Presumably, such a view has its foundation in the scattered, more famous instances of attempted repression of particular poets, especially Wordsworth and Keats. But the simple fact is that the reviewers were on the whole not only favorable toward but also proud of their contemporary literature, indicating that something is radically amiss in the abovementioned viewpoint.

Before proceeding, however, it should be remarked that the function of reviewing puts the Romantic reviewers in a separate category in the history of English literary criticism. Their job required them to describe and evaluate individual works of immediately contemporary literature. Most of the reviewers did not have the space to set forth creative and critical theories, and reviewing policies often militated against them in any case. Those writing for the quarterlies were in a more advantageous position as regards both space and policies. Even so, there could not be much theorizing of the sort that is found in such works as Coleridge's *Biographia Literaria* or Wordsworth's Preface to the *Lyrical Ballads*.

Theories of literary criticism and creativity are often considered as falling within the limits of that much-abused term 'criticism'; such theories, in fact, usually take precedence in histories of literary criticism. And so it is important to distinguish the critical function of the reviewers: in current parlance it would be called practical criticism. This form of criticism, which is etymologically the only one entitled to be called criticism, involves applying a set of values, either explicit or assumed, to a literary work and judging that work as it conforms to them.

The literary values of the Romantic reviewers were in general those that had come down the classical tradition from Aristotle through Horace, Dryden, and Samuel Johnson. Art was, in this traditional view, imitative and it was moral; criticism relied heavily on reason and experience. When the tradition was restated in the Renaissance, the tendency, which can be seen in Sidney's *Defense of Poesy*, was toward the codification of hard-and-fast rules, such as those concerning the unities. But, as Walter Jackson Bate has pointed out, English criticism in this tradition became more rather than less flexible during the eighteenth century.[1] The Romantic reviewers, I believe, were an extension of that later tradition.

When commentators on the Romantic reviewers remark that they resemble literary critics of the eighteenth century, the commentators are, of course, correct, if they are referring to critics, such as Johnson, working in the same tradition. But the criticism of the reviewers also resembles the practical criticism of other critics of their own age as well. Coleridge's criticism of Wordsworth's poetry in the *Biographia Literaria*, for example, had for the most part been made before by the reviewers; and William Hazlitt's reviews, such as his critique of Wordsworth's *Excursion* in the *Examiner* or of Shelley's *Posthumous Poems* in the *Edinburgh*, do not differ in basic approach from those of other reviewers. They were all working in the same tradition and held in practice the same general critical presuppositions.

Towards the end of the seventeenth century in England, the late Renaissance restatement of the classical tradition in part was made by a group of critics—denominated by Bate as 'Neoclassical Rationalists' and typified by Thomas Rymer—who sought to evaluate literature guided by a set of strict rules. If later commentators mean to place the reviewers in such a category (and the usual implications are that they do), they are clearly wrong. For the reviewers, a century after Rymer, had no such respect for rules. If they had been rule-ridden, which of the Romantic poets would have received critical approval at their hands? And yet, as we have seen, all of them did receive such approval, even though the allotment was at times disproportionate to respective merits.

A similarity between the reviewers and Dr. Johnson has already been suggested; and the flexibility of the reviewers, their emphasis

[1] Walter Jackson Bate (ed.), *Criticism: The Major Texts* (New York: Harcourt, Brace, 1952), pp. 10–11. See also J. W. H. Atkins, *English Literary Criticism: 17th and 18th Centuries* (London: Methuen, 1951), pp. 356–57.

on the human in literature, their reliance on reason and experience, and their firm belief in the morality of literature would seem to augment such a similarity. There were, in fact, many more references to Johnson in the reviews than to any previous literary critic, a statistic which would imply the operation of considerable influence by Johnson on their critical thinking. And yet they did not, taken either singly or as a whole, measure up to Dr. Johnson as critics of literature; indeed, that would have been a high standard to approach. In certain respects, however, their occupation of reviewing—a special kind of criticism—perhaps required different capabilities. George Saintsbury, arguing later in the nineteenth century against the proposition that reviewers should be specialists, observed:

> The perfect reviewer would be . . . the Platonic or pseudo-Platonic philosopher who is 'second best in everything', who has enough special knowledge not to miss merits or defects, and enough general knowledge to estimate the particular at, and not above, its relative value to the whole.[1]

That, I submit, is not an unfair description of the majority of the Romantic reviewers.

[1] George Saintsbury, *Essays in English Literature 1780–1860*, p. xxiv.

Appendix I

British Reviewing Periodicals 1802–24

AjR — *Antijacobin Review and Magazine* (1798–1821). See text, pp. 45–46.

Album — *Album* (1822–25). See text, p. 65.

AR — *Annual Review* (1802–8). See text, pp. 52–54.

AugR — *Augustan Review* (1815–16). A monthly Review published in London: 'Printed for the Proprietors; Sold by Law and Whittaker.' The size ranged around 112 pages, with mostly reviews, but also some regular departments, such as Public Affairs and the Monthly Register of Arts, Sciences, and Literature. The reviews were generally short (three to ten pages). It claimed (Preface to Vol. I, iv.) to have no political creed, but in its literary reviews it seems to have had a liberal bias.

LaBA — *La Belle Assembleé* (1806–32). A monthly fashionable magazine published in London by John Bell until 1823, when G. and W. B. Whittaker took over publication. It was edited by Laman Blanchard in the 1820's (F. Sper, *The Periodical Press of London* [Boston, 1937], p. 19). See text, p. 54.

BC — *British Critic* (1793–1826). See text, pp. 44–45.

BLM — *British Lady's Magazine* (1815–18). A London monthly magazine of eighty double-column pages, published by John Souter. It had regular departments, and the reviews, which are found in The Lady's Cabinet of Literature, run from about two to four pages. Mary Lamb wrote articles for the *BLM* (E. V. Lucas, *The Life of Charles Lamb*, 5th ed. [London, 1921], p. 427).

BM — *Blackwood's Edinburgh Magazine* (1817–). See text, pp. 60–63.

LeBM — *Le Beau Monde* (1806–10). A monthly fashionable magazine published in London by John Browne Bell. It had about sixty-four double-column pages with regular departments, including a Review of Literature, which usually contained one or two fairly long reviews. It was begun as a competitor to John Bell's

	LaBA. The only difference between the two was that the *LeBM* contained features for men as well as women, but this proved to be a disadvantageous mixture. After an attempt to reconstruct the magazine, it expired early in 1810. (S. Morison, *A Memoir of John Bell* [Cambridge, 1930], pp. 65–66.) See text, p. 54.
BR	*British Review* (1811–25). See text, pp. 51–52.
Cab	*Cabinet* (1807–9). A London fashionable magazine published by Mathews and Leigh. At first a magazine of seventy-two pages with regular departments including Reviews of Books, its size increased to ninety-six pages in the new series in 1809, just before it expired. It placed great emphasis on the theater. See text, p. 54.
Champ	*Champion* (1814–22). See text, pp. 68–70.
CO	*Christian Observer* (1802–74). See text, pp. 46–47.
CR	*Critical Review* (1756–1817). See text, pp. 42–44.
EcR	*Eclectic Review* (1805–68). See text, pp. 47–49.
EdM	*Edinburgh Magazine* (1817–26). A continuation or new series of *SM* (*q.v.*). See text, p. 56.
EM	*European Magazine and London Review* (1782–1826). See text, pp. 56–57.
EMR	*Edinburgh Monthly Review* (1819–21). As its title indicates, it was a monthly Review published in Edinburgh (by Waugh and Innes), but it was also published in London by G. and W. B. Whittaker and John Warren. Although it had about the same number of pages (120) as the other monthlies, it followed the trend set by the *ER* in having longer (about ten to thirty pages) reviews. Its only other novelty was the substitution of an abstract of its reviews for the usual simple index. In July, 1821, it became a quarterly, the *NER* (*q.v.*). It had a conservative political bias.
ER	*Edinburgh Review* (1802–1929). See text, pp. 8–22.
Exam	*Examiner* (1808–81). See text, pp. 66–68.
GM	*Gentleman's Magazine* (1731–1868). See text, pp. 54, 55–56.
GR	*General Review of British and Foreign Literature* (1806). A London monthly Review published by William Nicholson, an inventor and freelance scientist—one of the advertisements inside announced that besides

publishing another (philosophical) journal, he ran an 'establishment for Twenty Pupils'. The *GR* stuck closely to the format typified by the *MR* (one hundred pages and twenty to thirty reviews per issue) and lasted only six months. Along with an outdated (by 1806) format, other problems led to its early demise: Southey wrote William Taylor (April 23, 1806), 'Nicholson's Review has set out badly, and unless his name be strong enough to support it till he gets a more certain supply of better articles, it must drop' (J. W. Robberds, *Memoir of . . . William Taylor* [London, 1843], II, 123).

IM — *Imperial Magazine* (1819–34). A London monthly magazine of ninety to one hundred pages (two columns per page with each column numbered as a separate page). It had the usual magazine format, including some chronicles. Its biases are not difficult to discover; the Preface to Volume I states: 'To every form in which anarchy can appear, whether theological, moral, intellectual, or civil, we declare our decided hostility; and our best endeavours will always be exerted to defend the Bible. . . .' It claimed non-sectarianism, however.

Indic — *Indicator* (1819–21). A London eight-page weekly published on Wednesdays by Joseph Appleyard, edited by Leigh Hunt and probably written mostly by him (title to the second volume reads 'By Leigh Hunt'). It was strictly a literary periodical, with essays, stories, and poems—Keats' 'La Belle Dame Sans Merci' was first published in the *Indic*. The three important reviews contained were of Keats' *Lamia* volume, Shelley's *The Cenci*, and Lamb's *Works* (review reprinted from the *Exam*): all three reviews were written by Hunt. It was a very successful periodical, and when Hunt ended the run in March, 1821, two other publishers took up the name (Louis Landré, *Leigh Hunt* [Paris, 1936], I, 103–5; II, 188, 192).

Invest — *Investigator* (1820–24). See text, p. 65.

IR — *Imperial Review* (1804–5). A monthly Review published in London by T. Cadell and W. Davies. For a monthly, it was large (160 pages), probably showing the influence of the *ER*; but this bulk cannot have been very successful, for by the fifth volume it had decreased to its normal number of 100–112 pages. Its one great novelty was 'a marked attention to the LITERATURE OF IRELAND' ('Prospectus'—quoted in a note to the Introduction, I [Jan., 1804], v).

JB — *John Bull* (1820–92). An eight-page Sunday paper published in London by E. Shackell. In December, 1820, the year of the trial of Queen Caroline, *JB* was begun in order to counteract the popular enthusiasm for the Queen that was encouraged by the Opposition. It was at first edited by Theodore Hook, a minor writer of the period; and its chief conductors were R. H. Barham, T. Haynes Bayley, and James Smith (*QR*, LXXII [May, 1843], 76; F. Sper, *The Periodical Press of London* [Boston, 1937], p. 24). For an account of its founding, see Walter Graham, *English Literary Periodicals* (New York, 1930), p. 387. Although mainly a political (Ultra-Tory) journal, it had the other usual features of the weeklies. There were, however, few literary reviews, and they were starkly partisan.

The success of *JB* must have been phenomenal. In 1821, its first year, the circulation, estimated on the yearly amount of stamps purchased, was about 9000 (*Journals of the House of Commons*, LXXVII [May 1, 1822], 930–31).

LC — *Literary Chronicle and Weekly Review* (1819–29). See text, p. 72.

LG — *Literary Gazette* (1817–62). See text, pp. 70–72.

LitExam — *Literary Examiner* (1823). A sixteen-page (8vo) Saturday paper, edited and published by Henry Leigh Hunt, nephew of Leigh Hunt. As the title might suggest, this paper was begun to supplement the *Exam* on the literary side (after the *Liberal* was abandoned); it contained essays and verse. A review section was a regular feature, but the reviews were not really so much criticisms as they were 'previews' of works. (Louis Landré, *Leigh Hunt* [Paris, 1936], I, 162.)

LitMus — *Literary Museum* (1822–24). A sixteen-page Saturday paper published in London by John Miller until August 2, 1823, and by John Warren afterward. It had the usual format of the weekly literary Review begun by the *LG*.

LitReg — *Literary Register* (1822–23). A sixteen-page Saturday paper published in London by J. Fraser, until May, 1823, after which date no publisher is given. See text, p. 72.

LJ — *Literary Journal* (1803–6). It began (Vol. I; January–June, 1803) as a sixteen-page weekly; then (Vols. II–III; July, 1803 to June, 1804) became a thirty-two page fortnightly—sixty-four pages by column pagination; then (Vols. IV–VII; July, 1804 to July, 1806) it became a fifty-six-page monthly—112 pages by column pagination. It was published in London by Charles R. Baldwin and edited by James Mill, the Utilitarian philosopher. David Macpherson was one of the literary reviewers (Alexander Bain, *James Mill* [London, 1882], pp. 46–47).

LJGM — *Literary Journal, and General Miscellany* (1818–19). A sixteen-page weekly published by J. Limberd and others (joint publishers alternate). It had the usual format of the literary weekly begun by the *LG*.

LM — *London Magazine* (1820–29). See text, pp. 63–65.

Gold's *LM* — *London Magazine; and Monthly Critical and Dramatic Review* (1820–21). See text, p. 65.

LMM — *Lady's Monthly Museum* (1798–1828). A fifty to sixty-page fashionable monthly magazine published in London consecutively by Vernor and Hood; Vernor, Hood, and Sharp; and Dean and Munday. The reviewing section alternated in size and title. According to the *British Stage* (I [July, 1817], 115), the *LMM* about the year 1817 changed proprietors and editors almost every volume. See text, p. 54.

LP — *Literary Panorama* (1806–19). See text, p. 59.

LR — *London Review* (1809). See text, pp. 50–51.

LS — *Literary Speculum* (1821–23). See text, p. 54.

LSB — *Literary Sketch-Book* (1823–24). A sixteen-page Saturday paper published in London by W. Crawford. It contained essays, poetry, and a few reviews, and lasted only thirty-seven numbers.

LSMS — *Literary and Statistical Magazine for Scotland* (1817–22). At first a 112-page monthly (1817–19), then a 112-page quarterly (1820), and finally, under the new title

Scottish Episcopal Magazine and Review, a 160-page quarterly (1821–22). It was published in Edinburgh by Macredie, Shelly, and Co., and it had the regular departments found in most magazines. Michael Russell, later Bishop of Glasgow, was for some time an editor. According to one source, the theology of the magazine was High Episcopal, but the *LSMS* never became the organ of the Scottish Episcopal Church (William Walker, *Three Churchmen* [Edinburgh, 1893], pp. 42–44).

MC — *Monthly Censor* (1822–23). A 120-page monthly Review. It was published in London by N. C. and J. Rivington and G. and W. B. Whittaker. Divided into four sections (Theology, Polity, Physics, and Philology), it had a regular reviewing department under the last section. Its politics were moderately conservative.

MLR — *Monthly Literary Recreations* (1806–7). An eighty-page monthly magazine published in London by B. Crosby. It had the usual magazine format typified by the *GM*. Byron reviewed Wordsworth's *Poems in Two Volumes* (R. E. Prothero, ed., *The Works of Lord Byron: Letters and Journals* [London, 1898–1901], V, 452). Since Crosby published both the *MLR* and Byron's *Hours of Idleness* and since Byron's work received a favorable review in the *MLR*, it is possible that puffery was involved (see L. Marchand, *Byron* [London, 1957] I, 134).

MM — *Monthly Magazine* (1796–1825). See text, pp. 57–58.

MonMir — *Monthly Mirror* (1795–1811). See text, p. 57.

MR — *Monthly Review* (1749–1845). See text, pp. 40–42.

NBTM — *New Bon Ton Magazine* (1818–21). See text, p. 54.

NEM — *New European Magazine* (1822–24). A ninety-six-page monthly magazine published in London by John Letts, Jr. The editor's name was given as 'Percy Somerset', probably a pseudonym like the 'Sylvanus Urban' of the *GM*. The *NEM* had the usual magazine features with reviews interspersed in the fashion later set by *BM*. It was ultra-conservative in politics.

NER — *New Edinburgh Review* (1821–23). A 320-page quarterly Review—continuation of the *EMR* (*q.v.*), with the same format and publishers. One change was the substitution of an index for the abstract of reviews.

NMM	*New Monthly Magazine* (1814–36). See text, pp. 59–60.
NR	*New Review* (1813–14). A 96–120-page monthly Review published in London. It was a regular monthly Review in the tradition of the *MR*. One unusual feature, however, was a section entitled 'Index of all the books reviewed, in the numbers of the Reviews and Magazines, published' on the first of every month. Thomas N. Talfourd wrote an article for the *NR* in defense of young poets (III, 345–50).
NUM	*New Universal Magazine* (1814–15). An eighty-page monthly magazine published in London by J. Stratford, and Sherwood, Neely, and Jones. It was a continuation of the *UM* (*q.v.*), and was in fact stated to be an attempt to provide a lighter kind of reading, since the diffusion of information provided by the *UM*, *MM*, and other magazines was considered no longer useful in light of the increase in books published (see Preface to Vol. I).
OR	*Oxford Review* (1807–8). See text, pp. 49–50.
PR	*Poetical Register* (1801–14). An annual published in London by F. and C. Rivington. Beginning as a 500-page publication, it grew to 646 pages in the final volume. Along with its increased bulk, the *PR* got further behind in its reviews in each issue (the last volume, for 1810–11, was published in 1814). Most of each volume is given over to a collection of fugitive verse; the comparatively short reviewing section comes at the end of every volume. In the Advertisement to the first volume occurs the following statement: 'For the critical opinions, delivered in this work, unless otherwise specified, the Ed. alone must be held responsible.' Most of the reviews are very short, usually limited to one paragraph.
QR	*Quarterly Review* (1809–). See text, pp. 22–38.
Sat	*Satirist* (1807–14). A monthly magazine of 112 pages first published in London (Vols. I–V) by Samuel Tipper, then (Vol. VI) by W. N. Jones, and finally by anonymous 'Proprietors'. Much more political than most magazines, the *Satirist*'s literary reviews nevertheless contain indiscriminately unfavorable judgments, especially severe after George Manners,

the original proprietor and editor, sold the magazine to William Jerdan (later editor of the *LG*) in 1812. Hewson Clarke was probably the reviewer of both editions of Byron's *Hours of Idleness*; at least Byron believed him to be the culprit (L. Marchand, *Byron* [New York, 1957], I, 155; R. E. Prothero, ed. *The Works of Lord Byron: Letters amd Journals* [London, 1898–1901], I, 321n). The *Sat* contained political cartoons by George Cruikshank.

Scourge — *Scourge* (1811–16). A monthly magazine of eighty to eighty-eight pages published in London by W. N. Jones, who had earlier published the *Sat*. Like that magazine, the *Scourge* was politically oriented; and though at the beginning it claimed to be middle of the road in its politics, it took a liberal position after 1813. Hewson Clarke may have been a contributor (L. Marchand, *Byron* [New York, 1957], I, 138). Like the *Sat*, it contained political cartoons by George Cruikshank.

SM — *Scots Magazine* (1739–1817). See text, p. 56. It changed its title to the *EdM* (*q.v.*) and began a new series in 1817.

TI — *Theatrical Inquisitor* (1812–21). A monthly magazine of eighty pages published in London by C. Chapple. It was conducted in 1814 by George Soane (L. M. Jones, 'The Essays and Critical Writing of John Hamilton Reynolds', Harvard diss. [1952], p. 11n. See also F. Sper, *The Periodical Press of London* [Boston, 1937], p. 15). It had the usual magazine features, except for chronicles, but was, as its title implies, weighted in the direction of drama. It nevertheless contained a considerable number of literary reviews.

UM — *Universal Magazine* (1747–1814). A monthly magazine with an average of eighty-eight to ninety-six pages, published in London by H. D. Symonds (1802–8) and Sherwood, Neely, and Jones (1808–14). It had the usual magazine features in the tradition of the *GM*. There was a regular reviewing section entitled 'Original Criticism', with reviews longer than usual for such a magazine. It was continued as the *NUM* (*q.v.*).

UR — *Universal Review* (1824–25). A 200–250-page

quarterly Review published in London by G. B. Whittaker. It placed special emphasis on foreign books.

YD *Yellow Dwarf* (1818). An eight-page (4to) Saturday paper published in London by John Hunt. It was largely a political paper, though essays, poetry, and reviews were included. William Hazlitt was the main contributor, and J. H. Reynolds is thought to have been involved also (P. P. Howe, *The Life of William Hazlitt* [London, 1947], pp. 225–26). There were only three important literary reviews in the twenty-one issues printed: one of *Beppo*, hardly more than a notice; one of Moore's *Fudge Family*; and another of *Childe Harold* (IV). The last two were written by Hazlitt (P. P. Howe, *The Complete Works of William Hazlitt* [London, 1930–34], VII, 287; XIX, 35).

Appendix II

Reviews of Romantic Literature

This list is arranged (1) alphabetically by author of the works reviewed, (2) works by each author chronologically listed according to their publication dates, (3) reviews of those works chronologically by the dates (or known appearance) of each. (The dates of the appearance of issues of the *Quarterly Review* are taken from Hill and Helen Shine, *The Quarterly Review Under Gifford* [Chapel Hill, N.C., 1949]—information cited at the beginning of each issue on their list.) The full titles of the reviewing periodicals can be found in Appendix I; in a few instances in which periodicals carried few reviews the titles of the Reviews are spelled out in the lists. Attributions of authorship of the reviews, when known or suspected, are placed in parentheses after the citation of each review; authorities for these attributions are given in Chapters 1 and 2 (or, in the case of very minor periodicals, in Appendix I) under the appropriate periodical. Asterisks adjacent to page numbers indicate misnumbering.

BYRON

Reviews of *Hours of Idleness* (1807): *MLR*, III (July, 1807), 67–71; *CR*, XII 3s (Sept., 1807), 47–53 (John Higgs Hunt); *LeBM*, II (Sept., 1807), 88–90; *UM*, VIII 2s (Sept., 1807), 235–37; *BC*, XXX (Oct., 1807), 436–37; *Sat*, I (Oct., 1807), 77–81 (H. Clarke?); *MR*, LIV (Nov., 1807), 256–63 (G. E. Griffiths); *EcR*, III–ii (Nov., 1807), 989–93; *LP*, III (Nov., 1807), 273–75; *AjR*, XXVIII (Dec., 1807), 407–8; *GM*, LXXVII (Supp., 1807), 1217–19, LXXVIII (Mar., 1808), 231–33; *AR*, VI (1808), 529–31 (L. Aikin); *ER*, XI (Jan., 1808), 285–89 (H. Brougham); *MonMir*, III 2s (Jan., 1808), 28–30; *Sat*, III (Aug., 1808), 78–86 [rev. of 2nd ed.] (H. Clarke?); *PR*, Vol. for 1806–7 (1811), pp. 538–39.

Reviews of *English Bards and Scotch Reviewers* (1809): *AjR*, XXXII (Mar., 1809), 301–6; *GM*, LXXIX (Mar., 1809), 246–49, LXXX–i (Feb., 1810), 156; *BC*, XXXIII (Apr., 1809), 410–11; *CR*, XVII 3s (May, 1809), 78–85; *EcR*, V–i (May, 1809), 481–84; *LP*, VI (June, 1809), 491–96; *Cab*, I 2s (June, 1809), 527–29; *LeBM*, I (June, 1809), 245–46; *AjR*, XXXVII (Sept., 1810), 84–87; *PR*, Vol. for 1808–9 (1812), pp. 607–8; *LJGM*, Apr. 19, 1818, pp. 49–50, May 3, 1818, pp. 86–87, May 10, 1818, pp. 98–99.

Reviews of *Childe Harold* I & II (1812): *ER*, XIX (Feb., 1812), 466–77 (F. Jeffrey); *LP*, XI (Mar., 1812), 417–30 (C. Dallas); *Scourge*, III (Apr., 1812), 305–13; *MR*, LXVIII (May, 1812), 74–83 (T. Denman); *BC*, XXXIX (May, 1812), 478–82; *GM*, LXXXII–i (May, 1812), 448–54; *QR*, VII (Mar., 1812), 180–200 [pub. after May 9, 1812] (G. Ellis); *BR*, III (June, 1812), 275–302 (W. Roberts); *CR*, I 4s (June, 1812), 561–75; *EcR*, VIII–i (June, 1812), 630–41; *CO*, XI (June, 1812), 376–86; *AjR*, XLII (Aug., 1812), 343–65; *Sat*, XI (Oct., 1812), 344–58, (Dec., 1812), 542–50; *Town Talk*, III (Oct., 1812), 372–77; *General Chronicle*, VI (Nov., 1812), 323–35; *LaBA*, VI 2s (Supp. to Vol. VI, 1812), 349–54; *MM*, XXXIV (Jan. 30, 1813), 650–52.

Reviews of *Waltz* (1813): *BC*, XLI (Mar., 1813), 301–2; *CR*, III 4s (Mar., 1813), 330–31; *MR*, LXX (Apr., 1813), 432–33 (C. L. Moody); *Sat*, XII (Apr., 1813), 385–87; *GM*, LXXXIII–i (Apr., 1813), 348–49; *LMM*, XIV 2s (Apr., 1813), 232–34; *NR*, I (June, 1813), 636–38; *LC*, July 14, 1821, pp. 441–42.

Reviews of *The Giaour* (1813): *MR*, LXXI (June, 1813), 202–7 (T. Denman); *Drakard's Paper*, June 27, 1813, pp. 199–200; *ER*, XXI (July, 1813), 299–309 (F. Jeffrey); *CR*, IV 4s (July, 1813), 56–68; *Sat*, XIII (July, 1813), 70–88; *AjR*, XLV (Aug., 1813), 127–38; *TI*, III (Aug., 1813), 48–50; *Town Talk*, V (Aug., 1813), 55–59; *GM*, LXXXIII–ii (Sept., 1813), 246–47; *BR*, V (Oct., 1813), 132–45 (W. Roberts); *SM*, LXXV (Oct., 1813), 769–73; *LaBA*, VIII 2s (Oct., 1813), 120–22; *Reasoner*, I (Oct., 1813), 250–55; *EcR*, X (Nov., 1813), 523–31; *CO*, XII (Nov., 1813), 731–37; *BC*, XLII (Dec., 1813), 611–13; *NR*, II (Dec., 1813), 674–75; *QR*, X (Jan., 1814), 331–54 [pub. between March 25 and April 7, 1814] (G. Ellis).

Reviews of *The Bride of Abydos* (1813); *CR*, IV 4s (Dec., 1813), 653–58; *LaBA*, VIII 2s (Dec., 1813), 257–60; *Drakard's Paper*, Dec. 12, 1813, p. 391; *MR*, LXXIII (Jan., 1814), 53–63 (J. Hodgson); *BC*, 1 2s (Jan., 1814), 34–50; *TI*, III (Jan., 1814), 355–60; *SM*, LXXVI (Jan., 1814), 48–51; *GM*, LXXXIV–i (Jan., 1814), 51–53; *Reasoner*, I (Jan., 1814), 357–64; *Tradesman*, XII (Jan., 1814), 43–46; *BR*, V (Feb., 1814), 391–400 (W. Roberts); *EcR*, I 2s (Feb., 1814), 187–93; NR, III (Feb., 1814), 111–17; *Sat*, XIV (Feb., 1814), 145–59; *AjR*, XLVI (Mar., 1814), 209–37; *ER* XXIII (Apr., 1814), 198–229 (F. Jeffrey); *LP*, XV (Apr., 1814), 370–78; *QR*, X (Jan., 1814), 331–54 [pub. between Mar. 25 and Apr. 7, 1814] (G. Ellis); *Variety*, Sept. 10, 1814, p. 5.

Reviews of *The Corsair* (1814): *MR*, LXXIII (Feb., 1814), 189–200 (J. Hodgson); *CR*, V 4s (Feb., 1814), 144–55; *BR*, V (Feb., 1814), 506–11 (W. Roberts); *GM*, LXXXIV–i (Feb., 1814), 154; *SM*, LXXVI (Feb., 1814), 124–27; *TI*, IV (Feb., 1814), 105–8; *EM*, LXV (Feb.,

1814), 134–35; *LaBA*, IX 2s (Feb., 1814), 81–83; *UM*, XXI 2s (Feb., 1814), 129–136*; *BC*, I 2s (Mar., 1814), 277–96; *AjR*, XLVI (Mar., 1814), 209–37; *Sat*, XIV (Mar., 1814), 246–50; *NMM*, I (Mar., 1814), 149–51; *ER*, XXIII (Apr., 1814), 198–229 (F. Jeffrey); *EcR*, I 2s (Apr., 1814), 416–26 (J. Conder); *CO*, XIII (Apr., 1814), 245–57; *NR*, III (Apr., 1814), 339–43; *Reasoner*, I (Apr., 1814), 549–57; *QR*, XI (July, 1814), 428–57 [pub. after Oct. 20, 1814] (G. Ellis); *Mentor*, Aug. 16, 1817, pp. 149–53, Aug. 23, 1817, pp. 161–64.

Reviews of *Lara* (1814): *CR*, VI 4s (Aug., 1814), 203; *SM*, LXXVI (Aug., 1814), 608–11; *TI*, V (Aug., 1814), 101–13; *NUM*, I (Aug., 1814), 123–26; *Entertaining Magazine*, II (Aug., 1814), 432–36, (Sept., 1814), 486–90; *MR*, LXXV (Sept., 1814), 83–92 (J. Hodgson); *NMM*, II (Sept., 1814), 156–57; *LaBA*, X 2s (Sept., 1814), 131–32; *BC*, II 2s (Oct., 1814), 401–13; *EcR*, II 2s (Oct., 1814), 393–400 (J. Conder); *QR*, XI (July, 1814), 428–57 [pub. after Oct. 20, 1814] (G. Ellis); *LMM*, XVII 2s (Nov., 1814), 290–94.

Reviews of *Ode to Napoleon Buonaparte* (1814): *MR*, LXXIII (Apr., 1814), 433–35; *CR*, V 4s (May, 1814), 524–29; *BC*, I 2s (May, 1814), 545–47; *EcR*, I 2s (May, 1814), 516–20; *AjR*, XLVI (May, 1814), 441–47; *Scourge*, VII (May, 1814), 410–17; *TI*, IV (May, 1814), 286–89; *NR*, III (May, 1814), 502–4; *GM*, LXXXIV-i (May, 1814), 477; *LP*, XV (May, 1814), 531–32; *UM*, XXI 2s (May, 1814), 399–401; *Reasoner*, I (July, 1814), 735–38.

Reviews of *Hebrew Melodies* (1815–16): *TI*, VI (May, 1815), 377–78; *BLM*, I (May, 1815), 358–60; *BC*, III 2s (June, 1815), 602–11; *EcR*, IV 2s (July, 1815), 94–96 (J. Conder); *AugR*, I (July, 1815), 209–15; *EM*, LXVIII (July, 1815), 37; *NUM*, III (July, 1815), 37–38; *CR*, II 5s (Aug., 1815), 166–71; *CO*, XIV (Aug., 1815), 542–49; *GM*, LXXXV-ii (Aug., 1815), 141; *BR*, VI (Aug., 1815), 200–8 (W. Roberts); *MR*, LXXVIII (Sept., 1815), 41–47 (F. Hodgson); *LMM*, II 3s (Sept., 1815), 169–72; *CR*, III 5s (Apr., 1816), 357–66; *TI*, VIII (June, 1816), 442–44.

Reviews of *The Siege of Corinth* and *Parisina* (1816): *MR*, LXXIX (Feb., 1816), 196–208; *CR*, III 5s (Feb., 1816), 146–54; *Champ*, Feb. 11, 1816, pp. 45–46; *EcR*, V 2s (Mar. 1816), 269–75 (J. Conder); *NMM*, V (Mar., 1816), 148–49; *GM*, LXXXVI-i (Mar., 1816), 241–43; *BLM*, III (Mar., 1816), 181–83; *LaBA*, XIII (Mar., 1816), 127–30; *Stage*, Mar. 2, 1816, pp. 155–58, Mar. 9, 1816, pp. 167–69; *BC*, V 2s (Apr., 1816), 430–36; *AugR*, II (Apr., 1816), 380–88; *TI*, VIII (Apr., 1816), 276–83; *BR*, VII (May, 1816), 452–69 (W. Roberts); *EM*, LXIX (May, 1816), 437–38; *LP*, IV 2s (June, 1816), 417–20.

Reviews of *Poems on His Domestic Circumstances* (1816): *LaBA*, XIII

2s (Apr., 1816), 177–78; *Br*, VII (May, 1816), 510–13 (W. Roberts); *NMM*, V (May, 1816), 344–45; *AugR*, II (May, 1816), 551–52; *Scourge*, XI (May, 1816), 376–80; *EcR*, V 2s (June, 1816), 595–99 (J. Conder); *GM*, LXXXVI-i (Supp. to Vol. LXXXVI-i [June 1816?]), 613; *MR*, LXXXI (Sept., 1816), 95–96; *AjR*, LI (Dec., 1816), 374.

Reviews of *Monody on the Death of Sheridan* (1816): *Exam*, Sept. 22, 1816, pp. 602–3 (L. Hunt); *MR*, LXXXI (Nov., 1816), 319–21; *EcR*, VI 2s (Nov., 1816), 502–6; *AugR*, III (Nov., 1816), 474–82; *NMM*, VI (Dec., 1816), 441; *TI*, XI (Nov., 1817), 362–67.

Reviews of *Childe Harold* III (1816): *MR*, LXXXI (Nov., 1816), 312–19; *CR*, IV 5s (Nov., 1816), 495–506; *SM*, LXXVIII (Nov., 1816), 849–54; *Portfolio*, Nov. 23, 1816, pp. 73–77, Nov. 30, 1816, pp. 97–102; *Champ*, Nov. 24, 1816, p. 374; *ER*, XXVII (Dec., 1816), 277–310 (F. Jeffrey); *BC*, VI 2s (Dec., 1816), 608–17; *MM*, XLII (Dec., 1816), 447–49; *GM*, LXXXVI-ii (Dec., 1816), 521–24; *LP*, V 2s (Dec., 1816), 409–13; *LaBA*, XIV 2s (Supp. for 1816), 338–41; *BLM*, V (Jan., 1817), 17–26; BR, IX (Feb., 1817), 1–23 (W. Roberts); *LSMS*, I (Feb., 1817), 75–81; *QR*, XVI (Oct., 1816), 172–208 [pub. Feb. 11, 1817] (W. Scott); *EcR*, VII 2s (Mar., 1817), 292–304 (J. Conder); *CO*, XVI (Apr., 1817), 246–59; *Christian Miscellany*, II (June, 1817), 270–77, (July, 1817), 317–24.

Reviews of *The Prisoner of Chillon, and other Poems* (1816): *ER*, XXVII (Dec., 1816), 277–310 (F. Jeffrey); *MR*, LXXXI (Dec., 1816), 435–38; *CR*, IV 5s (Dec., 1816), 567–81; *BC*, VI 2s (Dec., 1816), 608–17; *Champ*, Dec. 1, 1816, pp. 382–83; *Portfolio*, Dec. 7, 1816, pp. 125–28; *MM*, XLII (Jan., 1817), 546; *GM*, LXXXVII-i (Jan., 1817), 41; *TI*, X (Jan., 1817), 43–48; *BLM*, V (Jan., 1817), 17–28; *NMM*, VII (Feb., 1817), 57; *QR*, XVI (Oct., 1816), 172–208 [pub. Feb. 11, 1817] (W. Scott); *EcR*, VII 2s (Mar., 1817), 292–304 (J. Conder).

Reviews of *Manfred* (1817): *CR*, V 5s (June, 1817), 622–29; *BM*, I (June, 1817), 289–95 (J. Wilson); *SM*, LXXIX (June, 1817), 449–53; *Monitor*, I (June?, 1817), 170–76, 177–82; *LG*, June 21, 1817, pp. 337–38; *Champ*, June 22, 1817, p. 197; *MR*, LXXXIII (July, 1817), 300–7; *BC*, VIII 2s (July, 1817), 38–47; *EcR*, VIII 2s (July, 1817), 62–66 (J. Conder); *MM*, XLIII (July, 1817), 547; *GM*, LXXXVII-ii (July, 1817), 45–47 (quoted from *The Day and New Times*); *Knight Errant*, July 19, 1817, p. 46; *ER*, XXVIII (Aug., 1817), 418–31 (F. Jeffrey); *BR*, X (Aug., 1817), 82–90 (W. Roberts); *EM*, LXXII (Aug., 1817), 150–52; *TI*, XI (Aug., 1817), 120–27; *LMM*, VI 3s (Aug., 1817), 90–95; *LaBA*, XVI 2s (Supp. for 1817), 342–43.

Reviews of the *Lament of Tasso* (1817): *LG*, July 26, 1817, p. 49; *MR*, LXXXIII (Aug., 1817), 424–27; *EdM*, I 2s (Aug., 1817), 48–49; *GM*,

LXXXVII–ii (Aug., 1817), 150–51; *EcR*, VIII 2s (Sept., 1817), 291–92 (J. Conder); *MM*, XLIV (Sept., 1817), 153; *BLM*, I 2s (Sept., 1817), 176–77; *Edinburgh Observer*, Sept. 13, 1817, p. 12; *BC*, VIII 2s (Nov., 1817), 488–93; *BM*, II (Nov., 1817), 142–44 (J. Wilson).

Reviews of *Beppo* (1818): *ER*, XXIX (Feb., 1818), 302–10 (F. Jeffrey); *MR*, LXXXV (Mar., 1818), 285–90; *BC*, IX 2s (Mar., 1818), 301–5; *LG*, Mar. 14, 1818, pp. 162–64; *YD*, Mar. 28, 1818, pp. 101–2; *Champ*, Mar. 29, 1818, p. 203; *EdM*, II 2s (Apr., 1818), 348–51; *LJGM*, Apr. 5, 1818, pp. 17–18; *BR*, XI (May, 1818), 327–33 (W. Roberts); *LP*, VIII 2s (May 1818), 239–42; *EcR*, IX 2s (June 1818), 555–57; *MM*, XLV (July, 1818), 535; *Edinburgh Reflector*, July 1, 1818, p. 6; *GM*, LXXXVIII–ii (Aug., 1818), 144–45 (quoted from the *New Times*).

Reviews of *Childe Harold* IV (1818); *BC*, IX 2s (May, 1818), 540–54; *BM*, III (May, 1818), 216–18* (J. Wilson); *EdM*, II 2s (May, 1818), 449–53; *Catholic Gentleman's Magazine*, I (May, 1818), 255–60, (June, 1818), 347–48; *LG*, May 2, 1818, pp. 273–77; *YD*, May 2, 1818, pp. 142–44 (W. Hazlitt); *LJGM*, May 3, 1818, pp. 81–83, May 10, 1818, pp. 99–100; *ER*, *XXX* (June, 1818), 87–120 (J. Wilson); *MM*, XLV (June, 1818), 434–36; *EcR*, X 2s (July, 1818), 46–54 (J. Conder); *GM*, LXXXVIII–ii (July, 1818), 45–47 (quoted from the *New Times*); *BR*, XII (Aug., 1818), 1–34 (W. Roberts); *LP*, VIII 2s (Aug., 1818), 718–22; *TI*, XIII (Sept., 1818), 217–21, (Oct., 1818), 289–94; *NMM*, X (Sept., 1818), 156–60; *QR*, XIX (Apr., 1818), 215–32 [pub. in Sept., 1818] (W. Scott); *MR*, LXXXVII (Nov., 1818), 289–302; *BLM*, I 3s (Nov., 1818), 221–24, (Dec., 1818), 266–68; *La BA*, XVIII 2s (Supp. for 1818), 340–42.

Reviews of *Mazeppa* (1819): *MM*, XLVIII (Aug., 1819), 57; *MR*, LXXXIX (July, 1819), 309–21; *BM*, V (July, 1819), 429–32 (J. Wilson?); *TI*, XV (July, 1819), 43–47, (Aug., 1819), 86–91; *GM*, LXXXIV–ii (July, 1819), 43–45 (quoted from the *New Times*); *LG*, July 3, 1819, pp. 417–19; *LC*, July 3, 1819, pp. 97–99, July 10, 1819, pp. 117–19; *Green Man*, July 3, 1819, pp. 53–56, July 10, 1819, pp. 62–63; *Theatre*, July 10, 1819, pp. 1–4; *Champ*, July 25, 1819, pp. 471–72; *EcR*, XII 2s (Aug., 1819), 147–56; *EMR*, II (Aug., 1819), 214–18; *NMM*, XII (Aug., 1819), 64–67; *EdM*, V 2s Aug., 1819), 145–52; *BLM*, III 3s (Aug., 1819), 82–85; *LaBA*, XX 2s (Supp., for 1819), 341–42.

Reviews of *Don Juan* I and II (1819): *EM*, LXXVI (July, 1819), 53–56; *MR*, LXXXIX (July, 1819), 309–21; *LG*, July 17, 1819, pp. 449–51, July 24, 1819, pp. 470–73; *LC*, July 17, 1819, pp. 129–30, July 24, 1819, pp. 147–49; *Green Man*, July 17, 1819, p. 69; *Champ*, July 25, 1819, pp. 472–73, Aug. 1, 1819, pp. 488–90 (J. Thelwall?); *BR*, XIV (Aug., 1819), 266–68 (W. Roberts?); *BC*, XII 2s (Aug., 1819), 195–205;

BM, V (Aug., 1819), 512–18 (J. G. Lockhart?); *MM*, XLVIII (Aug., 1819), 56; *NMM*, XII (Aug., 1819), 75–78; *GM*, LXXXIX–ii (Aug., 1819), 152; *NBTM*, III (Aug., 1819), 234–39; *EMR*, II (Oct., 1819), 468–86; *Miniature Magazine*, III (Oct., 1819), 236–39; *Exam*, Oct. 31, 1819, pp. 700–2 (L. Hunt); *EdM*, IX 2s (Aug., 1821), 105*–108*; *Invest*, III (Oct., 1821), 353–60.

Reviews of *Letter to [John Murray]* (1821): *LC*, Mar. 31, 1821, pp. 193–96; *LG*, Apr. 7, 1821, pp. 213–15; *Exam*, Apr. 29, 1821, pp. 267–69 (A. Fonblanque?); *BC*, XV 2s (May, 1821), 463–74; *BM*, IX (May, 1821), 227–33 (H. Matthews); *EMR*, V (May, 1821), 616–26; *MM*, LI (May, 1821), 365; *LM*, III (June, 1821), 593–607 (W. Hazlitt); *AjR*, LX (Aug., 1821), 577–83.

Reviews of *Marino Faliero* (1821): *BM*, IX (Apr., 1821), 93–103 (J. Wilson?); *LG*, Apr. 28, 1821, pp. 259–63; *LC*, Apr. 28, 1821, pp. 257–62; *MR*, XCV (May, 1821), 41–50; *BC*, XV 2s (May, 1821), 463–74; *LM*, III (May, 1821), 550–54 (W. Hazlitt); Gold's *LM*, III (May, 1821), 489–98; *EM*, LXXIX (May, 1821), 437–43; *MM*, LI (May, 1821), 368; *Exam*, May 6, 1821, pp. 285–86 (A. Fonblanque?); *BR*, XVII (June, 1821), 439–52 (W. Roberts); *EcR*, XV 2s (June, 1821), 518–27; *Drama*, I (June, 1821), 89–92, (July, 1821), 114–20; *ER*, XXXV (July, 1821), 271–85 (F. Jeffrey); *NER*, I (July, 1821), 237–56; *MM*, LI (July, 1821), 524–28; *QR*, XXVII (July, 1822), 476–524 [pub. in Oct., 1822] (R. Heber).

Reviews of *The Prophecy of Dante* (1821) are usually contained in reviews of *Marino Faliero*, but the following are separate reviews: *NMM*, I 2s (1821), 725–28; *LG*, May 5, 1821, pp. 277–79.

Reviews of *Sardanapalus*, *The Two Foscari*, and *Cain* (1821)—unless otherwise indicated, each review includes criticism of all three plays: *GM*, XCI–ii (Dec., 1821), 537–41, (Supp. for Vol. XCI–ii), 613–15; *LG*, Dec. 22, 1821, pp. 808–12, Dec. 29, 1821, pp. 821–22, Jan. 5, 1822, pp. 4–5; *LC*, Dec. 22, 1821, pp. 799–802, Dec. 27, 1821, pp. 815–17, Jan. 5, 1822, pp. 6–8; *Exam*, Dec. 23, 1821, pp. 808–10, Dec. 30, 1821, pp. 827–28 (A. Fonblanque?); *MR*, XCVII (Jan., 1822), 83–98*; *BM*, XI (Jan., 1822), 90–92 (J. G. Lockhart); *LM*, V (Jan., 1822), 66–71 (T. N. Talfourd); *GM*, XCII–i (Jan., 1822), 59–61; *EdM*, X 2s (Jan. 1822), 102–14; *EM*, LXXXI (Jan. 1822), 58–70; *LMM*, XV 3s (Jan., 1822), 38–41 (*Cain* only); *ER*, XXXVI (Feb., 1822), 413–52 (F. Jeffrey); *BM*, XI (Feb., 1822), 212–17 (J. Matthews); *MM*, LIII (Feb., 1822), 10–15; *LS*, I (Feb., 1822), 257–60 (*Cain* only); *Republican*, Feb. 8, 1822, p. 192 (R. Carlile) (*Cain* only); *BR*, XIX (Mar., 1822), 72–102 (W. Roberts); *London Christian Instructor*, V (Apr., 1822), 202–6 (*Cain* only); *IM*, IV (Apr., 1822), 379 (*Cain* only);

BC, XVII 2s (May, 1822), 520–40; *EcR*, XVII 2s (May, 1822), 418–27 (*Cain* only); *Evangelical Magazine*, XXX (May, 1822), 192–93 (*Cain* only); *Invest*, V (Oct., 1822), 315–71; *QR*, XXVII (July, 1822), 476–524 [pub. in Oct., 1822] (R. Heber).

Reviews of *Don Juan* III–V (1821): *MR*, XCV (Aug., 1821), 418–24; *BM*, X (Aug., 1821), 107–15 (signed 'Henry Franklin'); *EM*, LXXX (Aug., 1821), 181–85; *EdM*, IX 2s (Aug., 1821), 105*–8*; *LG*, Aug. 11, 1821, pp. 497–500, Aug. 18, 1821, pp. 516–17; *LC*, Aug. 11, 1821, pp. 495–97, Aug. 18, 1821, pp. 514–16; *Exam*, Aug. 26, 1821, p. 538; *BC*, XVI 2s (Sept., 1821), 251–56; *MM*, LII (Sept., 1821), 124–29; *IM*, III (Oct., 1821), 945–48; *Invest*, III (Oct., 1821), 353–60; *LS*, I (Nov., 1821), 1–5; *BR*, XVIII (Dec., 1821), 245–65 (W. Roberts?); *GM*, XCII–i (Jan., 1822), 48–50; *Invest*, V (Oct., 1822), 315–71; *BM*, XIV (July, 1823), 88–92 (W. Maginn and J. G. Lockhart).

Reviews of the *Liberal* #1 [*The Vision of Judgment*] (1822): *LS*, II (Oct., 1822?), 422–32; *GM*, XCII–ii (Oct., 1822), 348–51 (quoted from the *St. James Chronicle*); *NEM*, I (Oct., 1822), 354–63; *Lady's Magazine*, III (Oct., 1822), 565–69 (T. N. Talfourd); *Exam*, Oct. 13, 1822, pp. 648–52 (A. Fonblanque?); *LG*, Oct. 19, 1822, pp. 655–58, Oct. 26, 1822, pp. 678–81, Nov. 2, 1822, pp. 693–95; *LC*, Oct. 19, 1822, pp. 655–58, Oct. 26, 1822, pp. 675–77; *LitReg*, Oct. 19, 1822, pp. 241–43, Oct. 26, 1822, pp. 260–61; *LitMus*, Oct. 19, 1822, pp. 405–6, Oct. 26, 1822, pp. 422–23; *British Luminary and Weekly Intelligencer*, Oct. 20, 1822, p. 754; *EdM*, XI 2s (Nov., 1822), 561–73; *MM*, LIV (Dec., 1822), 452; *IM*, IV (Dec., 1822), 1139–42; *Invest*, VI (Jan., 1823), 76–108; *MC* II (Apr., 1823), 452–58.

Reviews of *Werner* (1822): *LG*, Nov. 23, 1822, pp. 740–42; *LC*, Nov. 30, 1822, pp. 753–57; *LitReg*, Nov. 30, 1822, pp. 340–42; *LitMus*, Nov. 30, 1822, pp. 497–500; *MR*, XCIX (Dec., 1822), 394–405; *BM*, XII (Dec., 1822), 710–19 (J. G. Lockhart?); *Lady's Magazine*, III (Dec., 1822), 662–68 (T. N. Talfourd); *Exam*, Dec. 1, 1822, pp. 754–57, Dec. 8, 1822, pp. 771–74 (A. Fonblanque?); *EdM*, XI 2s (Dec., 1822), 688–94; *NEM*, I (Dec., 1822), 517–27; *Drama*, III (Dec., 1822), 324–32; *NMM*, VI 2s (1822), 553–55; *NER*, IV (Jan., 1823), 159–79; *MM*, LIV (Jan., 1823), 504–7; *EM*, LXXXIII (Jan., 1823), 73–76; *EcR*, XIX 2s (Feb., 1823), 136–55; *BC*, XIX 2s (Mar., 1823), 242–53; *MC*, II (Apr., 1823), 452–58.

Reviews of the *Liberal* #2 [*Heaven and Earth*] (1823): *Exam*, Dec. 29, 1822, pp. 818–22 (A. Fonblanque ?); *BM*, XIII (Jan., 1823), 72–77 (J. Wilson); *GM*, XCIII–i (Jan., 1823), 41–44; *Lady's Magazine*, IV (Jan., 1823), 19–23 (T. N. Talfourd); *LG*, Jan. 4, 1823, pp. 2–5; *LC*, Jan. 4, 1823, pp. 8–11, Jan. 11, 1823, pp. 26–28; *LitMus*, Jan. 4, 1823, pp. 1–3; *LitReg*, Jan. 4, 1823, pp. 5–6, Jan. 11, 1823, pp. 22–23; *ER*, XXXVIII (Feb., 1823), 27–48 (F. Jeffrey?); *MM*, LV (Feb., 1823), 35–39; *EcR*, XIX 2s (Mar., 1823), 216; *MC*, II (Apr., 1823), 452–58; *NMM*, VII 2s (1823), 353–58.

Reviews of the *Liberal* #3 (1823): *LC*, Apr. 26, 1823, pp. 257–59; *LitMus*, Apr. 26, 1823, pp. 257–59; *LG*, May 3, 1823, p. 275; *LitReg*, May 3, 1823, pp. 273–75; *JB*, May 4, 1823, pp. 141–42.

Reviews of the *Liberal* #4 (1823): *LitExam*, July 26, 1823, pp. 49–58; *LC*, Aug. 2, 1823, pp. 481–83; *LitMus*, Aug. 2, 1823, pp. 486–88.

Reviews of *Don Juan* VI–VIII (1823): *MR*, CI (July, 1823), 316–21; *LitExam*, July 5, 1823, pp. 6–12, July 12, 1823, pp. 23–27; *LG*, July 19, 1823, pp. 451–53; *LC*, July 19, 1823, pp. 451–53; *LitMus*, July 19, 1823, pp. 452–53; *LitReg*, July 19, 1823, pp. 33–35; *JB*, July 20, 1823, p. 229; *BC*, XX 2s (Aug., 1823), 178–88; *EdM*, XIII 2s (Aug., 1823), 190–99; *NEM*, III (Aug., 1823), 126–28; *British Magazine*, I (Aug., 1823), 273–76; *MM*, LVI (Sept., 1823), 112–15; *GM*, XCIII–ii (Sept., 1823), 250–52.

Reviews of *Don Juan* IX–XI (1823): *LitExam*, Aug. 2, 1823, pp. 65–68, Aug. 9, 1823, pp. 81–85, Aug. 16, 1823, pp. 105–10, Aug. 23, 1823, pp. 120–23; *LC*, Aug. 30, 1823, pp. 553–55; *LSB*, Aug. 30, 1823, pp. 44–45, Sept. 6, 1823, pp. 56–58; *BM*, XIV (Sept., 1823), 282–93 (J. G. Lockhart); *EdM*, XIII 2s (Sept., 1823), 357*–360*; *GM*, XCIII–ii (Sept., 1823), 250–52; *British Magazine*, I (Sept., 1823), 296–99; *LitMus*, Sept. 6, 1823, pp. 564–65; *LG*, Sept. 6, 1823, pp. 562–63; *MR*, CII (Oct., 1823), 217–20; *BC*, XX 2s (Nov., 1823), 524–30; *MM*, LVI (Dec., 1823), 414–17.

Reviews of *Don Juan* XII–XIV (1823): *LitExam*, Nov. 8, 1823, pp. 289–94, Nov. 15, 1823, pp. 305–9, Nov. 22, 1823, pp. 321–25, Nov. 29, 1823, pp. 337–41; *BC*, XX 2s (Dec., 1823), 662–68; *NEM*, III (Dec., 1823), 530–34; *LG*, Dec. 6, 1823, pp. 771–73; *LC*, Dec. 6, 1823, pp. 768–71; *LitMus*, Dec. 6, 1823, pp. 769–70; *LSB*, Dec. 6, 1823, pp. 257–58, Dec. 20, 1823, pp. 296–97; *MR*, CIII (Feb., 1824), 212–15.

Reviews of *The Age of Bronze* (1823): *Exam*, Mar. 30, 1823, pp. 217–18; *MR*, C (Apr., 1823), 430–33; *BM*, XIII (Apr., 1823), 457–60 (J. Wilson); *EdM*, XII 2s (Apr., 1823), 483–88; *LG*, Apr. 5, 1823, pp. 211–13; *LC*, Apr. 5, 1823, pp. 209–10; *LitMus*, Apr. 5, 1823, p. 209; *LitReg*, Apr. 5, 1823, pp. 209–10; *MM*, LV (May, 1823), 322–25; *British Magazine*, I (May, 1823), 114–19.

Reviews of *The Island* (1823): *Exam*, June 16, 1823, pp. 394–96 (A. Fonblanque?); *LC*, June 21, 1823, pp. 385–87; *LitMus*, June 21, 1823, pp. 385–86; *LitReg*, June 28, 1823, pp. 405–6; *MR*, CI (July, 1823),

316–21; *BC*, XX 2s (July, 1823), 16–22; *NEM*, III (July, 1823), 47–51; *British Magazine*, I (July, 1823), 195–200; *NMM*, VIII 2s (1823), 136–41.

Reviews of *The Deformed Transformed* (1824): *Exam*, Feb. 15, 1824, pp. 104–6 (A. Fonblanque?); *LG*, Feb. 28, 1824, pp. 131–33; *LC*, Feb. 28, 1824, pp. 129–31; *MR*, CIII (Mar., 1824), 321–24; *LM*, IX (Mar., 1824), 315–21; *EdM*, XIV 2s (Mar., 1824), 353–56; *NEM*, IV (Mar., 1824), 255–60; *BC*, XXI 2s (Apr., 1824), 403–14; *LaBA*, XXIX (Apr., 1824), 170; *UR*, I (May, 1824), 239–46.

Reviews of *Don Juan* XV–XVI (1824); *Exam*, Mar. 14, 1824, pp. 163–64, Mar. 21, 1824, pp. 179–80; *MR*, CIII (Apr., 1824), 434–36; *LG*, Apr. 3, 1824, pp. 212–13; *LC*, Apr. 3, 1824, pp. 215–17.

COLERIDGE

Reviews of the third ed. of Coleridge's *Poems* (1803): *AR*, II (1804), 556; *PR*, Vol. for 1804 (1806), p. 485.

Review of *The Friend* (1809–10): *EcR*, VII–ii (Oct., 1811), 912–31 (J. Foster).

Reviews of *Remorse* (1813): *Republican*, Feb. 13, 1813, pp. 96–99; *Sat*, XII (Mar., 1813), 269–83; *TI*, II (Mar., 1813), 111–16; *CR*, III 4s (Apr., 1813), 402–5; *CO*, XII (Apr., 1813), 228–38; *MR*, LXXI (May, 1813), 82–93 (F. Hodgson); *BR*, IV (May, 1813), 361–70; *QR*, XI (Apr., 1814), 177–90 [pub. July, 1814] (J. T. Coleridge).

Reviews of the *Christabel* vol. (1816): *CR*, III 5s (May, 1816), 504–10; *Champ*, May 26, 1816, pp. 166–67; *EcR*, V 2s (June, 1816), 565–72 (J. Conder); *Exam*, June 2, 1816, pp. 348–49 (W. Hazlitt); *AugR*, III (July, 1816), 14–24; *LP*, IV 2s (July, 1816), 559–63; *AjR*, L (July, 1816), 632–36; *Scourge and Satirist*, XII (July, 1816), 60–72; *BR*, VIII (Aug., 1816), 64–81 (W. Roberts); *BLM*, IV (Oct., 1816), 248–51; *ER*, XXVII (Sept., 1816), 58–67 [pub. Nov., 1816]; *EM*, LXX (Nov., 1816), 434–37 (G. F. Mathew); *MR*, LXXXII (Jan., 1817), 22–25.

Reviews of *The Statesman's Manual* (1816): *ER*, XXVII (Dec., 1816), 444–59 (W. Hazlitt); *Exam*, Dec. 29, 1816, pp. 824–27 (W. Hazlitt); *MM*, XLII (Jan., 1817), 545.

Reviews of *Blessed Are Ye That Sow* (1817): *Monthly Repository*, XII (May, 1817), 299–301; *MM*, XLIII (May, 1817), 34; *CR*, V 5s (June, 1817), 581–86.

Reviews of the *Biographia Literaria* (1817): *ER*, XXVIII (Aug., 1817), 488–515 (W. Hazlitt); *NMM*, VIII (Aug., 1817), 50; *LG*, Aug. 9, 1817, pp. 83–85; *MM*, XLIV (Sept., 1817), 154; *BM*, II (Oct., 1817),

3–18 (J. Wilson); *BC*, VIII 2s (Nov., 1817), 460–81; *MR*, LXXXVIII (Feb., 1819), 124–38.

Reviews of *Sibylline Leaves* (1817): *LG*, July 26, 1817, pp. 49–51; *MM*, XLIV (Sept., 1817), 156; *EdM*, I 2s (Oct., 1817), 245–50; *BC*, VIII 2s (Nov., 1817), 460–81; *MR*, LXXXVIII (Jan., 1819), 24–38; Gold's *LM*, II (July, 1820), 70–74.

Reviews of *Zapolya* (1817): *LG*, Nov. 15, 1817, pp. 307–8; *Champ*, Nov. 16, 1817, p. 365; *EdM*, I 2s (Dec., 1817), 455–59; *NMM*, VIII (Jan., 1818), 544; *MM*, XLIV (Jan., 1818), 541; *TI*, XII (Feb., 1818), 107–11; *Edinburgh Observer*, Feb. 7, 1818, p. 237.

Review of the second ed. of *The Friend* (1818): *EM*, LXXV (Feb., 1819), 141–42.

CRABBE

Reviews of *Poems* (1807): *GM*, LXXVII–ii (Nov., 1807), 1033–40, LXXVIII–i (Jan., 1808), 59; *CR*, XII 3s (Dec., 1807), 439–40; *AjR*, XXVIII (Dec., 1807), 337–47; *AR*, VI (1808), 514–21; *OR*, III (Jan., 1808), 87–96; *ER*, XII (Apr., 1808), 131–51 (F. Jeffrey); *MR*, LVI (June, 1808), 170–79 (T. Denman); *BC*, XXXI (June, 1808), 590–95; *UM*, X 2s (Nov., 1808), 434–38, (Dec., 1808), 513–18, XI 2s (Jan., 1809), 39–45, (Feb., 1809), 127–32; *EcR*, V-i (Jan., 1809), 40–49 (J. Montgomery); *PR*, Vol. for 1806–7 (1811), p. 538.

Reviews of *The Borough* (1810): *ER*, XVI (Apr., 1810), 30–55 (F. Jeffrey); *MR*, LXI (Apr., 1810), 396–409 (T. Denman): *GM*, LXXX–i (May, 1810), 445–47, (June, 1810), 548–54, (Supp. for 1810), 633–41; *EcR*, VI–i (June, 1810), 546–61; *CR*, XX 3s (July, 1810), 291–305; *LaBA*, II 2s (July, 1810), 36–40; *MM*, XXIX (Supp. for July 31, 1810), 633–34; *MonMir*, VIII 2s (Aug., 1810), 126–34, (Oct., 1810), 280–84; *QR*, IV (Nov., 1810), 281–312 [pub. late Dec., 1810] (R. Grant); *BC*, XXXVII (Mar., 1811), 236–47; *CO*, X (Aug., 1811), 502–11; *LaBA*, II 2s (Supp. to Vol. II 2s, 1811), 353–54; *PR*, Vol. for 1810–11 (1814), p. 554.

Reviews of *Tales in Verse* (1812): *GM*, LXXXII–ii (Sept., 1812), 241–45, (Oct., 1812), 346–49; *Scottish Review*, I (Sept., 1812), 60–94; *BR*, IV (Oct., 1812), 51–64; *ER*, XX (Nov., 1812), 277–305 (F. Jefffrey); *Scourge*, IV (Nov., 1812), 386–94; *MR*, LXIX (Dec., 1812), 352–64 (T. Denman); *CR*, II 4s (Dec., 1812), 561–79; *EcR*, VIII-ii (Dec., 1812), 1240–53; *NR*, I (Feb., 1813) 176–78; *UM*, XIX 2s (Feb., 1813), 128–33, (Mar., 1813), 219–24; *BC*, XLI (Apr., 1813), 380–86.

Reviews of *Tales of the Hall* (1819): *ER*, XXXII (July, 1819), 118–48 (F. Jeffrey); *BM*, V (July, 1819), 469–83 (J. Wilson); *GM*, LXXXIX–ii

(July, 1819), 45–47; *LG*, July 3, 1819, pp. 424–26; *LC*, July 10, 1819, pp. 113–15, July 17, 1819, pp. 133–34; *Green Man*, July 17, 1819, pp. 68–69; *BC*, XII 2s (Sept., 1819), 285–301; *NMM*, XII (Sept., 1819), 198–205, (Oct., 1819), 324–28; *EMR*, II (Sept., 1819), 287–302; *MM*, XLVIII (Sept., 1819), 155; *BLM*, III 3s (Sept., 1819), 133–34; *CO*, XVIII (Oct., 1819), 650–68; *MR*, XC (Nov., 1819), 225–38; *EcR*, XIII 2s (Feb., 1820), 114–33; *LaBA*, XX 2s (Supp. for 1819), 343–44.

HAZLITT

Reviews of *An Essay on the Principles of Human Action* (1805): *AR*, IV (1806), 657–64; *GR*, I (Mar., 1806), 225–35; *AjR*, XXVI (Jan., 1807), 17–22; *EcR*, III-ii (Aug., 1807), 698–704.

Reviews of *The Eloquence of the British Senate* (1807): *CR*, XIII 3s (Mar., 1808), 290–302; *MR*, LIX (June, 1809), 166–74 (S. Jones); *BC*, XXXVI (Aug., 1810), 124–37.

Reviews of *A Reply to the Essay on Population* (1807): *MR*, LVI (May, 1808), 53–62 (S. Jones); *ER*, XVI (Aug., 1810), 464–76 (T. Malthus?).

Review of *Memoirs of the Late Thomas Holcroft* (1816): *GM*, LXXXVI–i (Apr., 1816), 341–42.

Reviews of *The Round Table* (1817): *SM*, LXXIX (Feb., 1817), 127–31; *CR*, V 5s (Mar., 1817), 244–53; *EcR*, VII 2s (Apr., 1817), 385–86 (J. Conder); *MM*, XLIII (Apr., 1817), 246–47; *BLM*, V (May, 1817), 297–99; *BC*, VII 2s (June, 1817), 554–69; *NMM*, VII (July, 1817), 540; *QR*, XVII (Apr., 1817), 154–59 [pub. in Aug., 1817] (J. Russell?); *EdM*, I 2s (Nov., 1817), 352–61 (W. Hazlitt?); *LSMS*, I (Nov., 1817), 362–72; *BR*, XIII (May., 1819), 313–39.

Reviews of *Characters of Shakespear's Plays* (1817): *Champ*, July 20, 1817, pp. 230–31, July 26, 1817, p. 237 (J. H. Reynolds); *ER*, XXVIII (Aug., 1817), 472–88 (F. Jeffrey); *NMM*, VIII (Aug., 1817), 51; *Exam*, Oct. 26, 1817, p. 683, Nov. 2, 1817, pp. 697–98, Nov. 23, 1817, pp. 746–48 (L. Hunt); *EdM*, I 2s (Nov., 1817), 352–61 (W. Hazlitt?); *BC*, IX 2s (Jan., 1818), 15–22; *QR*, XVIII (Jan., 1818), 458–66 [pub. in June., 1818] (J. Russell?); *BR*, XIII (May., 1819), 313–39; *MR*, XCII (May, 1820), 53–68 (W. Taylor).

Reviews of *Lectures on the English Poets* (1818): *Champ*, May 24, 1818, pp. 330–32; *MM*, XLV (July, 1818), 534; *LJGM*, July 25, 1818, pp. 271–73, Aug. 1, 1818, pp. 291–93; *MM*, XLVI (Sept., 1818), 158; *LP*, VIII 2s (Sept., 1818), 1073–85; *BC*, X 2s (Dec., 1818), 600–11; *QR*, XIX (July, 1818), 424–34 [pub. in Jan., 1819] (E. S. Barrett and W. Gifford); *BR*, XIII (May, 1819), 313–39; *MR*, XCII (May, 1820), 53–68 (W. Taylor).

Reviews of *A View of the English Stage* (1818): *Champ*, May 24, 1818, pp. 330–32; *British Stage*, II (June, 1818), 124–26; *MM*, XLVI (Sept., 1818), 158; *BC*, X 2s (Oct., 1818), 441–45; *BR*, XIII (May, 1819), 313–39.

Review of *A Letter to William Gifford, Esq.* (1819): *Exam*, Mar. 7, 1819, p. 156, Mar. 14, 1819, pp. 171–73 (L. Hunt).

Reviews of *Lectures on the English Comic Writers* (1819); *Exam*, Apr. 18, 1819, pp. 250–51, June 6, 1819, pp. 362–63 (L. Hunt); *LSMS*, III (May, 1819), 197–208; *British Stage*, III (June, 1819), 163–65; *MR*, XCII (May, 1820), 53–68 (W. Taylor).

Reviews of *Political Essays* (1819): *LC*, Aug. 21, 1819, pp. 209–11; *MM*, XLVIII (Sept., 1819), 154–55; *QR*, XXII (July, 1819), 158–63 [pub. in Nov., 1819] (W. Gifford?); *Champ*, Nov. 7, 1819, p. 711; *AjR*, LVII (Dec., 1819), 312–24; *EMR*, III (Mar., 1820), 297–309; *MR*, XCIII (Nov., 1820), 250–58.

Reviews of *Lectures Chiefly on the Dramatic Literature of the Age of Elizabeth* (1820): *LM*, I (Feb., 1820), 185–91 (J. Scott); Gold's *LM*, I (Mar., 1820), 281–88; *Exam*, Mar. 19, 1820, p. 190 (L. Hunt); *MM*, XLIX (May, 1820), 356; *MR*, XCIII (Sept., 1820), 59–67 (W. Taylor); *ER*, XXXIV (Nov., 1820), 438–49 (T. N. Talfourd?).

Reviews of *Table Talk* (1821–22): *LC*, Apr. 14, 1821, pp. 225–27, Apr. 21, 1821, pp. 248–50; *LM*, III (May. 1821), 545–50 (T. N. Talfourd); *MM*, LI (May, 1821), 367–68; *BC*, XV 2s (June, 1821), 629–34; Gold's *LM*, III (June, 1821), 618–24; *NER*, I (July, 1821), 100–21; *GM*, XCI–ii (Nov., 1821), 448; *QR*, XXVI (Oct., 1821), 103–8 [pub. in Dec., 1821] (J. Matthews); *LitMus*, July 13, 1822, pp. 177–79, July 20, 1822, pp. 195–96; *LitReg*, July 27, 1822, pp. 53–56, Aug. 3, 1822, pp. 66–68; *BM*, XII (Aug., 1822), 157–66 (E. E. Crowe); *BC*, XVIII 2s (Aug., 1822), 174–78; *Exam*, Sept. 8, 1822, pp. 569–71; *MC*, I (Dec., 1822), 830–35; *MR*, CI (May, 1823), 55–62 (W. Taylor); *LM*, VII (June, 1823), 689–93.

Reviews of *Liber Amoris* (1823): *Exam*, May 11, 1823, pp. 313–15 (A. Fonblanque); *LitReg*, May 17, 1823, pp. 305–8, May 24, 1823, pp. 322–25; *LG*, May 31, 1823, pp. 339–40; *LitMus*, May 31, 1823, pp. 338–39; *BM*, XIII (June, 1823), 640–46 (J. G. Lockhart?); *NEM*, II (June, 1823), 518–21; *LC*, June 28, 1823, p. 409.

Reviews of *Characteristics* (1823): *NMM*, IX 2s (1823), 363; *LitExam*, July 12, 1823, pp. 27–29; *LitReg*, July 19, 1823, pp. 40–41; *MM*, LVI (Sept., 1823), 167; *MR*, CIII (Feb., 1824), 221–22.

HUNT

Reviews of *Critical Essays on the Performers of the London Theatres* (1807): *MonMir*, III 2s (Feb., 1808), 105–9; *Sat*, II (Mar., 1808), 75–84; *LMM*, V 2s (July, 1808), 42–43; *CR*, XIV 3s (Aug.. 1808), 374–79; *MR*, LVII (Dec., 1808), 423–29 (J. H. Merivale); *Cab*, I 2s (Feb., 1809), 141–48; *AjR*, XXXIII (June, 1809), 191; *LR*, II (Aug., 1809), 1–21 (R. Cumberland).

Reviews of *An Attempt to Shew the Folly and Danger of Methodism* (1809): *CR*, XIX 3s (Jan., 1810), 86–88; *MonMir*, VII 2s (Apr., 1810), 275–84.

Review of verses in the *Examiner* (1814): *Sat*, XIV (Feb., 1814), 161–63.

Reviews of *The Feast of the Poets* (1814): *Champ*, Feb. 20, 1814, pp. 62–63; *CR*, V 4s (Mar., 1814), 293–303; *NR*, III (Apr., 1814), 337*–339*; *Sat*, XIV (Apr., 1814), 327–31; *BC*, I 2s (May, 1814), 549–51; *EcR*, I 2s (June, 1814), 628–29; *NMM*, II (Aug., 1814), 58; *MR*, LXXV (Sept., 1814), 100–3; *NUM*, I (Oct., 1814), 297; *AugR*, II (Mar., 1816), 287–91.

Reviews of *The Descent of Liberty* (1815): *CR*, I 5s (Mar., 1815), 284–88; *Champ*, Mar., 26, 1815, p. 102 (J. Scott); *TI*, VI (Apr., 1815), 289–98; *BLM*, I (Apr., 1815), 277–81; *EcR*, III 2s (May, 1815), 517–21; *MR*, LXXVII (Aug., 1815), 434; *BC*, IV 2s (Aug., 1815) 205–10; *AugR*, II (Mar., 1816), 287–91.

Reviews of *The Story of Rimini* (1816): *NMM*, V (Mar., 1816), 149; *EcR*, V 2s (Apr., 1816), 380–85; *BLM*, III (Apr., 1816), 239–42; *QR*, XIV (Jan., 1816), 473–81 [pub. in May, 1816] (J. W. Croker); *BR*, VII (May, 1816), 452–69; *AugR*, II (May, 1816), 474–79; *ER*, XXVI (June, 1816), 476–91 (F. Jeffrey?); *MR*, LXXX (June, 1816), 138–47; *LP*, IV 2s (Sept., 1816), 936–44; *BM*, II (Nov., 1817), 194–201 (J. G. Lockhart).

Reviews of *Foliage* (1818): *LG*, Apr. 4, 1818, pp. 210–12; *MM*, XLV (May, 1818), 346; *QR*, XVIII (Jan., 1818), 324–35 [pub. in June, 1818], (J. W. Croker?); *BC*, X 2s (July, 1818), 90–96; *NMM*, X (Sept., 1818), 162–65; *EcR*, X 2s (Nov., 1818), 484–93.

Review of *Hero and Leander; & Bacchus and Ariadne* (1819): *LM*, II (July, 1820), 45–55 (P. G. Patmore).

Reviews of the *Literary Pocket-Book* (1819–24): *BM*, VI (Dec., 1819), 235–47 (J. Wilson?); *LC*, Dec. 30, 1820, pp. 834–35; *LM*, III (Jan., 1821), 62–66.

Reviews of *Amyntas* (1820); *LG*, July 22, 1820, pp. 467–69; *MM*, L

(Aug., 1820), 64–65; *MR*, XCIII (Sept., 1820), 17–31; *EdM*, VII 2s (Sept., 1820), 215–18.

For reviews of the *Liberal* 1–4, see above under Byron.

Reviews of *Ultra-Crepidarius* (1823): *LitExam*, Dec. 13, 1823, pp. 369–72; *LitMus*, Dec. 27, 1823, pp. 821–22; *BM*, XV (Jan., 1824), 86–90 (J. Wilson?); *BC*, XXI 2s (June, 1824), 647–57.

KEATS

Reviews of *Poems* (1817): *Champ*, Mar. 9, 1817, p. 78 (J. H. Reynolds?); *MM*, XLIII (Apr., 1817), 248; *EM*, LXXI (May, 1817), 434–37 (G. F. Mathew); *Exam*, June 1, 1817, p. 345, July 6, 1817, pp. 428–29, July 13, 1817, pp. 443–44 (L. Hunt); *EcR*, VIII 2s (Sept., 1817), 267–75 (J. Conder); *EdM*, I 2s (Oct., 1817), 254–57; *BM*, III (Aug., 1818), 519–24 (J. G. Lockhart).

Reviews of *Endymion* (1818): *LJGM*, May 17, 1818, pp. 114–15, May 24, 1818, p. 131; *BC*, IX 2s (June, 1818), 649–54; *Champ*, June 7, 1818, pp. 362–64 (J. H. Reynolds?); *BM*, III (Aug., 1818), 519–24 (J. G. Lockhart); *QR*, XIX (Apr. 1818), 204–8 [pub. Sept., 1818], (J. W. Croker); *Exam*, Oct. 11, 1818, pp. 648–49 (J. H. Reynolds); *LM*, I (Apr., 1820), 380–89 (P. G. Patmore); *ER*, XXXIV (Aug., 1820), 203–13 (F. Jeffrey); *EdM*, VII 2s (Aug., 1820), 107–10, (Oct. 1820), 313 16.

Reviews of *Lamia, Isabella, The Eve of St. Agnes, and Other Poems* (1820): *MR*, XCII (July, 1820), 305–10; *LC*, July 29, 1820, pp. 484–85; *Exam*, July 30, 1820, pp. 494–95 (C. Lamb) [quoted from the *New Times*]; *ER*, XXXIV (Aug., 1820), 203–13 (F. Jeffrey); *EdM*, VII 2s (Aug., 1820), 107–10, (Oct., 1820), 313–16; Gold's *LM*, II (Aug., 1820), 160–73; *Indic*, Aug. 2, 1820, pp. 337–44, Aug. 9, 1820, pp. 345–52 (L. Hunt); *Guardian*, Aug. 6, 1820 (no p. nos. given); *LM*, II (Sept., 1820), 315–21 (J. Scott); *BC*, XIV 2s (Sept., 1820), 257–64; *EcR*, XIV 2s (Sept., 1820), 158*–71*; *NMM*, XIV (Sept., 1820), 245–48; *MM*, L (Sept., 1820), 166.

LAMB

Reviews of *John Woodvil* (1802): *MonMir*, XIII (Apr., 1802), 254–56; *BC*, XIX (June, 1802), 646–47; *AR*, I (1803), 688–92; *MM*, XIV (Jan. 25, 1803), 600; *ER*, II (Apr., 1803), 90–96 (T. Brown); *MR*, XL (Apr., 1803), 442–43 (J. Ferriar).

Reviews of *Tales from Shakespear* (1807): *AjR*, XXVI (Mar. 1807), 298; *CR*, XI 3s (May, 1807), 97–99; *MonMir*, II 2s (July, 1807), 39; *LP*, III (Nov., 1807), 294–95; *GM*, LXXVIII (Nov., 1808), 1001; *BC*, XXXIII (May, 1809), 525.

Reviews of *Mrs. Leicester's School* (1807): *CR*, XV 3s (Dec., 1808), 444; *BC*, XXXIII (Jan., 1809), 77; *EcR*, V-i (Jan., 1809), 95; *LP*, V (Feb., 1809), 876.

Reviews of *The Adventures of Ulysses* (1808): *EM*, LIV (Nov., 1808), 384; *CR*, XV 3s (Dec., 1808), 443; *BC*, XXXII (Dec., 1808), 648–49; *AjR*, XXXII (Jan., 1809), 80–81; *MR*, LIX (May, 1809), 105–6 (T. Denman); *EcR*, V–ii (Oct., 1809), 973.

Reviews of *Specimens of English Dramatic Poets* (1808): *AR*, VII (1809), 562–70; *MR*, LVIII (Apr., 1809), 349–56 (T. Denman); *BC*, XXXIV (July, 1809), 73; *CR*, XX 3s (May, 1810), 80–82; *PR*, Vol. for 1808–9 (1812), p. 572.

Reviews of *Poetry for Children* (1809): *CR*, XVIII 3s (Oct., 1809), 223; *EM*, LVI (Nov., 1809), 378; *MR*, LXIV (Jan., 1811), 102 (Mrs. Barbauld).

Reviews of *The Works of Charles Lamb* (1818): *BLM*, II 2s (June, 1818), 262–64; *LJGM*, July 4, 1818, pp. 223–25, July 25, 1818, pp. 275–76; *BM*, III (Aug., 1818), 599–610 (J. Wilson); *MM*, XLVI (Sept., 1818), 158; *LP*, VIII 2s (Jan., 1819), 1646–53; *BC*, XI 2s (Feb., 1819), 139–47; *Exam*, Mar. 21, 1819, pp. 187–89, Mar. 28, 1819, pp. 204–6 (L. Hunt); *EM*, LXXV (Apr., 1819), 346–47; *Champ*, May 16, 1819, pp. 313–14, May 23, 1819, pp. 328–30 (T. N. Talfourd); *GM*, LXXXIX–ii (July, 1819), 49–51, (Aug., 1819), 138–40 (G. Dyer); *LG*, Aug. 14, 1819, pp. 516–17; *MR*, XC (Nov., 1819), 253–59; *Indic*, Jan. 31, 1821, pp. 129–36, Feb. 7, 1821, pp. 137–39 [quoted from *Exam*] (L. Hunt).

Reviews of *Elia*: *Essays Which Have Appeared under That Signature in the London Magazine* (1823): *MM*, LV (Feb., 1823), 62–63; *MR*, CI (June, 1823), 202–10; *BC*, XX 2s (July, 1823), 83–92.

MOORE

Reviews of the *Poetical Works of Thomas Little* (1801): *BC*, XVIII (Nov., 1801), 540–41; *MonMir*, XII (Nov., 1801), 316–17; *PR*, Vol. for 1801 (1802), p. 431; *CR*, XXXIV 2s (Feb., 1802), 200–5; *MM*, XIII (Supp. for July 20, 1802), 658; *MR*, XXXIX (Oct. 1802), 174–79 (J. Ferriar).

Reviews of the *Epistles, Odes and Other Poems* (1806): *UM*, V 2s (May, 1806), 428–33; *LJ*, I 2s (June, 1806), 646–57; *ER*, VIII (July, 1806), 456–65 (F. Jeffrey); *AjR*, XXIV (July, 1806), 263–71; *MLR*, I (July, 1806), 84–85; *MR*, LI (Sept., 1806), 59–70 (J. Ferriar); *MonMir*, XXII (Sept., 1806), 182–83; *CR*, IX 3s (Oct., 1806), 113–28; *EcR*, II–ii (Oct., 1806), 811–15 (J. Montgomery); *LeBM*, I (Nov., 1806), 37–41,

(Dec., 1806), 97–101; *AR*, V (1807), 498–99 (R. Southey); *Flowers of Literature*, Vol. for 1806 (1807), pp. 500–1; *PR*, Vol. for 1806–7 (1811), p. 499.

Reviews of the *Irish Melodies* I-IX (1808–24): *QR*, VII (June, 1812), 374–82 [pub. between July 10 and Aug. 14, 1812] (H. Twiss); *MR*, LXXI (June, 1813), 113–26 (F. Hodgson); *MR*, LXXIV (June, 1814), 183–87 (J. Hodgson); *TI*, VII (Aug., 1815), 128–31; *LJGM*, Oct. 10, 1818, pp. 448–49; *MR*, LXXXVII (Dec., 1818), 419–33; *British Stage*, II (Dec., 1818), 268–71; *Edinburgh Reflector*, Dec. 23, 1818, p. 223; *Exam*, Jan, 3, 1819, p. 11, Jan. 17, 1819, pp. 43–44; *LG*, May 12, 1821, pp. 290 91; *LM*, III (June, 1821), 659–63; *British Stage*, V (June, 1821), 165–68; *LC*, Nov. 10, 1821, pp. 705–7; *BM*, XI (Jan., 1822), 62–67 (E. E. Crowe); *QR*, XXVIII (Oct., 1822), 138–44 (H. Taylor); *NMM*, XII 2s (1824), 555; *LG*, Nov. 6, 1824, p. 705; *LaBA*, XXX (Dec., 1824), 260; *LMM*, XX 3s (Dec., 1824), 336.

Reviews of *Corruption and Intolerance* (1808): *MonMir*, IV 2s (Sept., 1808), 173–76; LeBM, IV (Sept., 1808), 119–21; *BC*, XXXII (Nov., 1808), 517–18; *AjR*, XXXI (Nov., 1808), 308–9; *MR*, LVIII (Apr., 1809), 418–22 (C. L. Moody and J. H. Merivale); *Sat*, VII (July, 1810), 80–89; *PR*, Vol. for 1808–9 (1812), p. 569.

Reviews of *The Sceptic* (1809): *MR*, LX (Sept., 1809), 103–4; *PR*, Vol. for 1810–11 (1814), p. 581.

Review of *A Letter to the Roman Catholics of Dublin* (1810): *Sat*, VII (July, 1810), 80–89.

Reviews of the *Intercepted Letters* (1813): *MR*, LXX (Apr., 1813), 436–38 (F. Hodgson); *CR*, III 4s (Apr., 1813), 421–26; *Drakard's Paper*, Apr. 4, 1813, p. 101; *Scourge*, V (May, 1813), 390–400; *Sat*, XIII (Dec., 1813), 553–57; *AjR*, XLVI (Mar., 1814), 266–68.

Review of *Lines on the Death of* [*Sheridan*] (1816): *TI*, XI (Nov., 1817), 362–67.

Reviews of *Sacred Songs* (1816): *CR*, III 5s (June, 1816), 607–16; *BR*, VIII (Aug., 1816), 164–69; *BM*, I (Sept., 1817), 630–31; *EMR*, I (Jan., 1819), 41–47; *MR*, XC (Dec., 1819), 413–20; *Christian Pocket Magazine*, II (Feb., 1820), 89–91.

Reviews of *Lalla Rookh* (1817): *Champ*, May 25, 1817, p. 165; *LG*, May 31, 1817, pp. 292–95; *Sale-Room*, May 31, 1817, pp. 173–75; *MR*, LXXXIII (June, 1817), 177–201, (July, 1817), 285–99; *CR*, V 5s (June, 1817), 560–81; *BC*, VII 2s (June, 1817), 604–16; *BM*, I (June, 1817), 279–85, (Aug., 1817), 503–10 (J. Wilson); *MM*, XLIII (June, 1817), 450–51; *GM*, LXXXVII-i (June, 1817), 535–37; *EM*, LXXII

(July, 1817), 55–58; *SM*, LXXIX (July, 1817), 528–31; *Knight Errant*, July 5, 1817, pp. 5–9; *BR*, X (Aug., 1817), 30–54; *NMM*, VIII (Aug., 1817), 52; *LSMS*, I (Aug., 1817), 297–307; *LP*, VI 2s (Sept., 1817), 897–913; *BLM*, I 2s (Sept., 1817), 180–81; *EcR*, VIII 2s (Oct., 1817), 340–53 (C. Neale?); *ER*, XXIX (Nov., 1817), 1–35 (F. Jeffrey); *Asiatic Journal*, IV (Nov., 1817), 457–67.

Reviews of *National Airs*, I–IV (1818–24): *Exam*, Feb. 13, 1820, p. 105; *MM*, LIII (June, 1822), 448; *Exam*, Dec. 1, 1822, p. 774; *LG*, Dec. 14, 1822, p. 785.

Reviews of *The Fudge Family in Paris* (1818): *MR*, LXXXV (Apr. 1818), 426–32; *LG*, Apr., 25, 1818, pp. 265–67; *YD*, Apr. 25, 1818, pp. 132–35 (W. Hazlitt); *Champ*, Apr. 26, 1818, pp. 267–68; *LJGM*, Apr. 26, 1818, pp. 71–72, May 3, 1818, pp. 87–89; *BC*, IX 2s (May, 1818), 496–501; *BM*, III (May, 1818), 129–36 (J. Wilson); *MM*, XLV (May, 1818), 342–44; *NBTM*, I (May, 1818), 49–52; *EM*, LXXIII (June, 1818), 517–19; *EdM*, II 2s (June, 1818), 553–58; *GM*, LXXXVIII–i (June, 1818), 527–28; *BLM*, II 2s (June, 1818), 273–74.

Reviews of *Tom Crib's Memorial to Congress* (1819): *LG*, Mar. 13, 1819, pp. 163–65; *Champ*, Mar. 21, 1819, p. 190, Apr. 4, 1819, pp. 220–21, Apr. 11, 1819, pp. 236–37 (J. Thelwall?); *MR*, LXXXVIII (Apr., 1819), 436–40; *MM*, XLVII (Apr., 1819), 254; *EdM*, IV 2s (Apr., 1819), 300–4; *LP*, IX 2s (June, 1819), 685–88; *Miniature Magazine*, I 2s (Sept., 1820), 165–67.

Reviews of *The Works of the Late Richard Brinsley Sheridan* (1821): *LC*, Apr. 7, 1821, pp. 209–10; *LG*, Apr. 21, 1821, 245–46.

Reviews of *The Loves of the Angels* (1823): *LG*, Dec. 28, 1822, pp. 815–17, Jan. 4, 1823, pp. 9–11; *LC*, Dec. 28, 1822, pp. 817–19; *LitMus*, Dec. 28, 1822, pp. 561–63; *NMM*, IX 2s (1823), 74–75; *MR*, C (Jan., 1823), 79–95; *BM*, XIII (Jan., 1823), 63–71 (J. Wilson); *GM*, XCIII–i (Jan., 1823), 41–44; *NEM*, II (Jan., 1823), 17–25; *LitReg*, Jan. 4, 1823, pp. 1–3; *Exam*, Jan. 5, 1823, pp. 6–9 (A. Fonblanque?); *JB*, Jan. 5, 1823, pp. 5–6, Jan. 12, 1823, pp. 13–14; *ER*, XXXVIII (Feb., 1823), 27–48 (F. Jeffrey?); *LM*, VII (Feb., 1823), 212–15 (J. H. Reynolds); *MM*, LV (Feb., 1823), 35–39; *IM*, V (Feb., 1823), 182–86; *EcR*, XIX 2s (Mar., 1823), 210–17; *EM*, LXXXIII (Mar., 1823), 256–59; *MC*, II (Mar. 1823), 335–41; *BC*, XIX 2s (June, 1823), 636–46.

Reviews of *Fables for the Holy Alliance* (1823): *BM*, XIII (May, 1823), 574–79 (J. G. Lockhart); *EM*, LXXXIII (May, 1823), 453; *LG*, May 10, 1823, pp. 289–91; *LC*, May 10, 1823, pp. 289–91; *LitMus*, May 10, 1823, pp. 292–94; *JB*, May 11, 1823, pp. 149–50; *Exam*, May 25, 1823, pp. 346–48 (A. Fonblanque?); *LitReg*, May 31, 1823, pp. 342–44; *BC*,

XIX 2s (June, 1823), 636–46; *British Magazine*, I (June, 1823), 153–59; *MM*, LV (July, 1823), 491; *EcR*, XX 2s (Aug., 1823), 181–84.

Reviews of *Memoirs of Captain Rock* (1824): *NMM*, XII 2s (1824), 216; *BC*, XXI 2s (Apr., 1824), 421–45; *NEM*, IV (Apr. 1824), 347–55; *LG*, Apr. 17, 1824, pp. 243–44; *LC*, Apr. 17, 1824, pp. 241–44; *Exam*, Apr. 25, 1824, pp. 257–59; *BM*, XV (May, 1824), 544–51 (J. Anster) ; *MM*, LVII (May, 1824), 347; *EdM*, XIV 2s (May, 1824), 513–25; *UR*, I (May, 1824), 340–49; *EM*, LXXXV (June, 1824), 543–46; *ER*, XLI (Oct., 1824), 143–53 (S. Smith); *BR*, XXII (Nov., 1824), 419–46.

SCOTT

Reviews of the *Minstrelsy of the Scottish Border* (1802–3): *SM*, LXIV (Jan., 1802), 68–71; *AR*, I (1803), 635–43; *PR*, Vol. for 1802 (1803), p. 447; *ER*, I (Jan., 1803), 395–406 (J. Stoddart); *MM*, XIV (Jan. 25, 1803), 598; *LJ*, II, Aug., 16, 1803, 144–47; *MR*, XLII (Sept., 1803), 21–33 (L. Muirhead); *CR*, XXXIX 2s (Nov., 1803), 250–59; *AR*, II (1804), 533–38; *PR*, Vol. for 1803 (1804), p. 462; *BC*, XXIII (Jan., 1804), 36–43; *MM*, XVII (July 28, 1804), 666; *MR*, XLV (Oct., 1804), 126–34 (L. Muirhead).

Reviews of *Sir Tristrem* (1804): *ER*, IV (July, 1804), 427–44 (G. Ellis); *CR*, III 3s (Sept., 1804), 45–52 (W. Taylor); *AR*, III (1805), 555–63 (R. Southey); *BC*, XXV (Apr., 1805), 361–68; *MR*, XLVIII (Oct. 1805), 196–203 (L. Muirhead); *PR*, Vol. for 1806–7 (1811), pp. 557–58.

Reviews of *The Lay of the Last Minstrel* (1805): *AR*, III (1805), 600–4 (Mrs. Barbauld); *SM*, LXVII (Jan., 1805), 37–45; *IR*, IV (Jan., 1805), 90–104; *LJ*, V (Mar. 1805) 271–80; *ER*, VI (Apr., 1805), 1–20 (F. Jeffrey); *CR*, V 3s (July, 1805), 225–42; *MM*, XIX (July 28, 1805), 658; *BC*, XXVI (Aug., 1805), 154–60; *EcR*, II–i (Mar., 1806), 193–200; *MR*, XLIX (Mar., 1806), 295–303 (L. Muirhead); *MonMir*, XXII (Dec., 1806), 385–95; *PR*, Vol. for 1805 (1807), p. 484.

Reviews of *Ballads and Lyrical Pieces* (1806): *SM*, LXVIII (Oct., 1806), 767–68; *CR*, IX 3s (Dec., 1806), 342–48; *MonMir*, XXII (Dec., 1806), 401–4; *AR*, V (1807), 494–97; *Flowers of Literature*, Vol. for 1806 (1807), p. 498; *OR*, I (Jan., 1807), 74–83; *MM*, XXII (Jan. 25, 1807), 641–42; (*LeBM*, I (Feb. 1807), 206–12; *EcR*, III-i (May, 1807), 374–80; *MR*, LIII (June, 1807), 183–91 (J. Finlay); *LaBA*, II (Supp. for 1807), 33–34; *BC*, XXXII (July, 1808), 72; *PR*, Vol. for 1806–7 (1811), pp. 499–500.

Reviews of *Marmion* (1808): *SM*, LXX (Mar. 1808), 195–202; *ER*, XII (Apr., 1808), 1–35 (F. Jeffrey); *CR*, XIII 3s (Apr., 1808), 387–401; *LP*,

IV (Apr., 1808), 53–63; *LaBA*, IV (Apr., 1808), 177–83; *Sat*, II (Apr., 1808), 186–93; *EcR*, IV–i (May, 1808), 407–22 (J. Montgomery); *MR*, LVI (May, 1808), 1–19 (J. H. Merivale); *UM*, IX 2s (May, 1808), 410–20; *LeBM*, III (May, 1808), 263–70, (June, 1808), 315–21 (H. Twiss?); *Cab*, III (May, 1808), 321–32, IV (July, 1808), 33–36; *BC*, XXXI (June, 1808), 640–48; *MM*, XXV (July 30, 1808), 594–95; *MonMir*, IV 2s (Aug., 1808), 85–92; *AR*, VII (1809), 462–73; *LR*, I (Feb., 1809), 82–122 (H. Twiss); *English Censor*, I (Feb., 1809), 144–50; *Cab*, II, 2s (Aug., 1809), 115–23; *AjR*, XXXVIII (Mar., 1811), 225–48; *PR*, Vol. for 1808–9 (1812), p. 547.

Reviews of *The Works of John Dryden* (1808): *SM*, LXX (May, 1808), 355–59; *Sat*, II (July, 1808), 518–26, III (Aug., 1808), 66–71; *ER*, XIII (Oct., 1808), 116–35 (H. Hallam); *AR*, VII (1809), 765–75; *MM*, XXVI (Jan. 30, 1809), 636–37; *MR*, LVIII (Feb., 1809), 137–60 (C. Symmons); *LR*, I (Feb., 1809), 42–65 (H. Pye); *BC*, XXXV (Feb., 1810), 97–109, (Mar., 1810), 272–88, (May, 1810), 465–74, (June, 1810), 574–84.

Reviews of *The State Papers and Letters of Sir Ralph Sadler* (1809); *ER*, XVI (Aug., 1810), 447–64 (M. Napier?); *CR*, XXI (Oct., 1810), 165–79, (Nov., 1810), 267–83; *QR*, IV (Nov., 1810), 403–14 [pub. late Dec., 1810] (E. Lodge).

Review of *Lord Somers' Collection of Tracts* (1809–12): *LP*, VI (June, 1809), 418–24.

Reviews of *The Lady of the Lake* (1810): *SM*, LXXII (May, 1810), 359–64; *LaBA*, I 2s (May, 1810), 245*–252*; *LaBA*, II 2s (Supp. 1811), 351–52; *MR*, LXII (June, 1810), 178–94 (F. Hodgson); *CO*, IX (June, 1810), 366–89; *Weekly Register*, June 30, 1810, pp. 1451–52; *EcR*, VI–ii (July, 1810), 577–602; *MonMir*, VIII 2s (July, 1810), 36–51; *QR*, III (May, 1810), 492–517 [pub. between July 3 and 17, 1810] (G. Ellis); *MM*, XXIX (July 31, 1810), 631–32; *ER*, XVI (Aug. 1810), 263–93 (F. Jeffrey); *CR*, XX 3s (Aug., 1810), 337–57; *BC*, XXXVI (Aug., 1810), 119–24; *EM*, LVIII (Nov., 1810), 363–69, (Dec., 1810), 443–48; *LP*, VIII (Nov., 1810), 1231–43; *AjR*, XXXVIII (Mar., 1811), 225–48; *UM*, XV 2s (May, 1811), 393–97; *PR*, Vol. for 1810–11 (1814), p. 548.

Reviews of the *Poetical Works of Anna Seward* (1810): *EM*, LVIII (Aug., 1810), 119–24, (Sept., 1810), 201–4, (Oct., 1810), 291–93; *EcR*, VII–i (Jan., 1811), 19–32 (J. Montgomery); *LP*, IX (Mar., 1811), 466–74; *BC*, XXXVII (May, 1811), 493–500; *CR*, XXIII 3s (July, 1811), 225–38; *SM*, LXXIII (July, 1811), 520–35; *BR*, II (Sept., 1811), 171–88; *AjR*, XLI (Apr., 1812), 372–86; *MR*, LXIX (Sept., 1812), 20–34

(C. L. Moody); *General Chronicle*, VI (Nov., 1812), 305–6; *PR*, Vol. for 1810–11 (1814), p. 560.

Reviews of *The Vision of Don Roderick* (1811): *MR*, LXV (July, 1811), 293–307 (F. Hodgson); *ER*, XVIII (Aug., 1811), 379–92 (F. Jeffrey); *CR*, XXIII 3s (Aug., 1811), 337–49; *EcR*, VII–ii (Aug., 1811), 672–88; *UM*, XVI 2s (Aug., 1811), 126–34; *General Chronicle*, II (Supp. Aug., 1811), 503–18; *BC*, XXXVIII (Sept., 1811), 280–84; *Scourge*, II (Sept., 1811), 224–35; *Edinburgh Quarterly Review and Magazine*, I (Sept., 1811), 411–27; *QR*, VI (Oct., 1811), 221–35 (W. Erskine); *CO*, XI (Jan., 1812), 29–33; *Military Panorama*, I (Jan., 1813), 329–32; *PR*, Vol. for 1810–11 (1814), pp. 603–4.

Reviews of *The Border Antiquities* (1812–17): *AjR*, XLII (Aug., 1812), 337–43; *EdM*, I 2s (Dec., 1817), 450–55; *EcR*, X 2s (Oct., 1818), 305–22 (J. Foster).

Reviews of *Rokeby* (1813): *SM*, LXXV (Jan., 1813), 46–51; *QR*, VIII (Dec., 1812), 485–507 [pub. between Jan. 25 and Apr. 7, 1813] (G. Ellis); *Drakard's Paper*, Jan. 31, 1813, pp. 31–32; *MR*, LXX (Feb., 1813), 113–32, (Mar., 1813), 225–40 (F. Hodgson); *TI*, II (Feb., 1813), 41–51; *Scourge*, V (Feb., 1813), 154–62; *CR*, III 4s (Mar., 1813), 240–58; *EM*, LXIII (Mar., 1813), 223–26; *LaBA*, VII 2s (Mar., 1813), 126–33; *AjR*, XLIV (Apr., 1813), 377–90; *BR*, IV (May, 1813), 270–82; *Sat*, XII (May, 1813), 464–73; *EcR*, IX–i (June, 1813), 587–605 (J. Montgomery); *LP*, XIII (June, 1813), 737–53; *BC*, XLII (Aug., 1813), 110–23; *NR*, II (Sept., 1813), 228–30.

Reviews of *The Bridal of Triermain* (1813): *SM*, LXXV (Apr., 1813), 282–86; *CR*, III 4s (May, 1813), 473–82; *Town Talk*, IV (July, 1813), 437–39; *QR*, IX (July, 1813), 480–97 [pub. 6 weeks late] (G. Ellis); *EcR*, IX-ii (Oct., 1813), 368–78; *Drakard's Paper*, Dec. 18, 1813, pp. 398–99; *MR*, LXXIII (Mar., 1814), 237–44 (F. Hodgson); *LMM*, XVII 2s (Dec., 1814), 340–43; *MM*, XLVIII (Oct., 1819), 255–56.

Reviews of the *Life and Works of Jonathan Swift* (1814): *SM*, LXXVI (Nov., 1814), 847–54; *ER*, XXVII (Sept., 1816), 1–58 (F. Jeffrey).

Reviews of *The Lord of the Isles* (1815): *SM*, LXXVII (Jan., 1815), 42–49; *EM*, LXVII (Jan., 1815), 48–50; *TI*, VI (Jan., 1815), 55–67; *Champ*, Jan. 15, 1815, p. 21; *MM*, XXXVIII (Supp. Jan. 30, 1815), 649–58; *ER*, XXIV (Feb., 1815), 273–94 (F. Jeffrey); *BC*, III 2s (Feb., 1815), 130–47; *GM*, LXXXV–i (Feb., 1815), 148–50; *NMM*, III (Feb., 1815), 54; *BLM*, I (Feb., 1815), 118–23; *MR*, LXXVI (Mar., 1815), 262–81 (F. Hodgson); *LaBA*, XI 2s (Mar., 1815), 125–28; *LP*, II 2s (Apr., 1815), 12–26; *Tradesman*, V 2s (Apr., 1815), 313–17; *AugR*, I (May, 1815), 1–11; *EcR*, III 2s (May, 1815), 469–80 (C. Neale?);

CR, II 5s (July, 1815), 58–77; *BR*, VI (Aug., 1815) 87–107; *QR*, XIII (July, 1815), 287–309 [pub. Nov. 2 to Dec. 6, 1815] (G. Ellis); *AjR*, L (Feb., 1816), 105–27; *Mentor*, Oct. 11, 1817, pp. 245–52, Oct. 25, 1817, pp. 269–72, Nov. 1, 1817, pp. 281–86.

Reviews of *The Field of Waterloo* (1815): *MR*, LXXVIII (Nov., 1815), 251–60; *CR*, II 5s (Nov., 1815), 457–63; *BC*, IV 2s (Nov., 1815), 528–32; *AjR*, XLIX (Nov., 1815), 471–79, (Dec., 1815), 521–37; *CO*, XIV (Nov., 1815), 750–60; *AugR*, I (Nov., 1815), 785–94; *Champ*, Nov. 5, 1815, p. 358; *EcR*, IV 2s (Dec., 1815), 570–78 (J. Conder); *LP*, III 2s (Dec., 1815), 392–98; *Scourge*, X (Dec., 1815), 437–51; *TI*, VII (Dec., 1815), 452–59; *BLM*, II (Dec., 1815), 393–94; *LMM*, II 3s (Dec., 1815), 329–31; *EM*, LXIX (Feb., 1816), 141–42; *LaBA*, XII 2s (Supp. for 1815), 340–42.

Reviews of *Harold the Dauntless* (1817): *SM*, LXXIX (Feb., 1817), 131–34; *LG*, Mar. 15, 1817, pp. 117–18; *CR*, V 5s (Apr., 1817), 379-84; *BM*, I (Apr., 1817), 76–78; *NMM*, VII (Apr., 1817), 251; *EcR*, VII 2s (May, 1817), 457–63; *MR*, LXXXIV (Sept., 1817), 10–18; *MM*, XLVIII (Oct., 1819), 255–56.

Review of *The Provincial Antiquities* (1818): *LC*, Nov. 27, 1819, pp. 433–34.

Reviews of *Patrick Carey's Trivial Poems and Triolets* (1819); *LG*, May 27, 1820, pp. 337–38; *LMM*, XII 3s (July, 1820), 35; *MR*, XCV (June, 1821), 212–15.

Reviews of *Halidon Hill* (1822): *LG*, June 29, 1822, pp. 399–401; *LC*, June 29, 1822, pp. 401–4; *LitMus*, June 29, 1822, pp. 145–47; *MR*, XCVIII (July, 1822), 309–15; *EdM*, XI 2s (July, 1822), 27–37; *GM*, XCII-ii (July, 1822), 49–52; *NER*, III (July, 1822), 264–81; *NEM*, I (July, 1822), 31–33; *LitReg*, July 6, 1822, pp. 3–6; *Gazette of Fashion*, July 13, 1822, pp. 173–76; *LM*, VI (Aug., 1822), 174–81 (A. Cunningham?); *MM*, LIV (Aug., 1822), 23–27; *EM*, LXXXII (Aug., 1822), 154–56; *LMM*, XVI 3s (Aug., 1822), 102, (Sept., 1822), 154–59; *MC*, I (Aug., 1822), 330–35; *LS*, II (Aug., 1822?), 195–200; *EcR*, XVIII 2s (Sept., 1822), 259–79; *LSMS*, III (Sept., 1822), 457–63; *BC*, XVIII 2s (Oct., 1822), 353–61; *NMM*, VI (1822), 363–64.

SHELLEY

Reviews of *Zastrozzi* (1810): *GM*, LXXX–ii (Sept., 1810), 258; *CR*, XXI 3s (Nov., 1810), 329–31.

Reviews of *Original Poetry; by Victor and Cazire* (1810): *AjR*, XXXVII (Oct., 1810), 206; *LP*, VIII (Oct., 1810), 1063–66; *BC*, XXXVII (Apr., 1811), 408–409; *PR*, Vol. for 1810–11 (1814), p. 617.

Reviews of *St. Irvyne* (1811): *BC*, XXXVII (Jan., 1811), 70–71; *LP*, IX (Feb., 1811), 252–54; *AjR*, XLI (Jan., 1812), 69–71.

Reviews of *Queen Mab* (1813): *Theological Inquirer*, I (Mar., 1815), 34–39, (Apr., 1815), 105–110, (May, 1815), 205–9, (July, 1815), 358–62 (Ronald Crawford Ferguson?).

Reviews of *Alastor* (1816): *MR*, LXXIX (Apr., 1816), 433; *BC*, V 2s (May, 1816), 545–46; *EcR*, VI 2s (Oct., 1816), 391–93 (J. Conder); *BM*, VI (Nov., 1819), 148–54 (J. G. Lockhart).

Reviews of *A Proposal for Putting Reform to the Vote* (1816): *QR*, XVI (Jan., 1817), 511–52 [pub. in Apr., 1817] (R. Southey). Although the work is listed as one of several being reviewed, it is never mentioned by name. For possible references to Shelley in the review, see K. N. Cameron, 'Shelley vs. Southey: New Light on an Old Quarrel', *PMLA*, LVII (1942), 489–512.

Review of *Laon and Cythna* (1817): *QR*, XXI (Apr., 1819), 460–71 [pub. in Sept., 1819] (J. T. Coleridge).

Reviews of *The Revolt of Islam* (1818): *Exam*, Feb. 1, 1818, pp. 75–76, Feb. 22, 1818, pp. 121–22, Mar. 1, 1818, pp. 139–41 (L. Hunt); *MM*, XLV (Mar., 1818), 154; *BM*, IV (Jan., 1819), 475–82 (J. G. Lockhart); *MR*, LXXXVIII (Mar., 1819), 323–24; *QR*, XXI (Apr., 1819), 460–71 [pub. in Sept., 1819] (J. T. Coleridge).

Reviews of *Rosalind and Helen* (1819): *Exam*, May 9, 1819, pp. 302–3 (L. Hunt); *BM*, V (June, 1819), 268–74 (J. G. Lockhart); *GM*, LXXXIX–i (Supp. June, 1819), 625–26 (quoted from the *New Times*); *MR*, XC (Oct., 1819), 207–9.

Reviews of *The Cenci* (1819): *Exam*, Mar. 19, 1820, pp. 190–91 (L. Hunt); Gold's *LM*, I (Apr., 1820), 401–7; *MM*, XLIX (Apr., 1820), 260; *TI*, XVI (Apr., 1820), 205–18; *LG*, Apr. 1, 1820, pp. 209–10; *LM*, I (May., 1820), 546–55 (J. Scott); *NMM*, XIII (May, 1820), 550–53; *EMR*, III (May, 1820), 591–604; *MR*, XCIV (Feb., 1821), 161–68; *Independent*, Feb. 17, 1821, pp. 99–103; *BR*, XVII (June, 1821), 380–89; *Indic*, July 26, 1820, pp. 329–36 (L. Hunt).

Reviews of *Prometheus Unbound* (1820): *BM*, VII (Sept., 1820), 679–87 (J. G. Lockhart); Gold's *LM*, II (Sept., 1820), 306–7, (Oct., 1820), 382–91; *LG*, Sept. 9, 1820, pp. 580–82; *MR*, XCIV (Feb., 1821), 168–73; *QR*, XXVI (Oct., 1821), 168–80 [pub. in Dec., 1821] (W. S. Walker).

Reviews of the pirated edition of *Queen Mab* (1821): Gold's *LM*, III (Mar., 1821), 278–80; *JBBJ*, Mar. 11, 1821, p. 22; *LG*, May 19, 1821, pp. 305–8; *MM*, LI (June, 1821), 460–61; *LC*, June 2, 1821, pp.

344–45; *Republican*, Feb. 1, 1822, pp. 145–48 (R. Carlile); *Investigator*, V (Oct., 1822), 315–71.

Reviews of *Epipsychidion* (1821): *Gossip*, June 23, 1821, pp. 129–35, July 14, 1821, pp. 153–58; *Gazette of Fashion*, Aug. 17, 1822, pp. 41–42.

Reviews of *Adonais* (1821): *BM*, X (Dec. 1821), 696–700 (G. Croly); *LC*, Dec. 1, 1821, pp. 751–54; *LG*, Dec. 8, 1821, pp. 772–73; *LitReg*, Sept. 28, 1822, pp. 193–94.

Review of *Hellas* (1822): *General Weekly Register*, June 30, 1822, pp. 501–3.

Reviews of *Posthumous Poems* (1824): *Exam*, June 13, 1824, p. 370 (A. Fonblanque?); *ER*, XL (July, 1824), 494–514 (W. Hazlitt); *EdM*, XV 2s (July, 1824), 11–17; *LG*, July 17, 1824, pp. 451–52; *LaBA*, XXX 2s (Aug., 1824), 81; *Knight's Quarterly Magazine*, III (Aug., 1824), 182–95; *LMM*, XX 3s (Aug., 1824), 106.

SOUTHEY

Reviews of *Thalaba* (1801): *BC*, XVIII (Sept., 1801), 309–10; *MonMir*, XII (Oct., 1801), 243–47; *PR*, Vol. for 1801 (1802), pp. 427–28; *MM*, XII (Jan., 1802), 581–84; *ER*, I (Oct., 1802), 63–83 (F. Jeffrey); *MR*, XXXIX (Nov., 1802), 240–51 (F. Jeffrey); *CR*, XXXIX 2s (Dec., 1803), 369–79 (W. Taylor).

Reviews of *The Works of Thomas Chatterton* (1803): *AR*, I (1803), 672; *BC*, XXI (Apr., 1803), 367–73; *MM*, XV (July 28, 1803), 636; *ER*, IV (Apr., 1804), 214–30 (W. Scott).

Reviews of *Amadis of Gaul* (1803): *LJ*, II (Sept. 16, 1803), 263–64; *ER*, III (Oct., 1803), 109–36 (W. Scott); *MonMir*, XVI (Nov., 1803), 318–20; *AR*, II (1804), 600–3; *CR*, I 3s (Jan., 1804), 45–52 (W. Taylor); *MM*, XVI (Jan. 25, 1804), 636; *BC*, XXIV (Nov., 1804), 471–81; *MR*, XLVII (May, 1805), 13–25 (L. Muirhead).

Reviews of the *Metrical Tales and Other Poems* (1805): *LJ*, V (Feb., 1805), 157–65; *CR*, IV 3s (Feb., 1805), 118–21 (J. H. Hunt?); *EcR*, I-i (Apr., 1805), 279–81; *MonMir*, XIX (May, 1805), 316–18; *BC*, XXV (May, 1805), 553–55; *MR*, XLVIII (Nov., 1805), 323–24 (J. Ferriar); *AR*, IV (1806), 579–81 (W. Taylor); *PR*, Vol. for 1805 (1807), p. 487.

Reviews of *Madoc* (1805): *LJ*, V (June, 1805), 621–36; *MM*, XIX (July 28, 1805), 656–58 (W. Taylor); *UM*, IV 2s (Aug., 1805), 149–53; *IR*, V (Oct., 1805), 417–26, (Nov., 1805), 465–73; *MR*, XLVIII (Oct., 1805), 113–22 (J. Ferriar); *EM*, XLVIII (Oct., 1805), 279–82; *ER*, VII (Oct., 1805), 1–28 (F. Jeffrey); *EcR*, I-ii (Dec., 1805), 899–908; *AR*,

IV (1806), 604–13 (W. Taylor); *CR*, VII 3s (Jan., 1806), 72–83 Le (C. Grice); *GR*, I (June, 1806), 505–26; *BC*, XXVIII (Oct., 1806), 395–410, (Nov., 1806), 486–94; *PR*, Vol. for 1805 (1807), pp. 483–84.

Reviews of *Specimens of the Later English Poets* (1807): *OR*, I (May, 1807), 558–65; *UM*, VIII 2s (July, 1807), 32–36; *MM*, XXIII (July 30, 1807), 640–41; *BC*, XXX (Sept., 1807), 245–49; *EcR*, III–ii (Oct., 1807), 845–55 (J. Montgomery); *ER*, XI (Oct., 1807), 31–40; *Literary Annual Register*, I (Oct., 1807), 467–68; *AR*, VI (1808), 557–60; *PR*, Vol. for 1806–7 (1811), p. 558.

Reviews of the *Letters from England* (1807): *MonMir*, II 2s (Sept., 1807), 177–82; *OR*, II (Sept., 1807), 284–97; *ER*, XI (Jan., 1808), 370–90 (F. Jeffrey); *AR*, VI (1808), 637–42 (W. Taylor); *UM*, IX 2s (Jan., 1808), 42–43; *MM*, XXIV (Jan. 30, 1808), 633–34; *BC*, XXXI (Feb., 1808), 168–78; *CR*, XIII 3s (Mar., 1808), 282–83; *Cab*, III (Apr., 1808), 260–62; *MR*, LV (Apr., 1808), 380–86 (C. L. Moody); *GM*, LXXVIII (Supp. for 1808), 1169–74; *AjR*, XXXIV (Nov., 1809), 274–89.

Reviews of *Palmerin of England* (1807): *CR*, XII 3s (Dec., 1807), 431–37; *MM*, XXIV (Jan. 30, 1808), 630; *AR*, VII (1809), 575–85; *GM*, LXXIX (May, 1809), 438–43; *MR*, LX (Oct., 1809), 157–59 (F. Hodgson).

Reviews of *The Remains of Henry Kirke White* (1807 & 1822): *AR*, VI (1808), 548–53; *GM*, LXXVIII (Jan., 1808), 45–46; *CR*, XIII 3s (Mar., 1808), 320–26; *Cab*, III (Mar., 1808), 177–82; *EcR*, IV–i (Mar., 1808), 193–207; *AjR*, XXXII (Apr., 1809), 352–57; *MR*, LXI (Jan., 1810), 71–84 (T. Denman & G. E. Griffiths); *PR*, Vol. for 1808–9 (1812), pp. 550–51; *NMM*, VI (1822), 365; *LG*, June 15, 1822, pp. 367–68; *EM*, LXXXII (July, 1822), 62; *MM*, LIII (July 18, 1822), 552; *EcR*, XVIII 2s (Sept., 1822), 209–16; *BR*, XX (Sept., 1822), 165–75; *LitMus*, Sept. 14, 1822, pp. 323–24; *MC*, I (Oct., 1822), 597–99; *MR*, XCIX (Dec., 1822), 445–47; *LC*, Dec. 14, 1822, pp. 791–92.

Reviews of the *Chronicle of the Cid* (1808): *AjR*, XXXI (Oct., 1808), 151–65, (Nov., 1808), 234–45; *AR*, VII (1809), 91–99 (S. Turner); *CR*, XVI 3s (Jan., 1809), 1–18, (Feb., 1809), 155–69; *QR*, I (Feb., 1809), 134–53 (W. Scott); *GM*, LXXIX (Mar., 1809), 237–45; *EcR*, V–i (Mar., 1809), 201–18 (J. Foster); *BC*, XXXIII (May, 1809), 458–67, (June, 1809), 610–18; *MR*, LXIV (Feb., 1811), 131–44 (W. Taylor).

Reviews of *The Curse of Kehama* (1810): *MM*, XXX (Jan. 31, 1811), 673–75; *MonMir*, IX 2s (Feb., 1811), 122–35; *ER*, XVII (Feb., 1811), 429–65 (F. Jeffrey); *Sat*, VIII (Feb., 1811), 168–74, (Mar., 1811), 249–56; *QR*, V (Feb., 1811), 40–61 [pub. Mar., 1811] (W. Scott and G. Bedford); *CR*, XXII 3s (Mar., 1811), 225–51; *EcR*, VII–i (Mar.,

1811), 185–205, (Apr., 1811), 334–50 (J. Foster); *General Chronicle and Literary Magazine*, I (Mar., 1811), 273–85; *MR*, LXV (May, 1811), 55–69, (June, 1811), 113–28 (F. Hodgson); *LP*, IX (June, 1811), 1044–59; *LaBA*, IV 2s (Supp. for 1811), 373–76; *BC*, XXXIX (Mar., 1812), 272–82; *PR*, Vol. for 1810–11 (1814), p. 547.

Reviews of *The History of Brazil* (1810, 1817, 1819): *CR*, XXI 3s (Sept., 1810), 27–43; *EcR*, VI-ii (Sept., 1810), 788–800; *QR*, IV (Nov., 1810), 454–74 [pub. late Dec., 1810] (R. Heber); *MM*, XXX (Jan. 31, 1811), 654–55; *GM*, LXXXI–i (May, 1811), 458–60; *MR*, LXIX (Dec., 1812), 337–52 (J. Lowe); *CR*, V 5s (Apr., 1817), 327–48; *LG*, Apr. 26, 1817, p. 213; *GM*, LXXXVII–i (June, 1817), 528–29; *QR*, XVIII (Oct., 1817), 99–128 [pub. Feb., 1818] (R. Heber); *BC*, IX 2s (Mar., 1818), 225–45, (Apr., 1818), 369–91; *MR*, LXXXVII (Nov., 1818), 267–78; *LG*, Oct. 30, 1819, pp. 689–90, Nov. 6, 1819, pp. 710–11, Nov., 13, 1819, pp. 727–29, Nov. 20, 1819, p. 743; *LC*, Dec. 11, 1819, pp. 467–69, Dec. 18, 1819, pp. 486–87, Dec. 25, 1819, pp. 503–5; *MR*, CI (July, 1823), 326–27.

Reviews of *Omniana* (1812): *BC*, XL (Nov., 1812), 540–41; *CR*, III 4s (Feb., 1813), 205–9; *MR*, LXXIII (Jan., 1814), 108–11 (C. L. Moody); *EM*, LXV (Feb., 1814), 130.

Reviews of the *Life of Nelson* (1813): *LP*, XIII (July, 1813), 959–61; *CR*, IV 4s (July, 1813), 11–26; *AjR*, XLV (July, 1813), 72–89, (Aug., 1813), 138–60; *GM*, LXXXIII–ii (Aug., 1813), 137–38; *BC*, XLII (Oct., 1813), 360–66; *BR*, V (Oct., 1813), 167–96; *EcR*, I 2s (June, 1814), 606–22 (J. Montgomery?).

Reviews of the *Carmen Triumphale* (1814): *ER*, XXII (Jan., 1814), 447–54 (F. Jeffrey?); *Scourge*, VII (Feb., 1814), 122–30; *TI*, IV (Feb., 1814), 103–4; *CR*, V 4s (Feb., 1814), 203–8; *MR*, LXXIII (Apr., 1814), 428–31 (C. L. Moody); *EcR*, I 2s (Apr., 1814), 431–36; *EM*, LXVI (Nov., 1814), 427–28.

Reviews of the *Congratulatory Odes* (1814): *BC*, II 2s (July, 1814), 95–98; *Tripod*, XV (July, 1814), 42–52; *EcR*, II 2s (Aug., 1814), 179–81; *LP*, XV (Aug., 1814), 1045–52; *CR*, VI 4s (Sept., 1814), 313; *GM*, LXXXIV–ii (Oct., 1814), 359.

Reviews of *Roderick* (1814): *TI*, V (Dec., 1814), 389–93; *Champ*, Jan. 1, 1815, pp. 423–24 (J. Scott); *NMM*, II (Jan., 1815), 549; *CR*, I 5s (Jan., 1815), 28–38; *MR*, LXXVI (Mar., 1815), 225–40 (J. H. Merivale); *BC*, III 2s (Apr., 1815), 353–89 (J. Coleridge); *EcR*, III 2s (Apr., 1815), 352–68 (J. Montgomery); *ER*, XXV (June, 1815), 1–31 (F. Jeffrey); *QR*, XIII (Apr., 1815), 83–113 [pub. June 20, 1815] (G. Bedford); *AugR*, I (Aug., 1815), 380–93; *CO*, XIV (Sept., 1815), 592–616; *BR*,

VI (Nov., 1815), 287-306; *Catholicon*, III (Nov., 1816), 175–79, (Dec., 1816), 225–27.

Review of *The Minor Poems of Robert Southey* (1815): *MR*, LXXVIII (Oct., 1815), 181–85.

Reviews of *The Poet's Pilgrimage to Waterloo* (1816): *CR*, III 5s (May, 1816), 470–82; *Champ*, May 19, 1816, p. 158; *MR*, LXXX (June, 1816), 189–99; *AjR*, L (June, 1816), 521–37; *AugR*, III (July, 1816), 45–54; *BC*, VI 2s (July, 1816), 27–40; *EcR*, VI 2s (July, 1816), 1–18 (J. Conder); *Scourge and Satirist*, XII (Aug., 1816), 129–41; *EM*, LXX (Nov., 1816), 438–39.

Reviews of the *Carmen Nuptiale* (1816): *ER*, XXVI (June, 1816), 441–49 (F. Jeffrey); *Champ*, June 30, 1816, p. 206; *BC*, VI 2s (July, 1816), 40–45; *CR*, IV 5s (July, 1816), 16–26; *Exam*, July 7, 1816, pp. 426–28, July 14, 1816, pp. 441–43 (W. Hazlitt); *AugR*, III (Aug., 1816), 151–55; *BR*, VIII (Aug., 1816), 189–93; *EcR*, VI 2s (Aug., 1816), 196–204 (J. Conder); *NMM*, VI (Aug., 1816), 55; *MR*, LXXXII (Jan., 1817), 91–97.

Reviews of *Wat Tyler* (1817): *CR*, V 5s (Feb., 1817), 187–89; *Monthly Repository*, XII (Mar., 1817), 172–74; *ER*, XXVIII (Mar., 1817), 151–74 (F. Jeffrey); *MR*, LXXXII (Mar., 1817), 313–17; *Exam*, Mar. 9, 1817, pp. 157–59 (W. Hazlitt); *Black Dwarf*, Mar. 26, 1817, pp. 139–43; *LG*, Mar. 29, 1817, pp. 147–48; *NMM*, VII (Apr., 1817), 250; *Monitor*, I (Apr.?, 1817), 37–43; *TI*, X (May, 1817), 370–75; *BC*, VII 2s (May, 1817), 437–48.

Reviews of *A Letter to William Smith* (1817): *ER*, XXVIII (Mar., 1817), 151–74 (F. Jeffrey); *CR*, V 5s (Apr., 1817), 390–95; *BC*, VII 2s (May, 1817), 437–48; *Monthly Repository*, XII (May, 1817), 274–76, 301–2; *Exam*, May 4, 1817, pp. 284–87, May 11, 1817, pp. 298–300, May 18, 1817, pp. 315–18 (W. Hazlitt); *MR*, LXXXIII (June, 1817), 223–24; *NMM*, VII (June, 1817), 444.

Review of *The Byrth, Lyf and Actes of King Arthur* (1817): *MR*, LXXXVII (Dec., 1818), 370–82.

Reviews of the *Life of Wesley* (1820): *LG*, Mar. 25, 1820, pp. 203–6, Apr. 1, 1820, pp. 213–15, Apr. 8, 1820, pp. 231–33, Apr., 15, 1820, pp. 246–48, Apr. 22, 1820, pp. 263–66; *EdM*, VI 2s (May, 1820), 405–8; Gold's *LM*, I (May, 1820), 529–33; *AjR*, LVIII (May, 1820), 257–66, (June, 1820), 329–44, (Aug., 1820), 505–17; *IM*, II (June, 1820), 475–79, (July, 1820), 546–54, (Sept., 1820), 759–65; *MM*, XLIX (June, 1820), 448–49; *LMM*, XI 3s (June, 1820), 333–34; *GM*, XC-i (June, 1820), 532–35; *BR*, XV (June, 1820), 455–92; *BC*, XIV 2s (July, 1820), 1–32, (Aug., 1820), 164–85; *LSMS*, IV (Aug., 1820), 282–300; *LM*, II

(Aug., 1820), 190–94 (G. Croly?); *Invest*, I (Sept., 1820), 367–409; *CO*, XIX (Nov., 1820), 738–60; *QR*, XXIV (Oct., 1820), 1–55 [pub. Dec., 1820] (R. Heber); *EcR*, XV 2s (Jan., 1821), 1–30; *MR*, XCVI (Sept., 1821), 26–43; *BM*, XV (Feb., 1824), 208–19 (J. G. Lockhart?).

Reviews of *A Vision of Judgement* (1821): *LG*, Mar. 17, 1821, pp. 161–63; *LC*, Mar. 24, 1821, pp. 180–83; Gold's *LM*, III (Apr., 1821), 393–401; *LM*, III (Apr., 1821), 428–30 (B. W. Proctor?); *GM*, XCI–i (Apr., 1821), 342–43; *MM*, LI (Apr., 1821), 270; *Exam*, Apr. 29, 1821, pp. 257–60 (A. Fonblanque?); *EMR*, V (May, 1821), 609–16; *MR*, XCV (June, 1821), 170–78; *AjR*, LX (June, 1821), 325–33; *BR*, XVII (June, 1821), 321–37; *ER*, XXXV (July, 1821), 422–36 (F. Jeffrey); *EcR*, XVII 2s (May, 1822), 418–27.

Reviews of *The Expedition of Orsua* (1821): *LG*, July 7, 1821, pp. 421–22, July 14, 1821, pp. 436–38; *MM*, LII (Aug., 1821), 70; *EcR*, XVI 2s (Sept., 1821), 250–56; *LC*, Sept., 15, 1821, pp. 576–78; *MR*, XCVII (Feb., 1822), 211–13.

Reviews of the *History of the Peninsular War*, Vol. I (1823): *LG*, Dec. 14, 1822, pp. 783–84, Dec. 21, 1822, pp. 802–4; *LC*, Dec. 21, 1822, pp. 801–4, Dec. 28, 1822, pp. 819–21; *LitMus*, Dec. 21, 1822, pp. 545–47, Dec. 28, 1822, pp. 563–65; *MM*, LIV (Jan., 1823), 532–33, LV (Feb., 1823), 65; *Exam*, Jan. 12, 1823, pp. 28–29 (A. Fonblanque?); *EdM*, XII 2s (Feb., 1823), 208–22, (Mar., 1823), 325–37; *MC*, II (Mar., 1823), 278–92; *MR*, CI (June, 1823), 113–27; *EcR*, XX 2s (July, 1823), 1–22; *QR*, XXIX (Apr., 1823), 53–85 [pub. Sept., 1823] (G. Procter & J. W. Croker).

Reviews of *The Book of the Church* (1824): *NMM*, XII 2s (1824), 220–21; *BM*, XV (Feb., 1824), 208–19 (J. G. Lockhart?); *LC*, Feb. 7, 1824, pp. 85–87, Feb. 14, 1824, pp. 100–2, Feb. 21, 1824, pp. 121–22; *GM*, XCIV-i (Mar., 1824), 246–48; *UR*, I (Mar., 1824), 81–91; *BC*, XXI 2s (May, 1824), 449–63; *BR*, XXII (May, 1824), 315–44; *MM*, LVII (May, 1824), 346–47; *LMM*, XX 3s (Sept., 1824), 162; *Exam*, Oct. 17, 1824, pp. 660–61.

WORDSWORTH

Reviews of the first edition of the *Lyrical Ballads* (1798): *CR*, XXIV 2s (Oct., 1798), 197–204 (R. Southey); *MonMir*, VI (Oct., 1798), 224–25; *Analytical Review*, XXVIII (Dec., 1798), 583–87; *MM*, VI (Supp. for 1798), 514; *MR*, XXIX (June, 1799), 202–10 (C. Burney); *BC*, XIV (Oct., 1799), 364–69; *AjR*, V (Apr., 1800), 334 (W. Heath).

Reviews of the second edition of the *Lyrical Ballads* (1800): *BC*, XVII (Feb., 1801), 125–31; *MonMir*, XI (June, 1801), 389–92; *MR*, XXXVIII (June, 1802), 209.

Reviews of the *Poems in Two Volumes* (1807): *MLR*, III (July, 1807), 65–66 (Byron); *CR*, XI 3s (Aug., 1807), 399–403; *LeBM*, II (Oct., 1807), 138–42; *ER*, XI (Oct., 1807), 214–31 (F. Jeffrey); *Literary Annual Register*, I (Oct., 1807), 468–69; *Sat*, I (Nov., 1807), 188–91; *LP*, III (Nov., 1807), 271–72; *EcR*, IV-i (Jan., 1808), 35–43 (J. Montgomery); *AR*, VI (1808), 521–29 (L. Aikin); *Cab*, III (Apr., 1808), 249–52; *BC*, XXXIII (Mar., 1809), 298–99; *PR*, Vol. for 1806–7 (1811), pp. 540–41.

Reviews of the *Convention of Cintra* tract (1809): *EcR*, V-ii (Aug., 1809), 744–50 (J. Montgomery); *BC*, XXXIV (Sept., 1809), 305–6; *LR*, II (Nov., 1809), 231–75 (H. C. Robinson).

Reviews of the *Excursion* (1814): *Exam*, Aug. 21, 1814, pp. 541–42, Aug. 28, 1814, pp. 555–58, Oct. 2, 1814, pp. 636–38 (W. Hazlitt); *NMM*, II (Sept., 1814), 157; *Variety*, Sept. 10, 1814, pp. 5–6; *ER*, XXIV (Nov., 1814), 1–30 (F. Jeffrey); *Philanthropist*, V (1815), 342–63; *EcR*, III 2s (Jan., 1815), 13–39 (J. Montgomery); *QR*, XII (Oct., 1814), 100–11 [pub. Jan. 14, 1815] (C. Lamb and W. Gifford); *MM*, XXXVIII (Supp. to Vol. XXXVIII, Jan. 30, 1815), 638–49; *MR*, LXXVI (Feb., 1815), 123–36 (J. H. Merivale); *BC*, III 2s (May, 1815), 449–67; *LaBA*, XI (May, 1815), 224–25; *BR*, VI (Aug., 1815), 50–64; *AugR*, I (Aug., 1815), 343–56; *LG*, Dec. 30, 1820, p. 837 [rev. of the 1820 ed.].

Reviews of the *White Doe* (1815): *TI*, VI (June, 1815), 445–50; *Champ*, June 25, 1815, pp. 205–6 (J. Scott); *BLM*, II (July, 1815), 33–37; *NMM*, III (July, 1815), 546; *AugR*, I (Aug., 1815), 343–56; *ER*, XXV (Oct., 1815), 355–63 (F. Jeffrey); *MR*, LXXVIII (Nov., 1815), 235–38; *BR*, VI (Nov., 1815), 370–77; *GM*, LV-ii (Dec., 1815), 524–25; *EcR*, V 2s (Jan., 1816), 33–45 (J. Conder); *EM*, LXIX (Mar., 1816), 237–39; *QR*, XIV (Oct., 1815), 201–25 [pub. Mar., 1816] (W. R. Lyall); *BM*, III (July, 1818), 369–81 (J. Wilson).

Reviews of the *Collected Ed.* of 1815: *AugR*, I (Aug., 1815), 343–56; *MR*, LXXVIII (Nov., 1815), 225–34; *QR*, XIV (Oct., 1815), 201–25 [pub. Mar., 1816] (W. R. Lyall).

Reviews of *A Letter to a Friend of Robert Burns* (1816): *MR*, LXXX (June, 1816), 221–22; *CR*, IV 5s (July, 1816), 51–58; *BM*, I (June, 1817), 261–66 (J. Wilson).

Reviews of the *Thanksgiving Ode* (1816): *EcR*, VI 2s (July, 1816), 1–18 (J. Conder); *BC*, VI 2s (Sept., 1816), 313–15; *Champ*, Oct. 20, 1816, pp. 334–35; *MR*, LXXXII (Jan., 1817), 98–100.

Reviews of *Peter Bell* (1819): *BM*, V (May, 1819), 130–36; *EdM*, IV 2s (May, 1819), 427–29; *GM*, LXXXIX-i (May, 1819), 441–42; *EM*,

LXXV (May, 1819), 445–48; *TI*, XIV (May, 1819), 369–76, (June, 1819), 441–46; *LG*, May 1, 1819, pp. 273–75; *Exam*, May 2, 1819, pp. 282–83 (L. Hunt); *LC*, May 29, 1819, pp. 20–21; *BC*, XI 2s (June, 1819), 584–603; *MM*, XLVII (June, 1819), 442; *EcR*, XII 2s (July, 1819), 62–76; *BLM*, III 3s (July, 1819), 34–35; *MR*, LXXXIX (Aug., 1819), 419–22; *LSMS*, III (Aug., 1819), 314–19; *EMR*, II (Dec., 1819), 654–61.

Reviews of *The Waggoner* (1819): *TI*, XIV (June, 1819), 447–49; *BM*, V (June, 1819), 332–34; *EM*, LXXV (June, 1819), 531–33; *LG*, June 12, 1819, pp. 369–71; *MM*, XLVII (July, 1819), 540; *EcR*, XII 2s (July, 1819), 62–76; *BLM*, III 3s (Aug., 1819), 85–86; *NMM*, XII (Aug., 1819), 81; *GM*, LXXXIX-ii (Aug., 1819), 143–44; *LSMS*, III (Aug., 1819), 314–19; *MR*, XC (Sept., 1819), 36–40; *BC*, XII 2s (Nov., 1819), 364–79; *EMR*, II (Dec., 1819), 654–61.

Reviews of the *River Duddon* vol. (1820): *LG*, Mar., 25, 1820, pp. 200–3; *BM*, VII (May, 1820), 206–13 (J. Wilson or J. G. Lockhart?); *EM*, LXXVII (June, 1820), 523–25; Gold's *LM*, I (June, 1820), 618–627; *LC*, July 1, 1820, pp. 420–22; *LSMS*, IV (Aug., 1820), 323–28; *LMM*, XII 3s (Aug., 1820), 95; *EcR*, XIV 2s (Aug., 1820), 170–84; *BR*, XVI (Sept., 1820), 37–53; *GM*, XC-ii (Oct., 1820), 344–46; *MR*, XCIII (Oct., 1820), 132–43; *BC*, XV 2s (Feb., 1821), 113–35.

Review of the *Collected Ed.* of 1820: *LG*, Oct. 7, 1820, p. 641.

Reviews of the *Ecclesiastical Sketches* (1822): *LG*, Mar. 30, 1822, pp. 191–92; *MM*, LIII (May, 1822), 343–44; *General Weekly Register*, May 5, 1822, pp. 184–85; *Monthly Repository*, XVII (June, 1822), 360–65 (John Bowring?); *BM*, XII (Aug., 1822), 175–91 (J. Wilson); *BC*, XVIII 2s (Nov., 1822), 522–31; *LC*, Dec. 14, 1822, p. 791; *MC*, II (Mar., 1823), 324–35.

Reviews of the *Memorials of a Tour* (1822): *LG*, Apr. 6, 1822, pp. 210–12; *MM*, LIII (May, 1822), 343–44; *LitMus*, May 18, 1822, pp. 52–53; *Monthly Repository*, XVII (June, 1822), 360–65 (John Bowring?); *BM*, XII (Aug., 1822), 175–91 (J. Wilson); *BC*, XVIII 2s (Nov., 1822), 522–31; *ER*, XXXVII (Nov., 1822), 449–56 (F. Jeffrey); *BR*, XX (Dec., 1822), 459–66; *LC*, Dec. 14, 1822, p. 791; *MC*, II (Mar., 1823), 324–35.

Review of *A Description of the Scenery of the Lakes* (1822): *NEM*, I (Dec., 1822), 490–97.

Works Pertaining to the Romantic Reviews

Abbreviations Used

BNYPL	*Bulletin of The New York Public Library*
BUSE	*Boston University Studies in English*
ELH	*Journal of English Literary History*
JEGP	*Journal of English and Germanic Philology*
K SJ	*Keats Shelley Journal*
MLN	*Modern Language Notes*
MLQ	*Modern Language Quarterly*
MLR	*Modern Language Review*
MP	*Modern Philology*
N&Q	*Notes and Queries*
PMLA	*Publications of the Modern Language Association of America*
PQ	*Philological Quarterly*
RES	*Review of English Studies*
SAQ	*South Atlantic Quarterly*
SP	*Studies in Philology*
TLS	*Times Literary Supplement*

Aikin, Lucy. *Memoir of John Aikin, M.D.* 2 vols. London, 1823.

Alden, Raymond M. (ed.). *Critical Essays of the Early Nineteenth Century.* New York: C. Scribner's Sons, 1921.

Altick, Richard D. *The English Common Reader: A Social History of the Mass Reading Public, 1800–1900.* Chicago: University of Chicago Press, 1957.

Amarasinghe, Upali. *Dryden and Pope in the Early Nineteenth Century.* Cambridge: Cambridge University Press, 1962.

Ames, Alfred C. 'Contemporary Defense of Wordsworth's Pedlar', *MLN*, LXIII (1948), 543–45.

Anon. 'The Centenary of the "Quarterly Review" ', *Quarterly Review*, CCX (1909), 731–84, CCXI (1909), 279–324.

——. 'The *Edinburgh Review* (1802–1902)', *Edinburgh Review*, CXLV (1902), 275–318.

——. *Libel. Sir John Carr against Hood & Sharpe.* London, 1808.

——. *Memoirs of the Public and Private Life of Sir Richard Phillips.* [By a Citizen of London, and Assistants] London, 1808.

Anon. 'Writers in the *Edinburgh Review*', *Gentleman's Magazine*, XXIII n.s. (May, 1845), 496–500.

——. 'Writers in the *Edinburgh Review*', *Gentleman's Magazine*, XXIV n.s. (December, 1845), 585–89.

Arnould, Joseph. *Memoir of Thomas, First Lord Denman.* 2 vols. London, 1873.

Aspinall, Arthur. 'The Circulation of Newspapers in the Early Nineteenth Century', *RES*, XXII (1946), 29–43.

——. *Politics and the Press c. 1780–1850.* London: Home and Van Thal, 1949.

——. 'The Social Status of Journalists at the Beginning of the Nineteenth Century', *RES*, XXI (1945), 216–32.

Atkinson, R. H. M. B., and Johnson, G. A. (eds). *Brougham and His Early Friends.* 3 vols. London: Privately printed, 1908.

Auden, W. H. 'Portrait of a Whig', *English Miscellany*, III (1952), 141–58.

Bagehot, Walter. 'The First Edinburgh Reviewers', in *Literary Studies.* 2 vols. London, 1879.

Bagot, Captain Josceline. *George Canning and His Friends.* 2 vols. London: J. Murray, 1909.

Bain, Alexander. *James Mill. A Biography.* London, 1822.

Baker, Herschel. *William Hazlitt.* Cambridge, Mass.: Harvard University Press, 1962.

Bald, R. C. 'Francis Jeffrey as a Literary Critic', *Nineteenth Century and After*, XCVII (1925), 201–5.

Ball, Margaret. *Sir Walter Scott as a Critic of Literature.* New York: Columbia University Press, 1907.

Barham, R. H. *The Life and Remains of Theodore Edward Hook.* 2 vols. London, 1849.

Barrow, Sir John. *Autobiographical Memoir of Sir John Barrow.* London, 1847.

Bates, William. *The Maclise Portrait-Gallery.* London, 1873.

Bauer, Josephine. *The London Magazine 1820–29.* Copenhagen: Rosenkilde and Bagger, 1953.

Beattie, William. *The Life and Letters of Thomas Campbell.* 2d ed., 3 vols. London, 1850.

Beatty, J. M., Jr. 'Lord Jeffrey and Wordsworth', *PMLA*, XXXVIII (1923), 221–35.

Beavan, A. H. *James and Horace Smith*. London, 1899.

Beloe, William. *The Sexagenarian, or, The Recollections of a Literary Life*, ed. Thomas Rennell. 2 vols. London, 1817.

Besterman, Theodore. *The Publishing Firm of Cadell & Davies*. Oxford: Oxford University Press, 1938.

Bloom, E. A. 'Labour of the Learned: Neoclassic Book Reviewing Aims and Techniques', *SP*, LIV (1957), 537–63.

Blumenthal, Walter Hart. 'Barbs and Bludgeons', *American Book Collector*, VII (1957), 23–31.

Blunden, Edmund. *Keats's Publisher: A Memoir of John Taylor*. London: Jonathan Cape, 1940.

——. *Leigh Hunt and His Circle*. London: Harper and Brothers, 1930.

—— (ed.). *Leigh Hunt's 'Examiner' Examined*. London: Cobden-Sanderson, 1928.

Boyle, A. 'The Publisher—Sir Richard Phillips', *N & Q*, CXCVI (1951), 361–66.

Briggs, Harold E. 'Keats's Conscious and Unconscious Reactions to Criticisms of *Endymion*', *PMLA*, LX (1945), 1106–29.

Brightfield, M. F. *John Wilson Croker*. Berkeley: University of California Press, 1940.

Broman, W. E. 'Factors in Crabbe's Eminence in the Early Nineteenth Century', *MP*, LI (1954), 42–49.

Brooks, Elmer L. 'Byron and the *London Magazine*', *K–SJ*, V (1956), 49–67.

Brougham, Henry. *The Life and Times of Henry Lord Brougham, Written by Himself*. 3 vols. Edinburgh and London, 1871.

Butterworth, S. 'The Old "London Magazine" ', *Bookman* (London), LXIII (1922), 12–17.

Caine, T. Hall. *Cobwebs of Criticism*. London, 1883.

Cameron, K. N. 'Shelley vs. Southey: New Light on an Old Quarrel', *PMLA*, LVII (1942), 489–512.

Campbell, O. J., Peyre, J. F. A., and Weaver, B. *Poetry and Criticism of the Romantic Movement*. New York: F. S. Crofts and Co., 1932.

Carnall, Geoffrey. 'The Monthly Magazine', *RES*, V n.s. (1954), 158–64.

——. *Southey and His Age*. Oxford: Clarendon Press. 1960.

Carver, P. L. 'The Authorship of a Review of "Christabel" Attributed to Hazlitt', *JEGP*, XXIX (1930), 562–78.

Carver, P. L. 'Hazlitt's Contributions to *The Edenburgh Review*', *RES*, IV (1928), 385–93.

Chew, S. C. *Byron in England: His Fame and After-Fame*. London: J. Murray, 1924.

Churton, Edward. *Memoir of Joshua Watson*. 2 vols. London, 1861.

Clark, Roy B. *William Gifford: Tory Satirist, Critic, and Editor*. New York: Columbia University Press, 1930.

Clive, John. *Scotch Reviewers: The Edinburgh Review 1802–1815*. London: Faber and Faber, 1957.

——. 'The Earl of Buchan's Kick: A Footnote to the History of the *Edinburgh Review*', *Harvard Library Bulletin*, V (1951), 362–70.

——. '*The Edinburgh Review*: 150 Years After', *History Today*, II (1952), 844–50.

Cockburn, Lord Henry. *Life of Lord Jeffrey*. 2d ed., 2 vols. Edinburgh, 1852.

——. *Memorials of His Time*. London, 1856.

Cohen, B. Bernard. 'William Hazlitt: Bonapartist Critic of *The Excursion*', *MLQ*, X (1949), 158–67.

Coles, William A. 'Thomas Noon Talfourd on Byron and the Imagination', *K–SJ*, IX (1960), 99–113.

Collins, Arthur S. *The Profession of Letters, 1780–1832*. London: G. Routledge and Sons, Ltd., 1928.

Conder, Eustace R. *Josiah Conder, A Memoir*. London, 1857.

Conder, Josiah [pseud. John Charles O'Reid]. *Reviewers Reviewed*. Oxford, 1811.

Constable, Thomas. *Archibald Constable and His Literary Correspondents*. 3 vols. Edinburgh, 1873.

Cooper, Duff [Viscount Norwich]. 'Keats and His Critics', *Essays by Divers Hands*, XXVIII (1956), 1–19.

Copinger, W. A. *On the Authorship of the First Hundred Numbers of the Edinburgh Review*. Manchester, 1895.

Cornelius, R. D. 'Two Early Reviews of Keats's First Volume', *PMLA*, XL (1925), 193–210.

Corson, J. C. *A Bibliography of Sir Walter Scott*. Edinburgh: Oliver and Boyd, 1943.

Cox, R. G. 'The Great Reviews', *Scrutiny*, VI (1937), 2–20, 155–75.

——. 'Nineteenth Century Periodical Criticism: 1800–60', unpublished dissertation, Cambridge University, 1939.

Crawford, Thomas. *The Edinburgh Review and Romantic Poetry (1802–29)*. Auckland University College Bulletin No. 47, English Series No. 8, 1955.

Cross, Maurice. *Selections from The Edinburgh Review*. 4 vols. London, 1833.

Curry, Kenneth (ed.). *New Letters of Robert Southey*. 2 vols. New York: Columbia University Press, 1965.

——. 'Southey's Contributions to the Annual Review', *Bulletin of Bibliography*, XVI (1939), 195–97.

Curwen, Henry. *History of Booksellers*. London, 1873.

Daniel, Robert. 'Jeffrey and Wordsworth: the Shape of Persecution', *Sewanee Review*, L (1942), 195–213.

Davies, Hugh Sykes. *The Poets and Their Critics*. Vol. II 'Blake to Browning'. London: Hutchinson and Co., 1962.

——. 'Wordsworth and His Critics', *Listener*, XLIII (1950), 1015–16.

De Fonblanque, E. B. *Life and Labour of Albany Fonblanque*. London, 1874.

Derby, R. 'The Paradox of Jeffrey: Reason versus Sensibility', *MLQ*, VII (1946), 489–500.

Dibdin, T. F. *Reminiscences of a Literary Life*. 2 vols. London, 1836.

Douady, Jules. *Liste Chronologique des œuvres de William Hazlitt*. Paris, 1906.

Doughty, Oswald. 'The Reception of Wordsworth by his Contemporaries', *English Miscellany*, XIII (1962), 81–95.

Dowden, W. S. 'A Jacobin Journal's View of Lord Byron', *SP*, XLVIII (1951), 56–66.

——. 'Thomas Moore and the Review of "Christabel" ', *MP*, LX (1962), 47–50.

Dudek, Louis. *Literature and the Press*. Toronto: Ryerson Press, 1960.

Duncan, Robert W. 'Byron and the London *Literary Gazette*', *BUSE*, II (1956), 240–50.

Dwyer, J. Thomas. 'Check List of Primary Sources of the Byron–Jeffrey Relationship', *N&Q*, VII n.s. (1960), 256–59.

Dyer, George. *The Privileges of the University of Cambridge*. 2 vols. London, 1824.

Edgcumbe, Richard. 'Byronic Literature', *N&Q*, II 7th ser. (1886), 284–85.

Elliott, Arthur R. D. 'Reviews and Magazines in the Early Years of the Nineteenth Century', *The Cambridge History of English Literature*, ed. A. W. Ward and A. R. Waller. Vol. XII, Chap. vi, Cambridge: Cambridge University Press, 1915.

Elsner, Richard. *Francis Jeffrey . . . und Seine Kritischen Prinzipien.* Berlin, 1908.

Elton, Oliver. *Survey of English Literature 1780–1830.* 2 vols. London: E. Arnold, 1912.

Elwin, Malcolm. 'The Founder of the "Quarterly Review"—John Murray II', *Quarterly Review*, CCLXXXI (1943), 1–15.

Erdman, David V. 'Immoral Acts of a Library Cormorant: the Extent of Coleridge's Contributions to the "Critical Review" ', *BNYPL*, LXIII (1959), 433–54, 515–30, 575–87.

Everts, W. W. *John Foster.* London, 1884.

Fetter, Frank Whitson. 'A Probable Source of Copinger's "On the Authorship of the First Hundred Numbers of the Edinburgh Review" ', *The Library*, IX, 5th ser., No. 1 (1954), 49–53.

Fisher, Walt. 'Leigh Hunt as Friend and Critic of Keats: 1816–1859', *Lock Haven Review*, Ser. 1, No. 5 (1963), 27–42.

Foster, John. *Contributions, Biographical, Literary, and Philosophical to the Eclectic Review.* 2 vols. London, 1844.

Garlitz, Barbara. 'The Baby's Debut: The Contemporary Reaction to Wordsworth's Poetry of Childhood', *BUSE*, IV (1960), 85–94.

Gates, Lewis Edwards. *Three Studies in Literature.* New York, 1899.

Gilfillan, George. *Galleries of Literary Portraits.* 2 vols. Edinburgh, 1856.

Gillies, R. P. *Memoirs of a Literary Veteran.* 3 vols. London, 1851.

Gordon, Martha H. *Christopher North: A Memoir.* 2 vols. Edinburgh, 1862.

Graham, Walter. 'Contemporary Critics of Coleridge', *PMLA*, XXXVIII (1923), 278–89.

——. *English Literary Periodicals.* New York: T. Nelson and Sons, 1930.

——. 'Robert Southey as Tory Reviewer', *PQ*, II (1923), 97–111.

——. 'Shelley's Debt to Leigh Hunt and the *Examiner*', *PMLA*, XL (1925), 185–92.

——. 'Some Infamous Tory Reviews', *SP*, XXII (1925), 500–17.

——. *Tory Criticism in the Quarterly Review 1809–1853.* New York: Columbia University Press, 1921.

Gregory, Olinthus. *Memoirs of the Life, Writings, and Character, Literary, Professional, and Religious, of John Mason Good.* London, 1828.

Greig, James A. *Francis Jeffrey of the Edinburgh Review.* Edinburgh: Oliver and Boyd, 1948.

Grierson, Sir H. J. C. *Sir Walter Scott, Bart.* London: Constable and Co., 1938.

—— (ed.). *The Letters of Sir Walter Scott*, 12 vols. London: Constable and Co., 1932–37.

Griggs, Irwin, Kern, John D., and Schneider, Elisabeth. 'Early Edinburgh Reviewers: a New List', *MP*, XLIII (1946), 192–210.

Guyer, Byron. 'Francis Jeffrey's *Essay on Beauty*', *Huntington Library Quarterly*, XIII (1949–50), 71–85.

——. 'The Philosophy of Jeffrey', *MLQ*, XI (1950), 17–26.

Halpern, Sheldon. 'Sydney Smith in the *Edinburgh Review:* a New List', *BNYPL*, LXVI (1962), 589–602.

Haney, John Louis (ed). *Early Reviews of English Poets.* Philadelphia: The Egerton Press, 1904.

Hildyard, M. C. (ed). *Lockhart's Literary Criticism.* Oxford: B. Blackwell, 1931.

Hoadley, Frank T. 'The Controversy over Southey's *Wat Tyler*', *SP*, XXXVIII (1941), 81–96.

Hodgart, Patricia, and Redpath, Theodore (eds.). *Romantic Perspectives.* London: Harrap and Co., 1964.

Hodgson, James T. *Memoir of the Rev. Francis Hodgson, B.D.* 2 vols. London, 1878.

Holland, John, and Everett, James. *Memoirs of the Life and Writings of James Montgomery.* 7 vols. London, 1854–56.

Holland, Lady. *Memoir of the Reverend Sydney Smith.* 2d ed., 2 vols. London, 1855.

Holloway, Owen E. 'George Ellis, *The Anti-Jacobin* and the *Quarterly Review*', *RES*, X (1934), 55–66.

Horner, Leonard (ed.). *Memoirs and Correspondence of Francis Horner.* 2 vols. London, 1853.

Houghton, Walter E. (ed.). *The Wellesley Index to Victorian Periodicals 1824–1900.* Toronto: University of Toronto Press, 1966.

Houtchens, Lawrence Huston, and Houtchens, Carolyn Washburn. *Leigh Hunt's Literary Criticism*, New York: Columbia University Press, 1956.

Houtchens, Lawrence Huston, and Houtchens, Carolyn Washburn. *Leigh Hunt's Political and Occasional Essays*. New York: Columbia University Press, 1962.

Howe, P. P. (ed.). *The Complete Works of William Hazlitt*. 21 vols. London: J. M. Dent and Sons, 1930–34.

——. 'Hazlitt and "Blackwood's"', *Fortnightly Review*, CXII (1919), 603–15.

——. *The Life of William Hazlitt*. 3d ed. London: H. Hamilton, 1947.

Hughes, M. Y. 'The Humanism of Francis Jeffrey', *MLR*, XVI (1921), 243–51.

Hughes, T. Rowland. 'John Scott: Author, Editor and Critic', *London Mercury*, XXI (1930), 518–28.

——. 'The London Magazine'. Unpublished dissertation, Oxford University, 1931.

Humphreys, A. L. *Picadilly Bookmen: Memorials of the House of Hatchard*. London, 1893.

Hunt, Leigh. *Autobiography*, ed. J. E. Morpurgo. London: Cresset Press, 1949.

——. *The Correspondence of Leigh Hunt*, ed. Thornton Hunt. 2 vols. London, 1862.

Hutchinson, Thomas. 'Coleridge's "Christabel"', *N&Q*, X 9s (1902), 388–90; XI 9s (1903), 170–72.

[Innes, Cosmo]. *Memoir of Thomas Thomson, Advocate*. Edinburgh, 1854.

Ireland, Alexander. *A List of the Writings of William Hazlitt and Leigh Hunt*. London, 1868.

Jack, Ian. *English Literature 1815–1832*. Oxford: Clarendon Press, 1963.

Jeffrey, Francis. *Contributions to the Edinburgh Review*. 4 vols. London, 1844.

Jennings, L. J. (ed.). *The Croker Papers*. 3 vols. London, 1884.

Jerdan, William. *Autobiography*. 4 vols. London, 1852–53.

Jerrold, Walter. *Thomas Hood*. London: A. Rivers, 1907.

Johnson, E. D. H. 'Don Juan in England', *ELH*, XI (1944), 135–53.

Johnson, Reginald Brimley (ed.). *Famous Reviews*. London: Sir. I. Pitman and Sons, 1914.

——. *Shelley—Leigh Hunt; Being Reviews and Leaders from the 'Examiner'*. London: Ingpen and Grant, 1928.

Jones, Leonidas M. 'The Essays and Critical Writing of John Hamilton Reynolds.' Unpublished dissertation, Harvard University, 1952.

Jordan, Hoover, H. 'Thomas Moore and the Review of *Christabel*', *MP*, LIV (1956), 95–105.

Joyce, Michael. *Edinburgh, the Golden Age, 1769–1832*. London: Longmans Green, 1951.

Kendall, Lyle H., Jr. 'John Murray to J. W. Croker: An Unpublished Letter on Keats', *K-SJ*, XII (1963), 8–9.

Kennedy, Virginia, and Barton, Mary. *Samuel Taylor Coleridge. A Selected Bibliography*. Baltimore: The Enoch Pratt Free Library, 1935.

Knight, Charles. *Passages of a Working Life*. 3 vols. London, 1863–65.

Landré, Louis. *Leigh Hunt: Contribution a l'histoire du Romantisme anglais*. Société Française d'Édition 'Les Belles-lettres', 2 vols. Paris, 1936.

Lane, William G. 'Keats and "The Smith and Theodore Hook Squad" ', *MLN*, LXX (1955), 22–24.

Lane-Poole, Stanley. *Life of Stratford Canning*. 2 vols. London, 1888.

Lang, Andrew. *The Life and Letters of John Gibson Lockhart*. 2 vols. London, 1897.

Lawson, Strang. 'Crabbe Thanks Jeffrey', *N&Q*, CXCV (1950), 538–39.

Le Bas, C. W. *Life of T. F. Middleton*. 2 vols. London, 1831.

Le Breton, Anna L. *Memoir of Mrs. Barbauld*. London, 1874.

Le Breton, P. H. *Memoirs, Miscellanies, and Letters of the Late Lucy Aikin*. London, 1864.

Lochhead, Marion Cleland. *Lockhart*. London: J. Murray, 1954.

Lockhart, J. G. *Life of Sir Walter Scott, Bart*. 10 vols. Edinburgh, 1882.

[Lockhart, J. G.]. 'Theodore Hook, A Sketch', *Quarterly Review*, LXXII (1843), 53–108.

Logan, J. V. *Wordsworthian Criticism: A Guide and Bibliography*. Columbus, Ohio: The Ohio State University Press, 1947.

Lucas, E. V. *The Life of Charles Lamb*. 5th ed. London: Methuen and Co., 1921.

Macbeth, G. *John Gibson Lockhart: A Critical Study*. Urbana: The University of Illinois Press, 1935.

McDonald, W. A., Jr. 'A Letter of Sir Walter Scott to William Scott on the Jeffrey–Swift Controversy', *RES*, XII n.s. (1961), 404–8.

MacGillivray, J. R. *John Keats: A Bibliography and Reference Guide*. Toronto: University of Toronto Press, 1949.

Mackintosh, R. J. (ed.). *Memoirs of the Life of the Right Honourable Sir James Mackintosh*. 2 vols. London, 1835.

MacManus, M. J. *A Bibliographical Hand-List of the First Editions of Thomas Moore*. Dublin: A. Thom and Co., 1934.

Marriott, J. A. R. *George Canning and His Times, a Political Study*. London: J. Murray, 1903.

Marsh, George L. 'The Early Reviews of Shelley', *MP*, XXVII (1929), 73–95.

——. 'L. Landré's Leigh Hunt', *MP*, XXXV (1937), 92–95.

——. 'The Writings of Keats's Friend Reynolds', *SP*, XXV (1928), 491–510.

Marsh, George L., and White, Newman I. 'Keats and the Periodicals of His Time', *MP*, XXXII (1934), 37–53.

Marshall, William H. *Byron, Shelley, Hunt, and The Liberal*. Philadelphia: University of Pennsylvania Press, 1960.

Mason, Francis Claiborne. *A Study in Shelley Criticism*. Mercersburg, Pa.: Privately printed, 1937.

Mineka, F. E. *The Dissidence of Dissent*. Chapel Hill: The University of North Carolina Press, 1944.

Mordell, Albert (ed.). *Notorious Literary Attacks*. New York: Boni and Liveright, 1926.

Morgan, Peter F. 'Taylor and Hessey: Aspects of their Conduct of the *London Magazine*', *K-SJ*, VII (1958), 61–68.

Morison, Stanley. *John Bell*. Cambridge: Cambridge University Press, 1930.

Nangle, B. C. *The Monthly Review, Second Series, 1790–1815: Indexes of Contributors and Articles*. Oxford: Clarendon Press, 1955.

Napier, Macvey. *Selections from the Correspondence of the Late Macvey Napier*. London, 1879.

New, Chester. *The Life of Henry Brougham to 1830*. Oxford: Clarendon Press, 1961.

Noel, R. *Life of Lord Byron*. London, 1890.

Noyes, R. *Wordsworth and Jeffrey in Controversy*. Indiana University Publications, Humanity Series No. 5, 1941.

Oliphant, Margaret. *Annals of a Publishing House*. 2 vols. Edinburgh, 1897.

——. *The Literary History of England*. 3 vols. London, 1882.

Overton, J. H. *The English Church in the Nineteenth Century (1800–1833)*. London, 1894.

Owen, W. J. B. 'Wordsworth and Jeffrey in Collaboration', *RES*, XV (1964), 161–67.

Parker, W. M., and Hudson, D. 'Thomas Barnes and "The Champion" ', *TLS* (Jan. 1 and 15, 1944), pp. 7, 29.

Paston, George. *Sidelights on the Georgian Period*. London: Methuen and Co., 1902.

Pearson, John. *The Life of William Hey*. 2d ed. 2 vols. London, 1823.

Peck, W. E. 'Shelley's Reviews Written for the *Examiner*', *MLN*, XXXIX (1924), 118–19.

Peek, Katherine M. *Wordsworth in England*. Bryn Mawr, 1943.

Peyre, Henri. *Writers and Their Critics*. Ithaca: Cornell University Press, 1944.

Pierce, Frederick E. *Currents and Eddies in the English Romantic Generation*. New Haven: Yale University Press, 1918.

Poole, William Frederick. *Index to Periodical Literature*. 3d ed. Boston, 1882.

Pratt, J. H. *Eclectic Notes*. London, 1865.

Prideaux, W. F. 'Coleridge's "Christabel" ', *N&Q*, X 9s (1902), 429–30; XI 9s (1903), 269–72.

Prothero, Rowland E. (ed.). *The Works of Lord Byron: Letters and Journals*. 6 vols. London, 1898–1901.

Raffles, T. S. *Memoirs of Dr. Thomas Raffles*. London, 1864.

Ransom, H. 'William Jerdan, Editor and Literary Agent', *Studies in English*, XXVII (1948), 68–74.

Raysor, Thomas M. 'The Establishment of Wordsworth's Reputation', *JEGP*, LIV (1955), 61–71.

Redding, Cyrus. *Literary Remains and Memoirs of Thomas Campbell*. 2 vols. London, 1860.

——. *Fifty Years Recollections Literary and Personal*. 3 vols. London, 1858.

Rede, Leman Thomas. *Memoir of the Right Honorable George Canning*. 2 vols. London, 1827.

Rees, Thomas. *Reminiscences of Literary London*. London, 1896.

Rice, Richard A. 'Lord Byron's British Reputation', *Smith College Studies in Modern Languages*. Vol. 5, No. 2, 1924.

Rivington, Septimus. *The Publishing Family of Rivington*. London: Rivingtons, 1919.

——. *The Publishing House of Rivington*. London: Rivington, Percival, and Co., 1894.

Robberds, J. W. *A Memoir of the Life and Writings of the Late William Taylor of Norwich*. 2 vols. London, 1843.

Roberts, Arthur. *The Life, Letters, and Opinions of William Roberts*. London, 1850.

Robinson, Henry Crabb. *Henry Crabb Robinson on Books and Their Writers*, ed. E. J. Morley. 3 vols. London: J. M. Dent and Sons, 1938.

——. *Diary of H. C. Robinson*, ed. T. Sadler. 3 vols. London, 1869.

Rollins, Hyder E. 'Keats's Elgin Marbles Sonnets', *University of Missouri Studies*, XXI (1946), 163–66.

Roper, Derek. 'Coleridge and the "Critical Review" ', *MLR*, LV (1960), 11–16.

——. 'The Politics of the *Critical Review*, 1756–1817', *Durham University Journal*, XXII n.s. (1961), 117–22.

Ryland, J. E. *The Life and Correspondence of John Foster*. 2 vols. London, 1846.

Saintsbury, George. *Essays in English Literature 1780–1860*. 2d ed. London, 1891.

——. *A History of Nineteenth Century Literature (1780–1895)*. London, 1896.

——. *A History of Criticism and Literary Taste in Europe*. 3 vols. Edinburgh: W. Blackwood, 1900–4.

Schneider, Elisabeth W. 'Tom Moore and the *Edinburgh* Review of "Christabel" ', *PMLA*, LXXVII (1962), 71–76.

——. 'The Unknown Reviewer of *Christabel*: Jeffrey, Hazlitt, Tom Moore', *PMLA*, LXX (1955), 417–32.

——. Irwin Griggs, Kern, John D. 'Brougham's Early Contributions to the *Edinburgh Review*: a New List', *MP*, XLII (1945), 152–73.

Scott, Sir Walter. *Familiar Letters of Sir Walter Scott*, ed. David Douglas. 2 vols. Edinburgh, 1894.

Severn, Joseph. 'The Vicissitudes of Keats's Fame', *Atlantic Monthly*, XI (1863), 401–7.

Shine, Hill, and Shine, Helen Chadwick. *The Quarterly Review under Gifford*. Chapel Hill: University of North Carolina Press, 1949.

Sikes, Herschel M. 'Hazlitt, the *London Magazine*, and the "Anonymous" Reviewer', *BNYPL*, LXV (1961), 159–74.

Simmons, Jack. *Southey*. London: Collins, 1945.

Smiles, Samuel. *A Publisher and His Friends: Memoir and Correspondence of John Murray*. 2 vols. London, 1891.

Smith, D. Nichol (ed.). *Jeffrey's Literary Criticism*. London: Henry Frowd, 1910.

Smith, Elsie (ed.). *An Estimate of Wordsworth by His Contemporaries 1793–1822*. Oxford: B. Blackwell, 1932.

[Smith, Horace]. 'A Graybeard's Gossip', *New Monthly Magazine and Humorist*, LXXXI (1847), 415–24.

Smith, Sydney. *The Letters of Sydney Smith*, ed. N. C. Smith. 2 vols. Oxford: Clarendon Press, 1953.

Southey, C. C. *Life and Correspondence of Robert Southey*. 6 vols. London, 1849–50.

Sper, Felix. *The Periodical Press of London 1800–1830*. Boston: The F. W. Faxon Co., 1937.

Stephen, Sir Leslie. 'The First Edinburgh Reviewers', in *Hours in a Library*. 3 vols. London, 1892.

Stevens, William. *A Short Account of the Life and Writings of William Jones*. London, 1801.

Stevenson, E. (ed.). *Early Reviews of Great Writers (1789–1832)*. London, 1886.

Stout, George D. 'Leigh Hunt on Wordsworth and Coleridge,' *K-SJ*, VI (1957), 59–73.

——. 'The "Literary Examiner" and "The Inquisitor" ', *TLS* (1925), p. 521.

——. 'The Political History of Leigh Hunt's Examiner Together with an Account of the "Book" ', *Washington University Studies*, n.s. (Language and Literature), No. 19, 1949.

Strout, Alan L. *A Bibliography of Articles in Blackwood's Magazine, 1817–25*. Texas Technological College Library Bulletin 5, Lubbock, Texas, 1959.

——. 'Hunt, Hazlitt, and "Maga" ', *ELH*, IV (1937), 151–59.

—— (ed.). *John Bull's Letter to Lord Byron*. Norman: University of Oklahoma Press, 1947.

——. 'John Wilson, "Champion" of Wordsworth', *MP*, XXXI (1934), 383–94.

Strout, Alan L. 'Lockhart, Champion of Shelley', *TLS* (1955), p. 468.

——. 'Maga, Champion of Shelley', *SP*, XXIX (1932), 95–119.

Styles, John. *Early Blossoms*. London, 1819.

Sutherland, James. *On English Prose*. Toronto: University of Toronto Press, 1947.

Swann, Elsie. *Christopher North—John Wilson*. Edinburgh: Oliver and Boyd, 1934.

Tave, Stuart M. 'The London Magazine, 1820–29', *MP*, LII (1954), 139–41.

Taylor, Olive M. 'John Taylor', *London Mercury*, XII (1925), 258–67.

Thomas, P. G. *Aspects of Literary Theory and Practice 1550–1870*. London: Heath, Cranton, 1931.

Thorpe, Clarence D. 'An Early Review of Keats', *JEGP*, XLIII (1944), 333–36.

Tillet, N. S. 'Elia and "The Indicator" ', *SAQ*, XXXIII (1934), 295–310.

Timperly, C. H. *Encyclopedia of Literary and Topographical Anecdotes*. 2d ed. London, 1842.

Tredrey, F. D. *The House of Blackwood 1804–1954*. Edinburgh: W. Blackwood, 1954.

Trueblood, Paul G. *The Flowering of Byron's Genius*. Stanford: Stanford University Press, 1945.

Turnbull, J. M. 'Keats, Reynolds, and *The Champion*', *London Mercury*, XIX (1929), 384–94.

Wain, John (ed.). *Contemporary Reviews of Romantic Poetry*. London: G. G. Harrap and Co., 1953.

Walker, Hugh. *The English Essay and Essayists*. London: J. M. Dent and Sons, 1915.

Walker, William. *Three Churchmen*. Edinburgh, 1893.

Waller, A. R. and Glover Arnold. *The Collected Works of William Hazlitt*. 13 vols. London: J. M. Dent and Sons., 1902–6.

Ward, W. S. 'Byron's "Hours of Idleness" and Other than Scotch Reviewers', *MLN*, LIX (1944), 547–50.

——. 'The Criticism of Poetry in British Periodicals, 1798–1820'. Unpublished dissertation, Duke University, 1943; Microcards, University of Kentucky, 1955.

——. 'An Early Champion of Wordsworth: Thomas Noon Talfourd', *PMLA*, LXVIII (1953), 992–1000.

——. *Index and Finding List of Serials Published in the British Isles 1789–1832.* Lexington: University of Kentucky Press, 1953.

——. 'Lord Byron and "My Grandmother's Review" ', *MLN*, LXIV (1949), 25–29.

——. 'Periodical Literature' in *Some British Romantics*, ed. James V. Logan *et al.* Columbus: Ohio State University Press, 1966.

——. 'Shelley and the Reviewers Once More', *MLN*, LIX (1944), 539–42.

——. 'Some Aspects of the Conservative Attitude toward Poetry in English Criticism, 1798–1820', *PMLA*, LX (1945), 386–98.

——. 'Wordsworth, the Lake Poets, and Their Contemporary Magazine Critics, 1798–1820', *SP*, XLII (1945), 87–113.

Warren, Alba H. *English Poetic Theory 1825–1865.* Princeton: Princeton University Press, 1950.

Warter, John Wood (ed.). *Selections from the Letters of Robert Southey.* 4 vols. London, 1856.

Watson, E. H. L., (ed.). *Contemporary Comments.* London: Eyre and Spottiswoode, 1931.

Watts, Alaric Alfred. *Alaric Watts: A Narrative of his Life.* 2 vols. London, 1844.

Waugh, Arthur. 'The English Reviewers. A Sketch of their History and Principles', *The Critic*, XL (1902), 26–37.

Welker, John James. 'The Position of the Quarterlies on Some Classical Dogmas', *SP*, XXXVII (1940), 542–62.

Wellek, René. *A History of Modern Criticism 1750–1950.* 2 vols. New Haven: Yale University Press, 1955.

Wheeler, Paul M. 'The Great Quarterlies of the Early Nineteenth Century and Leigh Hunt', *SAQ*, XXIX (1930), 282–303.

White, Newman Ivy. *The Unextinguished Hearth.* Durham, N.C.: Duke University Press, 1938.

Winchester, C. T. *A Group of English Essayists of the Early Nineteenth Century.* New York: The Macmillan Co., 1910.

Woolf, Virginia. 'Lockhart's Criticism', in *The Moment and Other Essays.* London: Hogarth Press, 1947.

Zeitlin, Jacob. 'The Editor of the *London Magazine*', *JEGP*, XX (1921), 328–54.

——. 'Southey's Contributions to "The Critical Review" ', *N&Q*, IV 12s (1918), 35–36, 66–67, 94–96, 122–25.

Index

www.ingramcontent.com/pod-product-compliance
Lightning Source LLC
LaVergne TN
LVHW020612110826
845149LV00002B/463

* 9 7 8 1 1 3 8 1 9 3 8 2 6 *